THE
RULE OF
LAWS

A 4,000-YEAR QUEST
TO ORDER THE WORLD

FERNANDA PIRIE

BASIC BOOKS
NEW YORK

Basic Books
Hachette Book Group
1290 Avenue of the Americas, New York, NY 10104
www.basicbooks.com

Printed in the United States of America

First Edition: November 2021

Published by Basic Books, an imprint of Perseus Books, LLC, a subsidiary of Hachette Book Group, Inc. The Basic Books name and logo is a trademark of the Hachette Book Group.

The Hachette Speakers Bureau provides a wide range of authors for speaking events. To find out more, go to www.hachettespeakersbureau.com or call (866) 376-6591.

The publisher is not responsible for websites (or their content) that are not owned by the publisher.

Print book interior design by Trish Wilkinson.

Library of Congress Control Number: 2021942287

ISBNs: 9781541617940 (hardcover), 9781541617957 (ebook)

TR

10 9 8 7 6 5 4 3 2 1

CONTENTS

CONTENTS

THE PROMISE OF LAW

In 1497 the Portuguese explorer Vasco da Gama sailed around the Cape of Good Hope and into the Indian Ocean. He was on a mission to open up a sea passage to the rich eastern trading networks. His journey also opened European eyes to the rich and sophisticated world of Asia, with its extensive commercial and technological developments, complex governing structures, and laws. The Portuguese docked at Calicut, on the west coast of India, where grains, sugar, spices, coffee, textiles, metals, and horses were loaded and unloaded every day on their way to and from the Spice Islands, the Indian plains, and ports in East Africa and the Arabian Gulf. Eager to participate in this trade, da Gama visited the court of the local ruler. The Zamorin was none too impressed by his gifts and sent the European delegation packing. But the Portuguese persisted, and after further missions and threats of violence, they established trading posts on the Indian coast.[1]

The merchants and adventurers who followed da Gama were impressed by the goods brought by Chinese traders, dazzled by the luxury and sophistication of the Muslim courts at Isfahan and Delhi, and intrigued by reports of the ancient Asian laws. In their distant capital at Beijing, Chinese rulers maintained a legal system that dated back to the third century BCE. The Zamorin of Calicut, like other Hindu rulers, took advice from religious scholars, brahmins, who consulted the Dharmashastras. These centuries-old legal texts had their origins in the philosophical and ritual traditions of India's Vedic period. Muslim legal experts referred to an extensive textual jurisprudence based on Muhammad's revelations in the seventh century CE. In the courts of the sultans, well-trained judges dispensed justice, while scholars issued legal opinions and jurists conducted esoteric debates over ancient legal texts. The Europeans had nothing to compare in legal sophistication. Their own laws were still little more than heterogeneous collections of local customs and courts interspersed with the remnants of Roman jurisprudence.

By the early eighteenth century CE, everything had begun to change. The Qing had established a powerful new dynasty in China, the Mughal emperor Shah Jahan had built the Taj Mahal and extended a network of roads throughout India, and the Ottomans had threatened Vienna. But the Asian regimes were already faltering. The French legal philosopher Montesquieu still spoke with admiration of China's sophisticated and stable legal system, but he also condemned it as 'despotic'. Enlightenment philosophers had persuaded European rulers that their political systems followed the most rational principles, while their laws promoted superior regimes of private property. And, as their industrial and military achievements outstripped those of Asia, European rulers became convinced that their political, educational, and legal systems were the best in the world. The intricate scholarship of the Muslim jurists, the learning of the Hindu brahmins, and the elaborate codes of Chinese law were, to their minds, the irrational and outdated institutions of a degenerate Orient.

The national legal systems now found throughout the world are almost all modeled on those developed by European nations in the eighteenth and nineteenth centuries. During two hundred years of colonial rule, they exported and imposed their laws

2

throughout the world and promoted a new international order of clearly demarcated states. Today, the leaders who take their seats at the United Nations are expected to maintain their own systems of laws and courts, as well as upholding democracy, human rights, and the rule of law. But within the long history of human civilizations, the rise and dominance of the state and systems of national law form just the latest chapter. The Europeans displaced legal systems that were already ancient when da Gama arrived in India, and even the Romans were inspired by earlier precedents. There is nothing inevitable about the shape that most legal systems take around the world today.

MOST LAWS THROUGHOUT history were very different from those considered appropriate in a modern state. For a start, laws have not always recognized territorial boundaries. Often, they travelled with merchants or religious scholars to new lands, where they generally came to coexist with local customs and rules. What is more, law and religion have often not been distinct. Particularly within the Hindu, Jewish, and Islamic traditions, legal rules have shaded imperceptibly into moral and religious guidance. Many ancient, and even quite recent, laws also defy the apparently basic requirements of efficiency, authority, and efficacy. Historically, many judges ignored the laws of their rulers, and plenty of laws were never enforced. Yet, highly impractical rules, which could hardly have contributed to the smooth running of their societies, were carefully written out on expensive parchment or chipped onto stone slabs. Time and again, historians have puzzled over what ancient laws were intended to do. Sometimes they have seemed little more than attempts to copy an older or grander civilization. Yet the Chinese traders, Hindu kings, and Muslim sultans that da Gama encountered all respected the rules of ancient legal systems. Their laws

were just the latest examples of a technique that had been taken up repeatedly since it first emerged over four thousand years ago.

The oldest laws were created in Mesopotamia, the fertile lands lying between the Tigris and Euphrates Rivers in what is now Iraq. In the third millennium BCE, the king of Ur ordered his scribes to write out a code of laws on a clay tablet. It followed a bold statement about the justice he could promise his people. Several centuries later, warlike leaders in central China inscribed ideograms onto bamboo strips and bronze vessels, which set out long lists of crimes and punishments. Their successors adopted the same methods to impose discipline on the officials and people of their expanding empires. On the plains of the Ganges, meanwhile, Indian scholars were crafting ritual texts based on the ancient wisdom of the Vedas. By the early centuries of the common era, brahmins were inscribing Sanskrit characters onto palm leaves to create the Dharmashastras, the foundational texts of Hindu law. Their successors travelled throughout South Asia, persuading rulers such as the Zamorin of Calicut to follow their rituals and adopt the Dharmashastras as codes of law. They were seeking to guide a body of religious adherents along a moral path.

The foundational legal systems that developed in Mesopotamia, China, and India were each distinct, in language, logic, and purpose. The Mesopotamian kings promised justice to their people, setting out rules that ordinary people could, at least in theory, rely upon; the Chinese rulers established systems of crimes and punishments to bring discipline and order to their expanding territories; and the Hindu brahmins sought to guide ordinary people along the path of the dharma, the cosmological order of their religious tradition. But, while each of these three legal systems was unique, together they provided the forms that all subsequent laws have adopted. It is arguably the crowning achievement of the modern state to have combined elements of all three within the legal systems that now dominate the world.

But this did not happen for many centuries. In the meantime, legal techniques travelled, inspiring kings and rulers with quite different ambitions. They were also taken up in much more local contexts, by princes, councils, villagers, and tribesmen.

THE EARLIEST LAWS were little more than pragmatic and mundane rules. Ostensibly intended for rulers trying to manage complex societies, most addressed the sorts of tensions that arise anywhere people live together, the consequences of killings, injuries, theft, and adultery. They attempted to regulate property use and ownership, inheritance, family relations, and responsibility for children, as most laws have done throughout human history. They dealt with the consequences of slavery, for long a widespread issue, and provided rules about using oaths and ordeals to resolve disputes of fact. Over the centuries, rulers found law a useful tool with which to manage their populations. Chinese emperors, Indian princes, and Islamic caliphs all conducted censuses, measured and mapped out fields and pastures, and used laws to categorize households, levy taxes, and raise armies. Village meetings and tribal councils also made constitutions to regulate social behaviour and resolve disputes.

But the aims of the first lawmakers were not just practical. The Mesopotamian kings wrapped their laws in grand statements about the social justice they were promising their people while also invoking the favour of the gods. The Chinese emperors claimed that, by enforcing their laws, they were maintaining the order of the cosmos. The Hindu brahmins explained that they were establishing rules to guide people according to the requirements of the dharma, the ideal order of the world. Many other respected sets of laws have been highly impractical in quite puzzling ways, including those developed by the authors of the Old Testament. Although inspired by the Mesopotamian tradition, where law was the work of kings, the Israelite priests were pursuing a distinctly religious project.

The Pentateuch (or Torah), the first five books of the Bible, probably took the form we know today between the ninth and fifth centuries BCE.[2] They describe how, after leading his people to safety, Moses gave them laws for worship, ritual, and sacrifice, along with an extremely complicated set of dietary rules. These forbade Israelites from eating 'abominable things', that is, animals, fish, and birds that were unclean, creating a set of distinctions that have puzzled scholars ever since.[3] Greek philosophers wondered whether the rules had medicinal purposes, preventing Jews from eating unsafe meat. But why should health, or even taste, have required that the Israelites avoid chameleons, moles, crocodiles, and most locusts (though not all), and what could possibly have been wrong with hares? The great Jewish theologian Maimonides despaired of finding meaning in the laws, declaring that 'those who trouble themselves to find a cause for any of these detailed rules are, to my eyes, devoid of sense'. Others supposed that the laws were an amalgam of earlier rules, which originally had hygienic, aesthetic, or religious purposes, or even that they were simply a set of commands that required discipline, obedience, and unreflective rule-following on the part of pious Jews. But the authors of Leviticus were obviously keen to promote an orderly society, so why should they have produced such an illogical list?[4] The answer must lie in the wider purposes of the laws. Many of them promoted physical perfection, so priests could not be disabled, for example. And they demanded ritual purity. Jews had to eat, sleep, dress, and have sex in the right ways; warriors' camps had to be set apart from the business of war, to avoid its polluting effects; and Jews were told they should not yoke together an ox and a donkey, or weave wool together with linen. This was to avoid confusing distinct categories. The laws, that is, told Israelites how to live holy lives by creating an order of categories and separating the pure from the impure, in physical as well as spiritual terms.

This larger purpose of the Israelites' laws sheds light on their distinctions between clean and unclean. The cattle, sheep, and goats that provided basic sustenance in the region were cloven-hoofed ungulates who chewed the cud, so the priests decided that these qualities should define the class of clean animals. As a result, it included some wild beasts, such as antelopes and wild goats, but not all domestic animals, most importantly pigs. They declared that fish without scales and fins were abominations, as were four-footed creatures that could fly, animals with hands that used them for walking, and anything that swarmed. To their minds, proper animals should walk, fish should swim, and birds should fly. Hopping was close enough to walking, so they declared that grasshoppers, crickets, and some locusts were clean. But swarming was not. Whatever the rationale behind their decisions, the rules were more important for what they symbolized, dividing pure from impure, than for the ways in which they might save Jews from unclean food. And they set the Israelites apart from gentiles, as people who followed God's laws. Behind them was a religious vision for a chosen people.

Hindu, Jewish, Islamic, and Christian scholars all made detailed and extensive laws as they developed their traditions. It is a consequence of the rift between church and state in medieval Europe that modern laws are considered to stand apart from religion. The distinction would have made little sense to the early lawmakers of the world's major religions.

Other lawmakers, pursuing apparently political projects, have been inspired by grander civilizations, setting out visions of social order in sets of laws that seem equally impractical. In the seventh and eighth centuries CE, the Tibetans who inhabited the vast plateau west of China were still warlike tribesmen. Strong leaders brought them together in military expeditions to China

and Central Asia, demanding oaths of loyalty, and the most successful eventually established themselves as kings. A royal dynasty set up a court and a bureaucracy, with offices and ranks
of ministers. Almost certainly inspired by the elaborate administration of the Chinese emperors, they also created laws. That
we know anything of this period is largely thanks to documents
crammed into a cave at Dunhuang, a trading post on a branch of
the silk roads that ran north of Tibet, discovered by local scholars in 1900. It had remained sealed since the eleventh century,
and when the Hungarian explorer Aurel Stein arrived in 1907,
he found almost forty thousand documents written in Chinese,
Tibetan, and other Asian languages.[5] Persuading the local scholars to give him access, he spent days leafing through the fragile
scrolls by candlelight and lamplight; eventually he carried away
caseloads of the most important documents, which he deposited
in the museums of Paris and London. Within this treasure trove
historians found some of the ancient Tibetan laws.

Two specified the compensation that was to be paid when
someone was injured on the hunting field, setting out long lists
of payments graded according to the ranks of both perpetrator
and victim.[6] Someone who killed one of the four great ministers was liable to pay ten thousand gold coins; for a minister
of the turquoise rank it was six thousand; for a gold-rank minister, five thousand; for the gilt, four thousand; for the silver,
three thousand; and for the brass and copper, two thousand
and one thousand, while the two classes of commoners received
three hundred and two hundred, respectively. But it was different if you killed someone of a significantly higher status, or if
the victim merely suffered a wound (although the severity of the
injury does not seem to have made a difference), or if you could
prove that the wound was an accident. The logic of the status
distinctions is clear: an aristocrat's life was worth more than
that of his servant. But gold coins were not common currency
when Dunhuang flourished, the differences seem excessive, and

the details are unrealistically complicated. For all the kings' desires to emulate their Chinese neighbours, Tibetan society can hardly have been so clearly stratified. On the vast plateau they depended on local tribal leaders to manage their populations, sending and receiving orders and letters over long distances via relays of horsemen. The laws symbolized the hierarchy the Tibetan kings wanted to create, their imagined state. They were mapping out a grander, more unified civilization. It was a map *for* civilization, not a map *of* an existing social order.[7]

Behind what are ostensibly functional laws there often hover grander ambitions and aims, in the modern period as much as in the ancient world. The US Constitution, for all its initial goal of establishing a practical means of coordination and government among the federal states, soon acquired a mythic aura as a symbol of the union's ideals and aspirations. Sometimes described as the foundation of America's 'civic religion', the original Constitution is carefully preserved and displayed in an elaborate vault in Washington, which some have likened to a sanctuary.[8] It symbolizes the foundations and order of the United States. And the text has inspired similar projects elsewhere. Following successful struggles for independence, most postcolonial states created brand new constitutions for their fledgling democracies. Each demonstrated the credentials of the new government and its claim to participate in the contemporary world order. The new states often lacked the court structures, professional resources, and political will to enforce the terms of their constitutions, yet their legal texts indicated a political coming of age, statehood, and leaders who could take their seats at the United Nations. Their projects were not so different from those of ancient kings who chiselled long lists of laws onto stone slabs, which no one seems to have applied, or those of medieval rulers who commissioned scribes to write out lists of impractically detailed compensation payments when literacy was rare and paper expensive. They were aspirations to a grander order.

Even contemporary laws formulated in response to a social problem are not always as pragmatic as our governments would have us believe. When a tragedy occurs involving handguns or dangerous dogs, or the media gets overexcited about criminals evading justice, politicians rush to legislate. But all too often the new laws are impractical or unenforceable. The problem of hate speech was the subject of legislation in the United Kingdom which many commentators thought could barely, if ever, be enforced.[9] But governments must be seen to be doing something. Passing a law gives their citizens the impression that politicians are in control of the situation. And, to be less cynical, it also expresses the moral revulsion of society at large. The laws set out, for all to see, the moral parameters of the civilized society our rulers claim they can create. They hold the promise of both justice and order.

NOT ALL SOCIETIES have created laws. Some people throughout history have formed social groups, managed their populations, and resolved their disputes without any laws. Bands of hunters and gatherers have practised tactics of avoidance rather than confrontation; tribes and lineages have pursued revenge relations, combining against adversaries but allowing mediators to settle feuds though compensation; homogeneous communities have preferred conciliatory mediation, trying to find compromises that satisfy all parties; and emergent leaders have centralized their powers, issuing orders and punishing those who disobeyed them. The variations have been endless, although patterns have repeated themselves, and they have produced forms of order that are stable and enduring without any explicit laws.

Even some complex and sophisticated societies have not made laws. The Old Kingdoms of ancient Egypt, the Aztec and Inca Empires in Central and South America, and the kingdoms that flourished in sub-Saharan Africa all maintained order without, as far as archaeologists have been able to discern, creating sets of rules or recording legal judgements as precedents. Ancient Egyptian documents and inscriptions indicate that for two thousand years pharaohs presided over complex fiscal systems in which officials kept detailed records of property holdings, temples, foundations, and revenues; scribes recorded royal decrees and orders; and judges heard legal cases and sentenced miscreants to penal labour, all without creating general rules.[10] The Old, Middle, and New Kingdoms flourished from the middle of the third millennium to the sixth century BCE with bureaucracies that were small, inefficient, and ramshackle.[11] High officials were appointed through patronage or inherited their titles, and they had to carry out wide-ranging duties at the request of the king. One inscription describes the duties of the vizier as if the king, the benevolent teacher, were passing on personal wisdom to his student. There must have been accepted ways of doing things and deciding cases, but the Egyptian records emphasize the personal discretion of those who acted as judges. It was only in the sixth century BCE that the Persian emperor Darius I ordered a legal codification in Egypt.

The first lawmakers were doing something different. Their laws may have been simple lists of punishments, compensation payments, and basic rules about contracts and divorce, but they were more than techniques of administration or means of judging cases. The Mesopotamian kings promised justice, Chinese emperors claimed they were upholding the order of the cosmos, and Hindu brahmins described the dharma that their rules enacted. From the earliest days, their laws represented a civilized world. Unlike the customs of nonliterate communities, the mediation of tribal conflicts, and the directions issued by Egyptian pharaohs, the new laws created objective standards, explicit sets of rules that other people could consult and quote. These laws could take on a life of their own. Some of the earliest

Mesopotamian lawmakers chiselled their laws onto stone slabs, fully intending them to last. And even if clay tablets were crushed, bronze vessels melted down, or palm leaves deteriorated, people could remember the rules and write them out again. Their laws had a permanence that could, and did, outlast the authority of the lawmakers.

Laws provide tools with which rulers can order and control their societies. But they also offer resources to which people can turn as they seek justice and resist the arbitrary exercise of power. When laws are written out, different people can read and refer to them. The Chinese rulers created laws as practical tools of government, but when scribes placed them onto long bamboo strips, which they pinned up on gateposts and at markets, ordinary people could quote the rules to argue about an abuse of power or appeal against an unfair sentence, to the discomfort of local officials. In India, scholars, judges, and litigants consulted legal texts as they pursued legal cases and debated how property ought to be distributed. Judges could not simply decide what amounted to wrongful conduct and what would produce justice; they had to apply the rules. Their laws were objective and authoritative.

This is why the apparently simple technique of lawmaking can give powerful arguments to ordinary people. On a practical level, laws guide behaviour in ways that may make complex relations more predictable, as international merchants have long found. They define classes, professions, and social relations and categorize actions as permitted or prohibited, effective, or invalid. Laws provide rules for moral conduct. They offer standards that people can refer to and means of making decisions. By referring to laws, judges can treat like cases alike, as lawyers insist they should. They can say with certainty what the outcome of a dispute should be, and explain the principles that emerged from earlier judgements, creating the system of precedent that lies at the heart of the common law. Both written laws and precedents create an order of rules and categories, even without ready means of enforcement. They order the world conceptually as well as physically. This is, in essence, what all laws do. And once made explicit, written on palm leaves or inscribed on clay tablets, laws become objective. They can be tools to exercise power, means to legitimate it, and resources for those who would resist it.

KINGS AND GOVERNMENTS have used law to cement their power, expand their domains, and discipline their populations. The Mesopotamian laws made liberal references to the death penalty; Chinese emperors used legally sanctioned sentences of penal labour to create an army of state slaves; brahmins supported the political projects of Indian kings; and Muslim caliphs enforced harsh criminal penalties, which they claimed were consistent with the directions of Islamic law. Laws help rulers to raise taxes and armies, requisition land and resources, and expand their empires. It was not just the Chinese rulers who used laws to create complex bureaucracies and manage their expanding territories. European powers also put law at the heart of their colonial projects. When the Persian, Mughal, and Ottoman Empires crumbled in the eighteenth and nineteenth centuries, and French and British forces unseated Muslim sultans and Hindu kings, colonial administrators declared that their laws would bring civilization to a 'despotic' Orient. Law legitimated their projects of conquest.

But law has never just been a tool for the powerful. People have also quoted laws to challenge government decisions, resist abuses of power, and seek justice. Over four thousand years, people have repeatedly put their faith in law to make the world a better place. Priests, village councils, and tribal leaders, along with reformers and campaigners, have crafted laws as they sought to promote a moral order, resolve conflicts, or pursue ambitious projects for justice. The innovation of the Mesopotamian kings, the Chinese emperors, and the Hindu brahmins was to create rules that would take on a life of their own. Once these laws were recorded and made public, people could appeal to them for justice. The determined dictator might tear up the rule book, but he could not do it unnoticed. Modern human rights laws are just the latest in a line of legal instruments designed to curb the wrongful use of power, and they do, on occasion, achieve this aim. This is the rule of law, and it is as ancient as law itself.

LAWS HAVE NEVER simply been rules. They have created intricate maps for civilization. Far from purely concrete or mundane, throughout their history laws have presented a social vision, promised justice, invoked the moral world ordained by God, and enshrined the principles of democracy and human rights. And, while laws have surely been an instrument of power, they have just as often been a means of resisting it. Yet the rule of law is neither universal nor inevitable. Some rulers have avoided submitting themselves to the constraints of law, as Chinese emperors did for two thousand years. The rule of law has a history, and we need to understand that history if we are to appreciate what law is, what it does, and how it can rule our world for better, as well as for worse.

PART I

VISIONS OF ORDER

CHAPTER ONE

MESOPOTAMIA AND THE
LANDS OF THE BIBLE

In 2112 BCE, an ambitious military leader, Ur-Namma, seized power in the Mesopotamian city of Ur. Ousting a successful but ruthless warlord, the new king introduced measures to relieve peasants, labourers, and artisans who had fallen into poverty, and he promised to redress social inequalities. He boldly declared, 'I did not deliver the orphan to the rich. I did not deliver the widow to the mighty. I did not deliver the man with only one shekel to the man with one mina [sixty shekels]. I did not deliver the man with only one sheep to the man with one ox. . . . I eliminated enmity, violence, and cries for justice.'[1]

Like many of his predecessors, Ur-Namma ordered scribes to write out his grand claims about justice on clay tablets. But he followed them with something new, a set of rules. From today's vantage point, the rules seem rather ordinary, little more than pragmatic directions about compensation payments and punishments. But they are the earliest laws that archaeologists have discovered anywhere in the world. And they lie at the origins of a legal tradition that developed over the next two thousand years, serving as examples for lawmakers in very different lands as they

pursued very different visions of order. Even after the Mesopotamian civilizations were finally overcome by Persian invaders,
their legal tradition lived on, indirectly inspiring the laws that
now dominate our world.

No one knows for sure whether Ur-Namma created the very
first laws. He may have been following the example of an even
earlier king. What is certain, however, is that in the fertile lands
between the Tigris and the Euphrates, the dry climate has preserved the earliest relics of any writing, cuneiform script, inscribed on stones and pressed onto clay tablets. And that writing
offers evidence that by the third millennium before the common
era, the Mesopotamian kings were making laws.

IRRIGATION BROUGHT PROSPERITY to the Fertile Crescent
in the fourth millennium BCE. By channelling water onto the
flat lands between the great rivers, which run through what is
now Iraq, farmers could cultivate barley and wheat, which they
ground, boiled, and roasted to create the staple foods of bread
and beer. Farther afield on the surrounding pastureland, livestock provided milk, meat, and wool. Women spun and wove
the wool into fine cloth, exchanging the most elaborate pieces for
silver in Anatolia, a journey of several weeks to the northwest.
Flourishing agriculture and successful trading allowed towns to
grow, and artisans became skilled in pottery and metalwork,
creating delicate jewellery and detailed inlaid patterns on the
pillars of their temples and palaces. By the end of the fourth
millennium BCE, the city of Uruk had perhaps twenty-five thousand people, their homes clustered around a central temple and
surrounded by 10 kilometers (about 6 miles) of walls.[2]

It was probably the priests who first developed cuneiform
writing, as a means to record the many donations made to
their goddess Inanna. People came from all over with offerings

of livestock, butter, and grain to fund the elaborate rituals the priests conducted at the temple. The technique of using styluses to press marks onto clay tablets was taken up by merchants, who recorded their stocks and noted down the arrangements they made with traders from distant lands. The city's governors realized they could use the same method to manage and pay the craftsmen who adorned their public buildings, and the labourers who fortified the walls of their cities. They used different symbols for metalworkers, spinners, weavers, potters, and merchants, noting the rations they were to receive.

The priests formed the elite in most early Mesopotamian cities, but in around 2900 BCE, a family in the city of Lagash established itself as royalty, the new kings claiming they could intercede with the gods for the benefit of the people. Soon, ambitious individuals in all the major cities of Mesopotamia followed suit. To establish legitimacy in the eyes of their people, the new rulers made grand claims about their devotion and their achievements. In elaborate dedications inscribed at their temples, they addressed both the gods and their descendants.[3] As well as recording their temple building and irrigation projects, the new rulers promised justice. An inscription on clay cones from Lagash dating to around 2450 BCE records the reforms of King Uruinimgina. Realizing that ordinary people were suffering at the hands of rapacious officials, who were taxing just about every activity imaginable, including funerals, the king sacked the corrupt, reduced taxes, and stopped exploitation of the poor, or so he claimed. 'Never', he promised the gods, 'would he allow the orphan or the widow to suffer at the hands of the powerful'.[4] Writing had become a means for kings to make grand statements about justice.

The cities of Mesopotamia were often embroiled in warfare as rulers competed for control of land and water resources. After the decline of Uruk and Lagash, the rulers of Ur came to power, leaving behind astonishing royal tombs; military conquest then saw the rise of the Akkadian warlord Sargon, who conquered city after city to create an empire on a new scale. His merchants traded with partners in the Arabian Peninsula and the distant Indus Valley, importing copper, cornelian, and lapis lazuli. Vast amounts of livestock and raw materials were moved around by boat. Sargon expanded his administration and large numbers of scribes found employment in government offices, where they wrote tax receipts, recorded population censuses, noted rations and wages, and inscribed royal edicts. The cities grew, professions became more specialist, and without systems of redistribution, the poor who fell on hard times had to borrow grain or food. Patterns of debt and credit developed, which allowed the wealthy to seize the property of the impoverished. It was these practices that had created the gap between rich and poor, which the king of Lagash claimed to redress. Practically all the new rulers used debt amnesties to try to redress the imbalances, and prophets of the gods even issued direct instructions to the kings to act justly whenever someone appealed to them for judgement.[5]

Late in the third millennium, Ur-Namma conquered Ur and 'liberated' the surrounding towns. He established control over most of the former Akkadian Empire, introducing systems of taxation, standardizing weights and measures, and promising justice to the people. Ordering scribes to record his projects of justice on clay tablets, he followed them by a set of laws. These specified how wrongdoing should be addressed, using a casuistic form: 'If . . . then . . .'. One provides, for example, that 'if a man (wrongfully) detains another he shall be imprisoned and he shall weigh and deliver fifteen shekels of silver'. The rules were intended to regulate future relations: instead of simply doing justice to those who came to him with petitions, Ur-Namma established rules that were supposed to last.

Thirty-seven of Ur-Namma's laws survive. They are far from comprehensive, and, certainly by later standards, they are not sophisticated. They direct punishment or compensation for murder, injury, false imprisonment, and sexual offences of different kinds; they specify what should happen to slaves who have relations with their owners or behave badly; and there are rules for divorce and marriage, oaths and accusations, and agricultural disputes. They are the sorts of rules that a judge could apply in a court. But there is no evidence that any judge ever did, which makes it difficult to discern how anyone could have used them in practice. There were courts in Ur, and surviving tablets record their decisions, but they never refer to Ur-Namma's laws. The laws probably did reflect existing practices—the issues people took to the judges and the ways they were resolved. Any complex society in which people form social and professional relationships, especially with those whom they do not know well, needs a means of resolving disputes. In all likelihood, the judges of Ur were mediators and conciliators who would cajole or pressure people to reach agreement along well-established lines following known customs. And the kings may have appointed a few specialist judges to decide on punishment for wrongdoers, which other powerful officials might enforce. In writing his laws, Ur-Namma was probably trying to regularize these practices, or even to institute new, more just traditions. But they were still more like statements of principle, examples of good practice, than rules to be enforced.

This does not mean, however, that the laws were empty promises. By now, it was well established that a king with divine sanction had to ensure justice for his people, even if his successes were built on warfare, plunder, and slavery. By making laws, Ur-Namma was promising that anyone wrongly imprisoned, or thrown into debt bondage, should get relief. He was trying to put Ur society on a new footing. By publicizing his laws for all to see, he made it easier for people to hold his officials to account. Anyone could now quote a law, which had been pronounced by the king. It was the beginning, indeed, of the rule of law.

Ur-Namma's innovation—assuming he was the first law-maker—was to create a list of rules in casuistic form, the pattern taken by all subsequent Mesopotamian law. It may not seem remarkable to modern eyes, as it is the form in which most contemporary legislation is drafted—even our criminal laws specify penalties for crimes, rather than simply instructing people not to commit them. But it was an innovation in Mesopotamia. The first law codes were statements of propaganda, but they also established a technique that would be taken up again and again over the following centuries and that would be put to many different uses. Ur-Namma's rules for divorce and agricultural disputes may not seem momentous, but the legal form claims an authority of its own. Legal rules can be quoted and misquoted, flaunted by rulers, and put at the heart of pleas for justice. They can shape human relations for both good and for bad.

THE FALL OF Ur to Elamite invaders at the turn of the millennium left Mesopotamia without a dominant king, and over the following centuries the rulers of different city-states formed alliances and competed for power. They occasionally raided one another's territories and carried away slaves, but in most cases people simply got on with their lives as farmers and herders, merchants and temple officials, artisans, sailors, and labourers. And the new kings also followed Ur-Namma's example and made laws. The ruler of Isin, Lipit-Ishtar, for example, created a new law code in around 1930 BCE. It dealt with similar subjects, albeit in more detail, and in the epilogue Lipit-Ishtar invoked blessings on future kings who honoured his laws. He intended them to last.

Other kings must have followed suit, because fragments of exercise tablets dating to around 1800 BCE record detailed rules for compensation payments. Scribes used the laws as examples when they learned their craft, and they dedicated their efforts, imperfect as they were, to their gods. Archaeologists have also found the remnants of a handbook to be used by scribes when they drew up contracts. Literacy had by now spread widely, and Mesopotamian citizens were using written agreements to commission construction projects, settle family disputes, make marriage and inheritance arrangements, agree on agricultural rents, organize navigation and the use of boats, and finalize sales of livestock and pledges. The handbook contains lists of useful phrases with grammatical variations, such as 'against', 'against him', 'he has a claim against him', and 'no one shall have a claim against him'. The writers were standardizing terms and bringing specificity to the sorts of arrangements by which merchants, and even ordinary citizens, regulated their interactions. Like the laws that rulers had promulgated before them, the scribes' practices helped to bring order to a complex society.

The Amorites arrived in Mesopotamia during this period. Nomadic herders from the lands of what are now Palestine and Syria, they gradually moved eastwards across the Euphrates, taking advantage of political fragmentation in the region to occupy new pastures. Some sold their herds and established towns, the most important of which grew into the city of Babylon. By around 1880 BCE, Babylonians had established their own royal dynasty, fortified their city, erected grand palaces, and extended their canals and irrigation channels far into the desert.

For over a century the Babylonian citizens lived a life that was stable, prosperous, and secure. But in 1793 BCE, when his father died, a young prince named Hammurabi decided to pursue grander ambitions. He quickly formed strategic alliances with surrounding kings and set off to raid the territories of more distant rivals. He confronted and defeated the Elamites, then the most powerful military force in Mesopotamia, and went on to conquer Eshnunna; then he turned south to incorporate the thriving city of Larsa into his empire. Finally, he set off with his armies to the north to attack Mari, the largest and most elaborately constructed city in the region, and the seat of his former ally Zimri-Lim. Having overcome its resistance, Hammurabi's soldiers plundered the city's riches, burnt down its monumental palaces, and enslaved its people. Back in Babylon, now the un-challenged king of all Mesopotamia, Hammurabi turned to new building projects, adorning the city with elaborate palaces and splendid temples. He also turned to his people, creating the laws that, he declared, would ensure justice in the region for genera-tions to come.

His ancestors may have been immigrants just a few generations earlier, but Hammurabi saw himself as a ruler in the Mesopota-mian tradition. In the prologue to his laws, he presents himself as a divinely inspired ruler whose military successes were due to the favour of the gods.[6] He describes himself as benevolent, providing for his people and guaranteeing them justice. In fact, he had already ordered several debt amnesties, concerned, like his predecessors, to rebalance destabilizing inequalities.[7] Ham-murabi ordered that his laws be inscribed onto tall stones and erected around his territories, where they could be seen and read out to anyone. On the grandest of these, a great granite slab, his stonemasons carved a picture of the king standing before the god of the sun, Shamash, obviously receiving divine authority. Beneath, the slab is covered by delicate cuneiform marks, which make up almost three hundred laws.

Hammurabi's legal text concludes with a long epilogue in which the king makes grand promises for the effects of his laws:

These are the judicial decisions that Hammurabi, the king, has established to bring about truth and a just order in his land. . . . Let any wronged man who has a lawsuit come be-fore my image, as king of justice, and have what is written on my stele read to him, so that he may understand my precious commands; and let my stele demonstrate his position, so that he may understand his case and calm his heart. . . . I am

Hammurabi, king of justice, to whom Shamash has granted the truth.[8]

The rules are far more detailed and elaborate than the rather rudimentary laws of Ur-Namma, but they take the same casuistic form. They clearly reflect the sorts of problems that must have given rise to disputes in Babylonian society. Although tribute and trade were responsible for much of Babylon's wealth, this was still a fundamentally agricultural society, and the rules deal with the many issues that must have arisen from cultivation, irrigation, and other farming activities. There are also a handful of rules relating to pastures and orchards. Farmers who were careless when irrigating their fields and flooded their neighbours' lands, for example, had to pay compensation for the damaged crops. Many of the rules are simple and straightforward:

If a man cuts down a tree in another man's date orchard, without his permission, he shall pay thirty shekels of silver.

If a man has given a field to a gardener to plant as a date orchard, when the gardener has planted it he shall cultivate it for four years. In the fifth year, the owner and gardener shall divide the yield in equal shares and the owner shall choose his share first.[9]

Local communities were probably enforcing these sorts of practices anyway, but writing them down may have given ordinary people a measure of protection against those who tried to cheat them. Quoting a rule from the great emperor's law stone was surely far more powerful than simply complaining about a careless neighbour.

It is evident that the farmers' lands and fields had, by this date, become commercial assets that could be bought, sold, rented, or mortgaged, and this led to new problems. Some rules specify the service obligations of those who held land leased to them by the palace—the king obviously owned extensive property in the city—while others deal with private tenancies and rent. Hammurabi also tried to give a measure of protection to farmers who got into debt and had to take out loans: 'If anyone owes a debt for a loan and the storm god Adat devastates his fields, or a flood sweeps away the crops, or the grain does not grow for lack of water, in that year he need not give his creditor any grain. He can suspend the contract and pay no interest for that year.'[10] Along with the debt amnesties, these laws would have helped to ensure that supplies of basic foodstuffs were not disrupted by the demands of unforgiving moneylenders.

As many citizens were involved in trade and commerce, the laws contain a long set of rules about interest rates, profits, debts, and the distraint (seizure) and custody of goods. Merchants were obviously entering into complex arrangements and using sophisticated financial instruments, and the rules prescribe harsh penalties for those who tried to cheat their partners. The profits and taxes generated by all this commercial activity would have funded much of Babylon's infrastructure and architectural splendour, but so, too, would plunder, and warfare generated its own problems. Hammurabi's campaigns, not long ended when he created his laws, had taken men away from their homes and families for months or years at a time, probably without easy means of communication. One set of laws deals with the sort of situation that might arise when a soldier returned unexpectedly. For example, 'If a man is taken prisoner in war and there are insufficient provisions in his house and his wife goes to another man's house and bears him children, and if later her husband returns to his home, then the wife shall return to her first husband, but the children shall inherit from their father.'[11] Family relations and inheritance were similarly complex issues, and the laws make detailed provisions for dowry, bridewealth, support for widows, and children's inheritance.

Hammurabi's laws reflect a stratified society in which people followed distinct professions as soldiers, civil servants, doctors, judges, and merchants. They divided people into three classes— freemen, dependent citizens, and slaves—who had different rights and privileges, and who were entitled to different amounts of compensation if they were injured. Slaves who integrated into Babylonian society, particularly concubines, caused particular difficulties. Liaisons between slaves and freemen were not forbidden, but could lead to problems upon death or divorce, and children needed to be carefully provided for: 'If a man's wife bears him children and his slave also bears him children, and the father, during his life, says to the children whom his slave has borne, "my children", and he counts them with the children of his wife; then if the father dies, the children of the wife and of the slave shall divide the paternal property equally between them. The children of the wife shall select and take the first share.'[12]

Hammurabi's laws address the sorts of problems that arise in a complex society in which not everything can be resolved by face-to-face mediation. But more than guidance for judges, the laws also gave structure to social relations, by specifying the different classes and professions people could belong to and how their members could and should relate to one another. They mapped out a set of rights, duties, activities, and social structures for Babylon's citizens.

So could Hammurabi's laws actually have brought peace and justice to Babylonian society? Whether by taking inspiration from previous rulers or by consulting his judges, Hammurabi seems genuinely to have tried to create rules that would enable his citizens to seek justice. But, like the laws of Ur-Namma, his rules do not ever seem to have been referred to in legal cases. The surviving records of the agreements and arrangements that followed legal disputes never make direct references to the laws; in fact, they show little direct correspondence with what the rules provided for.[13] The laws are also not comprehensive: the rules concerning agriculture outnumber by far those on pastoralism, for example, although herding activities must have been just as important as planting and harvesting crops, and probably led to just as many disputes. Doubtless these were resolved through time-honoured, unwritten processes of mediation. Some of the laws are inconsistent in the amounts of compensation they specify for injuries. Other are improbably harsh. The death penalty is ordained for false accusations of homicide and theft, for abducting the child of a nobleman, and for adultery.[14] There are also mutilation penalties: if a child strikes his father, one of his hands shall be cut off; and there shall be an eye for destroying the eye of a free man, and a tooth for breaking his tooth.[15] But what if a genuine victim of theft could not find anyone to identify his property, or was let down at the last minute by a malicious neighbour? If Babylonian judges were applying these laws with the sort of exactness we expect of courts in the modern world, they would have been meting out an extremely severe form of justice. Would the citizens of Babylon not have been indignant about the harshness of this 'justice'?

Rather than allowing the laws to confirm the familiar image of a tyrannical king, engaging in violent warfare, with armies of slaves, we should take Hammurabi's claims to be establishing justice for his people seriously. The laws probably aimed to make clear the sorts of offences that were considered to be the most serious. By specifying the death penalty, Hammurabi was putting the crimes of kidnapping and false accusation on a par with murder and theft. The laws told the Babylonians that it was as bad to make a false accusation of theft as it was to commit theft itself— after all, a false accusation could lead to the death of an innocent man or woman. Doubtless murderers, thieves, traffickers, and other scoundrels were sometimes—maybe often—put to death.

In a society in which armies plundered and sacked one another's cities and the defeated were carried off into slavery, powerful officials probably did enforce harsh penalties. But the physical brutality meted out on conquered populations would have destabilized Babylon if applied to its own citizens. We should not assume that in every case for which the laws prescribed the death penalty, the judges actually imposed it, or that Hammurabi intended that they should. He was most likely using the laws to indicate the sorts of cases in which it *might* be right to impose it, the sorts of conduct that were most to be discouraged in a peaceful and just society. The laws reflected past cases, telling the Babylonians how justice had already been handed out; but they also established principles for the future, using Ur-Namma's casuistic form. They provided examples, specified limits, and established exceptions, all against a background in which the basic principles of justice were known to all.

Hammurabi provided rules that would help people navigate complex social relations in a society divided into different social classes and professions. He claims in his epilogue that the rules are 'judicial decisions', apparently records of actual cases. And it is clear that he (or his advisers) selected examples that would demonstrate particular principles. One is the distinction between the three different statuses of Babylonian citizens. A rather touching group of laws stipulates that a doctor who saves a man's life by using a bronze knife should be rewarded: for the life of a freeman he should be given ten pieces of silver; for a dependent citizen, five; and for a slave he should receive two pieces from the slave's master.[16] These directions cannot always have been followed exactly—fluctuations in the value of money would quickly have made the actual rules obsolete. But they symbolized the difference between the three classes of citizens—a freeman was worth twice as much as a dependent citizen, and a slave less than half as much again, and his master was liable for the debt because the slave was the master's property. Another group of laws specifies the payments that a negligent doctor must make, drawing similar distinctions between classes.[17] These laws seem to be just as important for what they demonstrate in terms of class as for the exact penalties they prescribe in cases of medical negligence. The rules must, then, have given judges and mediators a starting point from which they could negotiate appropriate compensation in quite different cases. They express general principles about status and equivalence in terms of specific rules about compensation.

Another law from Hammurabi's code provides that if a slave falls ill with epilepsy within one month of being purchased, the owner should be able to send him back and recover what he has paid.[18] This may well reflect an actual case, but it would be bizarre if the principle only applied to epilepsy. The rule expresses a general principle: that sellers should guarantee the fitness of their slaves for a reasonable length of time. And although the rules for doctors only specify treatment using a bronze knife, surely the same principle must have applied to other successful cures. In the rules dealing with penalties and compensation due after an injury, there is one saying that if a man swears that he did not strike his victim intentionally, he merely has to cover the costs of the physician, rather than paying substantial compensation.[19] This rule confirmed an important principle, that judges and mediators should treat unintentional injuries less severely than deliberate harm. Another rule states that if a shepherd negligently allows disease to spread in an enclosure, he is to make restitution to the owner of the livestock, unless it was an epidemic or a lion that caused the loss, in which case it falls on the owner.[20] The laws are quite specific, reflecting decisions in real cases and indicating the sorts of predators that threatened Babylonian shepherds. But they demonstrate fundamental principles: unintentional injuries and unavoidable losses should be treated differently from deliberate striking and negligent damage. Hammurabi almost certainly did not intend that his judges should apply the rules literally, as we expect of contemporary legislation.

In practice, most legal disputes were probably resolved locally, through mediation or the interventions of officials, regional governors, or respected elders.[21] Farmers would have appealed to a local official if they felt that a moneylender was charging too much interest; a freeman in the city could have asked a government official to help recover his runaway slave; and an artisan might have gathered friends and neighbours to persuade a mediator that he was being unfairly accused of a scam. The mediators would have treated each individual case on its own facts, but they would have taken account of the general principles expressed in Hammurabi's laws.

Against the backdrop of traditional practices of justice in local courts, it was probably the case that the things everyone knew did not need to be spelled out. No one is likely to have denied that it was wrong to kill, to injure, or to steal, and that compensation should be paid by those who did. What the laws needed to do was to clarify best practice in difficult cases, such as when witnesses gave contradictory evidence, when a guilty party claimed his behaviour was an accident, or when a thief was caught red-handed and killed by an irate property-owner. Everyone knew that a father should leave his property to his children, but what if he also had a mistress, or children by a slave whom he had freed? The laws cover some of the more difficult cases, while the more basic principles are assumed. This explains many of the apparent gaps and inconsistencies.

In his epilogue Hammurabi demands that his laws should provide inspiration for a ruler 'who has discernment, and is capable of providing just ways for his land'. Future kings should use them as examples to provide justice for their subjects, in the way that Hammurabi had done for his. And he calls down a series of terrifying curses on any future king who does not respect them. Written in everyday language, his laws were accessible not only to all literate people who could read, but to all who were in hearing distance when they were read aloud, and they could be quoted back to anyone who tried to cheat or oppress them. They held the promise of justice for all. They were also supposed to last forever. Hammurabi was promising the rule of law.

THE POTENTIAL OF this new technique was quickly appreciated by other rulers in Mesopotamia and its surroundings. While Hammurabi and his successors held power in Babylon, practices of lawmaking spread into Anatolia, where they were adopted by the Hittite kings, who ruled from the seventeenth to twelfth centuries BCE. Their extensive sets of laws were copied over several generations, although apparently without the grand prologues of the Mesopotamian kings.[22] Hammurabi's own laws had a long legacy in the region and were largely adopted by his successors; they also inspired the dynasties that followed. After Hammurabi's dynasty fell in 1595 BCE, Assyrian invaders moved in from the east, and by 1400 they had settled in Babylon and established their own empire. One of the first things they did was to make laws, using a casuistic form similar to the earlier Mesopotamian laws, which they undoubtedly copied. Their empire lasted until around 950 BCE, during which time they continued to copy out their original laws.[23] Throughout, Hammurabi's text was used as a writing exercise, a model of legal writing for scribes learning their craft. The claims of longevity made by the early Mesopotamian kings were fulfilled by their successors a millennium later.

Ascendant Persian forces invaded Mesopotamia in 538 BCE under their leader Cyrus the Great. They swept away most of the region's civilizations, razing its cities, burning palaces, and enslaving much of its population, rather as rival Mesopotamian kings had treated one another. But no conqueror can govern through force alone. Cyrus was soon claiming he would bring justice to the Babylonians and restore their city and monuments. He made no new laws, but he ordered that copies of Hammurabi's code be made from the stele that had been carried off to western Persia by Elamite invaders. This was to be placed in a library near Babylon. He also maintained the tradition of appointing royal judges. When his son Cambyses wanted to marry one of his sisters, he sought their approval, and the judges disapproved, at least according to the Greek historian Herodotus writing a century later. Cambyses ultimately ignored the judges' opinion, but he had acknowledged their authority.

Cambyses's successor, Darius, saw himself as more of a lawmaker and adapted the Mesopotamian legal forms to his own purposes.[24] As he developed the administration of his empire, he was concerned to ensure that local leaders showed him loyalty and paid tribute. Like his Mesopotamian predecessors, he wanted to protect ordinary people as well. He explained that men should fear his laws, so that the strong would not attack the weak. Realizing that conquered populations needed to retain their own traditions, he also ordered that his scribes codify the largely unwritten Egyptian customs. And his successors apparently ordered their judges to teach Jewish law to the local populations in the Israelite province of Yehud, safeguarding what would grow into one of the world's major religious legal traditions.

Mesopotamian legal techniques, meanwhile, had spread farther afield. Since the time of Hammurabi in the 1770s BCE, Babylon had been a centre of trade and commerce, welcoming traders and other visitors from India, Central Asia, Persia, Arabia, Egypt, Armenia, and Greece. Merchants would have appreciated the benefits of using legal forms and transported legal ideas to their homelands. Around the turn of the seventh and sixth centuries, there was unrest in the city of Athens, and during a popular revolt against tyranny the citizens asked for a set of laws that would protect them against future tyrants.[25]

But the laws, created by Draco, an Athenian legislator, seem to have been harsh, failing to resolve tensions between rich and poor. This prompted a popular leader, Solon, to promise a better constitution. He ordered a debt cancellation, repealed almost all of Draco's laws, and replaced them with a new set, which promised to relieve agricultural poverty and address debt. Their content may have been designed to resolve particularly Athenian problems, but Solon adopted the casuistic form, almost certainly inspired by Mesopotamian laws. It was a technique that had travelled westwards, along with luxury goods, decorative arts, and the alphabet.[26]

Later Greeks were not enthusiastic lawmakers, although they did inscribe some laws on stone slabs, but they were proud of their legal traditions. And a century and a half later, the same legal tradition inspired a group of scribes from the small city of Rome on the Italian Peninsula. Charged with constitutional reform after a similar period of unrest and popular revolt, they produced laws that would later form the basis for one of the world's most influential legal traditions.

In the meantime, the Mesopotamian legal tradition had also inspired a very different group of people, the Israelite tribes who grazed their livestock on the lands of what are now Israel and Palestine.

WHILE THE RULERS of Mesopotamian cities were erecting superb palaces, laying out intricate canal systems, and developing sophisticated bureaucracies, six hundred miles to the west assorted herdsmen were tending sheep and goats on the grasslands that bordered the eastern Mediterranean. In the second millennium BCE they were divided into a number of distinct tribes, twelve according to the Old Testament, although the real number varied, as different groups expanded, contracted, combined, and disappeared. Many were nomadic, while others settled down and built houses next to fields and orchards, in which they grew grain, grapes, and olives.[27]

There are no records of any rulers in these lands until we meet Saul, David, and Solomon, the first kings to unite the Israelite tribes, at the turn of the first millennium BCE. According to the Old Testament, this was after the Israelites had returned from Egypt under the leadership of Moses, having spent many years wandering in the wilderness. The historical and archaeological evidence of this great journey is sparse, and the accounts that we find in the early books of the Bible were almost certainly compiled several centuries later. It was probably not until the time of the kings that these origin stories, including the exodus from Egypt, were written down in anything like their final form. But the writers may well have used older sources, reproducing written and oral accounts. Much of the detail, including the laws they describe, may well have had their origins in the ways of life and social organization of the Israelite tribesmen.[28]

The five books of the Pentateuch, or Torah, describe laws for worship, ritual, and sacrifice. Much of their moral guidance takes the form of proverbs and offers motivations for good conduct. Leviticus sets out the famously elaborate dietary rules. In the Book of Exodus we hear how Moses climbed a mountain to receive God's instructions and returned with the Ten Commandments and a set of practical laws for his people.[29] The commandments affirmed that the Israelites must worship a single god and listed the most important moral rules they should observe. The laws that followed told them about social relations, specifying how tribesmen should deal with cases of murder and assault, the injuries caused by wayward livestock, theft, seduction, and the like. There are other rules regulating agriculture and basic forms of trade. Still others tell the Israelites how to make arrangements for their slaves. In fact, in the rules he spelled out to Moses, God started with slaves, saying, 'Now, these are the laws that you shall set before them. When you buy a Hebrew servant, he shall serve six years, and in the seventh he shall go out free, for nothing. . . . If his master gives him a wife and she bears his children, the wife and her children shall be her master's and he shall go out alone.'[30] The first eleven verses concern slavery, in reality debt bondage, before turning to assaults and injuries.

The twenty-one or so laws of Exodus are far briefer than the Babylonian laws.[31] They deal with only a handful of basic issues, and there are nothing like the fine distinctions and exceptions found in the Babylonian code. It is fair to assume that most disputes were mediated locally, both during and after the time of the kings, when elders in Jerusalem and other towns decided cases 'in the gate', that is, in the marketplace just inside the town's gate.[32] The rules contained just some of the most important principles that threaded through their practices. As with the laws of Hammurabi, many also condone slavery, frequent use of the death penalty, and violent retribution.[33]

The world of the Israelite tribes was very different from that of Babylon. Hammurabi was a powerful ruler who presided over a literate society with a stable and bureaucratic government, complex finances, and flourishing commerce. The Israelites had nothing like a centralized state before Saul and David established their kingdoms in the tenth and eleventh centuries BCE, and even from this period, archaeology has revealed little in the way of urban infrastructure. Before then, the tribes' leaders would have been more like mediators than heads of a state. They were probably called upon to make peace after quarrels, or when fighting threatened the stability of their tribes, and they may have summoned councils to make strategic decisions about nomadic movements and pasture use. The sorts of disputes indicated by the laws, the injuries caused by small-scale fighting, arguments over grazing and wandering livestock, allegations of theft and adultery, and complaints about those who allowed their oxen to run wild—all of these must have been resolved locally and orally.

The Israelites used a similar casuistic form for their laws as the Mesopotamians, and many deal with similar subjects: how to treat slaves, the penalties that should be imposed for injuries and theft, and the consequences of adultery or seducing a virgin, although the details are different. For example, the laws provide that killing through ambush or treachery attracts the death penalty, whereas if it is in response to an attack, the perpetrator should be able to seek a safe haven. Causing injuries that later heal attracts compensation for loss of time and the costs of treatment. A stolen sheep must be compensated for with four sheep, and an ox with five oxen, but if the thief still has the animal, he may return it along with a second animal. Someone who seduces a virgin must pay the bridewealth and marry her, unless her father refuses, in which case he just has to pay the bridewealth. These were the sorts of practices and principles that could well have shaped the lives of the Israelites when they were still nomadic tribesmen.

The laws of the Pentateuch place considerable emphasis on retaliation. The verses on causing injuries during fighting famously conclude, 'Life for life, eye for eye, tooth for tooth, burn for burn, wound for wound, and stripe for stripe'.[34] The principle of retaliation may seem barbarous in the modern world, and it is far less prominent in Hammurabi's laws, designed as they were for a more centralized and urbanized society. But patterns of feuding are extremely common among nomadic tribesmen. On the steppes of Central Asia and in the deserts of North Africa, and even today on the open grasslands of eastern Tibet, practices of revenge make sense. Here it was, and still is, easy to ride up to a nomadic encampment and drive away a few choice oxen, or a herd of sheep, while their unsuspecting owner is asleep in his tent. Animals are not fixed in the way that fields are. Pastoralists anxious to deter raiding let it be known that retaliation will be swift and severe, and that not only the injured party, but all his kinsmen, will combine to take revenge. Feuding, or the threat of a feud, is a form of defence. It requires that tribesmen are unquestioningly loyal to their leaders, ready to throw down their tools and ride off to avenge a wrong at a moment's notice. In the books of the Pentateuch, both God and Moses talk frequently about loyalty among the Israelite tribesmen and the revenge they can or must take for wrongs committed by strangers and enemies. The Book of Numbers carefully delineates the different Israelite tribes and their lands, but God also orders that the tribes should combine to wage war on their enemies the Midianites in revenge for past wrongs. And it is only from their enemies that they may take true slaves.[35]

But no society shaped by feuding relations condones indiscriminate retaliation. Revenge must always be proportionate, so that feuds do not escalate with terrible consequences for both sides. This is almost certainly what Moses (on God's instructions) meant when he declared 'a life for a life'. It was a law designed to limit retaliation, rather than an order that his people should always take revenge for a wrong. It was designed to ensure that feuds did not get out of hand. In the different parts of the world where people practise feuding, in East Africa, the Middle East, and the shores of the Mediterranean, there are always elaborate practices of mediation. Skilled mediators negotiate between warring factions to achieve peace through the payment and acceptance of compensation: blood money is paid for a death, and a wound price for injuries. This explains what Moses meant when he went on to declare 'an eye for an eye, a tooth for a tooth'. He was setting out a rule of equivalence, the starting point for a negotiated settlement in what might be the messy aftermath of a long-running feud. In this context, the laws were perfectly logical, emphasizing the right ways to make peace in a region subject to periodic outbreaks of feuding. Several centuries later, when Jesus declared 'love thy neighbour', he was introducing a seismic shift in social dynamics among the Israelites.

BUT BEFORE JESUS revolutionized the Middle East, and the world, much changed in the lands of Israel and Judah. The first Israelites to write down their laws were probably specialist scribes working at the courts of the kings who succeeded David and Solomon in the eighth century BCE. By then, the population had grown, towns had been built, and something of an urban elite had formed around the kings, who were starting to centralize their governments. The kingdoms of Israel and Judah had also become separate states, in the north and south. The laws of Exodus do not refer to kings, but they do talk of judges deciding appropriate penalties, which suggests that there were specialists to whom people could go with difficult cases. In the Books of Numbers and Deuteronomy, God orders that the Israelites should build cities which are to be places of refuge for those fleeing from vengeance, where their cases can be properly judged. They needed protected spaces if they were to take advantage of the law stipulating that an accidental killing should not attract a reciprocal death. The laws on debt bondage, more elaborate in Deuteronomy than Exodus, may well date from this period. As in Mesopotamian cities, the Israelites were finding that more centralized societies, money, and practices of lending resulted in more debt and debt bondage. But, although the Book of Deuteronomy tells the Israelites to select a king to rule over them, tribal ways almost certainly persisted into this era, and people must have continued to hold allegiance to their old family groups. An instinct for revenge probably lingered, and the basic pattern of compensation for injuries must have been maintained among groups to whom tribal loyalties mattered.

The laws of Exodus may have been written down in stages during this period, successively revised, combined, and supplemented. But when the scribes eventually put the laws into the form they now take in the Old Testament, they chose words and phrases that are strikingly similar to those which Hammurabi had used on his law stone:

> If a man puts out the eye of another man, his eye shall be put out.
> If he breaks another man's bone, his bone shall be broken.
> . . .
> If a man knocks out the tooth of his equal, his tooth shall be knocked out.[36]

Several of the laws on slavery are also remarkably similar to the rules written by the Babylonian king, and biblical scholars have noted more subtle correspondences.[37] The Israelites had very different lifestyles from the urban Babylonians and spoke a mutually incomprehensible language. The cuneiform script on Hammurabi's law stone would have been unreadable to most Israelites in the first millennium. Yet they adopted both the Mesopotamians' legal techniques and much of their laws' substance.[38] Of course, some problems arise almost everywhere that people live together. Every society must decide how to respond to an accidental killing, how to deal with conflicting evidence about the loss of property, and what penalties to apply for rape, and it should not be a surprise if different people came up with similar solutions. But some of the details are too particular to be the result of coincidence. Through the centuries, merchants and soldiers travelled over long distances, and they would have transported slaves, wives, and assistants with them. Mesopotamians could have quoted important oral rules in new places, which were taken up by others and made their own. Equally, well-travelled Israelites may have seen some of the many law stones and tablets onto which Hammurabi's laws were copied over the centuries and, like the Greek lawmakers, been impressed by what they read or heard read aloud. Whatever the mechanisms,

Mesopotamian laws travelled into a very different context, a society still shaped by tribal dynamics, where they were adopted by religious leaders concerned, above all, to distinguish their people from the surrounding gentiles.

For several centuries, Assyrian kings dominated the lands of Israel and Judah. According to one scholarly theory, it was a small and literate Israeli elite who wrote the laws of Exodus under Assyrian domination, partly to resist the domineering practices of their rulers, who were paying little respect to their history and traditions. Creating a code of laws was one way to show their conquerors, and, indeed, their own people, that the Israelites had a long history as independent tribes. Gathering together origin stories, narratives, proverbs, and ancient wisdom, as well as tribal laws and customs, they set out to create a permanent written record of who they were. As they travelled through Assyrian-dominated lands, literate Israelites may well have seen or heard examples of Hammurabi's laws and decided to use them as a model when they created their own. In their account of God's commandments to Moses, they accordingly started by copying parts of these famous laws, simplifying, improving, and adapting the rules to suit their own circumstances and practices.[39] It was simultaneously a mark of respect for the ancient civilization of Babylon and a gesture of defiance towards their own rulers.

The writing of the earliest books of the Bible is largely lost in the mists of time, and scholars are still debating their sources and origins. Did writers, in this or an earlier period, gather together old texts and oral traditions that had developed and changed over time, adding a few new phrases and laws to create a code in a form inspired by Hammurabi's laws? Was it the work of urban scribes under the Assyrian kings? Or did an Israeli elite put them together under later Babylonian domination, after King Nebuchadnezzar rose to power in Babylon, besieged Jerusalem, and took away scores of Israelites as prisoners?

It is extremely difficult to say for certain when the laws were made, and by whom, not to mention how they might actually have been used. But it seems likely that they had their roots in basic principles of social organization which the Israelites thought were important: ideas of equivalence and just compensation. These were defining principles for tribal people, whose livelihoods and social structures were constantly in flux, but who held a common vision of justice. Revenge should be proportionate, unintentional killing should not be avenged by death, injuries should be appropriately compensated for, women and children should be respected and protected, and slaves should be fairly treated. This is what the rules promised, and what they might actually have helped to achieve. Respected as matters of wisdom, they were repeated over the generations and finally written down by literate scribes under the domination of a later empire. Now more familiar with the work of specialist judges, and facing the contemporary problem of debt bondage, the writers combined their ancient traditions and practices of justice with the laws and legal forms developed by Mesopotamian rulers, laws that had acquired prestige throughout the region.

Whatever their history, the Israelite authors were using legal techniques to reinforce their account of who they were: independent people, loyal to their tribes, proud of their homeland, considerate to the poor, and worshipping a single god.

Law started out as a project of justice. The earliest lawmakers wrote out rules to accompany grand statements about their achievements, their religious devotion, and their commitment to a just society. In societies where the rich could force the poor into debt bondage and officials levied exploitative taxes, populist rulers, such as Uruinimgina, presented themselves as reformers.

But when Ur-Namma created rules that were supposed to curb wrongdoing and define just compensation, he was making promises about the future. His reforms and his reputation were supposed to last, and his text was meant to impress later generations as well as the gods.

Successive Mesopotamian kings appreciated the potential of written rules and used them to regulate their societies, create predictability for their merchants, and address social problems. The substance may often have been mundane, specifying penalties for basic crimes, compensation for injuries, and rules for contracts and family relations, but they created a new form of order. By defining classes and professions, rights and duties, like the scribes who developed standard forms for commercial relations, they were creating an order of rules and categories. They were classifying people and things, specifying relations between them, and giving a more permanent structure to society. The simple casuistic form of the Mesopotamian laws created objective standards that anyone could refer to.

The earliest laws were not just practical instruments to regulate city life and address the problems of individual petitioners. Judges and mediators did not need laws to resolve disputes; nor did kings primarily intend them to give officials ways of raising taxes, suppressing crime, and keeping undesirable people off the streets. It was the people who needed laws as resources for justice, standards that they could quote against anyone who might try to oppress them—and this was what Hammurabi claimed he was giving them. In the lengthy epilogue to his laws, the king described the terrible curses and misfortunes that would be heaped upon the head of any future ruler who failed to respect the justice of his laws. Line after line invoked the gods to punish such a person: to 'break his sceptre', 'curse his destiny', 'destroy his land by famine and want', 'shatter his weapons', and 'strike down his warriors'. Hammurabi was telling the world at large not just that he was an important ruler who enjoyed the favour of the gods, but that his laws would ensure justice into the future. This was the rule of law.

The same possibilities for creating practical order and mapping out routes to justice were grasped by others in distant lands, where Mesopotamian legal techniques were taken up by religious leaders with very different ambitions. The Israelite priests were trying to bring together scattered tribes to form a single people. Their laws specified what it was to lead a good and ritually correct life, mapping out duties and obligations more than rights, but also telling Israelites how to stand up for themselves and their religion in the face of powerful kings and rival tribes.

The casuistic form of law established in Mesopotamia was to have a long history, after it was adopted and adapted by the citizens of Rome. But in the meantime, legal techniques were invented, quite independently, farther to the east. Indian brahmins and Chinese rulers were also aspiring to order the world, but their visions were fundamentally different, and the laws they developed took quite distinct forms.

CHAPTER TWO

INDIAN BRAHMINS
The Order of the Cosmos

The laws crafted on the Indian plains were written by religious specialists, brahmins, whose mission was to uphold the cosmological order revealed in the Vedas, the ancient Sanskrit texts. They specified duties more than rights, and these were duties people had to fulfil if they were to uphold the dharma, the ideal order of the world. In the Hindu tradition there was never any clear divide between law and religion. The legal texts, the Dharmashastras, presented rules for daily life, specifying how people should live in accordance with their caste, along with instructions about ritual, purity, commercial activities, and rules of evidence. And the brahmins always remained the highest legal authorities, claiming that their laws should guide even the king. Over the centuries, they relied on powerful rulers for protection and support, but, at least in theory, a good Hindu king was supposed to observe the brahmin's laws. He could enact law, but he could not make it.

THE BRAHMINS CRAFTED their first legal texts in the second century of the common era, but their rules and principles were rooted in traditions that stretched back to the very origins of the Vedas more than a thousand years earlier. This was when ritual specialists first built up a body of oral texts and knowledge, which they passed on through the generations.

The Harappan Empire, the first great civilization of South Asia, was already in decline when a group of Aryan tribesmen swept into northern India. Debates about the origins of these warlike horsemen have raged for decades, but their horses suggest Central Asia. They arrived on the plains of the river Ganges between around 1500 and 1300 BCE and pushed the indigenous people into the surrounding forests and marshlands.[1] The Aryans frequently engaged in fighting, raiding one another's livestock, and their chiefs, the *raja*s, were more like warlords than heads of state. They rode around in fast two-wheeled chariots, used bows and arrows, drank alcohol, and led raiding expeditions.[2] The Aryans depended on their animals and animal products for nourishment and household goods, but they also had silver, gold, copper, and bronze, with which they crafted ornaments, ritual objects, and weapons.

The rajas distributed largesse in grand ceremonies, often involving elaborate animal sacrifices. Unlike the Mesopotamian kings, who claimed divine authority as direct recipients of the gods' favour, the Aryan rulers supported a distinct class of ritual specialists to conduct these sacrifices. These may originally have been prophets, oracles, wandering shamans who claimed to be able to placate troublesome sprits, or simply local priests who carried out rites to ensure good fortune in battle and plentiful monsoon rains. Whatever their origins, it is fair to assume that they gave people a sense that there was a right way to do things. They may have talked of an afterlife, and they almost certainly promised to address the threat of natural disasters. Supported by the rajas, these priests built up a body of mantras and invocations which they passed on orally, claiming they had been revealed to the most learned after profound meditation. These were the earliest of the Vedas.

At around the turn of the first millennium BCE, the Aryans moved eastwards onto the Doab, the area of marshland and monsoon forests between the Ganges and Jamuna Rivers. Here, they found lands they could cultivate using new iron tools, and many settled and became farmers. They grew rice and developed irrigation techniques. Successful agriculture can produce surpluses, which often allows a small class of people to accumulate wealth and set themselves up as rulers and protectors of the population at large. So it was with the Aryans. Communal pasturelands, which had probably been allotted each year on the throw of a dice, now gave way to landholdings, which could be accumulated, leased out, and bought or sold. Later texts mention farms extending to one hundred acres, with five hundred ploughs and forty thousand cattle.[3] The figures may be exaggerated, but these were more than smallholdings. The chiefs accumulated surplus animals, rice, and ghee, and successful farmers could use their wealth to engage in trade and buy fine pottery with delicate floral and geometric designs.

The Aryans eventually clustered into towns and cities, which developed the trappings of urban civilization. Although theirs was still largely a rural culture, some specialized as soldiers, merchants, shopkeepers, craftsmen, elephant- and horse-trainers, and stage managers for the rajas' ceremonies. The merchants' networks probably extended as far as Babylon to the west and to what is now Sri Lanka to the south. With trade came coinage, banking, and literacy. As in Mesopotamia over a thousand years earlier, the complexity of trade relations prompted the development of a written script, first in the form of marks used for accounting purposes, and, by around the sixth century BCE, in letters that could be used to keep records, send messages, and draw up contracts.

The most successful rulers now governed cities, into which people clustered from different areas. As their wealth increased, the rajas built up substantial retinues, with multiple wives, military commanders, charioteers, bards, butchers, cooks, and the *purohita*, the ruler's priest, who rode in his chariot and chanted mantras to keep him safe in combat.[4] They were now kings of defined territories, rather than leaders of clans, and they insisted on passing their positions on to their sons. As they explained, people without a raja would languish in a state of anarchy. But each new ruler was also consecrated by a priest. The kings needed their blessing.

Gradually, Aryan society became more stratified. A historical sense of superiority, of warrior over peasant, now solidified into a class distinction between the *kshatriyas* (the rajas and power-holders), on the one hand, and the *vaishyas* (the farmers, merchants, and craftsmen), on the other. The clansmen of the raja, retaining old loyalties, probably regarded themselves as above everyone else. The more successful farmers and traders began to employ servants, who came to form an underclass, the *shudras*. The shudras also included landless peasants, wage labourers, and slaves, both the inhabitants of conquered lands and those who had fallen into debt bondage.

As the social stratification sharpened, the priests insisted that they were the only ones who could consume the remains of an animal sacrifice, and then they banned shudras from these ritual events altogether. They gradually formed a hereditary class, calling themselves 'brahmins', those who knew the secrets of ritual efficacy and whose duty it was to preserve the wisdom of the Vedas. This wisdom largely consisted of mantras and invocations in an ancient version of Sanskrit that ordinary people could no longer understand. The most elaborate rituals, meanwhile, developed into lengthy ceremonies, on which the rajas lavished extensive resources, which served to demonstrate their power and legitimacy.

Over time, the classes formed a hierarchy of ritual purity, from the elite brahmins, to the kshatriyas, to the vaishyas, and finally the least pure, the shudras. These were the four *varnas*, which Vedic wisdom explained as being like parts of the human body, each with its own independent character. In practice, these distinctions allowed disparate groups of people, of different ethnic origins and engaged in different occupations, to form into a single social and ritual structure. It is the basis of India's caste system, which endures to this day.

This period, the middle of the first millennium before the common era, is known as 'the formative phase of India culture'.[5] The brahmins, who had been passing on their wisdom orally in mantras and *sutras* (instructions for rituals), now wrote them down in texts, which gradually became more elaborate and more esoteric. These coalesced into the four primary Vedas, along with the Brahmanas, commentaries on sacrificial rituals, and the Upanishads, more esoteric philosophical treatises. Concerned with ritual correctness more than rules for behaviour in ordinary life, let alone matters of politics and administration, the brahmins nevertheless offered a sense of ritual order to ordinary people. They promoted the idea that the whole of life was governed by a mysterious and immutable law, the dharma, which people needed to observe in order to maintain the world in its ideal state. The dharma provided standards for ethical behaviour, social conduct, and judicial processes. The requirements of the dharma would later be explained in the Dharmashastras, the texts that formed Hindu law.[6]

BY THE MIDDLE of the sixth century BCE, small states had emerged on the Ganges plains and the most powerful rajas had fortified their cities.[7] Urban economies grew, coins became widespread, rulers standardized weights and measures, and potters innovated with new techniques. As rice cultivation expanded, the population increased, and smaller groups moved off in search of new lands. The varna system presided over by the brahmins now extended throughout the cities on the plains and gradually extended towards the peripheries.

Maintaining their status as guardians of the ritual order, some of the brahmins acquired considerable wealth and influence. However, in the fifth century BCE, a number of reformers in the new urban centres began to challenge their dominance.[8] Gautama Buddha, along with his contemporary Mahavira, founder of Jainism, initiated a concerted set of reactions against the brahmins. They turned their backs on traditional brahminical rituals and sacrifices and promoted more austere forms of religious practice, the principle of nonviolence, and ideas of ritual purity. While the Jains promoted extreme forms of asceticism, the Buddha promoted a 'middle way', emphasizing everyday ethical practices and a route to salvation. The Buddha's path, with its promise of a release from the inevitability of suffering, was the same for everyone, whatever their status. Although the Buddhists and Jains advocated different styles of ethical and religious practice, both rejected the hierarchy of the varna system.

Over the next centuries, different rulers battled for power and patronized different ritual specialists. Brahmins, Buddhists, and Jains gradually separated into distinct groups, any of which could have formulated laws that might have come to dominate in India. As it was, the ruler of Magadha, in present-day Bihar, declared war on his neighbours, annexing large territories with the help of armoured chariots and stone-hurling catapults. Next came the short-lived Nanda dynasty, whose ruler, Mahapadma, subjugated much of northern India with an army of two hundred thousand soldiers, twenty thousand horsemen, two thousand chariots, and three thousand elephants, at least according to reports by the Greeks, who were then moving into northwestern India. Even if the Greeks exaggerated their accounts,

Mahapadma's rule was on a large scale. But his sons were over-thrown by Chandragupta, who emerged from the west, where he had waged campaigns against outposts of Alexander's retreating army. Chandragupta seized the throne of Magadha in 320 BCE and conquered a swath of northern India, founding the Mauryan Empire, which was to last 150 years.

To maintain control over an empire of this size, the Mau-ryan rulers required new techniques of administration, which prompted Chandragupta's chief minister, Kautilya, to formulate advice for him on statecraft.[9] This was the basis of the *Artha-shastra*, a new style of text in which the minister advised the king on how to increase his power, weaken that of his enemies, and maintain the prosperity of his empire. Kautilya told the king to raise taxes, but he realized that the ruler had to look out for the welfare of his people and he offered guidance for judicial processes, suggesting specialist judges and rules for witnesses and evidence. The Arthashastra, although not initially written down, was to influence later legal writing.[10] Like the Mesopota-mian kings, the Mauryan rulers carved inscriptions onto stone slabs and pillars to record their conquests. But the most famous, Ashoka, who ruled from around 268 BCE, declared dramatically that he was renouncing all warfare. Persuading his ministers to support this new policy, he ordered that a series of stone pillars be erected throughout his empire instructing people to avoid eating meat and to extend goodwill to all foreigners. Later, Buddhists claimed Ashoka as the greatest royal patron of their religion, although he patronized brahmins as well. But when he forbade animal sacrifice, it threatened the brahmins' status. They were, after all, in charge of the important royal horse sacrifice.[11] The king also encouraged new Buddhist practitioners to set up mon-asteries to house the growing number of their followers, which attracted both people and resources.

It was still not clear whether any religious specialists would come to dominate, and none had yet written rules of law. After the last Mauryan ruler was assassinated by one of his generals during a parade of his troops in 185 BCE, power again shifted, and new regimes arose. The Kushan rulers took power in the north, at around the time of the birth of Christ, establishing an empire that extended from Central Asia down to the Ganges. Under their patronage, commerce, art, and high culture all continued to flourish, and trading networks extended far across the seas; people from distant regions exchanged cultural ideas and artefacts, and new artistic techniques flowed in from Persia. It was during this period that Indian writers put together the great epics, the Ramayana and the Mahabharata, with their tales of a heroic age. They also turned to secular poetry and drama, enjoying favours at the royal courts.[12] But the Kushans, like the Mauryan rulers, were not Aryans, and they were wary of the brahmins, preferring to patronize the more accessible ideas and rituals of Buddhism. This posed a threat to the brahmins, which may have inspired some of them to bring together their knowledge and write new texts.[13] Here they developed a distinctly brahmin-centred theory of dharma, which reemphasized the importance of the varnas. Like the Israelite priests, they expanded their guidance from ritual to the rest of life, including what people should eat and who they could marry. This was the beginning of their law.

BRAHMIN SCHOLARS WHO had previously clustered in their own small circles of learning, distrusting the innovations of the new urban centres and the universalist message of the Buddhists, now began to join forces. They developed their view of dharma gradually, building up a body of wisdom and ritual practices to create a sense that Hindus everywhere should live by the same principles and follow the same rules. The scholars were laying the foundations of what is now known as 'Hinduism', a quite varied set of beliefs and practices which cluster around a common group of deities and ritual techniques, along with reverence for ancient Sanskrit texts. The brahmins also created a new style of ritual texts, the Dharmasutras.[14] These used aphorisms, short and often cryptic sayings, to present ideas about the meaning and philosophy of dharma, expressing a sense of justice and right conduct.

The sutras presented individuals with rules for how to follow ritually correct lives. A person who travelled to a place where sacrificial ritual was in decline or heterodoxy was evident, for example, could become unclean, needing purification. But the sutras also gave guidance for daily life, concentrating on the elite, the brahmins themselves. A young man, they directed, should spend his formative years as a student, learning the Vedas and the meaning and practice of correct rituals, as well as the rules and principles of correct behaviour. Then he should marry and set up his own household, assuming an extensive array of ritual and practical obligations to his extended family and entourage, as well as associated business duties. Towards the end of his life, the brahmin should withdraw from the social world and become a hermit, eventually living as a wandering ascetic. In practice, of course, not all brahmins moved into caves, but the texts presented an ideal. The sutras claimed to be rooted in the ancient Vedas, which gave them a sense of timeless authority. In reality they probably drew much of their content from contemporary custom. Effectively, they were redescribing the practices of the upper classes in terms of a higher morality, creating an ideology that would dominate Indian social thought for centuries to come.[15]

Although primarily concerned with ritual, the new texts also launched into politics and the role of the kshatriyas, the ruling classes. The duty of the king, they declared, was to protect his people against enemies and those who disturbed the social order, the 'thorns' in society. The brahmins might be able to prescribe the correct penance for bad behaviour, but the kings were to make sure that criminals were punished. And at some point, probably towards the end of the second century CE, a confident scholar, or group of scholars, decided to write a text which would set out the advice of the Creator himself. Attributed to Manu, son of the creator god, Brahma, this was the first of the Dharmashastras. While the sutras were scholarly works, rather like the textbooks written for modern legal practitioners, the shastras set out specific rules. What they contained *was* the law, the wisdom of the Vedas in the form of legal rules.

Manu's Dharmashastra announces that it is the work of Brahma, the Imperishable One. It contains 2,694 two-line verses and presents much of its guidance as rules for daily life.[16] Like the sutras, although giving far more specific rules, it concentrates on the upper classes. The first section contains rules for the conduct of brahmins as they progress through the stages of life from child, to student, to husband, to parent, and finally, at least for those who choose it, to a state of renunciation. It tells them how to live a life of learning, ritual, and purity. The next section contains rules for the king, or kshatriya, class. The king is supposed to support the brahmins and protect his people, and a long section tells him, in some detail, how to address disputes and mete out punishments, setting out appropriate penalties for different crimes and rules for legal procedures. There is only a brief section on how the vaishyas should behave, largely by being diligent and properly learning their particular professions, and there is the briefest of directions for the shudras, whose duty was simply to act as servants to the brahmins. They were obviously supposed to hope for a better status in a later life.

The overwhelming emphasis of the text is on the correct behaviour of individuals according to their caste, family, and life stage, and it specifies their duties, rather than defining their rights.[17] It reflects and emphasizes the fact that individuals are born into a web of social relations and obligations. The young brahmin owes a debt to his teachers, duties of a son to his father, and obligations to carry out sacrifices to the gods. Throughout his life, an individual might take on further roles, as business partner, owner of property, mortgagee, guild member, husband, or father. Different statuses and roles entailed different duties. Above all, the text emphasizes the importance of the brahmin's household and the role of its head, especially at times of death or divorce. The text creates a sense that there is a right way to do almost everything, from eating and bathing to sleeping, marrying, having sex, conducting business, and being a student.

Legal rules, that is, general directions for behaviour, are scattered throughout the more general advice and examples given in the text. The most legalistic sections of Manu's Dharmashastra are those that tell the king how to approach judicial cases. Divided into eighteen sections, they contain rules for how he should mete out punishments, regulate commerce, and deal with disputes concerning marriage and other family relations. The first eight sections concern business matters, including nonpayment of debts, sale contracts, forms of partnership, appropriate wages, and the enforcement of rules by associations and corporations. Two concern the sorts of disputes that might arise out of herding activities and the organization of village property. Six describe what we might think of as crimes, such as assault, theft, insults, and adultery. And there are sections on marriage, inheritance, and gambling. The topics themselves are not surprising, and not so different from those that concerned Hammurabi when he set out rules for the Babylonians almost a millennium earlier. Both were urbanized societies in which trade, property, and family relations must have given rise to disputes and people were likely to fight for their interests.

Manu's text offers quite specific rules on how disputed debts should be handled, how interest rates should be determined, how pledges and sureties could be made and enforced, how partnerships should be managed, how boundary disputes should be resolved, and how judges should deal with thieves.[18] Some are casuistic: for example, 'If a pledge together with any profits has been furnished, the creditor shall not receive any interest on the loan.' But the authors—whoever they were—generally express their rules in the form of commands. This section continues: 'The creditor must not make use of a pledge by force. If he does, he forfeits the interest.'[19] In keeping with the rest of the text it concentrates on duties rather than rights.

During the Mauryan and Kushan periods most conflict must have been sorted out locally, through negotiation and consensus, but Manu's text describes the formal procedures that those with more intractable disputes needed to follow in the royal courts. The Mauryan emperors had already introduced measures to safeguard the welfare of their people, and they had almost certainly also established courts.[20] By the fourth and fifth centuries of the common era, judicial practices had become formal and rule-bound, and petitioners could appeal from the court of the guild or local community to that of the king.[21] Here, each party had to present his own case in accordance with rules that can be traced to the Arthashastra tradition.[22] These were obviously adversarial processes: as one of the later Hindu commentators says, 'In a legal procedure one person wins and another loses.'[23] Behind this lay the idea that the king should determine what was right and correct, applying the superior laws of the dharma as set out in the Dharmashastras.

THE BRAHMIN AUTHORS of Manu's text were clearly keen to defend their social and ritual privileges and to emphasize the special relationship between king and priest at the top of the Indian social hierarchy. Their agenda, as one contemporary writer has commented, was to tell brahmins how to behave as true brahmins, and to tell kings how to behave as true kings. The former were to be devoted to Vedic learning and virtue, whereas the latter were to be devoted to the brahmins and to ruling their people justly.[24] In the competitive religious environment of northern India, the brahmins were claiming knowledge of higher and eternal truths, which they could interpret for kings and princes, declaring what the law was in cases of uncertainty. The kings and their officials were supposed to enact the law, not make it. They were the servants of the dharma.

The Kushan rulers patronized Buddhism, and their king, Kanishka (r. c. 127–150 CE), dotted his territories with stupas (Buddhist monuments). But in a decisive move in around 150 CE, King Rudradaman of the Saka dynasty, who ruled land to the south of the Kushans, confirmed his commitment to brahminical wisdom. He ordered that a poem be engraved on a huge boulder to record his achievements, claiming he knew grammar, music, the shastras, and logic, as well as being a fine swordsman, boxer, horseman, charioteer, elephant rider, and poet. And he wrote it in Sanskrit.[25] This made the ancient ritual language, the preserve of the brahmins, into a symbol and expression of royal power. Before long, rulers throughout India had followed suit, making great efforts to express themselves elegantly in this complex language. It became a marker of a good king, one who could rule justly.[26] It also confirmed the brahmins' authority, and they set about writing new texts, along with collections and commentaries, with enthusiasm.

Scholars believe that Indian writers produced at least one hundred Dharmashastra texts, although only ten have survived. Frustratingly for historians, in the climate of tropical India manuscripts written on cloth or palm leaves, or even copper plates, deteriorate quickly. Only the most popular, those that were recopied and rewritten over the centuries, survive. But from the eighth and ninth centuries, scholars began to produce commentaries on earlier texts and digests of what they considered the most important of these writings, which helped to preserve the tradition and its learning. Medieval Indian kings probably ordered, and sponsored, many of these compilations, while the arrival of Muslim conquerors, who made incursions into India from the tenth century, provided yet another incentive for Hindu writers to consolidate and promote their historical legal tradition.

As creators and interpreters of the Dharmashastras, the brahmins were able to assert ritual authority in the face of powerful Hindu kings. But India was not politically unified until the Moghuls established their empire in the sixteenth century, and not all kings were willing to let the brahmins exercise their ritual authority unchecked.[27] So some set off to find patrons in distant parts. From the fourth century, when the Gupta Empire covered most of the north, many brahmins travelled southwards, beyond imperial borders, with their rituals and laws. By the sixth century, they had followed adventurous artisans to Kerala, a rich region on the western coast encompassing what became Calicut, where they introduced new ideas to the local rulers. Regional kings and powerful clan leaders were doubtless impressed by the brahmins' elaborate rituals, the quality of the deities they venerated, and the promise of the benefits to be gained from a life lived according to the rules of dharma. They probably also hoped to enhance their status by patronizing the now renowned religious specialists. As the brahmins converted local populations and their rulers to Hindu ritual ways and beliefs, they established themselves as religious authorities, founded temples, and built up substantial wealth.

After the Gupta Empire disintegrated in the late sixth century, a number of ascendant Muslim leaders made incursions into northern India, establishing a series of sultanates. But most allowed the Hindu kings to retain authority and continue to manage their own territories and people, in return for allegiance. The more pious continued to respect the authority of the brahmins and the guidance of the Dharmashastra texts and traditions.

The rules of the Dharmashastras were relatively limited in their scope, but later scholars, along with local rulers, guilds, and councils, worked out more detailed rules for social regulation and legal procedures. And in doing so, they followed the shastras' rules for judicial processes and guidance on such things as how claims for debt could be proved. The rules already specified the value of different documents and delineated who might be called as a witness in a legal case, how witnesses should be examined, how their evidence should be assessed, when and how judges should use oaths and ordeals, and the punishments they should impose for perjury.[28]

According to the Dharmashastras, it was for the brahmin to declare what the law was and for the kings to enforce it. In reality, many rulers must have been primarily concerned with maintaining power, standing up to their rivals, and establishing a stable economic base from which to raise taxes and secure services. And the stronger, more warlike, and most ruthless kings probably issued authoritarian commands and directed their officials to punish anyone who defied them, whatever the local brahmins advised. But in the chronicles they wrote and the inscriptions they made on stones and pillars, Hindu kings almost invariably claimed to be pronouncing local laws, hearing petitions, and resolving disputes in accordance with the requirements of the dharma.

Few case records survive, but the authors of medieval stories and poems described kings handling disputes. In practice, they could, and often did, consult councils of brahmins, *yogam*, on difficult points of textual and legal interpretation. By the sixteenth century Calicut was governed by a Zamorin, but the local brahmins had formed a yogam.[29] It sat in judgement in major legal disputes and heard accusations of the most serious crimes, and would refer its decisions and judgements to the Zamorin to enact punishment. In these ways, the brahmins maintained their status as guardians of the legal tradition, responsible for interpreting the old texts and adapting their ideas to new contexts. They pronounced on what the law was, while the ruler was responsible for implementing it, as the Dharmashastra texts had stipulated.

Over the centuries, councils of brahmins in different parts of India administered local rules and explained their meaning in new texts and commentaries. Sexual misconduct seems to have become a particular concern in eighteenth-century Kerala, for example, where some brahmins produced legal texts instructing the king, in elaborate detail, on how to deal with allegations of adultery.[30] A man who suspected his wife of adultery, they said, must take his case directly to the king, beseeching the monarch to 'protect and preserve the dharma'. The king should then appoint a brahmin to represent him in the investigation, which was to be conducted by an expert on the legal codes, another brahmin. There were to be four investigators, possibly representatives of the plaintiff, who briefed the expert. The expert was to go to the plaintiff's house with the king's brahmin and hide behind a wall. From behind the wall he would question the accused wife. The king's brahmin had to listen silently, his head covered by a veil, which he was supposed to drop if the expert made a mistake. Having concluded this investigation, the expert was to report to the king. Meanwhile, the king's brahmin continued to monitor the process and would indicate further disapproval, if necessary, via his veil. The process described in the Dharmashastra text seems impractically elaborate, but the central position of the brahmins is clear. And in all likelihood the drama served to impress on everyone the seriousness of the allegations and the moral and spiritual consequences of both the alleged crime and any attempts to lie or pervert the course of justice. This was the Hindu answer to the universal problem of adjudicating on allegations of sexual misconduct.

Well into the colonial period, Hindu kings continued to follow the advice of their brahmins and the legal procedures set out in the Dharmashastras. In the eighteenth century, for example, two wealthy individuals claimed ownership of a slave and her offspring in the region of Mithila, in what is now Bihar. The case went to the court convened by Madhu Sing, the local raja, where the judges repeatedly referred to the Dharmashastra texts when directing how the claim should be presented and how it could be denied, as well as how much time the court could allow for adjournments and evidence-gathering. They referred to the shastras to explain how they had weighed up the relative strength of the evidence provided for the claimant by another of his slaves, against the respondent's evidence of actual possession. In the end, as the scribe recorded in the case report, the court had no hesitation in rejecting the claim, and he carefully followed the guidance of the Dharmashastra texts when compiling his report.[31]

RELATIONS BETWEEN KINGS, brahmins, and local groups all depended on the regional dynamics and relative power of particular families and individuals. In many cases, brahmins would act as judges, hearing cases of murder, theft, and arson as well as religious offences. At times, powerful brahmin families could take direct responsibility for law and order. In the twelfth century, a powerful maharaja from Marwar (now Jodhpur in Rajasthan) assembled a group of brahmins from the eight regions of his area, along with local bankers and merchants, and demanded that they investigate cases of robbery from bards, orators, the king's doorkeepers, pilgrims, and goods' carriers. It seems very much as if this was an initiative by the king for the protection of his entourage, and he provided resources for their work. The brahmins agreed to direct their local councils to investigate these cases and said they would do this 'in accordance with the customs of the region'. If they failed, they would 'die like dogs', as the agreement put it.[32] In practice, many brahmins were better able than kings to enforce law and order, although even they had to rely upon powerful local families, occupation groups, and castes to investigate, identify, and punish wrongdoers.

Under the patronage of local rajas, some brahmin families became powerful landowners. In Kerala, some settled in Malabar, a region on the west coast, divided from the rest of the subcontinent by a long line of mountains, which had developed distinctive local traditions. By the sixteenth century, the Hindu Zamorin of Calicut, along with a number of lesser rajas from the region, concerned to promote maritime trade, welcomed the Portuguese and Dutch merchants who were settling in the coastal towns. The brahmins had brought copies of their Dharmashastra and other texts with them, which later scholars studied and translated into local languages. Some local scholars inscribed regional rules and customs in copies of their texts—to sanction the local custom of matriliny, for example—and gradually people came to think of these composite texts as their own laws.

In the southern portion of the region, the Brahmin Vanjeri family effectively ruled an almost autonomous territory, where they were trustees of an important Shiva temple.[33] As well as advising on ritual practices, their leaders demanded that people should follow standard forms in their legal transactions, particularly when buying, selling, and mortgaging land and in their business accounts.[34] Many of these forms used phrases and terminology that related closely to the language of the Dharmashastras. For example, if people needed to raise money, they could pledge not just their land but also its produce, which might include rice, coconuts, mangoes, ghee, or pepper, along with the taxes due to be paid by their sharecroppers, using a type of mortgage described in the shastra texts. When land was sold, the parties might mark the transaction by pouring out water, a signal of gift-giving in the ancient texts and a means of circumventing a technical prohibition on land sales. In these ways, legal forms derived from the Dharmashastras spread through the region. But the brahmins also asked groups of people to advise on local custom—for example, by deciding on the just price for a field, a garden, a house, or livestock. In addition, they took responsibility for investigating and adjudicating on crimes in their areas. In one case, the head of the Vanjeri family even obtained permission from the Zamorin to convene a council to try someone accused of murder, according to the laws in the area. But generally they referred offenders to the local raja for punishment, as decreed in the Dharmashastras.

In these ways, the influence of the brahmins, their ideas of ritual obligation and purity, the legal forms prescribed by the Dharmashastras, and the whole hierarchy envisaged by their texts filtered down from the ritual specialists into the practicalities of daily life. The brahmins controlled the interpretation of the Dharmashastras and the practices of the unwritten local law, largely by specifying the forms in which people could deal with land and take their cases to court. The terms used in the shastras to refer to rules, conventions, decrees, acts of dharma (religious donations), and royal directives all found their way into regional laws and texts.

SOME BRAHMINS ENJOYED a worldly life at the kings' courts, where they turned out long eulogies in praise of their royal patrons. These detailed illustrious genealogies, auspicious marriages, and heroic feats on the battlefield. But not all brahmins sought wealth. In contrast to these flamboyant poets, many eminent brahmins turned to more ascetic ways of life.[35] In the eleventh century CE, the Chalukya emperors of southern India patronized a sage named Vijnyaneshvara, who took decades to compile an extended commentary on an important Dharmashastra text. In all likelihood painfully thin, carrying a begging bowl and a staff made of three reeds tied together, the brahmin would have cut an incongruous figure at the court of the Hindu kings, with their parasol- and fan-bearers, generals and guards, queens and children, representatives of merchants' guilds, and diplomats from distant lands. Like other ascetics, Vijnyaneshvara was revered as representing the moral foundations of Hindu society.

All these ritual specialists were, at least in theory, guardians and interpreters of the immutable Vedic tradition, and it was the kings' duty to enforce and apply laws over which they claimed ultimate authority. But these ideas gave rise to tensions, particularly as the brahmins' influence began to extend beyond the Aryan heartlands and new groups of people were drawn into their cultural orbit. Scholars debated how powerful non-Aryan chiefs and warlords could be incorporated into the system of varna, and some were uncompromising. Strictly, outsiders could only ever be shudras; one brahmin claimed that even the *rajputs*, the leaders of the large and warlike clans in western India, were of mixed race and should be treated as shudras.

This opinion did not undermine the rajputs' power, but it did trouble them. In the mid-seventeenth century, one of the rajput warlords, Shivaji, rose to prominence.[36] Through battle, conquest, fort-building, and strategic alliances, he gradually acquired power to rival the Muslim chiefs who now dominated the region, and in 1674 he decided to assume the title of king. His status as a rajput was a problem, however, and even that may have been a fiction. As well as military and political power, he needed the status of kshatriya, so that he could claim the respect of the notoriously orthodox local brahmins and hold his head high next to the Moghul emperor, Aurangzeb. So Shivaji turned to a renowned brahmin and expert in Hindu law who was also nephew to the author of an important opinion on the status of the rajputs. Summoning him from Banaras, many miles away, the king made it clear that he expected a genealogy that would confirm his kshatriya heritage. The brahmin duly complied and delivered an opinion to the effect that Shivaji was descended from a high-status rajput clan whose members were proper kshatriya.

From the pen of such an expert, the opinion could hardly be challenged, and Shivaji duly rewarded the brahmin with an eye-watering amount of gold (to which he later declared he was indifferent). A spectacular ceremony was then organized, supposedly to restore Shivaji's unfortunately lapsed kshatriya status. Shivaji also remarried his wife (or wives) according to Vedic rituals and received the emblems of royalty, becoming 'The Lord who bears a Royal Umbrella'. Over seven days, courtiers, priests, musicians, visiting dignitaries, and a multitude of spectators participated in a coronation, an enthroning, and a triumphal procession. The events included baths and ritual meals and people from all over the region arrived to present the new king with cows, horses, elephants, jewels, and silks. Brahmins chanted mantras in Sanskrit, observers recorded the events for posterity, and the king's newly appointed ministers and generals gathered around him in displays of loyalty and support. When the ceremonies were over, the king went on tour, handing out gifts and sponsoring lavish feasts. The ordinary people could hardly fail to be impressed, although they later had to pay for the king's largesse. The ceremonies demonstrated his wealth and power to all the world—but first he had had to demonstrate that he was legally entitled to his status. And this had required confirmation by an eminent brahmin.

THE BRAHMINS CONTINUED to be unwavering in their ideas about caste. They insisted that each had its own occupation, even if caste status could be lost through immoral behaviour, most importantly killing, drinking, stealing, and sexual misconduct.[37] But occupations were proliferating even as the first shastras were being written, and new subcastes constantly formed. The match between occupation and caste was never perfect, but gradually occupations became hereditary. The new groups formed a ritual and economic hierarchy that in many ways endures to this day.[38] Unlike the message of the Buddha, which was essentially egalitarian, the brahmins linked all their laws to caste, life stage, gender, family situation, and profession. In these ways, the Dharmashastras' emphasis on mantras, fasting, meditation, and food offerings, along with the image of an ideal lifestyle which the members of their own class were supposed to follow, consolidated and reinforced a rigid caste hierarchy.[39] The system was also one that regarded women with considerable suspicion, prone to corrupting activities such as drinking, associating with the wrong people, wandering about, and living in other people's houses.[40]

Not surprisingly, many lower-caste people sought to challenge their classification or to dispute its implications, and some launched complex and entangled legal cases, especially in southern India, where the brahminical structures had to be reconciled with older family, occupational, and regional divisions.[41] In the twelfth century, Kammala craftsmen flourished thanks to a boom in temple-building.[42] Some commanded substantial incomes and eventually felt confident enough to claim they were of high status, members of the Rathakara caste. The Rathakaras, who built chariots and wagons and undertook carpentry, metalwork, house-building, and related crafts, had already established themselves as a high-status group, at times even rivalling the brahmins. So the religious specialists were concerned. They convened councils to consider the matter, invited argument, and consulted erudite texts, which did not always offer consistent opinions. In the end, two different councils reached similar conclusions, which they recorded for posterity in stone inscriptions. Each reached a compromise. The Kammala who were doing more menial work, they decided, were not entitled to adopt the craft and specialist construction activities of the Rathakaras, but those who could reasonably claim to be doing the more skilled work already could continue their trades. Since people could not change caste, however, the division between them would from then on be permanent. One council confirmed their right to practise sculpture and engineering; to make scientific instruments; to fashion statues, palaces, halls, and the monumental towers known as *gopurams*; to craft crowns, bracelets, and thread for the royal palace; and to paint idols and images.

In the light of these sorts of challenges, brahmins wrote further treatises confirming the immutable dharma of the shudras, entrenching the caste system, and their own position within it, in the face of the practical, economic, and moral forces that constantly threatened its authority.

THE BRAHMINS CONTINUED to read and reread, copy, comment upon, and collate their texts while new Indian kingdoms rose and fell, Muslim invaders established and lost an empire, and European merchants established a foothold in southern and eastern India. Particularly when sectarian tensions arose, those who pursued more scholarly activities would consult one another and call for opinions from distant parts. Councils and individuals in Maharashtra exchanged letters, legal judgements, and opinions with their counterparts in Banaras, building up extensive networks of learning. All the while, they promoted the ideal of the brahmin householder, someone who lived a ritually pure life in accordance with the ideal model of dharma, as explained in the rules of the shastras. Even if the lower castes could not follow the same rules, they could aspire to a higher status in a later life.

In these ways, the learning of the shastras and other Hindu texts created a sense of commonality among populations that were never united under a single Hindu king.

It was largely left to the kings and councils of much smaller social groups to create practical rules to regulate daily life, mete out justice, and resolve disputes. The shastras specified which communities should make their own rules and when, even granting 'heretics'—Buddhists and Jains—a measure of legal autonomy. Local laws, rooted in tradition, united groups of farmers, artisans, and traders and defined the behaviour expected of their members, but the Dharmashastras provided a common vision of social structures and relations. As one scholar put it, the Dharmashastra was a meta-level law, a source of ideas and arrangements that Indian people could use in different ways in very different places.[43] Those at the top of the caste hierarchy thus maintained a relatively unified set of ideas and rules throughout the patchwork of kingdoms and communities that made up premodern India.

The Dharmashastras set out detailed rules for the ways in which Hindus should live their lives and how the king should maintain social order, all in accordance with the hierarchy of the varnas, but they were never supposed to produce a functioning legal system. More importantly, they provided a sense of what united legal practices and the ideas and principles that should guide the judges in their enactment of justice. The shastras demonstrated the nature of Hindu law and the duties of those who were charged with implementing it. Eventually, Indian people who were scattered throughout a multiplicity of different towns, villages, guilds, and temples, with very different livelihoods and traditions, came to think of themselves and their obligations as good Hindus in terms of the roles, duties, and responsibilities appropriate to their caste as specified in the Dharmashastras.

THE LEARNING AND texts of the brahmins also provided inspiration for lawmakers in very different parts of Southeast Asia where kings and populations had already converted to different religions. About seven hundred years after Hindu brahmins created Manu's Dharmashastra, for example, Mon priests in what is now Myanmar took it as an example when their king asked them to create a legal text.[44] The kings had adopted Buddhism and were building fabulous stupas in their capital at Bagan. But, inspired by the sophisticated civilization of India across the Bay of Bengal, they now instructed their scholars to create their own legal texts. Writing in Pali, the language of Buddhism in Southeast Asia, the Mon priests created texts they called Dhammasattas. These followed the form of the Dharmashastras, arranging legal disputes into the same eighteen sections. But they had to invent a different origin story. The first Buddhist king, they said, was chosen by his people to end the civil chaos that had arisen in their land, and he turned to a hermit, Manu, to recite the law that he had learned in the celestial regions. In practice, the Mon scholars introduced many local customs into their texts, but they created the image of an ideal society governed by a universal law, like that of their brahmin counterparts in India. And, as there, the Buddhist kings were only supposed to interpret the law, not make it. By the time the wisdom of the Dhammasattas filtered down into local contexts, it was substantially reworked to suit custom and practice, but the texts were an important unifying force in this thriving kingdom. By the time it fell two centuries later, the Mon had produced over one hundred texts.

The Dharmashastras also reached Buddhist Thailand, several centuries later, and eventually Cambodia and Java. The Thai texts were divided into more sections, but in many details they resembled the Bagan laws, which the authors had clearly copied. In theory, the kings could issue decrees, but they could not officially make new laws. The Thai king was supposed to embody the law, or, as one modern writer has put it, 'the sovereign's commands, when they were proper acts, spelled out the law'.[45] It was the king's duty to maintain order in society by punishing those who disturbed it, but the ruler was himself subject to the principles of the dharma, like everyone else. This was the essence of the relationship between king and priest worked out centuries earlier by the Hindu brahmins. It was a form of the rule of law. Of course, many of the Thai and Burmese rulers, like the Indian kings, were absolute and authoritarian and readily deviated from the duties and principles spelled out in the legal texts. But, at least in theory, the law limited their powers and shaped their actions.

HINDU LAW WAS always a religious, rather than a political, project, rooted in a sense of immutable tradition. Behind it was the idea of cosmological order as enshrined in the wisdom of the ancient, obscure revelations of the Vedas. The duty of all humans was to maintain that order by complying with the rules of the dharma, which specified how they should behave, and it was this that the brahmins worked out in their legal texts. Simple and often mundane statements about duties and the consequences of events and activities created an order of rules and categories which, like the Mesopotamian laws, had a sense of fixity. But while the Mesopotamian kings were mapping out social justice, the brahmins were specifying individual duties with cosmological order in mind.

In practice, the Hindu tradition established and entrenched one of the world's most rigid social hierarchies. But there was always a sense that the religious law transcended political power. The brahmins could tell even the kings how to behave.

CHAPTER THREE

CHINESE EMPERORS
Codes, Punishments, and Bureaucracy

T he third of the great legal systems to emerge was that
of China. It, too, mapped out an order based on rules
and categories, but it was an order of discipline rather
than an order of duties or a project of social justice. For more
than two thousand years, Chinese legal systems were punitive,
disciplinary, and resilient. The longevity of the tradition they
formed is remarkable, although each ruling dynasty revised and
reformed the laws when it took power. And, just as remarkably,
the system they created completely disappeared over a very short
period of time in the twentieth century.

Law in China was always an instrument of power and control.
The ambitions of the rulers who first inscribed lists of punishments onto long bamboo strips were not so different from those
of the Mesopotamian kings several centuries earlier; and behind
their work hovered a sense of cosmological order that was similar, in some ways, to the ideas of the Indian brahmins. But the
Chinese produced a quite different system of law from either the
Mesopotamian kings or the Hindu religious specialists. The emperors never allowed a class of priests, or any other specialists, to

challenge their authority as lawmakers: they successfully avoided becoming, themselves, subject to the rule of law. And their vision of order was one of discipline and punishment.

AT LEAST SEVEN millennia before the common era, farmers in northern China were creating embankments along the Yellow River.[1] This allowed them to cultivate the rich silt along its banks, where they planted millet and raised pigs. As their settlements grew, they began to carve decorative items out of jade and fashioned copper and bronze tools. Their rulers also used oracle bones to foretell the future, eventually developing elaborate burial rituals. People over a large area shared common beliefs and practices by around 2000 BCE, and the stage was set for the emergence of the first small states. Little is known about the rulers of the earliest dynasty, the Xia, save that the last one was overthrown by the first of the Shang dynasty in 1600 BCE.

The Shang had to manage a population that was divided into clans whose members claimed common ancestry.[2] Some were nomadic, others created settlements, and over time they combined to establish small walled towns. The Shang kings amassed enough wealth to construct palaces and temples with enormous underground storage pits, and over the next five hundred years, their workshops turned out bronze, jade, and stone artefacts, along with pottery, ceramics, lacquerware, weapons, and musical instruments. Cowrie shells provided currency for the merchants, and there were diviners in every settlement who used turtle shells and cattle bones to predict the future and ascertain the most auspicious days for important events. The king himself was a diviner. As well as leading a powerful army, he made the most splendid offerings to the ancestors and deities, combining ritual status with political power in a pattern that continued throughout Chinese history.

The Shang ruled a relatively untroubled northern China for several centuries, but in 1027 BCE, Zhou invaders swept onto the central plains from the west. They overthrew the Shang and through a series of military campaigns brought a large area with a diverse population under their control. In order to govern these different people, they established a decentralized system not unlike the feudal patterns of medieval Europe. The kings rewarded loyal generals and officials with lands, and they dispatched sons, brothers, and other relatives to strategic states and border cities. When the first king appointed his brother as governor of one of the new states, he wrote him a letter of advice, the Kang Gao, which survives to this day.[3] In it, the king instructs his brother to investigate the activities of the former kings and learn from them how to protect and regulate his population. If Shang people brought legal cases to him, the king said, especially if they might require a death or mutilation penalty, he should refer them to specially appointed officials who knew the former rules and could apply them correctly. When it came to offences committed by Zhou people, the governor should impose punishments himself. But he should apply leniency and moderation, distinguishing intentional and persistent offenders, who merited harsher punishments, from those who offended unintentionally or on a single occasion. And the governor should treat family cases especially seriously. If sons did not respect their fathers and younger brothers the elder, the king said, 'the norms given by Heaven to our people will be brought into disorder'. The kings took it for granted that imposing punishments was the way to maintain order. They regularly complained that their officials were not fulfilling their duties properly and handing out correct punishments. Like the Aryans on the Indian plains, they had a sense of cosmological order, a divine ideal which people needed to respect, and kings should support, if their societies were to prosper.

The Zhou kings also entertained legal petitions, and they appointed judges to make decisions.[4] Military and other officials, along with members of aristocratic families, would bring complaints to them, often concerning land transfers, along with commercial transactions and allegations of theft or perjury. Many recorded the resulting decisions on the bronze vessels they used for sacrificial and food offerings during lineage ceremonies, which they kept in their temples and inscribed with records of important meetings and military campaigns. Surviving vessels from the tenth to eighth centuries BCE, buried when the Zhou fled westwards, indicate some patterns and formality in these processes. Judges regularly demanded that litigants swear oaths to conclude a case. One man found guilty of misappropriating land, for example, had to swear that he would return the fields, and that he would petition the deities to mete out retribution if he failed to do so. Servants of a man named Kuang stole a large quantity of grain from Hu, who lodged a complaint with the king's officials. The appointed judge ordered Kuang to repay the grain twice over, but the servants had absconded, and the unfortunate Kuang was unable to comply with the order. In a series of further hearings, he offered increasing numbers of fields and men by way of compensation, without being able to satisfy the insistent Hu. The judge demanded strict application of the rules.

Officials also made regulations about currency. Alongside the strings of cowrie shells, merchants regularly used bolts of silk, jade tablets, deer and tiger skins, and even servants as means of payment. But in one case a creditor claimed he could not transfer the horse and silk he had agreed to pay for the use of labour because it contravened new rules. Patterns must have emerged among these decisions, setting precedents for the first written laws, which appeared as the Zhou regime was already in decline.

IN 771 BCE, barbarians raided the Zhou capital and killed the king, forcing his successors to move eastwards to Chengzhou.

But the Zhou continued to claim authority over a large part of central China. Their kings conducted rituals, convened assemblies, and occasionally mustered armies to attack 'disobedient' kingdoms. The following centuries are known as the Spring and Autumn period. But although the Zhou kings exercised little control over their populations and delegated many activities to local rulers, or maybe even because of this, their people made great scientific and technological advances. After the introduction of iron, they developed agricultural techniques, created bronze coins, expanded trade, and crafted decorative and luxury goods. People also came to identify more closely with their family units than their old clans, especially in the towns, and in this way, scholars believe, they began to form a common identity as people of China.[5]

The Zhou kings continued to summon large conventions, at which lords would pledge allegiance to them in written covenants, which they buried along with sacrificial animals.[6] The kings, in other words, used legal documents to try to hold together a disintegrating kingdom. Meanwhile, the lords expanded their governments and punishments as they tried to maintain peace and stability. In the seventh century BCE, Guan Zhong, a minister in the state of Qi, wrote a treatise on politics in which he tried to persuade the king to institute new policies. The ruler should promote the growth of the population; exercise monopolies on salt, iron, and wine; and centralize the system of taxation, he declared, and a powerful ruler would be able to impose peace by using a strong army and a powerful set of rules. His treatise describes a political system that would regulate a vast range of behaviour. Other rulers established bureaucracies and began to write down laws. A new governor in the state of Jin drew up plans for wide-ranging administrative reforms in 620 BCE, proposing to systematize official posts, 'rectify' laws and offences, standardize legal processes, institute the use of contracts, restore distinctions of rank, and promote the most able individuals to official positions. He presented his plans to the Zhou king's most senior representatives, so that they could implement them throughout his state. We know little about the documents or laws they drew up, but it is clear that the governor's scheme assumed that the way to impose order was to introduce a raft of new laws to systematize punishments.

This was top-down reform. The governor was advising the king to organize his laws correctly. A tidy legal system would be the basis for a tidy state. Other rulers also systematized practices of punishment, often employing scribes to write out both orders and rules on long bamboo slips, one character wide, which they pinned up on large boards for the general population to see. These were to be displayed in townships, stations, and markets, on gateposts, and in hostels for travellers. But bamboo slips were notoriously liable to decay and at risk of fire, so those who had the resources etched them onto bronze cauldrons to create more durable, if less portable, texts. A minister in the state of Zheng transferred his *Book of Punishments* onto a bronze vessel in 536 BCE, and the Jin chancellor followed suit in 513. The practice soon became widespread.

No original texts survive from this period, but there is evidence that the 'books of punishment' presented penalties for different crimes and classes of offender, including forced suicide, banishment, and imprisonment for the nobility.[7] Like the Hindu brahmins, Chinese officials clearly believed that proper forms of behaviour were important to the maintenance of social order, and that people, activities, and offences should be divided into categories in order to transform a disorderly society into an orderly one. Chinese rulers insisted on the power of law to map out their society, but they also thought they needed to impose order through a system of punishment, rather than rules for ritual purity. They were far more ambitious, and more confident in the power of law than the Indian and Israelite rulers of the period, whose regions were just as politically fragmented. Many Chinese states were riven by factions and rebellions, but the rulers set out to bring order to the whole society through law.

AND YET, NOT everyone was happy with the activities of the Zhou kings and their allies. A number of influential thinkers expressed severe reservations about their harsh methods of government, among whom was Kong Fuzi, commonly known as Confucius. Living between 551 and 479 BCE, Confucius offered a radically new view of the state.[8] Rather than requiring a strong and authoritarian king, he argued, social stability depended upon basic relations between ruler and ruled, father and son, elder and younger brother, friend and friend, and husband and wife. He emphasized the importance of the cultivated and moral individual, the *junzi*, who would determine his fate by relying on his own abilities and efforts. This was the person most suitable to be a ruler. It was not for the king to impose order through laws and punishments. Rather, social order arose from the behaviour of individuals, who needed to follow codes of morality, properly conduct rituals and ceremonies, pursue education, and, above all, be loyal to their parents. He was describing a state that appeared, in many ways, like an extension of the basic family, not unlike the brahmins' insistence on the centrality of the householder. Confucius famously criticized the practice of issuing laws, on the basis that this would disrupt social hierarchies. Referring to one of the new codes, maybe that of the Jin, he said, 'The people will think only about the cauldron. How will they revere the noble? How will the nobles preserve their patrimony? Without a distinction between noble and base, how can there be a kingdom?'[9] On his view, order should flow from a stable social hierarchy rather than from laws that the rulers applied to everyone.

Confucius's ideas captured the imagination of many contemporary scholars. In a commentary known as the *Zuo zhuan*, the author, probably one of Confucius's disciples, launched into a lengthy diatribe against the Zheng code of laws. He pointed out that previous rulers had not made laws, lest they encourage people to be litigious.[10] Rather, they 'restrained them with rightness, bound them with [good] governance, and raised them with humanity'. While he was not against all forms of punishment, he thought that punishments—along with rewards—should be deployed humanely and firmly, not reduced to written texts. The king should be a guide and a model, while astute officials, trustworthy elders, and beneficent masters should ensure that order reigned. When people are aware of legal texts, the author argued, they lose respect for their superiors, becoming contentious, appealing to the laws, and conniving to achieve their goals. They cannot then be governed. Frenzied litigation will flourish and bribes will circulate. It is only when a state is about to fall, he concluded, that it introduces legislation.

This was largely the Confucian view of law. For the great philosopher and his followers, it was not so much the system of rewards and punishments that was problematic. The writer of the *Zuo zhuan* did not explicitly criticize the strong, even authoritarian, ruler, or the hierarchy of ministers and nobility. Rather, he criticized the act of writing down laws and making them publicly available. Recent history had clearly led him to mistrust laws. But, as a result, he rejected the rule of law, the idea that laws should exist and be enforced independently of power-holders. The Confucian scholars clearly had no faith in the ability of laws to constrain arbitrary power or prevent officials from favouring those who pleased them, even though the scholars were obviously chafing against the centralization of power by the new political classes.

Whatever his reasons, and although he was categorical about the dangers of written laws, the author of the *Zuo zhuan* did recognize that at times, particularly during periods of social change, the ruler might have to create written laws in order to promote peace and stability. Even he was not entirely opposed to what seemed obvious to Chinese officials, that rulers needed to control their populations and impose order through a system of rules and punishments.

DESPITE THE ZHOU rulers' efforts to terrify would-be rebels into obedience, serious and prolonged warfare broke out in 403 BCE, ushering in what is generally known as the Warring States period. In many areas, powerful ministers mobilized court factions to usurp power and even assassinated their governors. The idea of a moral ruler who could maintain peace through virtuous examples must have seemed like a distant dream. Those who managed to hold on to their positions saw an urgent need for new forms of control. In an attempt to preserve order and centralized power, they placed their faith in laws that were clear, universal, and consistently applied.

The Confucianists may not have had much success in persuading local rulers of the wisdom of their ideas, but political leaders still valued scholars' advice. The Qin state, to the west of the Zhou heartlands, suffered from power struggles that paralysed its government for decades, and when a new ruler assumed power in 361 BCE, he sent out an invitation to 'virtuous men' to serve as his officials. Many scholars contended for the privilege, inevitably promising to ensure that by implementing their ideas the ruler would achieve wealth and power. Shang Yang (Lord Shang), then a minister in another state, put himself forward and after several audiences persuaded the Qin ruler to implement his policies.[11] Shang took the view that social problems arose from the gap between law and reality, which led to inconsistent practices, a corrupt administration, and unaccountable ministers. Clear and consistent legal norms were therefore essential. He advised that the Qin should replace their old laws with new written statutes, which would use rewards and punishments to ensure that farmers worked hard and soldiers were loyal. These were the only pursuits the ruler should encourage. Shang poured scorn on the practices of merchants, artists, and craftsmen, along with most scholarship, ritual, and music. In his view, people had formerly lived in peace, without the need for any government, but in the current age, when disorder abounded, scholars had to create written laws with heavy punishments to help the king rule effectively. Punishment would deter crime if it was enforced uniformly on all classes. On Shang's view, law was an entirely pragmatic matter. Justice had little, if anything, to do with it; nor was there any merit in following ancient tradition.

Some of the Confucian scholars criticized these policies and warned of the dangers of centralizing power, but the new rulers ruthlessly swept them aside and ordered that all Confucian literature be burned. The Qin restructured their government on Lord Shang's recommendations to create an impersonal bureaucracy of salaried officials whose powers and duties were defined and controlled by the central government. They demanded that officials keep records and take censuses, organizing people into units of five or ten families, which would be combined into prefectures under magistrates appointed by the ruler. The head of each household had to register its members, so that officials could summon them in times of war and to provide labour for public projects. They were forbidden to change their residences without permission and even discouraged from travelling.

The rulers introduced these reforms gradually, over about a century and a half. They also introduced numerous laws designed to control members of their bureaucracy, demanding that officials apply them exactly and ordering that senior officials discipline any subordinate who failed to do the same. The kings inscribed their most important orders—for example, those pertaining to military conscription—on metal objects, and lesser rules and orders onto bamboo slips tied together with silken cords, which could easily be transported. They standardized weights and measures and even tried to control the language of administration, issuing lists of approved terms and phrases.

Through this system of tight controls, the Qin rapidly increased their power and wealth, eventually defeating their rivals and establishing, in 221 BCE, what is generally regarded as the first Chinese empire.

MOST OF WHAT we know about the Qin legal system, which lasted until their empire collapsed abruptly in 207 BCE, comes from manuscripts discovered in the tombs of Qin officials.[12] The tombs contained calendars, divinatory manuscripts, and works on mathematics as well as guides to official duties, but the bulk of the documents was legal.[13] One official, a man named Xi who had been appointed as a scribe in 244 BCE, at the age of nineteen, began trying legal cases nine years later. The documents buried with him indicate that he consulted dozens of different statutes on a daily basis.[14] Most concerned administrative matters, such as managing communal granaries, protecting the ruler's hunting parks, repairing roads, supervising horse- and cattle-breeding, and recording crop yields. Others concerned currency, markets, border control points, the requisitioning and enrollment of labour, the appointment of officials, the system of ranks, food rations for couriers, and the transmission of higher orders. Xi also consulted laws on punishment and commentaries on how they should be applied, and kept records of his investigations and interrogations. One case in his collection concerns a prefectural official who had failed to carry out his duties properly.[15] Among other things, he had neglected to forward an order for military service to the right people; in one case, he had failed to enforce the performance of military service on a man who was supposed to cultivate mandarin orange trees but had become a vagrant.

Moreover, the skylights of the storehouses in his prefecture were wide enough to let in birds; someone appointed as a scribe had started his work before the official had properly registered his appointment; and one hundred crossbows were missing from the government's arsenal.

The documents indicate that order was supposed to be maintained through an extensive system of criminal punishments. When problems arose, someone would generally charge another with misconduct and the case would go to one of the scribes, who acted as an investigator. The scribe then sent a report to the magistrate, who was supposed to apply the correct punishment according to the severity of the crime. In their ranking system, the lowest penalties were fines.[16] Next was banishment, then light penal labour as a guard, watchman, or servant. In these cases the criminal's beard would be shaved off as a stigmatizing mark. Following banishment was more severe penal labour as a 'firewood-gatherer' or 'rice-sifter', for men and women, respectively. After that was the most severe form of penal labour, as an 'earth-' or 'grain-pounder', accompanied by visible mutilation, which could involve cutting the nose, although this penalty could be transmuted into a fine for people of higher rank. Finally, there was the death penalty. In practice, the magistrates often reduced the penalties because of the offender's rank, particularly when it came to mutilation. But they had to navigate a sophisticated system for determining the correct punishment according to the different categories of crime and depending on factors such as the circumstances of a killing, with lesser punishments for those who had only assisted or conspired to commit an offence. They also had to reduce the penalty if the offender had reported his or her own crime, and there were rules about the minimum age at which children could be prosecuted. On the advice of Lord Shang, the Qin had introduced a system of collective responsibility, which meant that family members, or those who lived in the same five-family unit, could be punished as well, albeit more leniently than the principal offender.

In all their activities, officials had to follow correct procedures, from receiving and considering reports, to arresting suspects, to confiscating and evaluating the property of the most severe offenders. Further rules applied when they interrogated a suspect, and they had to be particularly careful in applying torture, so as not to extract a false confession. When the magistrates were unsure about the correct procedure, the assessment of the evidence, or the appropriate crime or penalty, they could refer the case to higher authorities. Many of these cases are recorded on the bamboo slips in Xi's tomb. Each time, the magistrate had first consulted a number of his colleagues, and where opinions were split he reported the facts, the evidence, and the different views to officers at the provincial level. But this was a risky process, as the provincial officials could decide that the decision of the magistrate was wrong and fine him for an error of judgement. None of the legal officials was an independent professional. They were all civil servants, whose primary duties were to the higher government authorities. There was no separation of powers between the government and the judiciary.

Most striking, at least to modern eyes, was that the whole legal system was based on crime and punishment. Although some of the cases involved what we might call 'civil' disputes—for example, over inheritance or the ownership of property—in the hands of the Chinese authorities they were assessed as crimes. In one case, a wealthy merchant of very high rank in a childless marriage had fathered two children by one of his female slaves, presumably a common occurrence in these times.[17] When his wife died, he freed the slave and treated her as his wife, after consulting members of his ancestral lineage, who accepted the situation. When the merchant died, however, she failed to report all his property to the authorities, apparently trying to hide some of his money for the benefit of her children. She later decided to confess, possibly fearing that someone would report her. The question faced by the legal officials was how to punish her. The crime of failing to report was serious, and a released slave would normally be sentenced to the most serious form of penal labour, as a grain-pounder. But the wife of a merchant of the fifth rank could receive a reduced conviction as a rice-sifter. Her confession reduced the penalty by another degree again. The question over which the officials hesitated was whether they should treat her as a wife, given that the merchant had not properly reported his marriage. While the government assumed responsibility for authorizing marriages, many people still looked to their lineage for confirmation instead. And this was not the end of the difficulties. Another servant claimed that the merchant had promised him a share of his property but had failed to record this in his will. The wife, meanwhile, claimed that the servant had tried to blackmail her into transferring the property to him. After the first round of interviews, the officials, faced with conflicting evidence, interrogated the servant again, presenting him with evidence of the merchant's wishes. Now the servant dropped his claim. The officials were still not sure that the evidence was clear enough to amount to blackmail, so they sent the case to the province for a ruling. The dispute in this case was between the wife and the servant of the merchant about who was entitled to his property. However, within the Qin legal system, it became a criminal case about reporting and bribery, in which both parties received punishments.

All Chinese litigants, including merchants with commercial disputes and peasants arguing about land use, had to squeeze their claims into the categories of the criminal laws. For those who took their cases to court, there must always have been a risk that they would find themselves being punished for a wrong, so most disputes probably never reached the magistrates. Disagreements over property, debts, contracts, and cases of minor fighting and assault were probably dealt with locally in the villages or in neighbourhoods, or by members of an ancestral lineage, in a pattern that continued into the modern era. But when they reached the courts, they were assessed against the extensive lists of crimes and punishments.

The cases buried with Xi and other Qin officials demonstrate meticulous control of public affairs. Officials managed not just armies, borders, roads, and waterways but also public granaries, storehouses, and markets. They pursued vagrants and those who absconded from proper employment as well as controlling systems of marriage and inheritance. The long arm of the government reached far into the everyday lives of most Chinese people. The Qin are now mostly remembered for the stupendous army of terracotta warriors they buried in a tomb complex at Xian, but they undertook other public works, building a large wall to the north of their empire and an elaborate system of roads. All this required considerable amounts of forced labour. This put a great strain on the peasantry and explains many of the laws concerning conscription, penal labour, and the offences of vagrancy and absconding. The emperors systematically centralized power in the hands of a small elite, which undermined the status and authority of local aristocrats. Eventually a few nobles were able to incite large numbers of discontented peasants to rebel against their rulers. In 207 BCE, less than two decades after the Qin established their empire, rebels took the opportunity presented by the death of the emperor to launch an attack on the capital and bring down the government.

THE REBELS' AMBITIOUS leader styled himself the emperor Gaozu and established what became the Han dynasty.[18] Although he strongly criticized the Qin and their system of government, not least for the harshness of their laws, Gaozu continued the former dynasty's policy of unifying China, expanding the structures of its government and maintaining many of its legal institutions. He founded a new capital near modern Xian, established markets, developed trade along the silk roads, and instituted examinations for the recruitment of officials. Drawn to the philosophy of Confucius, Gaozu and his successors styled themselves 'Sons of Heaven' and 'Leaders of the East', and they performed sacrifices and divination and continued the ancestral cults. Now free of persecution, Confucian scholars wrote extensive commentaries on the classics and persuaded the emperors that good education was essential for election to any government position. These ideas conflicted with legalistic institutions and practices of the bureaucracy, however, which most officials saw no reason to change. Throughout the rest of the Han period, debates continued between those sympathetic to Confucian ideas, who warned of corruption and growing disparities between rich and poor and who advocated leadership through moral example, and those who sought to strengthen government monopolies, control the population, and impose strict laws.

The Han emperors made much of the fact that their regime and its laws were more merciful and less complicated than those of their predecessors, but they only gradually relaxed the harshest Qin laws. They kept or copied Qin statutes on agriculture, the auditing of official records, transmission of orders, provision of services, establishment of offices, food rations, and markets. Like their predecessors, they used the legal system to manage the economy, control officials, maintain the flow of important information, requisition labour, control ideology and religious practices, monitor family structures, and manage inheritance and property relations. Individuals who wished to resist the control of the state were reduced to absconding, smuggling, conducting illicit affairs, organizing revolts, or using the legal system itself.

Under the Han, legal officials at quite low levels continued to exercise considerable power. They began their training at an early age and became familiar with a mass of statutes, difficult legal terminology, and types of documents. If someone made a complaint, they would conduct the initial investigation, record accusations, interrogate and cross-examine parties and witnesses, and even administer or supervise torture, if they thought it necessary to extract a confession. They then collated the evidence, assembled it into a case, and sent it to the magistrate for a decision. As in Qin times, the magistrates followed precise procedures and kept records of past cases, particularly those they referred to their superiors. Carefully recorded on bamboo strips, these established a system of precedent not unlike the English common law. About half of the cases discovered in one tomb at Hubei concerned officials who had failed in their duties, falsified books, committed theft or bribery, or obtained a wrongful conviction through torture.[19] Others had to do with captives and convicts who had absconded, been freed, or been beaten to death. One case involved a woman from the ruling family of a newly conquered territory who had eloped with her official escort on her way to the capital. In another, a man had unwittingly married an absconding slave. Generally, the cases raised questions about the correct degree of punishment when several finely defined crimes could have applied to the facts in question.

Four of the cases found in the tomb at Hubei offer graphic tales of courtroom drama, and these may have had literary, as well as legal, purposes. One document dating to the Qin period records how, in 241 BCE, a plague of locusts had devastated crops in the capital, and all able-bodied men were sent to the fields to beat off the pests, leaving the streets and markets empty.[20] An opportunistic robber chose the moment to attack a woman and snatch a large amount of cash, but he dropped a fragment of a silk merchant's contract at the scene. According to the record, this violent crime, committed in broad daylight, terrified the inhabitants of the city, and the officials sent scribes to investigate. Initial work produced no leads, so the magistrate called upon the hero of the case, a scribe named Julü, to investigate.

Careful questioning among the silk merchants who might know something about the contract fragment was inconclusive, so Julü moved on to 'lower elements of society', including juvenile delinquents, servants of market traders, male slaves, bond servants, and foreign wage labourers, observing their behaviour and looking for signs of suspicious activity. Eventually he sought out even more shadowy characters—black market traders, the homeless, the destitute, and male prostitutes. He finally found a pitiful suspect, a man named Kong whose contradictory and implausible statements he destroyed in cross-examination. His final triumph was to match the assault weapon with a scabbard that Kong had once owned. Now the suspect confessed, and Julü was nominated for promotion as a 'highly competent, incorrupt, conscientious, and dutiful' official. The scribe seems to have been more concerned to record, and possibly embellish, his heroics than the legal niceties of the case.

Another set of bamboo strips describes the case of a widow who was prosecuted for having illicit intercourse with a lover.[21] To add insult to injury, the two had been discovered in the house of her mother-in-law, next to the coffin of her deceased husband. The magistrates charged her with filial impiety towards her mother-in-law, on apparently incontrovertible grounds, and they were just about to pronounce sentence when a junior scribe returned to confront his superiors. Challenging the sentence, he proceeded to demolish the case against the widow and the magistrates' logic, demonstrating that the widow no longer owed any filial duty to her former mother-in-law. The scribes who compiled these cases almost certainly embellished the narratives to increase the drama and celebrate the heroism of their colleagues.

Other texts found in the Hubei tomb record dialogues between a ruler and one of his senior judges about the cases he presented for approval. The judge always starts with excerpts from the statutes and the facts of the case leading to his decision, and the ruler in each case initially expresses consternation and disapproval. The judge bravely persists, offering a detailed and persuasive account of the reasons for his verdict, which finally leaves the ruler with no choice but to approve his decision. Scribes may have compiled these records to serve as instructive precedents or to educate trainee officials, but some do look more like literary works because of the manner in which they cast legal officials as heroes. By burying them in a tomb, the bereaved were perhaps hoping they would continue to provide a source of amusement and satisfaction for a scribe in the afterlife.

Over the next four hundred years, the Han governments alternated between policies inspired by Confucian thought and the stricter laws that seemed more appropriate at times of unrest and disorder.[22] And all the while they passed new statutes and regulations. By 94 CE, there were 610 capital offences, 1,698 offences punishable by penal servitude, and 2,681 other offences. One emperor complained of the 'vexatiously numerous' laws and prolix system.[23] Still, perhaps troubled by Confucian criticisms, they never produced a streamlined and coordinated legal code, and the laws became more disorganized as they multiplied.

The later centuries of Han rule, in the first and second centuries of the common era, were marred by court intrigues, corruption, and the machinations of imperial regents, wives, mothers, and eunuchs. Literature continued to flourish, along with philosophy, the arts, and scientific and technological innovations, but social order disintegrated, and many lost their faith in the promises of Confucianism. It seemed unable to create stability. Some turned to Daoism, others to Buddhism, which had entered China in the second century BCE, and the Han regime eventually fell in 220 CE. Now China divided into three kingdoms, and there followed several centuries of political chaos. Despite the political turmoil, many of the Han statutes survived; rulers continued to create, amend, and repeal them to suit their own administrative needs; and several brave scholars attempted to organize them into more coherent groups.

IN 581 CE, Yang Jian, a general in the northern kingdom, ousted the heir apparent to the ruling family, killed fifty-nine of its princes, and proclaimed himself founder of a new dynasty, the Sui. Within a few years, he had conquered the southern kingdom and consolidated his rule over the whole of China. To mark the reunification of the country, he proclaimed a new legal code. Like earlier rulers, he declared that his intention was to introduce a more just system and abolish the most cruel punishments of his predecessors. But, in practice, his scribes simply copied out many of the 1,735 articles from the Han, several of which had their roots in Zhou and Qin times 700 or 800 years earlier. The basic shape of the system also continued to be overwhelmingly penal, demanding serious punishments for many crimes, albeit mitigated by possibilities for remission. But Yang Jian's ambitious plans to reunite the Chinese state and construct a grand canal to link north and south, along with his continuous military campaigns, demanded excessive labour and military conscription, which his people struggled to provide. Exhausted and oppressed, they staged a series of rebellions just a few decades later and overthrew the regime.

Among the contenders for power, one nobleman emerged to establish what became the Tang dynasty in 618. His son, Taizong, then secured the succession in 626 by killing his two brothers and all ten of their sons. Despite these violent beginnings, the later Tang emperors were careful rulers, selecting good advisers, and under their governance China prospered. Over the next 150 years, the capital, Chang'an (modern Xian), became the greatest city in the Far East and the largest in the world, with some one million inhabitants. Embassies arrived bringing tributes to the rulers, now styled Sons of Heaven, while students flocked to the Buddhist monasteries and Chinese pilgrims journeyed throughout Central Asia as far as India. Merchants and goods from Java and Iran flowed into Chang'an's markets and streets, which jostled with foreigners. Brilliant poets and artists flocked to the court and sought patronage from the wealthy, while artisans turned out delicate ceramics and porcelain. The first printed books appeared in this era, originally to reproduce scriptures for Buddhist monks.

The new rulers slowly unified the government of their empire, controlling urban markets and standardizing taxes on grain, cloth, and labour services. They revised the equal-field system, under which land was allotted to farmers, and expanded the tax registers, which soon recorded nine million households, representing a population of close to fifty million. The emperors also insisted on personal skills, rather than family connections or military achievements, for official positions. Candidates for the highest levels of government service studied the Confucian classics as they trained for their examinations, which taught them about loyalty, not least to the emperor. The ministry of personnel then allocated successful candidates to government posts, including the magistrates who headed the district offices in the far corners of the empire. The Tang system of government was designed to keep local families from amassing power.

The emperors also commissioned a team of legal experts to draft laws. In time-honoured tradition, they declared that their laws would be more lenient than those of their predecessors, but the draftsmen based their new code firmly on the laws of the Sui.[24] Officials continued to develop and improve the laws over the next three decades until they had created a substantial penal code, with articles, commentaries, and subcommentaries, many in the form of queries and answers.[25] These qualified and extended the basic rules, incorporating the wisdom of cases decided over many centuries, to create a complex set of crimes, often distinguished from each other in precise and subtle ways. The Tang Code started with different types of punishment: beatings of various kinds, penal labour, and the death penalty. It described the great crimes that merited the death sentence: rebellion, sedition, treason; major crimes against family members, teachers, employers, and officials; poisoning and sorcery; and not serving the emperor properly. It then described the people who were entitled to remission or who were permitted to substitute a fine for a physical penalty—such as relatives of the emperor, those who had given long service, and others renowned for great achievements. It dealt with the prosecution of anyone who conspired in or assisted a crime, and it delineated how officials should deal with multiple crimes, or mitigate sentences for youth, age, disability, and confession. The code indicates that many people could claim reductions in their sentences, meaning that in practice punishments were much less severe than the basic rules might suggest.

The next sections discussed property crimes, kidnapping, fraud, the effects of imperial amnesties, and collective responsibility and set out rules for servants and slaves. There followed twelve sets of articles on specific types of crimes, errors that might be committed by the imperial guard, misdemeanours in government office, household registration and composition, marriage, regulations for public stables and granaries, rules on theft and robbery as well as assaults and accusations, and various procedural rules about arrest, judgement, and imprisonment. Alongside this criminal code, officials drafted administrative statutes, regulations, and ordinances. As in all previous regimes, the laws were first and foremost concerned with the running of the state, raising taxes, managing land, regulating marriage among peasants, conscripting troops, maintaining stud farms and storehouses, and preventing forgeries and counterfeiting.

The introduction to the code reveals much about how the Tang rulers and their officials and advisers had come to see their legal system. The great rulers of the past, it claimed, had been chosen by the people, and they had made laws in accordance with the highest moral standards. After an original golden age, when morality alone could maintain order, the rulers had had to introduce punishments to inspire awe and dread among the stupid, the unthinking, and the downright criminal. But they had ensured that penalties were appropriate, recognizing 'heaven's great statute'. The Tang Code claimed that it followed 'the pattern of the former sages, whose regulations have not been lost, but have all been preserved, both great and small'. Like Hindu brahmins, the Chinese lawmakers invoked a sense of cosmological order as the foundation of their laws. These were the creation of men, but observed principles of morality and justice. And, putting the emperor at the centre, the Tang Code proclaimed his 'wide and great mercy'.

The code invoked both the Confucian sense of an ideal moral order and the legalistic approach of the Qin, claiming that 'virtue and ritual are the basis of the government's teaching, but punishments and chastisement are its instruments'. But it went much further than either the Mesopotamian or Indian laws in its insistence on the good order of rules and categories. The authors emphasized the importance of distinguishing between different kinds and degrees of crimes with laws that were both concise and durable, able to distinguish round and square, like a measuring stick or a balance, as they put it. And this was borne out by the structure of the articles with their fine distinctions and careful qualifications.

Not only did the Tang Code model itself on much previous law, but it set the scene for almost all later Chinese legal codes. Its rules were largely adopted by the subsequent Song (960–1279), Ming (1368–1644), and Qing (1644–1911) regimes. Over time, legal officials introduced new laws in order to deal with changing social issues, making the codes more and more complex. They also poured out commentaries and legal treatises, along with collections of cases, not to mention detective literature in which county magistrates often featured as resourceful heroes. As a result, the law was well known to those who could read—educated citizens, merchants, artisans, and a relatively large general public. And, despite substantial reorganization, much of its substance was still present in the version of the code maintained by the last Qing emperors at the beginning of the twentieth century.[26]

Throughout the changes in ruling dynasty, the Chinese law codes remained overwhelmingly penal. Anything that the government wanted to control and regulate, it made the subject of criminal sanctions. If local officials were supposed to transmit conscription orders throughout their regions, or keep birds out of their granaries, they made it an offence not to do so. If people were supposed to divide their property equally among their sons, it was a crime if they gave instructions to do something else. And the social hierarchy among government officials, soldiers, merchants, and artisans was made clear in the different punishments they would receive for the same crimes. This meant that people could not sue one another directly to enforce commercial contracts or property claims, or challenge relatives when divorce or death led to family disputes. If they wanted to use the official legal system, they had to accuse someone of a crime. Sometimes there was a suitable offence—for example, it was a crime for someone who had entered into a temporary property purchase, effectively a type of mortgage, not to allow the debtor to redeem it. This protected the right of the property-owner, as civil laws do elsewhere. But in other cases the laws were not so useful. Those embroiled in property disputes often had to rely on a general provision against 'stealing, selling, exchanging, falsely claiming, falsely contriving a price and drawing up a deed, conditionally selling or occupying another's land'.[27] This hardly helped anyone.

In practice, many people tried to avoid the formality and delays of the official system, along with the risk that they might, themselves, be found to be in breach of some rule.[28] Throughout the following centuries, most of what we might call 'civil' disputes were mediated locally, by village and guild councils, or by respected leaders, such as members of ancestral lineages, or even Daoist priests. Indeed, since at least Han times, the rulers explicitly encouraged these informal practices, on the basis that they upheld the Confucian values of harmony, conciliation, and forbearance. They were aspects of a more 'humane' or 'minimalist' government, as a succession of rulers liked to present it, the moral 'rule of men' as opposed to the harsh 'rule of law'. Even in the modern world, the Chinese state has continued to rely on local mediation and semiformal justice systems in the interest of creating a more 'harmonious society'.[29] Nevertheless, the classical legal codes remained penal in form, prescribing punishments for people who did not follow the rules, rather than giving citizens the right to make claims against one another.

The Chinese laws formed a system of discipline, providing rewards and punishments by which officials were supposed to induce correct behaviour. As one Chinese scholar put it, the legal system was like a net. If the holes were too small, it would catch everything and become unmanageable, but if they were too big, some fish would slip through. The experts knew how to manipulate the cords so as to strike the right balance.[30] But people continued to talk about Chinese law in Confucian terms, and the laws emphasized Confucian values, including respect for senior relatives, teachers, employers, and officials. In these ways, it had some parallels with the laws of the Hindu brahmins. But while the Dharmashastras emphasized individual duties and correct ritual behaviour, the Chinese thought of their law as a system of norms created by their rulers to bring order to a great empire. They seem to have internalized the words of the Tang ruler who declared that he had relied upon his 'estimation of heavenly principles and considerations of human compassion' to ensure that his code would embody universal and unchanging moral principles. He was the source of all law. This also meant that he was not constrained by it. Ironically, supported by the Confucianists' warnings about publicizing legal rules, the emperors resisted the 'rule of law', the possibility that they could be judged according to their own laws. This was a unique achievement among the world's major legal traditions.

LAW DEVELOPED QUITE independently in Mesopotamia, India, and China, at least as far as the historical record suggests. In each case, the lawmakers created basic rules that specified punishments and compensation, regulated family relations and contracts, and provided rules for evidence. Their substance reflected the social problems that mediators faced everywhere in complex societies. Their laws could, at least in principle, have been applied by judges, and they soon were by China's magistrates, but all the early lawmakers had higher aspirations. The Mesopotamian laws were casuistic, specifying the consequences of actions, events, and situations; the brahmins spelled out duties; and the Chinese defined appropriate punishments—and behind each legal system was a different vision of order. Their texts were more important for what they represented—statements about justice, a map for a social hierarchy, a system of discipline—than for the social order they actually produced.

As these three legal traditions developed and spread over the centuries, different lawmakers used forms and techniques from all of them and found that their rules offered pragmatic instruments to regulate daily life, create predictability, and resolve disputes. But the lawmakers of the great traditions that emerged in Rome, the Middle East, and Western Europe, largely the distant descendants of the Mesopotamian tradition, all had their own visions of order. Here, ideals of justice, duty, and discipline combined to form distinctly new traditions, those that dominate the modern world.

CHAPTER FOUR

ADVOCATES AND JURISTS
Intellectual Pursuits in Ancient Rome

R oman law was the project of Roman citizens. Like the
Athenians, just a few decades earlier, they were seeking
justice, probably inspired by what they had heard of the
Mesopotamian laws and their promises. Throughout most of
Roman history, assemblies of citizens had to gather to approve
any new laws. They were not in the gift of either the ruling elite
or a priestly class. But over time, legal scholars developed the
substance of the law, treating it as an intellectual exercise and
producing academic opinions. These were eventually brought together in the great compendium of Roman law that law students
still study today. Ultimately, powerful emperors managed to control both judges and scholars, but they never quite achieved the
lawmaking authority of their Chinese counterparts. There was
always a sense that law was made by and for Roman citizens and
that it held the promise of justice for all.

★

IN THE SEVENTH and sixth centuries BCE, there was little to distinguish the site of what would become one of the world's most powerful ancient cities at the mouth of the river Tiber. The local populations were still tending herds and fields untroubled by written rules or regulations, living in settlements of wattle-and-daub houses clustered on the hilltops. But across the Mediterranean people were exploring new trading possibilities. Adventurous Greeks established settlements in southern Italy, and an elite class emerged among the Italians to the north. Successful warrior clans consolidated their wealth, combined their villages into towns, and sent missions over the seas in search of luxury goods and cultural inspiration.[1]

Little is known about the Romans who lived during this period, but in Etruria, north of Rome, archaeologists have found ornate weapons, banqueting services, ivory ornaments, jewellery, and even ostrich eggs. Many of these items had been imported from Greece. The elite displayed their wealth during processions and at athletic competitions, horse races, and banquets, and they decorated their tombs with delicate murals. The Romans followed suit and began to construct substantial temples in their villages. At some point in the seventh century, they created a public space between the hills and constructed the foundations of a new urban centre, later known as the Forum.[2]

Throughout most of the following century, a series of kings, thought to be of Etruscan origin, governed Rome. They commanded large armies, raided their neighbours, and drew many of the surrounding populations into their sphere of control. The ambitious Servius Tullius embarked on extensive political and military reforms, introducing censuses, reorganizing the population into new groups, and establishing a military assembly. He may have been trying to limit the power of the aristocrats— he himself was probably of slave origin. But the wealthy classes were not happy and in 509 BCE they staged a coup against his successor, Tarquinius Superbus. Having removed the populist tyrant, they determined that Rome should have no more kings. This was the start of the Roman Republic, and it is here that the story of Roman law begins.

LATER ROMAN HISTORIANS described and embellished the events surrounding the overthrow of the Roman monarchy in stories involving the dramatic rape of the virtuous Lucretia by an arrogant king, and his final defeat twenty years later in a great battle outside Rome. It is now practically impossible to disentangle myth from reality, a common problem with early Roman history. But, possibly inspired by the Athenians, who deposed their tyrannical ruler in 510 BCE, the Roman elite established an oligarchy. They elected two consuls to manage their domestic affairs and military campaigns, and these men had to consult a larger assembly on important issues. The consuls also established an ad hoc group of advisers, which would later develop into Rome's Senate.

But the Roman elite were careless with the livelihoods of the poor, whose resources they severely depleted through constant warfare. A group of commoners decided to form their own assembly, the *consilium plebis*, in 494 BCE and elected their own leaders, tribunes. They took over one of the town's temples and refused to perform military service. This was the first of a series of strikes during which they demanded relief from both hunger and debt. The Roman economy had evolved systems of lending and credit, and, like their Mesopotamian counterparts, many of the poorest found themselves in debt bondage. As in Ur, debt and social inequality surrounded the emergence of laws. But in Rome lawmaking was the initiative of the people themselves.

By the middle of the century, the plebeians' assembly had established voting procedures and the tribunes were demanding better treatment from the wealthy classes—the patricians, as they became known—who were monopolizing the higher offices of government.[3] The tribunes also demanded that newly conquered territories be distributed fairly among them. They wanted laws that would apply to everyone, which would be written down for all to see. Responding to the plebeians' demands, in around 451 BCE the consuls suspended normal political offices and appointed a board of ten men, the *decimviri*, to collect, draft, and publish a set of laws. Later tradition has it that they took a trip to Athens to study Solon's text, written over a century earlier. Other scholars think it more likely that the Romans were inspired directly by Mesopotamian laws, which they knew about from Phoenician traders and diplomats. Certainly, the Roman laws follow a similar basic format and use a casuistic form.[4] In any event, it was a political crisis that led the Romans to commission the decimviri to write laws.

The subjects and content of the Twelve Tables, as they came to be known, carefully reconstructed by decades of later scholarship, were in fact rather mundane.[5] They made procedural rules for court cases and dealt with the sorts of subjects that almost certainly gave rise to disputes in the normal course of Roman life: compensation for injuries, theft, and other minor crimes; wills and inheritance; and debt, obligations, and damage to property. Some confirmed the status of the *paterfamilias*, the head of a household, while one limited funeral expenses, apparently to avoid conspicuous consumption. Others specified the circumstances in which debt bondage might be imposed. Although a couple of clauses concerned the organization of boundaries and roads, the beginnings of urban planning, for the most part the laws dealt with private relations. One of the rules directed that important cases, which probably meant those involving the death penalty, required the approval of 'the fullest possible assembly', that is, the *consilium* of the plebeians. They wanted all Rome's citizens to participate in the administration of justice.[6]

Historians have long debated the nature of the conflict between Rome's classes.[7] The creation of the Twelve Tables was certainly not the great plebeian victory that later Roman tradition claimed it to be, and the patrician elite continued to dominate the higher offices of government. Nor did the new laws demand, even on the face of it, equality among citizens, or general relief from debt. Still, they came to seem foundational to later Roman writers, probably because the laws promised, even if they could not guarantee, the right of every citizen to be treated fairly.

After some tensions and the drafting of the last two laws, the decimviri retired and two new consuls reestablished a government. In consultation with the plebeians, they formulated further laws, *leges* (pl. of *lex*), in 449 BCE, which recognized the plebeians' assembly. Its decisions now had the force of law, although, at least initially, members of the Senate could veto them. The consuls also recognized the status of the tribunes and confirmed that all citizens had rights of appeal. And they agreed that the Twelve Tables should be inscribed onto bronze tablets and nailed up in the Forum, the public centre of the town. Although few citizens were literate, simply by being written out and prominently displayed the laws signalled the fact that all Roman citizens had the right to refer to their laws. The plebeians also felt they should have access to government decisions and demanded that the Senate reveal its private decisions to two of their officials, the *aediles*.

The consuls, who effectively managed Rome's affairs, now had to convene an assembly if they wanted to introduce new laws. There were three of these, including the plebeians' consilium, which had different constituencies and overlapping jurisdictions. Initially, the consuls introduced very few laws, and when they did it was mostly on constitutional matters, such as a decision to go to war, to make peace, or to change legal procedures.[8] But the basic system for making new laws continued throughout the four centuries of the Roman Republic, and the summoning of assemblies confirmed the important fact that government decisions had to be debated and confirmed by the citizens at large.

POLITICAL TENSIONS CONTINUED in Rome over the following century. The economy struggled, and famines caused ongoing unrest among the plebeians. But in 396 BCE, Roman forces destroyed the Etruscan town of Veii, took over its productive agricultural lands, and distributed them among Rome's citizens.[9] Then, in the 380s and 370s, the tribunes successfully demanded that more land be allocated to the commoners.[10] But despite the consequent reduction in food shortages, the poorer citizens continued to descend into debt bondage, and the tribunes persuaded the assemblies to enact further laws to address the problem, albeit without wholly resolving it.[11] They also demanded that plebeians should be eligible for higher office. The result was the Licinian-Sextian law, approved in 367 BCE, which required that one of the two annually elected consuls be a plebeian. For a while, the patricians managed to hold on to control of the Senate, but the plebeians secured another victory in 339, when they passed the Ovinian law, which gave the censor, an elected official, power to remove and enroll new senators.[12] If anything, the Senate now increased in importance, debating political issues and exercising an influence on government officials, of whom there were still a very small number.[13]

In 387 BCE, a Gallic tribe from across the Alps invaded northern Italy and destroyed much of Rome. But the intruders did not stay, and the city soon recovered. If nothing else, the debacle confirmed to Rome's leaders the importance of maintaining their military capacity. Roman armies continued to pursue campaigns in the surrounding Latin region, moving on to southern Italy and forming alliances with more distant rulers, and by the third century BCE they had come to dominate more than half the Italian Peninsula. Rome was still, in the words of the Roman historian Livy, a city 'not yet adorned'. But trade was expanding, and with it the wealth of the *nobilitas*, the new aristocratic class, which was starting to include wealthy plebeians.[14]

The tribunes continued to agitate for political reform, and in 287 BCE the Senate relinquished its remaining control over their assembly.[15] Soon afterwards, the plebeians' consilium approved the Lex Aquilia, a set of systematic rules about how to deal with cases of killing, wounding, and damage to property. One of its most important provisions was the right of citizens to sit in judgement on a corrupt official. If someone was suspected or accused of a serious crime, a high-ranking official, generally a tribune, would call the suspect to an inquiry, which would be held in public, most likely in the open air of the Forum. Here, anyone interested in the case could listen and comment. If the tribune concluded by laying a charge, he would convene an assembly to hear the evidence and make the final decision.

For minor disputes, citizens could go to the aediles, the officials in charge of Rome's streets and markets, who would hear accusations of commercial and other misconduct, including usury, grain speculation, and prostitution.[16] In more serious cases, a citizen had to send a petition to a higher official. For this, the citizen had to use a precise form of words, stipulated by the *pontiffs*, the aristocratic religious experts. These words, the *legis actiones*, were often complicated, and any badly drafted petition would automatically fail.[17] Initiating a legal case, although available to all, was not a straightforward process. If the case involved a debt, an official might allow the creditor to seize what he was owed directly, but he sent other cases to a judge, or group of judges, *iudices*, who might demand that the petitioner support his or her claim by taking an oath. The judges were not legal experts, simply officials. And the Twelve Tables required petitioners to bring the defendant physically before the judge, which often caused difficulties.

The provisions of the Twelve Tables were rather sparse. But, like Hammurabi's laws, they set out general principles that could be applied to a range of cases. They stated, for example, that someone who killed a thief in his house in the middle of the night had a defence to a charge of homicide. The implication was that someone who surprised a thief during the day was supposed to show more restraint. The laws also set out a complicated process that creditors needed to follow before they could impose debt bondage, which probably did give a measure of protection to debtors, at least those educated and confident enough to quote the laws. And they established technical requirements for marriage and inheritance. The assemblies passed several further laws to regulate contracts and guarantees, the status of minors and illegitimate children, and inheritance and succession practices, which were a constant source of problems.[18] Even if ordinary citizens avoided the more complex legal procedures, the principles behind these laws surely made their way into the thinking of people who mediated local disputes. Rome was a small place, and the most important laws would have been known to all.

ROME WAS NOW effectively governed by members of the nobilitas, the wealthy class. They formed the Senate, which debated general policy and controlled the treasury, but its business was largely controlled by the consuls, who also exercised authority over the army. And the consuls, in turn, were elected by the assemblies, along with all other senior officials.[19] The body of citizens, through these gatherings, had the power to reject or approve new laws. The assemblies followed numerous rituals and procedures, not least for voting, which had to be conducted correctly before any appointment or decision could be made.[20] If a consul or a tribune wanted to propose a new law, he would start by sending notices to all voting citizens, men between the ages of seventeen and sixty, calling them to assemble in the Forum. In the days before the assembly, the bill's proposers would convene meetings in which they made strenuous efforts to win people over to their side. On the appointed day for the vote, generally chosen to coincide with one of Rome's markets, official observers carefully set up the voting baskets on a wooden platform in the Forum and an orator read out the proposed law. Meanwhile, the citizens assembled into tribes, the historical groups that formed to vote on these occasions. Another official brought in the pitcher used to draw lots to select the voting order among them. One by one, the members of the first tribe would step up to receive their voting slips, one from each basket for 'yes' and 'no', one of which they placed in the voting urn. When everyone from the tribe had voted, official enumerators counted the slips and declared the tribe to be for or against the law. Then the next tribe would vote. This continued until a majority of the tribes, eighteen out of thirty-five, had voted the same way and the result could be declared. The whole process could take several hours. Meanwhile, women, children, traders, foreigners, and slaves crowded the Forum and surrounding streets. They did not have voting rights, but they gathered to watch the spectacle, enjoying food and drink from circulating vendors and murmuring in anticipation as each result was announced. If the new law was controversial, emotions could run high.

The nobilitas exercised a disproportionate influence in the assemblies, even the plebeians' consilium, and their complex and cumbersome processes were hardly democratic. But, when coupled with the system of annual elections for major offices, the assemblies did effectively limit the powers of any one individual. And those who held high office and wanted to introduce changes had to have at least some understanding of the issues that faced the majority of the Roman people. The assemblies also gave orators an opportunity to shine and establish their reputations, as they tried to rouse the emotions of the gathered citizens. Above all, the laws were public statements, written down for everyone to see, after the citizens had had the opportunity to hear them debated.[21] The nobilitas dominated the higher offices of government, the army, and Rome's economic resources, but they could not simply govern at will.[22]

These structures and processes of government continued throughout the Republic—and they established a system of checks and balances between the consuls, the Senate, and the people. In the second century BCE, a Greek hostage named Polybius, who had settled in Rome, commented approvingly on its delicate political structures. At the centre of the Roman state, he said, the wealthy might dominate the most important offices and institutions, but the votes of the poor mattered, and had to be won.[23]

ROMAN ARMIES ENGAGED in almost continual warfare on the Italian Peninsula and beyond during the third and second centuries BCE. Most dramatic were the Punic Wars against Carthage, the second of which started with Hannibal's heroic crossing of the Alps in 218 BCE and saw him practically wipe out the Roman army. The campaigns drained Rome's treasury, and Carthage came very close to eliminating Roman power. Victory in North Africa in 202 BCE turned the tide, however, securing Rome's position as the most powerful force in the Mediterranean. Rome now had access to vast quantities of booty from North Africa and southern Spain.

Possibly a quarter of Rome's adult male population was now employed in its armies, and the soldiers brought back spectacular spoils from their successful campaigns. Conquest also meant captives, thousands of whom were set to work in the plantations and mines, as well as becoming domestic servants. As many as forty thousand slaves may have toiled to extract Spanish silver, which the Roman treasury used to mint coins, further stimulating the economy.[24] Wealthy citizens specialized their agricultural techniques, and many of them acquired vast estates, which produced olive oil and wine for export around the Mediterranean. They developed new foodstuffs—bread now replaced porridge—and new building materials, most famously concrete, which allowed them to adorn their city with monumental buildings. There were triumphal military processions and public feasts. The government could even afford to suspend taxes on Roman citizens by 167 BCE.

Rome's dramatic expansion raised new legal issues for its officials. Many soldiers, for example, settled in Spain, where they fathered children, and the Senate had to decide how to treat their progeny. Were they Roman citizens or not?[25] The laws of the Twelve Tables were by now over three hundred years old, and although they remained important in the minds of most Romans, they were hardly adequate to deal with contemporary problems. So the consuls and tribunes formulated new laws, which the assemblies approved.[26] The reforming tribune Gaius Gracchus fixed the price of grain in 127 BCE and built granaries to ensure a supply for the poorer citizens. In addition, he introduced new taxes on the colonies. Officials might ask the assemblies to rule in individual cases, particularly those that concerned citizens' status and rights. For example, in 186 BCE, one courtesan told her patrician lover about the Bacchanalian orgies she had witnessed. The man now refused to be initiated into the cult in question, to the horror of his family, who drove him out of their house. So he took his information to a consul, who interrogated the courtesan, dragging the information out of her with threats. He then took steps to repress the cult. The consul also suggested that the informers should be rewarded, and he asked the assembly of plebeians to decide, among other things, whether the courtesan should be granted new status and rights.[27]

The Twelve Tables had been intended to ensure a form of equality among Rome's people, and the laws guaranteed them certain freedoms and protections. But disparities in wealth and complicated distinctions in status and rights still created hierarchies and divided the population in ways that became more complex as the city grew. At the domestic level, the head of a family, the paterfamilias, had remarkably broad rights over members of his household. Women, meanwhile, did not vote or participate in government. The enslaved population increased massively, and some became trusted by their owners, who might grant them freedom, although, as freedmen, they retained duties towards their former owners. The nature of citizenship also changed, particularly after 89 BCE, when it was extended to the populations of the rest of the Italian Peninsula. Not everyone could travel to Rome to vote in an assembly, but the right to appeal to Roman law was an important marker of inclusion.

Roman laws did not just concern its citizens. By far and away the majority of the issues debated by the assemblies concerned political and procedural matters revolving around the conduct of officials. As Rome grew, so did the number of official positions, which the wealthy were eager to fill. An ambitious young man would generally start as a *quaestor*, a junior official, who might be given responsibility for financial matters. After this, he could hope to be enrolled in the Senate, then move on to an annual term as aedile. As such, he would be responsible for the day-to-day running of the city, the maintenance of buildings and streets, supervision of markets and shops, the conduct of games and festivals, and the maintenance of law and order. Election as a *praetor* might follow, and from there the most successful could hope to be elected as consul. The praetors initially acted as deputies to the consuls, issuing military commands, deputizing for them when they were away, and convening meetings of the Senate. But new overseas conquests produced colonies that needed to be governed, and in 227 BCE two new praetors were appointed to administer Sicily and Sardinia, followed by another two for Spain in 198 BCE.[28]

During the second century BCE, the urban praetors, those concerned with the affairs of Roman citizens, assumed the task of supervising the civil courts. And these officials, although not legally trained, became hugely influential in the development and expansion of Roman law. As the city grew and the affairs of its citizens became more complex, the judges, or iudices, began to require that applicants use a specific form of words, a *formula*, to begin a legal case, in place of the complicated legis actiones the pontiffs had stipulated. The urban praetors now decided which *formulae* could be used in which cases, effectively determining what an applicant had to prove in order to succeed in his claim. Like other government officials, each praetor would issue an edict at the beginning of his year in office setting out how he would fulfil his duties. On a large whitewashed board, he would write out, in red letters, the laws and orders he considered to be most relevant for Roman citizens, as well as the formulae they should use.[29] This board was set up in the Forum for all to see.[30] In this way, the praetors could deliberately develop Roman civil law, formulating new and innovative legal actions.

Now, a Roman citizen with a legal problem would approach the urban praetor, who would decide whether to make an immediate order.[31] He could grant an interdict, an injunction to forbid the use of force, for example, or make orders about burials, water rights, or other urgent matters. If he thought the case had been properly formulated, he would then send it to a judge for a decision. Both praetors and judges heard cases on a wooden platform in the Forum, where they sat in the shade of the surrounding temples. Litigants, or their advocates, would address them from the ground, where they might attract a circle of interested onlookers. Both the litigants and their advocates were expected to wear togas, rather than more informal daily wear, and to speak in proper Latin. As Cicero later explained, the advocates were supposed to avoid displaying anger or partiality, should not vomit from drunkenness, and should not allow themselves to be smothered in kisses by ardent admirers.[32]

Serious charges—those involving forgery, conspiracy, or treason—would be sent to the plebeians' assembly, which might impose physical penalties or bar a corrupt official from office. But in 149 BCE the assembly scandalized the consuls and the Senate when its members acquitted the praetor Servius Sulpicius Galba. Galba had betrayed eight thousand Lusitanians after inviting them to peace talks following a rebellion on the Iberian Peninsula, and the reforming tribune Gaius Gracchus seized the opportunity to introduce new legal procedures.[33] He proposed that in cases of official extortion, if the praetor considered the charge worthy of trial, he should establish a panel of jurors. To do this, he should first invite the accuser to nominate a hundred men, of which the accused would select fifty to hear the case. Further rules disqualified jurors with connections to either party. The praetor also had to help the accuser summon witnesses and produce documents, assign advocates, and examine witnesses. After a guilty verdict, he then helped with recovery of the penalty, twice the amount wrongly taken. These rules gave considerably more assistance to someone who accused an official of corruption than to people with ordinary civil claims. Civil claims were heard by a single judge, who provided no assistance with recovery. The perils of litigation were the subject of ridicule in the comedies of Plautus and Terence, written in the third and second centuries BCE.[34]

THE ANNUALLY ELECTED urban praetor was now, in the second century BCE, in charge of Rome's courts and determined how citizens could access the legal system. But the Twelve Tables still loomed large in the collective Roman imagination. The original bronze tablets had come to seem foundational to the establishment of their city and the freedoms of its citizens, representing an end to tyranny. Schoolboys had to memorize them and learned that their rules provided the basis of their rights. But the edicts of the more ambitious and creative praetors continued to develop the range of legal actions, and a group of scholars began to take an interest in the underlying legal principles. They set themselves up as expert jurists, *iurisconsulti*, and offered advice to both judges and ordinary people who were contemplating, or embroiled in, a court case.[35] By the first century BCE, the jurists were attending trials, invited by the praetors or judges to join their circles of advisers. They were also 'providing weapons for careful advocates', as Cicero put it.[36] They advised judges on the status and duties of partners, agents, husbands, and wives, and offered guidance on how to decide whether an action had been done 'in good faith', or 'as one ought to behave among good men'. They expressed opinions about what was 'fairer and better' in cases of fraud. These were all judgements that the laws required judges to make.[37] When the consul Quintus Mucius Scaevola set out to write a comprehensive commentary on Rome's laws in around 95 BCE, he used the Twelve Tables as his starting point. During the same period, the great orator Cicero, in several early speeches, referred to the Twelve Tables as the source of Rome's laws.[38] But in the hands of the praetors, the law was changing too fast for this idea to be maintained. By the middle of the first century BCE the laws of the Twelve Tables had come to have more moral than legal authority, and eventually they were dropped from the school curriculum.[39]

Those who staffed and used the courts now faced the problems of complexity and corruption. The praetors were not legal experts, but rather, ambitious men en route to higher political office, and some would use their positions for personal gain.

In one famous case, Cicero helped to prosecute Gaius Verres, a praetor in 74 BCE, for misconduct in office.[40] According to Cicero, Verres had ignored the edicts of his predecessors and accepted low standards of proof in inheritance cases in order to gratify individuals who might offer him personal favours. Even worse, Verres had freely ignored what he had stated in his own edict, making ad hoc decisions according to his will. It was only through the brave intervention of one of his junior colleagues, Cicero argued, that several litigants had been saved. There were now eight annual praetors, but their roles were determined by lot, so it was never certain that someone with legal knowledge would be appointed urban praetor, in charge of Rome's courts. Quite possibly as a result of pressure from the jurists, along with influential advocates, such as Cicero, the tribune Cornelius proposed a new law in 67 BCE requiring each new praetor to announce his edict in advance of taking office, and then to abide by its laws. Many of the senators who might have benefitted from the cosy corruption of a man like Verres opposed the law, but the tribune persisted and the law was passed. This effectively restricted the opportunities for bribery and corruption while also making the application of the law more predictable.

BY THE END of the first century BCE, another group of men, the orators, became involved in Roman legal processes. The many meetings and assemblies held in the Forum provided opportunities for displays of advocacy, as did gatherings of the Senate, where the most persuasive speakers could wield considerable influence.[41] Some litigants asked friends and relatives, or respected jurists, to present their legal cases, and as the art of oratory developed, men trained in rhetoric took over these roles. They had to understand the law and engage in protracted and technical arguments about the formulae that had been used and the facts that had to be proved. But the facts also had to be presented in a way likely to win a case, and matters of 'equity' and justice might be fundamental to a judge's decision. They certainly were in capital cases and charges of corruption. It was here that the orators came into their own, most notably Cicero, who proudly kept records of his speeches, several of which survive to this day. Many of these cases involved high politics, which were often fought out at trial as officials charged others with misconduct and ambitious men accused their rivals of corruption. These cases raised issues of good faith and honesty, *fides*, which were critical qualities in many arguments.

Cicero's speeches reveal an ambivalence towards the law. When he defended the praetor Murena, Cicero described him as a 'wise' man, someone who was impartial and considerate in his hearings and exercised fairness, integrity, and accessibility. And in another case, he spoke of the need for seriousness and conscientiousness on the part of the praetor. But he did not mention knowledge of the law.[42] Legal procedures and scholarly debate had become highly complex, and Cicero took pride in the power of his oratory to transcend the technicalities of the law. He quoted the words of the jurist Gaius Aquilius Gallus, who had said, probably intending it to be disparaging, that a certain case 'involved no law, so it is one for Cicero' ('nihil hoc ad ius, ad Ciceronem').[43] But at other times, Cicero was a great champion of the law and its importance, not least in his condemnation of the corrupt Verres—after his blistering prosecution speech Verres fled Rome without attempting a defence.

Aulus Caecina, the widower of a rich landowner, sought Cicero's advice over the ownership of a valuable farm of olive groves in the Etruscan territories north of Rome in 69 BCE.[44] Roman citizenship had been extended to all of Italy in 90 BCE, and with it came the right to appeal to Roman law.[45] Caecina was in a dispute with Sextus Aebutius, a friend and adviser to his deceased wife, from whom Aebutius claimed to have bought the farm shortly before her death. As soon as he learned that Caecina was claiming it under her will, Aebutius took up residence on it. Caecina then went to the praetor to seek an order for possession. In a series of complicated procedural moves, he asked Aebutius to agree that he, Caecina, could enter the farm and 'be led off in the time-honoured way'. This appears to have been an established drama, whereby the parties to such a dispute would use a formula designed for someone who had been forcibly expelled from his land, in order to initiate the appropriate legal case. It was a convenient process. Most adversaries cooperated with it, and in this instance Aebutius initially indicated that he would follow the protocol. Caecina duly turned up with some friends, however, only to be confronted by a band of men who threatened him with deadly violence. Showered with missiles, Caecina and his companions retreated in confusion. The men, it turned out, were current and former servants to Aebutius.

Caecina then faced a difficult legal problem. Because he had not, technically, been expelled from the estate—he had not set foot on it—Aebutius could claim that his case could not even get off the ground. Cicero, representing Caecina, had to use all his ingenuity to get around this technical obstacle. First, he presented the judge with a favourable legal opinion he had secured from one of the jurists. Then he launched into a passionate argument about the law, in which he claimed that the law, the *ius civile*, was an independent body of rules and institutions which formed 'the bonds of social welfare and life'. It was the basis for rights to ownership and legal relations. Law was the 'incorruptible guarantor' of these rights, he claimed, and its rules had to be 'uniform among all and identical for everyone', that is, set apart from ordinary political and social life. He continued by emphasizing the importance of the jurists. They stood between the law and the courts, he said, which are the most fallible of legal institutions. As interpreters of the law, they had the authority of the law itself, and they could not be attacked without the law also being attacked. The judges must respect their opinions, he concluded firmly.

Cicero was daring the judge to disregard the opinion of a jurist that was favourable to his client's case. The speech was a display of advocacy, possibly improved in the recounting, and he delivered it in the face of almost overwhelming procedural problems. In other speeches, he was distinctly more ambivalent about the jurists.[46] But Cicero must have been confident that his words in Caecina's case would be at least persuasive. In the Roman Republic, the elite had become convinced of the independence of the law and the authority of the jurists as its interpreters. They upheld, that is, the rule of law. History does not relate whether Cicero won the case for Caecina. But its inclusion in his collected speeches suggests pride in a victory against the odds.

As LEGAL SCHOLARS developed their expertise in Roman law, judges, praetors, and ordinary citizens all came to respect their authority.[47] In the late Republic, ambitious young Romans would seek careers in law, instead of the military, as long as they had the contacts to arrange training with a senior jurist.[48] Cicero describes how, in 90 BCE, at the age of sixteen, he went to study with the eminent jurist and former consul Quintus Mucius Scaevola.[49] Cicero stayed with Scaevola for two years. The jurist was a plainspoken and somewhat old-fashioned man, as Cicero described it, who used his legal knowledge to give opinions rather than appearing in court. But the stream of distinguished visitors to his house impressed the young student, who listened intently to their erudite and witty conversation. Sometimes they travelled to Scaevola's hunting lodges or country retreats, but most often they gathered in his grand house on the Palatine Hill above the Forum. In the brightly painted atrium with its mosaic floors, carefully adorned with sculptures and artworks to display its owner's refined taste—although without contravening the norms against ostentatious luxury—Scaevola dispensed legal advice, while senators, consuls, praetors, generals, and other distinguished men discussed affairs of state. The teacher's closest friends and most honoured guests would be welcomed into an inner room, perhaps the library, where they debated Greek philosophy as well as commenting on the latest Roman news and gossip. Many declared that intellectual conversation among friends provided solace after the chaos and political intrigues of public life.[50]

It was in these rarefied surroundings that jurists developed their opinions on Roman law and Cicero's contemporaries acquired their legal knowledge. Law, in their hands, became an academic and elite pursuit. Ordinary people might call on a jurist to advise on social issues, such as arranging a daughter's marriage, buying an estate, or cultivating a field, and Cicero describes how a citizen might approach a scholar to ask for advice when out walking. The jurists also drafted wills, contracts, and other legal documents, which enabled people to make complicated arrangements for inheritance or allowed them to buy livestock in a way that avoided falling afoul of regulations.[51] But as well as advising private citizens, the jurists spent hours debating among themselves about what the law was and should be. How did an action to recover property in one circumstance relate to rules about the use of farmland in different legislation? What should happen when an individual fell between two legal stools? The formulae of the praetors were sometimes limited, and the jurists had to be creative to find ways for their clients to pursue the remedies they desired. Among themselves, the jurists constructed hypothetical cases to test out how the laws might be applied, what their limits were, and how an action could be worded to take best advantage of all the legal requirements. To make the law work, they also had to use legal fictions.[52] One thing might have to be treated 'as if' it were another, so that a legal case could proceed smoothly. An unborn child might have to be treated as an already existing person, for example, to inherit under the laws of succession.[53] The jurists explained all these legal niceties in their *responsa*, the opinions they gave to citizens who came to them for legal advice.

The jurists sought to develop legal knowledge, *ius*, although this was, in theory, ancient and unchanging. They distinguished it from the leges, the assemblies' decisions, which represented the will of the people.[54] But the jurists' debates became increasingly esoteric. They spent hours picking over classifications and definitions, and the more they debated the details and the more interesting their hypothetical cases became, the more complex the rules, principles, and exceptions they constructed to hold together the whole legal edifice.[55] Already in the late Republic, Cicero could criticize the jurists and their opinions for being convoluted.[56] And grave inscriptions proclaimed, 'Let evil intent and jurists be gone.'[57] Complexity and obscurity are recurrent problems in developed legal systems.

Roman law had begun as an essentially practical system. The laws of the Twelve Tables, the legislation passed by the assemblies, and the formulae specified by the praetors were all created with contemporary problems in mind; they were designed to regulate the lives of Roman citizens and served as the basis for argument and decision-making during trials. They were resources for those who needed to fight legal cases. They also, from a very early period, symbolized the rights of all citizens to a measure of equality before the law. But in the hands of the jurists, law became an academic exercise. Learned men conducted debates in the rarefied surroundings of their aristocratic mansions, where they were free to develop their intellectual interests. Roman law had become an elite pursuit, insulated from the social and political pressures of Roman life as it unfolded in all its complexity outside their walls.

THIS WAS THE state of Roman law in the first decades of the first century BCE, during the tumultuous events that surrounded the end of the Republic and the political intrigues and civil warfare that led to the rise and fall of Pompey, Julius Caesar, and Mark Antony. In 27 BC, Gaius Octavius Thurinus established himself as the first emperor, calling himself Augustus. By now the population of the empire was at least forty million, while the number of citizens had risen to over five million.[58]

Initially, Augustus and his successors retained the political institutions of the Republic, the consuls and tribunes, the Senate, and the voting assemblies. For some time, they also maintained the structures and officials of the legal system. Augustus burned piles of religious literature, but he acknowledged the expertise of the jurists, and he formally conferred on a number of them the authority to give responsa.[59] Caligula, emperor from 37 to 41 CE, threatened to abolish their profession if the jurists gave too many unfavourable opinions. But in 125 CE, the emperor Hadrian ordered that the praetors' edict should be made permanent, and recognized the authority of the jurists' opinions. This announcement confirmed their status, and over the next decades their numbers expanded.[60] This was the heyday of the jurists and their law, the era of Gaius, Papian, Ulpian, Paulus, and Modestinus. But it was not to last.

When not plotting against their rivals in struggles for succession, or leading armies into battle against 'barbarians', most of the emperors were keen to consolidate their administrative powers. Augustus had accepted the title 'father of the land', *pater patriae*, supposedly on the insistence of the Senate and citizenry, and gradually the emperors promoted the idea that they were the origin of justice, as their Mesopotamian predecessors had done. An emperor might delegate this task to a judge, but he would claim to be ultimate arbiter in legal matters.[61] At the same time, the jurists were writing ever more complex opinions, which strayed ever further from the practical reality of court cases. In around 160 CE, the jurist Gaius, determined to present the law in a systematic way, produced a text known as his *Institutes*, in which he attempted to systematize the laws and opinions of the jurists. He divided the subject matter into sections on personal status, rights over property, wills and succession, legal proceedings, and obligations—what we would think of as contracts. But the jurists' scholarship continued to proliferate, with personal rivalries leading to disagreements and opposing opinions. This made it easier for the Severan emperors, who ruled from 193 to 235 CE, to select and integrate a number of scholars into their courts and begin to undermine their independence.

The Roman generals, meanwhile, continued to wage war against the rulers of distant lands, expanding the territories they controlled. Most of the inhabitants of these far-flung areas were not granted citizenship, which meant that they could not appeal to Roman laws when they made contracts, acquired property, entered into marriages, or made wills. Nor, indeed, did they have the right to vote in any of the Roman assemblies, although these were becoming less important as imperial power grew. Romans regarded law as a privilege that they only rarely extended to 'barbarians'. The ius was the basis of the Republic, as Cicero had put it.[62] Some of the new provinces and their cities actively aspired to Roman civilization, seeking the status of *civitas*, which meant adopting Roman styles of organization and civic regulation. But others, particularly the Greek cities, already had well-established legal structures and sought to retain their own laws, and merchants were often keen to preserve traditional commercial and maritime practices.[63]

In circumstances that are not entirely clear, and to the surprise of many contemporary writers, in 212 CE the emperor Caracalla suddenly extended Roman citizenship to the free inhabitants of all his territories. He claimed that he wanted to unify religious practices so that all people could join with him in thanking the gods for his safety, but one cynic commented that the emperor was primarily trying to improve his tax revenues.[64] Whatever the reasons, the result was to vastly expand the 'benefits' of Roman law, along with the number of people eligible for high government office. Change would have been gradual, as people and local officials in distant provinces became used to the new procedures and realized the possibilities of Roman law.[65] But over time, many of them started to refer to Roman laws and to follow Roman legal forms and processes.

The administration of Roman justice gradually changed, too, as the Severan emperors exerted more control over legal processes. By drawing the most prominent jurists into their court circles, the emperors turned them into advisers rather than independent legal authorities. A period of political upheaval followed in the second half of the third century CE, with a bewildering number of ambitious men seizing power in quick succession only to be swiftly deposed. Finally, the army declared Diocletian to be emperor in 284. During a reign of twenty years, the new emperor successfully stabilized his administration. He introduced a number of reforms, not least dividing Rome's sprawling territories into east and west. He also took steps to professionalize legal processes by appointing assessors, legal experts, to advise his judges. This bound them more tightly to the imperial administration, and they naturally felt more inclined to show loyalty to the emperors' wishes.[66] Diocletian also continued his predecessors' practice of issuing *rescripts*, legal opinions, which gradually became more important, and more authoritative, than the jurists' responsa.[67]

Roman law slowly flowed into the provinces, where local administrators published edicts and legal decisions, and quite ordinary citizens began to initiate legal processes.[68] Many regarded the legal system as a benefit of Roman occupation, along with improved architectural techniques, aqueducts, and baths, innovations that even reached the wilds of northern Britain. But some writers could see that Roman officials were using law as a tool of control. Tacitus, in his commentary on the administration of Britain, declared that what Britons mistook for 'civilization' was really an aspect of their slavery.[69] And, commenting on the Romans' difficulties in Germany, one second-century writer declared that 'it is more difficult to govern a province than to acquire one, for they are conquered by force, but they must be retained by law'. Two centuries later, another writer attributed Roman success in Arabia to the emperor Trajan, who had 'compelled [Arabia] to obey our laws, after having often crushed the arrogance of its inhabitants'.[70] Although nominally a benefit and an aspect of civilization, law had also become a tool of political control.

By the fifth century, emperors and their administrators in both east and west were making efforts to rationalize the complex edifice of Roman law. In 426, the western emperor Valentinian III specified the jurists whose opinions were to be regarded as authoritative, and in 438 the eastern emperor Theodosius II compiled a collection of imperial laws enacted over the previous century.[71] A century later, his successor, Justinian I, ordered a comprehensive codification, to include both imperial laws and jurists' opinions. Like the Chinese emperors, Justinian declared that his *Corpus Iuris Civilis* would bring law and order to the whole empire, that the laws would be valid for all time, and that he would allow no further juristic interpretations to muddy the legal waters. But it was a brash statement, an aspiration to unchallengeable legal authority, that ignored the status that law had already acquired.

★

OVER THE COURSE of a millennium, Roman law was and meant a great many different things. At the time of the Twelve Tables, the laws inscribed on bronze tablets gave Rome's citizens a set of basic rules about how they should be treated and punished and how they could bring cases to court and seek relief from debt. And these rights went along with their participation in great decision-making assemblies. Their laws, leges, were instruments of government, by which the citizens could influence public affairs and the activities of their officials. As legal procedures became more elaborate, judges and praetors stipulated precise formulae for legal cases. These then became subject to debate and a matter of scholarship in the hands of the jurists. They made the law, the ius, into an intellectual exercise. It was the sophistication of their opinions that would so impress medieval European scholars. But throughout most of Roman history, law was also a marker of civilization. The law was originally a tool that Rome's citizens used in their pursuit of justice, but by Cicero's time it was considered a benefit enjoyed by all citizens. And Caracalla munificently extended it to all free imperial subjects.

Later emperors claimed that 'the emperor is free from the laws', *princeps legibus solutus est*. But Justinian's *Corpus Iuris* also stated that the emperor should declare himself to be bound by the law, as a mark of his imperial authority. And it called jurisprudence 'knowledge of things human and divine'.[72] Justinian's assertion of absolute legal authority was tentative at best. A sense that law, ius, represented higher principles, that it should provide resources for citizens and constrain the ruler, was not eclipsed by even the most autocratic emperors.

When Justinian's *Corpus Iuris* was rediscovered, several centuries later, it came to represent civilization for medieval European scholars, too, inspiring the laws that eventually came to dominate the world. But elsewhere lawmakers pursued more cosmological visions of order, particularly as a new religion founded in the deserts of Arabia gave birth to the most recent of the great legal traditions to take shape.

CHAPTER FIVE

JEWISH AND ISLAMIC SCHOLARS
God's Path for the World

When the Persian emperor Cyrus led his armies into Mesopotamia in 538 BCE, he razed its cities and largely destroyed their ancient civilizations. But Mesopotamian legal techniques were not so easily eliminated. They had already served as models for the Israelite priests, who made laws with firmly religious purposes, working out the rules that God had given his chosen people. Adapting the Mesopotamian forms to realize a religious vision for their societies, the priests crafted rules for prayer, ritual observance, and cleanliness alongside social rules designed to ensure everyday justice. These were developed over the centuries into the great works of Jewish law.

The Jewish laws, in turn, inspired what became an entirely separate religious legal tradition, that of the Muslims. In both, religious experts were the interpreters of the divine law, as they remain to this day, explaining the rules that tell ordinary Jews and Muslims how to follow God's path for the world. As in the Hindu world, these laws concentrate on duties far more than on justice or discipline. And, like the Hindu brahmins in India, the legal scholars always claimed to be able to sit in judgement on kings, caliphs, and sultans.

THE LAWS IN the books of the Pentateuch instructed the Israelites how to live ritually pure lives, worshipping a single God in the right ways, eating only food that was clean, and acting justly towards their fellow Israelites. They were laws for a single people. But as religious leaders, the priests created laws with a very different purpose and character from those of the Greek and Roman citizens and, indeed, from those of the Mesopotamian lawmakers who had inspired them. Like the Hindu brahmins, they had a religious authority quite independent of the political power of Saul, David, and the other early kings. But the Israelite lawmakers were working in a very different social and political context to their Hindu counterparts and it was not their object to insist on a social hierarchy. Many of the Israelites were still nomadic, often at odds with neighbouring tribes, and they had just a few kings before their lands were taken over by powerful conquerors: Assyrians, Babylonians, Persians, and then Romans. Throughout these shifts in power, the Israelites' laws helped to create a sense of unity and identity among their scattered tribes, including the people captured and transported to distant lands.

Assyrians and neo-Assyrians dominated the lands of Israel and Judah into the sixth century BCE and may have inspired the earliest Israelite lawmaking. When the neo-Babylonian Nebuchadnezzar besieged Jerusalem, he transported many Israelites back to Babylon, where they worked, at least initially, as slaves. But some prospered and stayed on in the city, even when the Persian conqueror, Cyrus, allowed them to reestablish their own homeland. Meanwhile, others had formed colonies in Egypt after earlier periods of dislocation. So Jewish populations were already scattered when the Romans occupied Palestine in 63 BCE.[1]

After the Jewish revolt against imperial occupation in 70 CE, when the Romans destroyed their temple in Jerusalem, many Jews fled their homeland and joined the long-established colonies in Egypt. Others travelled to lands around the Mediterranean as far as Spain, or moved on from Egypt into North Africa. It did not cause an unprecedented flood of migration, but the second destruction of their temple made Jews more conscious of the distinction between themselves and the gentiles among whom most now lived. They felt it ever more important to insist upon their unique relationship with God and their responsibility towards 'all Israel', that is, to all Jews, wherever they lived.

New religious scholars now emerged, rabbis rather than temple priests, who were concerned about the threat to their people's identity and systems of belief. After their violent destruction of the temple in Jerusalem, the Roman authorities had softened their stance towards the Jews and recognized their leader, generally a rabbi, as a prince, the *nasi*, allowing him to establish his own court.[2] The Persians had also protected the Jews' academies in Babylon and recognized Jewish laws in the province of Yehud. Possibly inspired by the written laws quoted by Roman governors and administrators, the rabbis now decided to consolidate the unwritten norms and ritual practices of their people, which had grown up around the rather scanty laws of the Pentateuch. They realized they needed to create a systematic programme to which all could commit. As tradition has it, they gathered in a vineyard in Palestine, where they decided to record the teaching of the Torah, their law, for future generations.

The written Torah was found in the first books of the Hebrew Bible, particularly Exodus, Leviticus, Numbers, and Deuteronomy, with their detailed rules on ritual and dietary practices. But the oral Torah was enshrined in the customs and traditions of the Israelites as they had developed over the centuries. The scholars now worked through their texts, interpreting and extending the rules to incorporate what had become accepted custom. By

200 CE, just as Hindu scholars were writing the first Dharma-shastras, Rabbi Judah the Prince was able to bring this work together into a compendium that he called the Mishnah. Written in Hebrew, the language of scholarship, the text contained a concise set of laws in six parts: on 'seeds' (agriculture), 'feasts' (religious festivals), 'women' (betrothal, marriage, divorce, and adultery), 'damages' (criminal and civil claims and procedures), 'hallowed things' (temple dues), and 'cleanliness' (purity). It combined practical rules and religious laws into a single system.

Over the following centuries, the rabbis continued to interpret the Torah, writing commentaries in the widely spoken Aramaic and founding academies in both Palestine and Babylon. Here, in the fifth and sixth centuries CE, scholars produced two great works, the Jerusalem and Babylon Talmuds. In these elaborate texts, which they carefully inked onto valuable parchment, they placed a section of the Hebrew Torah in the centre of a page and surrounded it with Aramaic commentaries in a smaller script. The Italian glossators would do the same in their commentaries on Justinian's works several centuries later. By this stage, an important sect of Jews, the Qaraites, had already divided from those who followed the rabbis, the Rabbanites, and they rejected the authority of the Talmud. But the rabbis' collective body of work on law and religion, known as the *halakha*, became authoritative for the majority of Jews and continues to be recognized to this day.

Practically wherever the Jewish diaspora settled, their rabbis poured out further quantities of scholarship on the Talmud. Most recognized the rabbinical academies in Jerusalem and Babylon and sent queries to their leading scholars, the Geonim.[3] They asked for advice on tricky points of biblical or Talmudic interpretation, or on practical issues raised by the lives that Jewish people were now leading in very varied contexts, and the Geonim replied with written opinions. Their responsa, written in Hebrew, contained scholarly advice, rather like the opinions that Roman jurists had given and that the Indian brahmins were offering farther to the east. Pragmatically, the Geonim supported and encouraged the work of the rabbis' courts as they emerged among the diaspora, often referring approvingly to the decisions of Jewish elders or the tribunals convened by traders.[4]

Roman control over the Middle East eventually weakened. Byzantine armies were unable to withstand the onslaught of the Muslim Umayyads when they swept out of Arabia in the seventh century. Moving west, the Umayyads quickly conquered Palestine, where they established an important mosque. But they recognized the Jews as 'people of the book', that is, people who had monotheistic scriptures, and allowed their academies, along with their cultural activities and commercial ventures, to continue. From then on, the lives of Jews in the Middle East and North Africa were intertwined with those of the Muslims, as were their laws and their languages.

ISLAM WAS BORN in the seventh century CE on the fringes of the Arabian deserts. The Prophet Muhammad lived and worked here in the small trading cities of Mecca and Medina. He was a member of one of the most important Bedouin tribes, originally camel herders, who still routinely indulged in blood feuds. To the north of the Arabian Peninsula, Byzantine armies were still engaged in periodic warfare with the Sassanians as they vied for control over the fertile lands of Mesopotamia and Syria and the trade routes that connected west and east. Alexander's conquest was just one among a series of wars between the Persians and Greeks, during which armies, mercenaries, and merchants from both sides arrived and left. Later rulers established cities with monumental buildings, extensive irrigation systems, and expanding trade networks, in which pagans, Christians, Jews, and Zoroastrians, speaking Greek, Aramaic, and Persian, lived side by side.[5]

The Byzantine and Sassanian armies fought out their last great wars in the seventh century, just as Muhammad was establishing his religious movement on the Arabian Peninsula. Here, the Bedouin tribesmen had continued their pastoralist ways of life, relatively untroubled, in the vast expanses of empty desert. They lived comfortably off herding, supplemented by raiding campaigns, and dominated local trade routes. Thanks to this, their language and poetry spread throughout the peninsula. Even those who settled in the trading towns of Medina and Mecca retained their tribal identities. They mostly worshipped local divinities while tolerating the followers of monotheistic religions, the Christians, Jews, and Zoroastrians who travelled through and settled in the region. When Muhammad began receiving religious revelations in Mecca at the age of forty, in around the year 610, he became convinced that he should speak as a prophet. He proclaimed that Allah, the creator god who existed above and beyond any local deity, should be venerated to the exclusion of all others. Boldly brushing aside ridicule and accusations of private ambition, he promoted his message widely, calling on others to reject their former religious practices and follow his teaching.[6] He insisted, above all, on the moral responsibilities of human beings and their duty to obey God. Members of the poorer classes in Mecca, disadvantaged by growing differences in wealth, were readily attracted to his message, but Muhammad also found adherents among rich merchants and members of powerful families, who used their influence and resources to support his work.

In 622 the Prophet moved to Medina, where he acted for some time as a mediator. He continued to build a community of followers, the *umma*, and with their support he started to defy anyone who opposed his ideas. Eventually he was able to stand up to even the most powerful and hostile Meccan tribesmen. As it grew in number, the umma began to act like a tribe itself, waging wars against its rivals, and by 630 it had forced even the most hostile adversaries to capitulate. Over the next two years, before Muhammad's death in 632, the umma was able to unite practically all the major tribes of Arabia under his leadership.

Muhammad's original message in Mecca was about faith, piety, and moral responsibility before God, which he recorded in the Quran. But as he settled in Medina and the umma expanded, Muhammad realized he needed to establish a more uniform social order. After forbidding tribal feuds, he raised taxes to support the poor and made new rules for family relations. He prescribed forms of marriage, set out rules for adoption (which he effectively prohibited), introduced a measure of financial security for wives, and systematized practices of inheritance. But for the most part, the rules and directions he inscribed in the Quran gave moral guidance to people on how best to fulfil existing duties, rather than instituting a radically new social scheme. The rules Muhammad made told people how to arbitrate and enter into contracts, how to determine which enemies should be fought, and how booty should be distributed, and they told men how to treat women, children, orphans, relatives, and other dependents, including slaves.[7] But, at best, they were unsystematic directions for individuals, rather than rules about how governors should resolve disputes, or laws that administrators could use to maintain order. Muhammad made few provisions for criminal conduct. He specified penalties for theft, including amputation, and prohibited his followers from drinking wine, playing games of chance, and charging interest. The Quran also contains rules about retaliation and blood money, highway robbery, sexual misconduct, and false accusations of the same, along with directions about the procedures to be followed in contested cases. But the laws on criminal procedure were not at all comprehensive.

These general principles in scattered sections of the Quran might have helped to unite the new community, but Muhammad was not trying to undermine the deeply rooted tribal traditions and forms of mediation that had shaped social relations among the Arab tribes for centuries. His revolution, in these early days, was centred on piety, faith, and moral responsibility more than political control or social reform. But he was paving the way for a more centralized social order.

FOLLOWING MUHAMMAD'S DEATH in 632, his followers continued to consolidate their power.[8] They were soon challenging the Byzantine and Sassanian Empires to the north, incorporating the Arab populations into their new community. In a series of highly successful military campaigns, they gradually extended their power over a vast area, which eventually stretched from Egypt and the Mediterranean in the west to the Caspian Sea in the north, and it encompassed most of modern Iran by 656. By now, a caliphate, a single political realm centred on Medina, was forming, and in 661 the first Umayyad caliph assumed the reins of power and moved his capital west, to Syria. After a very troubled start, effectively a civil war, in which the Shi'i split off from the rest of the umma, this powerful family ruled for over a century. The Umayyads conquered al-Andalus (southern Spain), extended their territories across the Maghreb (northern Africa), and incorporated more of Central Asia. As Muhammad's message spread, Arabian tribes converted en masse to Islam. Byzantine and Sassanian subjects gradually followed suit, often adopting Arabian cultural practices as they did so. Soon the Arabs ceased to be an occupying force and became the ruling elite of a more unified population. The Umayyads built fabulous mosques and religious schools throughout the region, constructing the magnificent Great Mosque in Damascus, for example, and supported religious scholars, the *ulama*. In little more than a century, Islam had unified an extensive Middle Eastern population.

In their newly founded schools, the ulama directed forms of public worship and pursued studies in theology, grammar, history, and literary criticism. They also used their status to influence the new rulers in their management of public order, government, and law. The caliphs were now trying to establish a more elaborate administration in the lands they had conquered. They appointed local tribes to run the garrison towns in the more distant provinces, minted coins, introduced new ways of writing, and appointed judges, *qadis*, to settle disputes in place of the old tribal mediators. They had the examples of the Persians and Romans before them, who had built elaborate administrations and—especially in the case of the Romans—used law as a practical tool of government. But the qadis had little to guide them in the administration of justice. Muhammad had concentrated on moral norms, and the Quran offered few rules that judges could apply when resolving practical disputes, particularly on commercial matters, and it made only brief references to crime and punishment. So the new rulers and their judges generally adopted the norms and practices of the territories they had conquered. When they introduced death by stoning for sexual misconduct, for example, they were almost certainly inspired by Mosaic laws. The Muslims were occupying territories that had long-established legal and administrative traditions, and it made sense to recognize and adopt the most practical and respected among them, particularly when it came to the management of commerce and taxation. The qadis probably looked to Quranic norms as much as they could, depending on their own knowledge and religious orientation, but they also recognized and supported customary practices, using discretion and judgement to mete out justice.[9]

Over time, the qadis became more specialized. The more pious adopted overtly Islamic ways of life and incorporated religious and ethical ideas into their decisions, which earned them respect among the faithful. At the same time, the religious scholars, the ulama, began to reflect on the administrative practices of the caliphate and the norms that the qadis were applying, and to debate how well they corresponded with the Quranic revelation.[10] Like the Hindu brahmins and Israelite priests, they were concerned that legal practices should follow religious principles, and groups of scholars began to debate the legal norms set out in the Quran and what they might mean in practice. They formed educational institutions at Basra, Medina, and Kufa, along with smaller centres in Syria, Egypt, and Khurasan (in the former Sassanian territory, now eastern Iran). Each group of scholars developed its own theories, but ideas travelled easily through the region, and a relatively consistent set of principles developed. All scholars were concerned to give due attention to the Quran, and they carefully sought out contemporary traditions that they could properly project back to the time of the Prophet. In the eyes of the most puritanical, the qadis' more pragmatic rules and principles often strayed too far from the teachings of the Prophet. The judges needed to be strict and rigorous in their reasoning, the scholars argued, and to avoid putting too much weight on local customs or relying upon their own judgement and ideas. Eventually, even the more practically oriented qadis had to ascribe the legal principles they applied, where they could, to the Prophet.[11]

The ulama made a self-conscious effort to systematize legal practices and ideas and bring them into line with Muhammad's religious revelation. Still, they did not try to write a definitive legal text, or even an authoritative set of laws like those in the Pentateuch. Muhammad had already explained God's revelation in the Quran, and their duty was to interpret and explain it, not to create new laws. Islamic law never had a foundational legal text.

THE UMAYYAD CALIPHS ruled a unified realm for almost a century, and Muhammad's revelation seemed set to expand indefinitely. Divisions among different schools of legal thought emerged, however, and they mirrored more serious religious and political divisions. The Shi'is, as they came to be known, had developed a following by the 660s and began to oppose the Umayyads. Several of the most traditional scholars also voiced opposition to the more pleasure-loving caliphs and criticized them for adopting the administrative structures, economic order, legal standards, and artistry of their Hellenic predecessors, even though the rulers had often had little choice, given the absence of equivalent Arab traditions. Disgruntled religious leaders exploited discontent and tribal rivalries to foment rebellion. Eventually, by 750, they supported a rival family, the Abbasids, who seized power from the Umayyads.

Moving their capital 470 miles eastwards, to Baghdad, the Abbasids presided over what historians refer to as the 'high caliphate' of the Islamic world. For almost two centuries they largely avoided major warfare, and they stimulated tremendous economic, cultural, and commercial growth. More cosmopolitan than the resolutely Arab Umayyads, the Abbasids transformed a patchwork of conquered states into an empire in which Muslims became the majority in most cities, not just the ruling class. Caravans carried pilgrims, diplomatic envoys, scholars, soldiers, and merchants and their wares from the Mediterranean to the Oxus. Commodities, people, and ideas spread across physical and cultural divides to and from Spain, southern Europe, northern Africa, Central Asia, and into China and India. The rulers were able to gather plentiful taxes from the highly productive agricultural lands of Mesopotamia, which they supplemented with trading profits to support the expenses of their armies, diplomatic missions, and splendid courts. They also developed sugar production and copied techniques of papermaking from the Sogdian traders of Central Asia.[12] Paper replaced the more expensive papyrus and parchment, which allowed literacy to spread and with it philosophy, science, and history, works of theology, and collections of poetry, much of it translated from Greek sources. Administrators and qadis routinely recorded their orders and decisions in writing, and they kept meticulous records of their activities. Inspired by the Sassanians' ideal of the monarch who embodied social order, stability, and justice, the caliphs constructed an enormous palace in Baghdad where they patronized literature, poetry, and song, surrounding themselves with luxury and a swirl of courtly etiquette. They expected personal submission from all who came before them and demanded that their words be treated, in effect, as law.

Aware of the respect enjoyed by the ulama, however, the Abbasids promised to recognize the legal programme of the more influential among them, those regarded as the most pious, and they patronized new mosques and religious foundations. Enjoying the status that came with official recognition, the ulama now formed themselves into a distinct class and set about institutionalizing their systems of knowledge. Their project was to explain the *shari'a*, God's law for his people, and develop a religious programme that all Muslims would understand and accept. Their writings, like those of the Jewish scholars from whom they must have taken inspiration, combined practical social rules, *fiqh*, with directions for ritual observance and moral principles. Through their work, they hoped to apply the principles of Islam to the regulation of all the day-to-day matters and create a unified social order among a population of tens of millions.

The more traditional Sunni scholars built their ideas on the image of Medina as it had existed at the time of the Prophet and his ideal of a community in which each individual would take responsibility for his or her own actions before God. The scholars regarded the traditions of Muhammad's time, the *sunna*, as the proper basis for contemporary legal practices, and they gathered information about those traditions, along with reports of what Muhammad had said and done, which they combined to form the *hadith*. In reality, many of these sayings and stories reflected traditions that had developed in the intervening century, but the scholars worked hard to trace their words back through lines of teachers and students who had passed them down from one of the original Medina masters, if not the Prophet himself. Only these, they maintained, were properly authoritative.[13]

In the writings they produced during this period, the scholars created the rules of Islamic law, the fiqh. In stark contrast to Hindus in India, all Muslims were supposed to be equally subject to the requirements of the shari'a, which recognized no hereditary class structures and maintained no ideal of monasticism, asceticism, or even celibacy. But, as among the Hindus, the archetypal Muslim was a householder, the centre of an extended family diligently carrying out his or her duties, both to relatives and before God. Like the brahmins, the Islamic scholars concentrated on defining individual duties rather than specifying norms for public life or laws that could be used within the political and social administration of the caliphate. Like the authors of the Pentateuch, they concerned themselves, first and foremost, with acts of worship, which their rules regulated in the minutest detail, and around which they conducted protracted scholarly debates.[14] They also created an elaborate set of rules for family relations, inheritance, and the maintenance of religious foundations, *awaqf* (s. *waqf*).

While Hindu and Jewish scholars had initially created foundational texts, statements of general principle that were supplemented by later works of interpretation and explanation, the Islamic legal scholars were more practically minded, giving detailed guidance for individual problems, rules people could live by. Like the Roman jurists, they were inspired by the social issues they saw around them. They confronted problems not considered in the Quran, such as the validity of multiple marriages, the status of women captured during warfare and held as concubines, and the manumission of slaves.[15] Neither the Quran nor the sunna had much to say about matters of contract and commercial obligations, so the scholars worked creatively to elaborate useful rules for property relations that merchants could use in the ever-expanding sphere of commerce, but which could be regarded as firmly based upon the principles of the Prophet. In developing these guidelines, scholars resorted to the idea of 'legal fictions' or 'devices', *hiyal*, which could be used to circumvent inconvenient, but undeniable, Quranic rules, such as the prohibition on taking interest. One device they developed was to use a double sale, whereby property was sold and immediately sold back for a higher price, the difference representing the amount of interest. The Islamic legal devices were not unlike Roman legal fictions, and they were to become immensely important in the twentieth century as Islamic scholars developed ways for businessmen to participate in international commerce.[16]

Another problematic area for the scholars, even more for the qadis engaged in legal practice, was the bundle of rules on evidence. Possibly recognizing Bedouin tribal norms developed to preserve the dignity of an accused, the qadis required several trustworthy witnesses to prove anything that amounted to a wrongdoing.[17] The Quran and sunna also privileged oral over written evidence, a principle that became increasingly impractical as literacy spread and documents came to form the basis of most commercial transactions. So the scholars developed theories about the witnessing of documents, an oral act which could turn a written text into a source of evidence. This notion, in turn, gave rise to a body of professional witnesses who would assist merchants and laymen in creating transactions that followed proper legal forms. The scholars conducted extensive debates about legal categories and definitions, such as what was a sale or a gift, and the qualities and legal implications of different types of property. Gradually, they established a science of law that became known as the *usul al-fiqh*. The goal was to ensure that legal rules and practices were firmly based upon the practices and words of the Prophet and those closest to him by using proper legal reasoning. It was proper, for example, to use analogies (*qiyas*), as long as they were based on accepted legal principles. Matters of considered opinion (*ra'y*) were acceptable in some circumstances, while matters of personal judgement generally were not. The fiqh soon became a highly technical project that demanded strict reasoning, and some scholars took pride, as one writer has put it, in creating 'small masterpieces of legal construction'.[18]

The scholars also tended to associate themselves with an individual master, and in this way distinct traditions, known as *madhhabs*, formed. During the first two centuries of the Abbasid caliphate, those who followed Abu Hanifa in Iraq formed the Hanafi school, which soon spread to Syria and later to Afghanistan, India, and Central Asia. Meanwhile, the followers of Malik ibn Anas, initially based in Medina, spread to Egypt and thence to North and West Africa and Spain. One of the most influential scholars was the arch traditionalist al-Shafi'i, who lived and worked in Cairo. He founded his own school, which later spread throughout southern Arabia, the Swahili Coast, and parts of Southeast Asia.[19] Al-Shafi'i insisted, even more than others, on the authority of tradition. Any work of legal interpretation was illegal, he claimed, if it did more than draw conclusions from the Quran or the sunna of the Prophet using properly strict and systematic reasoning. It was largely under his influence that Sunni scholars put together large collections of authoritative hadiths, which came to form something like a legal canon, providing sources for the qadis and helping to unify legal practices. One of al-Shafi'i's disciples, Ahmad ibn Hanbal, formed another school, which advocated even more literal and traditional approaches, eventually coalescing into the Hanbali school, which now dominates the Arabian Peninsula. But all the Islamic legal traditions

pursued similar goals, emphasizing the ideal of individual responsibility before God, and they were generally tolerant of one
another. Most ordinary Muslims accepted the authority of the
madhhab that prevailed in their region, looking to its scholars for
guidance on their own legal problems and ethical dilemmas.[20]

Over time, Shafi'i's approach to the fiqh became widely accepted. Maybe without explicitly saying or even recognizing it,
the scholars became concerned about the proliferation of legal
ideas and the dangers of contradictions among them. This, after
all, was the problem that had faced Roman jurists in the later
empire. In theory, at least, Islamic scholars only recognized four
'roots', or sources, of law: the Quran itself, little though it had to
say about law; the sunna of the Prophet, or what were accepted
as records of his activities; the results of reasoning by analogy;
and the conclusions of an established community of scholars, on
the assumption that they had correctly reasoned from established
sources. Custom and practice inevitably contributed a great deal
to the reasoning of both scholars and judges, but these were not
officially recognized as sources of law.[21] Scholars continued to
develop new theories and interpretations of legal principles for
several centuries, but the idea that they should be strictly limited
and firmly grounded in the proper sources had taken hold.[22]

Given the emphasis in shari'a scholarship on personal above
public duties, the fiqh scholars had little to say about penal processes, taxation, and the political constitution.[23] They recognized the position of the caliphs and left matters of public policy
largely to them.[24] The caliphs, in turn, accepted recommendations of the scholars on the appointment of qadis and required
them to follow the shari'a, successfully persuading a number of
scholars to undertake these roles. In the cities, they delegated
the regulation of everyday public life to the *muhtasib*, technically market inspectors, who made local rules and heard minor
disputes among tradesmen, artisans, and ordinary household-
ers. At the same time, most caliphs held their own courts in

which they addressed individual wrongs. In these they generally listened to accusations of criminal conduct or allegations about corrupt officials.[25]

The more pious scholars were reluctant to allow the caliphs to have too much authority. They considered that they, the ulama, were the true heirs of the Prophet, and that the law was found in their reasoning, not in a caliph's decrees. It was they who should determine how people conducted prayers and rituals, how they should behave in markets and commercial ventures, and how they should act ethically as good Muslims. The duties of the caliph and his officers, in their view, were to maintain the mosques, preserve order in the market, and defend the frontiers of the realm.[26] The ulama insisted on the rule of law, and especially the word of God, which was authoritative above all else. Against this the actions of even the most powerful caliph ought to be judged.

The Abbasid caliphs had largely relied on military strength when they swept to power in the eighth century and fought out the later sectarian conflicts, but they always avowed commitment to the principles of Islam. This secured the loyalty of the major religious sects, but it also gave the ulama licence to criticize the caliphs' activities if they did not, in the scholars' view, properly adhere to the principles of the sunna.[27] Religion remained always above the law and in this sphere of life the scholars regarded themselves as independent of the caliphs.[28] Over the next one thousand years, these ideas led to troubled relations between religious scholars and caliphs, the priests and kings of the Islamic world, as wars were fought and lost, empires and caliphates rose and fell, and new converts and pretenders to power emerged to challenge the old political orders.

THE FIRST TWO centuries of Abbasid rule, from the mid-eighth to the mid-tenth centuries, saw the high point of the Islamic caliphate, a period of relative peace, economic success, and legal efflorescence. But political expansion introduced its own problems, and in the ninth century slaves from East Africa mounted a revolt at Basra, from which the Abbasid court drew most of its basic foods and received its taxes. By the beginning of the tenth century, the Abbasid court was struggling to keep control over its more far-flung provinces. Large parts of the western empire had already broken away with the collapse of the Umayyad dynasty, starting with the independent emirate of al-Andalus in modern-day Spain and Portugal. A local ruler in Morocco did the same forty years later, followed by others throughout North Africa, and, finally, Egypt.

For the most part, the new rulers modelled themselves on the Abbasid court, not least in their support of the ulama and patronage of Islamic institutions and centres of learning, building libraries, religious academies (*madrasas*), and schools of law for both Sunni and Shi'i scholars. Among the more successful were the Shi'i Fatimids, who rose to power in North Africa and in 969 conquered Egypt, where they based their caliphate for the next two hundred years. By now, the Buyids, invaders from northern Iran, had swept into Baghdad. They allowed the Abbasid rulers to retain their throne, but reduced them to little more than figureheads. Then, in the eleventh century, further Turkic tribes emerged from Central Asia. Recently converted to Sunni Islam, the Seljuks ousted the Buyids, going on to rule the central Islamic region for another century. During that time they made steady encroachments westwards, challenging the shaky Byzantine administration and finally defeating its armies in 1071. Alarmed, Christian leaders launched the first of their crusades against the Muslim 'infidels', but after initial, and much-lauded, success, their campaigns faltered. Within two centuries Muslim forces had again taken control of the Holy Lands. In the meantime, the Seljuks had fallen to the Ayyubid sultans, who were themselves overthrown by an army of their own slave soldiers, the Mamluks, in 1250.

In al-Andalus, the Almoravid rulers were relatively untouched by the crusading Christians. But in the middle of the twelfth century they were replaced by new Berber forces, the puritanical Almohads, who set about persecuting both Jews and Christians. Throughout these changes of political regime, Jews had formed their own communities in areas dominated by Muslim rulers. They interacted with the surrounding Muslim populations and their rulers, often harmoniously, particularly in the commercial realm, although occasionally they were brutally persecuted. Their stories form part of Chapter 8, along with those of some of the ordinary Muslims who lived in the Maghreb.

In the thirteenth century, the Mongols overran large parts of Central Asia, moving southwards and westwards into northern Iran and from there into Iraq, where they destroyed intricate irrigation systems, libraries, and mosques, finally sacking Baghdad in 1258. The Islamic world was now divided into three—the Almohad west, the Mamluk central regions, and the Mongol regions to the east. It would never again be politically reunited.

Amidst, and despite, all these political upheavals, particularly in the periods of peace guaranteed by one or other of the caliphs, jurists continued to work in their madrasas and debate their theories of fiqh.[29] The different Sunni madhhabs were now relatively well settled, each with its own central texts and structures of authority, although all claimed legitimacy from the Quran and the foundational teachings of the Prophet. And, in substance, their principles were not so different. The legal scholars learned and restated the basic legal principles established in Abbasid times, concentrating on broadly the same topics and using similar rules and terminology. They took the view that the fundamental principles of law had been settled and it was the work of their own generation of jurists to interpret them for ordinary Muslims. It was then the task of the qadis to apply their abstract version of the law, developed in the law schools, to the practical problems of real life.

Many jurists carefully preserved their writings, and some of these have survived. They demonstrate how Muslim jurists thought and wrote and reveal the subjects that concerned them. Yahya ibn Sharaf Muhyi al-Din al-Nawawi (Nawawi for short), for example, lived in Damascus under the Mamluk sultans between 1233 and 1277.[30] He trained in various madrasas of the Hanafi school before becoming a teacher and producing a large corpus of writing on fiqh in the form of commentaries on earlier texts. He also wrote works on language, hadith, and biography. Pious and ascetic, Nawawi was not afraid to confront the sultan when necessary. He maintained that the task of the jurist was to discover the universal principles of the law, which must be derived from the Prophet's revelations. Although generations of scholars and pious Muslims had already explored these principles, he explained that men's efforts were inevitably imperfect; thus later generations needed to refine and synthesize the earlier scholarship. He wrote treatises on the *zakat*, the obligatory giving of alms, with a particular focus on how much was correct, when and to whom alms should be given, and whether alms should be calculated on the basis of hidden wealth. These questions raised larger issues about the nature of property and its ownership. Nawawi discussed different classes of slaves and the complications that arose when a slave was only partly free, because he or she was jointly owned, and only one of the owners had granted him freedom. Nawawi also considered the position of a slave who had agreed to buy his own freedom.[31] And he discussed the types of animals that could be paid as zakat, a topic that belied the origins of Islamic law in the pastoralists' economy of the Prophet's time.

Elsewhere, Nawawi indulged in an extensive discussion of hermaphrodites and the basis on which they should be regarded as either men or women. This was not, we can assume, because her-maphroditism was a particularly widespread or practical problem in thirteenth-century Damascus, but because considering the sta-tus of those on the borders between the sexes could clarify the dis-tinction, important to so much Islamic family law, between the genders. Like the Roman jurists, Nawawi developed the law in-tellectually, using hypothetical examples to clarify categories and rules and draw distinctions between them. Many other scholars were, like Nawawi, concerned with clarifications and distinctions, considering such topics as the status of the children of divorced parents and whether a mother could retain custody of them. Such questions helped them to refine the categories used by earlier schol-ars and explain their significance. Their purposes were ostensibly practical, but theirs was, above all, an intellectual project. They also worried about the issue of authority, about which of the had-iths and other texts they could rely upon, and about which other scholars had used correct forms of reasoning, and how they might reconcile what different scholars had said on the same topic. At times, the level of detail and the complexity of their arguments were more like esoteric games than practical exercises, not unlike the more intricate opinions of the Roman jurists.[32]

Some of the Islamic jurists' writings were so technical that they could hardly have been comprehensible, let alone useful, to laymen, or even to qadis. In the hands of the most erudite scholars, fiqh became an art. It was mannered and intricate, its elaborate language more like the exquisite detail of a Moghul miniature than the ponderous prose of a dry legal treatise. And this was how the scholars themselves saw it. Nawawi described fiqh as both a 'predicament' and a 'delight'. Analysing the law was 'the most noble approach to God, the highest act of obedi-ence, the most pressing category of the good, the most secure act of worship, and the most worthy thing to do'. The law was a 'scintillating sea, a treasury of subtleties, a garden', and the task of the scholars was to make this 'multi-faceted jewel' sparkle.[33]

Most caliphs were generous patrons of the madrasas and many of the madrasas also received support from the donations of ordinary people. The most privileged scholars probably lived and worked in elegant surroundings, scouring the resources of their extensive libraries, where they rubbed shoulders with fellow jurists who were always ready to engage in challenging debate. Others became more involved in the practical administration of the law, acting as *muftis* or qadis. These were the legal advisers and judges—the Sunni and Shi'i had parallel divisions of legal labour. The jurists were, as Nawawi explained, primarily concerned with the abstract and universal principles of the law, while the task of the muftis was to apply these legal rules and principles in opinions that related to real life.[34] The muftis heard petitions from ordinary people and responded with *fatwas*, short legal opinions explaining what they could or could not do in particular situations. They advised on such things as correct procedures for inheritance and the enforcement of problematic contracts; they also provided opinions for qadis on tricky questions of evidence or law that arose in court. Jurists would often act as muftis, but their tasks when playing these two roles were distinct. As Nawawi said, the fatwa of a mufti was concerned with particulars, descending from the abstraction of the law into the reality of daily life.

Jurists might also act as qadis, bringing the benefits of their wisdom and learning directly into the courts. One such jurist was 'Ali ibn 'Abd al-Kafi al-Subki (Subki for short), who was, for a while, chief qadi of Damascus.[35] As a bright young scholar from Mamluk Egypt, Subki had travelled widely, teaching in Alexandria, Syria, and western Arabia. The Mamluk sultan appointed Subki as the chief qadi of Damascus in 1339, when Subki was already in his fifties, quite an old man in those days. He performed his task with enthusiasm and energy. His biographers describe him as pious, ascetic, effective, and strong-willed. In particular, he was reputed to be a judge who could resolve tricky and hotly contested inheritance disputes without incurring criticism. As well as hearing legal cases, he gave advice and opinions in the form of fatwas to all sorts of people—his judicial deputies, individual petitioners, members of the elite, and ordinary citizens, sometimes intervening in public debates, sometimes addressing individual problems. According to one contemporary, 'horsemen carried his writings and his fatwas to all corners of the land'.[36]

Subki obviously took some pride in his performance as chief qadi, but in his writings he made it clear that there was a hierarchy among the jurist, the mufti, and the qadi. The jurist's was the highest authority, he explained, because the scholar dealt in universals, coming closest to the divine law, while the mufti's work was complicated by the consideration of particulars. The qadi was even closer to the messy reality of daily life. At one point, Subki even advised young scholars not to accept judicial appointments. The opinions of the ulama, he said, are accepted, while those of the qadis are 'contaminated with suspicion'.[37] Elsewhere he made it clear that the qadi was subordinate to the mufti, who, as the heir to the Prophet, could explain and clarify God's ruling.[38] This was not to cast aspersions on the quality of any particular legal judgement. There could be excellent qadis, and many scholars, like Subki himself, played multiple roles. But it was to insist on a hierarchy of legal knowledge, at the top of which the jurist dealt directly with divine law. Islamic law had its origins in the guidance that God had given to humanity, found in the Quran and the sunna of the Prophet, which it was the business of the jurists to interpret for all.

Over the following centuries, Islamic scholars continued to debate the principles and procedures of Islamic law, while Muslim rulers, officials, judges, and individuals all turned to the muftis for legal advice. The muftis and qadis were largely kept busy advising individuals, confirming duties and obligations as much as resolving disputes. But conflicts between rival religious sects and political families were, on occasion, fought out in the courts. Most Muslim rulers were serious about their piety and tried to base their systems of government, at least nominally, on the shari'a, appointing qadis to apply Islamic law and patronizing madrasas. Throughout, religious and legal scholars, on the one hand, and political rulers, on the other, negotiated a delicate balance of power and authority.

LIKE JEWISH LAW, the Islamic fiqh was a religious project. In both, lawmakers adopted casuistic forms when they gave guidance to ordinary people and included rules that judges could use to resolve disputes and regulate social relations, and that merchants could use to shape contracts. But like the Hindu brahmins, the scholars were more concerned with duties than rights, and the most powerful rulers never seriously challenged the hierarchy of religious authority. This put the Geonim and mufti firmly above the judges and qadis.

The Jewish and Islamic systems of law never had any lasting central authority, or even, in the case of the shari'a, foundational legal texts. They endured and developed during periods of repeated political turmoil, when jurists held their own against confident sultans and invading warlords. Based on a moral vision for the world, they proved their resilience time and again. To this day, Jewish and Islamic legal scholars study, develop, and disseminate forms of law and legal reasoning that are very different from the state laws that dominate our world. But much happened before any European state was able to challenge the powerful Islamic caliphs.

CHAPTER SIX

EUROPEAN KINGS
Courts and Customs After the Fall of Rome

W hen the Roman armies withdrew from northern Europe in the fifth century of the common era, they took with them their systems of government and their laws. Gallic, Celtic, and Anglo-Saxon tribesmen had little use for complex sets of legal rules. Roman systems of administration lingered for some time in southern Europe, after the western empire collapsed in 476, but even here court processes were forgotten, libraries ransacked, and precious parchment burned or crumbled. Impressive cities, grand monuments, and sophisticated literary techniques still reminded people of past glories, and the eastern Roman emperors maintained their courts, palaces, and armies in Constantinople. But the new governors of the western Roman territories were leaders of nomadic tribes, used to moving around with small groups of trusted noblemen and engaging in long-running feuds with their rivals. They, too, had little use for elaborate processes of government. Still, they were impressed by the grandeur of the Roman emperors and decided to create their own legal codes. Initially, they did little more than write out basic lists of injuries and compensation, but they were promising justice, as the Romans had done before them. Eventually, their assorted rules, customs, and ideas developed into the sophisticated European systems that came to dominate the world. But it was centuries before they produced anything like a coherent body of law.

WHEN THE ROMAN Empire was at its height, judges, jurists, and litigants in North Africa, Egypt, the Middle East, and Armenia as well as southern Europe all referred to Roman legal texts and ideas. But even the Roman Empire had its limits. East of Babylon, south of the Sahara, and north of the Rhine there were people who remained beyond the control of Rome's armies and administrators.[1] In northern Europe, Germanic tribes threatened Roman outposts, and in the early fifth century one of their leaders, Alaric, gathered a coalition of tribes, invaded Italy, and sacked Rome. A few years later, his successor moved with the Visigoth tribes into Aquitaine (southwestern France). The Huns, meanwhile, had emerged from the East Asian steppes with fearsomely effective military cavalry and gradually moved westwards, pushing many of the Germanic tribes before them. Crossing the frozen Rhine in 406, they moved into Gaul (modern France), Burgundy, and the Iberian Peninsula. One contingent crossed the sea to Morocco and went on to seize Carthage in 439. Alarmed, the eastern emperor sent an army to try to recapture all the North African provinces, but when Attila invaded the Balkans with his army of Huns, the Roman troops hurried to defend their eastern lands and left Africa to its new rulers. In Gaul, the Roman general Aetius defended Roman territory for some time, forming coalitions with a number of the new tribes. But when Aetius was murdered, his army was left in disarray. One of the Germanic leaders, Odovacar, decided to depose the last Roman emperor in 476. Dispatching his imperial robes to the court in Constantinople, Odovacar informed Zeno that the west no longer needed an emperor.

Throughout these upheavals, Roman law continued to flourish in the east, where the emperors presided over well-developed structures of government. Theodosius II ordered a compilation of laws to form the code that bears his name, which was completed in 438. The western Roman generals, meanwhile, tried to continue their predecessors' policy of using law to 'pacify' the barbarians. Aetius ordered the compilation of a set of laws for the Bretons, whom he had recently subdued, and probably another for the Franks.[2] But these initiatives were very different from the previous practice of extending Roman law to all new citizens. They were new sets of laws, formulated specifically for the barbarians. The Breton laws, according to surviving reports, forbade vengeance, specified compensation payments, regulated relations between the military and civilians, and criminalized tax fraud, homicide, adultery, theft, and illegal grazing.

By the second half of the fifth century, the Merovingian Franks had settled in the productive farmlands of Gaul in what is now northern France. Meanwhile, the Visigoths, ascendant under their leader Euric, were taking control in most of Spain. A new coalition of Gothic tribes that now emerged in the east— the Ostrogoths, as they became known—conquered Italy and deposed Odovacar in the 490s. At around the same time, the Frankish king, Clovis, moved south and seized almost all the Visigoth territory in Gaul, then turned to the Burgundian lands.

Partly Romanized through long association with the imperial armies, and doubtless wishing to emulate the impressive civilization of the eastern Roman Empire, the Visigoth leader, Euric, ordered a code for his people in around 475. His laws clearly reflected local concerns, particularly the relations between different classes of nobles, but Euric's adviser, Leo, had trained as a Roman lawyer and gave the code a distinctly Roman veneer. Since law applied to people, rather than territories, the new rulers also felt they should have different laws for themselves and their Roman subjects. Euric's son Alaric duly compiled a set of Roman laws and juristic opinions into a *Breviarium Alaricianum* (Breviary of Alaric) for his Roman subjects. The Burgundian kings took the same approach, employing members of the old Roman elite as advisers and scribes. Resigning themselves to their new status as subjects of barbarian invaders, educated Romans encouraged their new rulers to respect the traditions of Roman law. As long as they maintained their language and their laws, they could feel that civilization was not altogether lost.[3]

In Italy, the Ostrogoth king, Theodoric the Great, saw himself as a successor to the Roman emperors and employed senior Roman officials to run his administration. Declaring that people could still rely upon Roman laws, he gathered a collection of them into his *Edictum Theodorici* (Edict of Theodoric) for his judges and other officials. As he confirmed in a letter to the Genoese Jews, 'the true mark of civilitas is the observance of law. It is this . . . which separates men from beasts'.[4] Law remained an important marker of civilization, even competition, among the new rulers.

Farther north, where the Latin influence was lighter, the Frankish king, Clovis, ordered a code which incorporated the laws drafted under Aetius several decades earlier along with prescriptions and procedural rules made by his predecessors.[5] The prologue to this code, known as the Lex Salica, declares that with the aid of God the Franks had decided to establish peace and prevent litigation, so that they might surpass their neighbours in the quality of their justice as well as the force of their arms. The first clause orders penalties for anyone who fails to appear when summoned to court, possibly copying the first law of the Roman Twelve Tables. But there the resemblance ends, and the code continues with the compensation payments typical of tribal dynamics. There is a long list of penalties for different types of theft, beginning with pigs and other animals, followed by provisions on injuries, killing, sexual misconduct, false accusations, marriage arrangements, and slavery. It reads very much as a record of customs, which it probably was, and reflects the practices of a feuding society, one without a strong state, where offences were matters of private wrong.

There is no evidence that any of these codes had a direct impact on the resolution of disputes. Written in Latin, they were more like gestures to Rome, markers of civilization, and attempts to create a common identity among the new coalitions of tribal groups than practical instruments designed to assist judges resolving conflicts.

DESPITE THEIR ATTEMPTS at lawmaking, the new rulers were still 'barbarians' in the eyes of the eastern Roman emperors, who made periodic attempts to recover their lost western territories. Justinian sent his armies to win back the Italian Peninsula in the 530s, initiating a series of bloody conflicts that continued for three decades. He was only briefly successful, and the rump of his remaining armies was defeated by another wave of Germanic invaders, the Lombards, who swept into northern Italy in 568. Hoping to restore Rome's imperial greatness, Justinian also set dozens of scribes to work on three new legal texts. His *Codex Justinianus* (Code of Justinian) brought Theodosius's work up to date by incorporating new laws and edicts; the *Institutiones Justinian* (Institutes of Justinian), based on the jurist Gaius's second-century text, served as an elementary textbook; and the monumental, confusingly named *Digesta* (Digest) collected together hundreds of jurists' opinions.[6] With some fanfare, Justinian proclaimed in 533 that these three books, together known as his *Corpus Iuris Civilis* (Body of civil law), contained all of Roman law and would remain valid for all time, throughout the whole of his empire. But most of the west was already in the hands of barbarian kings, who ignored it, and the Greek-speaking Byzantine lawyers could not easily understand the legal Latin. Although they made a monumental translation effort in the tenth century, there is little evidence that the *Corpus Iuris* made any impact on legal practices of the time.

What had been the western Roman Empire was now dominated by three major powers: the Franks, based in Gaul; the Lombards, in northern Italy; and the Visigoths, who maintained a kingdom in Spain until 711, when the ascendant Umayyads sailed across the Mediterranean to absorb Andalusia into their caliphate. But the Germanic intruders generally remained a minority within their new lands and for the most part maintained Roman systems of administration. These were well suited to the centralized governments they were now trying to establish. In the Latin-speaking south, both Ostrogoth and Visigoth leaders could claim they were reestablishing Roman rule. Here, Roman legal ideas, practices, and institutions were well entrenched. The church had also established courts, in which judges still followed the Roman civil law and its procedures.[7] The popes gradually expanded their influence, eventually converting the Visigoths and Lombards from their Arian Christian 'heresy'.[8]

Farther north, relations of vengeance probably continued for some time among the Frankish elite. But Clovis had been persuaded by the bishop of Rheims to convene councils to debate matters of policy, and his successors ordered their scribes to draft legal codes for their new subjects as they extended their dominions to the east. These codes aspired to reflect local customs. The kings heard the most important legal cases, but Roman systems of taxation had largely broken down, and with them the capacity for extensive centralized administration. Urban councils and local landowners therefore took responsibility for settling most conflicts.[9] Notaries continued to use Roman legal forms to record important transactions, including sales and gifts of land, divorces, adoptions, and disputes over labour, keeping alive parts of the Roman legal tradition.[10] But judges mostly decided individual cases on their own merits, settling appropriate amounts of compensation according to established traditions and using oaths and ordeals, themselves recognized in the laws, to determine guilt and innocence.[11]

If they wanted to introduce new practices, the Frankish kings now issued edicts, known as *capitularies*. Some of these confirmed decisions made by councils of bishops; others were rules for the whole population, to be read out at local assemblies. The majority simply contained instructions to administrators. These repeatedly ordered officials to enact justice properly and avoid bribery. As for Clovis's code, the Lex Salica, it may not have been of great practical use, but it remained important to the Frankish kings, who added further clauses to it over the next two centuries. Some dealt with new topics, such as disputes over social status, land transactions by the church, slave manumission, sureties, and debt. Pippin III brought them together into a code with a hundred clauses in 763, although it was still rather haphazard. Charlemagne ordered yet another revision when he took the throne a few years later. In a decree of 802, Charlemagne also demanded that his judges base their judgements on the written law, rather than on their personal opinions. But almost simultaneously he produced another version of the Lex Salica, which largely reverted to Clovis's text. His scribes updated the language but not the currency for compensation payments, which were now wildly out of date. They ignored the additions of later kings, in fact reintroducing contradictions and inconsistencies that intervening versions had removed.[12] So, although Charlemagne cared that his judges should heed his decrees, govern honestly, and in his name, they could not apply his laws in any detail.

Why did Charlemagne and his successors, the Carolingian kings, think it worthwhile to put all this time and so many resources into lawmaking? After successful campaigns against the

Visigoths and Burgundians in 774, Charlemagne moved on to Italy and deposed the Lombard kings. He was then able to negotiate with Pope Leo III to recognize him as emperor. Disillusioned with imperial plots in the east and concerned about attempts on his own life, the pope crowned Charlemagne Roman emperor in 800. Now Charlemagne needed to adopt an appearance of imperial dignity. He did not have the administrative apparatus to reproduce Roman systems of government, with its Senate, officials, judges, and courts, but he could make laws. The Lex Salica might have started as a list of penalties and tribal customs, but a Latin text could be presented as something grander, the work of an authoritative king. It demonstrated that the ruler was governing properly, as the Roman emperors had done before him. Lawmaking, as one scholar has put it, was an exercise in image-building.[13]

TO THE NORTH, in the British Isles, the Romans' influence had petered out more completely with the retreat of their armies in 410. Subsequent waves of migration from continental Europe changed the composition and organization of the local populations, and Anglo-Saxons now vied for power with Britons, Celts, and Picts. Most people belonged to tribes, among whom there were traditions of revenge, compensation, and blood money. It was only in the mid-sixth century that more stable patterns of settlement and landholding emerged. By the end of that century, small kingdoms had formed in Kent, Wessex, and Mercia, and when the Kentish king, Aethelberht, married a Christian Frankish princess, Pope Gregory sent the Benedictine prior Augustine on an evangelizing mission to Britain. In Canterbury in 597, the monk persuaded Aethelberht to adopt Christianity and then embarked on a massive project of conversion.

Possibly under Augustine's influence, Aethelberht also created a set of laws, the earliest document known to have been written in English.[14] The ninety clauses of this code specify compensation payments for 'affronts', both material harm and insults to a freeman's honour, such as sleeping with a high-status woman from his household. The laws recognized status, specifying certain privileges for the king and his men, granting various protections to the churchmen, and distinguishing freemen from slaves. Aethelberht added a few clauses on religious misconduct, recognizing his duty to protect the new church as well as his people. But the code was little more than a list of monetary equivalents for different injuries. In this way it was not entirely dissimilar from Clovis's code, reflecting practices of compensation that must have been common among the Kentish tribes. In practical terms, these laws might have made it easier for the king to persuade vengeful people to make peace. He was also making a claim about his authority. Like other Anglo-Saxon kings, Aethelberht was little more than a grand freeman. But he could summon assemblies, where he discussed warfare and other important issues with his nobles and bishops and sought approval for new decrees.[15] His laws defined what mattered among the Kentish freemen, most importantly the levels of compensation they could honourably accept, so that they could live together in peace.

Gradually, the kings began to control more areas of public life, defining more crimes and developing more complex legal procedures. The codes produced for the later Kentish kings Hlothhere and Eadric describe the ways in which Kentish people could buy property in London. The laws of King Wihtred, written at the end of the seventh century, include provisions to protect church property and rules on sexual misconduct, fasting, devil-worship, and stealing, as well as directions on how oaths and accusations should be made and tested. The early English kings must have been aware of the lawmaking activities of their counterparts to the south: King Ine of Wessex made a substantial code in seventy-six clauses at around the same time. These imposed penalties on anyone who tried to wreak revenge without seeking justice in court. Ine's code stood until King Alfred ordered another two centuries later.

Although largely occupied by his campaigns against the Vikings, Alfred took a keen interest in the government of his kingdom. In his coronation oath, he promised to maintain peace, to forbid robbery and other injustices, and 'to be just and merciful in his own judgements'.[16] Probably on the advice of his bishops, he ordered a substantial new legal code. The long introduction cites the Ten Commandments, the biblical Book of Exodus, and the Acts of the Apostles. Moses, of course, had made laws to confirm the independence and religious commitment of his people, and Alfred believed he was doing the same for his kingdom. And, like his Germanic counterparts, Alfred used prestigious Roman forms for his laws, but they reflected existing traditions. All the kings confirmed the tribal order at the heart of their new kingdoms by making explicit important practices of compensation. But Alfred went further, not just invoking the laws of the Bible but also recording a number of the judgements made by his councils.

One rule in Alfred's laws directs that if a man is walking along with a spear over his shoulder and turns carelessly, injuring a passerby, he has to pay compensation more or less depending on the angle of the spear. This passage must reflect a real case, given the specificity of the law—that it only applies to an accident involving a spear, and only if it is carried over the shoulder. But it must have been included among the laws because it expressed an important principle about accidental injuries and the level of carelessness that might be implied by something as ordinary as the angle of a spear. Like the authors of the Frankish and Lombard laws, and those of Hammurabi over two thousand years earlier, Alfred's lawmakers used real cases to express general principles and adopted the casuistic form to make rules that could be widely applied. His laws combined rules based on custom with records of real cases, which gave the laws a somewhat haphazard form. But, written in the Anglo-Saxon vernacular, they were relatively accessible to the local populations.[17]

Like other Anglo-Saxon kings, Alfred was fully aware of his duty to maintain the order ordained by God. Kings had to uphold minimum standards of Christian observance if they were to avoid plagues and overcome their enemies. It was their duty to ensure peace, and this primarily meant controlling theft. Alfred's code did not forbid violence per se, but it did try to limit the possibilities for vengeance by restricting when it was permitted and who its targets could be. It also insisted that everyone had a duty to denounce thieves and help recover stolen property. Alfred's son Edward the Elder made another code at the beginning of the tenth century, which dealt primarily with legal procedures, warranties, and witnesses. His successor, Aethelstan, ordered no fewer than six codes on the advice of his bishops. The new laws covered witchcraft, ordeals, commerce, coinage, attendance at assemblies, responsibilities concerning slaves and servants, the duties of the reeves (government officials), warranties, sanctuary, and the obligation on everyone to pursue thieves. The provisions reflected the expanding reach of royal government.

In 927, having successfully led his armies to the north of the island, Aethelstan declared that he was 'King of Britain'.[18] His successors followed suit. Aethelred (r. 978–1013) asked Wulfstan II, Archbishop of York, to draft a new set of laws for his whole kingdom.[19] The bishop brought together a number of earlier codes and, not surprisingly, wrapped them in highly moralizing language, emphasizing the Christian penance that any murderer had to undertake for this gravest of sins. He also introduced new restrictions on revenge: priests were fair game, but monks were not. In the early eleventh century, the Danish invader Cnut, who ruled England from 1016 to 1035 (as well as Denmark and Norway), also turned to Wulfstan, asking him to draft a new set of laws for his kingdom. English laws were now supposed to apply to all who lived east of the Welsh borders and south of the Tees.

WHILE THE ANGLO-SAXON kings were writing laws for an English kingdom, another story was unfolding on the Italian Peninsula.[20] When the Lombards defeated the remaining Byzantine forces in 568, the emperors' hopes of a reunified Roman imperium finally faded and the Germanic Lombards introduced their own customs. Like the Franks and Visigoths to the north and west, the Lombards formed distinct tribes. Compensation for killings and injuries loomed large among the issues faced by their mediators. King Rothari issued the *Edictum Rothari* (Edict of Rothari), effectively a legal code, in 643, setting out long lists of compensation payments. Starting with treason, treachery, and desertion, it then catalogued different types of personal injury. Its 388 clauses stipulated complex processes of oath-taking to establish guilt and innocence. Rothari may have hoped his laws would impress his army and strengthen its loyalty as it embarked on a major campaign into Liguria. But he was also trying to limit the powers of rival lords and, in an explicit attempt to deter blood feuds, he increased the level of compensation payments. Like the Franks, Rothari employed Latin-speaking scribes, but they littered their text with Germanic terms for which they could evidently find no Latin equivalents.

As in the Visigothic and Burgundian territories, the new rulers expected that Roman citizens would continue to rely upon Roman laws. But the administrative classes had been devastated by the turmoil of the previous decades, and intricate Roman rules and practices must soon have seemed irrelevant. The southern part of the Italian Peninsula, as well as the area around the cities of Ravenna and Rome, remained beyond the control of the Lombards, and people in these areas maintained contact with Byzantium for some time. Scholars imported copies of Justinian's *Corpus Iuris* and circulated his *Institutiones* among their students. But Roman law was extravagantly complicated. Years of study were needed before any scholar could understand the more esoteric juristic opinions, let alone get to the point where they could apply them effectively. Even in this region, Roman legal influence gradually faded.

Meanwhile, successive Lombard kings issued supplements and additions to Rothari's Edict. Many of their laws read like records of court cases, which they may have been. Like the Frankish and Anglo-Saxon laws, they were not always consistent. Despite the example of Justinian's texts, the kings did not think it important to employ scholars to tease out and systematize the principles underlying their laws. Notaries in Lombard towns did keep alive something of the Roman legal tradition. When they drafted charters to record important transactions, such as the manumission of slaves, sales of land, leases, and marriages, they insisted on precise words and phrases, which might have served to give their documents authority in legal disputes. Roman legal forms, in this way, continued to shape social relations. But even these practices may have disappeared had it not been for a series of chance events that led to the 'rediscovery' of Roman law.

The Lombard kings chose Pavia as their capital, and Charlemagne moved into its palace after his armies swept across the Alps to rout the Lombards in 774.[21] He also founded a school in which notaries could train. Some notaries were already intervening in legal disputes, consulted about the correctness and interpretation of written documents, and some litigants had begun to ask them to act as judges in more complex cases. By the middle of the ninth century, the Carolingian emperors were appointing notaries to act as their *iudices sacri palatii*, judges of the sacred palace. To consider the most serious cases, they would gather in groups of sixteen, sometimes up to thirty, particularly when monastic property was at stake.

Following the fall of the Carolingian rulers, Pope John XII crowned the Saxon king Otto I as emperor, in 951. The new emperor did not try to change the Lombard laws in any significant way, but he did not care much for Roman bureaucratic practices. He favoured the custom of trial by battle, which reduced legal argument to a trial of physical skill. He also moved his capital away from Pavia. The judges now lost their royal patronage, but they did not give up their work. They began to travel around northern Italy, where they were asked to hear cases in different towns, and they commissioned a collection of local Lombard laws, the *Liber Legis Langobardorum* (Book of the Law of the Lombards), which they could carry with them. They scribbled notes and comments in their pocket editions, which included scattered references to Roman principles. As the judges continued their work, they trained students and debated among themselves about what the law was and should be. In all likelihood inspired by the work of the Roman jurists, they discussed which laws should apply to all people and which concerned men rather than boys, or freemen but not slaves. They argued about whether they had to stick to the literal words of a Lombard law or could look for underlying principles to expand its reach. Like the Roman jurists, some now claimed they could extend rules by using hypothetical examples and general principles, which they extracted by comparing the words in different laws. In other words, the judges saw the law as a system with a logic of its own. Some even argued that where there were gaps in the laws they could apply Roman laws and principles directly. They sought out copies of Justinian's *Institutiones* to construct a commentary on the Lombard laws and completed this work, their *Expositio* (Exposition), in the late eleventh century.

It had now been over four centuries since Justinian had written his great *Corpus Iuris*, and the most extensive of his texts, the Digest, had practically been forgotten, its collection of complex and abstract opinions being of little use in contemporary Italy. Judges hardly had the time to delve into its intellectual masterpieces when they had petitioners with practical problems in front of them. Italian texts had been lost, damaged, or forgotten, and Byzantine libraries were destroyed in the Seljuk conquest in the eleventh century. But careful librarians had kept a copy of the Digest safe at a library in Pisa, and one of them now invited inquisitive scholars to examine the text. The more intellectually ambitious were delighted to rediscover this treasure trove of legal reasoning. Scholars from Pavia, Mantua, Modena, and Bologna journeyed to Pisa to examine the Digest, and they made their way laboriously through its pages to study the arguments of the Roman jurists. Some of them persuaded their patrons to commission copies for their own libraries.

Irnerius, a jurist from Bologna, was one such scholar. He had a powerful patron in Matilda of Canossa, who probably encouraged him to pursue his work in Bologna. Here he helped to develop what became the most famous legal school in Italian history.[22] Irnerius tackled the dense scholarship of the Digest, writing glosses on each of its books and using these to teach new techniques of analysis to his students. Roman law soon became a subject for study in its own right. Lombard law was not forgotten, and for practical purposes the schools continued to teach its rules. But the scholars sought out new legal ideas.

The great conflict between church and state known as the Investiture Crisis was then raging. It led to a standoff between Pope Gregory VII and the emperor Henry IV in 1072, and it was outside of Matilda's castle at Canossa that the excommunicated Henry did penance in the snow. The controversy rippled out in tensions between church and secular leaders. Meanwhile, increasing commercial activity brought its own opportunities, challenges, and sources of power. Growing diversity among different classes of people also called into question many of the older laws and legal categories. People began to question patterns of land distribution, trading practices, and traditions of inheritance, and they began to bring more problems to the courts. All of this encouraged the judges to look beyond the Lombard laws, seeking inspiration in the ideas and principles of the Roman texts and the writings of the jurists who were studying them.

The Bologna law school flourished as the jurists worked their way through the Roman texts. They enjoyed the intellectual challenge of the new legal science, the civil law, as their Roman predecessors had done almost a millennium earlier. Chaplains sent by their bishops joined other hopeful young men on the arduous journey to learn at the feet of the most eminent Italian masters. When the emperor Frederick Barbarossa stopped at Bologna on the way to his coronation in 1155 to seek the jurists' approval for his new laws, he called the students 'pilgrims for the sake of study'. They formed a powerful guild and proceeded to make so many demands of the city government that the pope had to intervene.[23] Over the next 150 years the scholars poured out commentaries, opinions, and glosses on the *Corpus Iuris*, and when the jurist Accursius gathered them together in 1240, his collection included 96,000 texts. For centuries to come, kings, judges, scholars, and scribes turned to its pages to find out what the civil law was. The scholars had once again established themselves as authorities on the law.

Bologna's success led to a proliferation of law schools and scholars, in both Italy and beyond, where teachers used summaries of Justinian's Digest and translated them into different languages.[24] At the same time, the church was developing its own rules and legal practices, largely based on Roman sources. Its courts asserted authority over any issue that touched on a matter of sin, including adultery, perjury, forgery, family law, even loans and interest. At first, the Bologna scholars were disdainful of the rather chaotic jumble of ecclesiastic rules and practices that made up the 'canon law' and largely ignored it, but in 1140 a monk named Gratian published a collection of texts. His *Decretum* (Decree) made the canon law look much more systematic, and the scholars began to take it seriously, embarking on interminable debates about its relation to the 'civil law'. Most universities now taught both. In England, the Archbishop of Canterbury recruited a Lombard scholar to assist him with the resolution of disputes, and the text this scholar compiled for his students became the basis for legal training in the new university at Oxford. The civil law had now acquired such prestige that no European university thought it worthwhile to teach any of the laws that were actually applied in their national or regional courts, something that did not change until the seventeenth century.[25]

MOST OF EUROPE was now divided into three parts. There was the Holy Roman Empire under the successors to Otto I, who were crowned as emperors by the popes, and then there were the emerging Kingdom of France and Angevin England. And in all three, kings and their advisers debated the nature of royal power and authority in terms of the law. Did the ruler simply have power, or did he only have the power to declare what was lawful? Or did the people have this power? Behind these debates was often a sense that the law was set apart from royal power, that the king could not simply declare what was lawful. And the protagonists on all sides turned to Roman sources to justify their arguments. The civil law had an authority, based on its ancient history and intellectual sophistication, that even the emperors respected.

At the same time, rulers and judges were inspired by the example of Justinian to create new codes for their people, either looking to the substance of the *Corpus Iuris*, via one of the many summaries or commentaries, or by copying material from the Visigothic or Burgundian codes. The Holy Roman Emperor

Frederick II commissioned the *Liber Augustalis* for his subjects in Sicily in 1231, and in Spain the kings Ferdinand III and Alfonso X created the *Siete Partidas* a few decades later, drawing on the Visigothic code. In France, Philip Augustus had transformed a small feudal state into one of the most prosperous and powerful countries in Europe. His Parlement, both a political and a judicial council, adopted a version of the legal procedures that the church courts had developed, which in turn were based on Roman precedents. Those who could afford to litigate before the Parlement now sought skilled men to represent them, and it was not long before the judges were adopting the substance of the Roman civil law in their decisions.

THERE WAS ONE place, however, in which both people and events conspired to resist the influence of classical Roman law. In England, the Anglo-Saxon kings had based their law codes largely upon custom and their own edicts. After the conquest of 1066, the new Norman king, William I, issued some new edicts, but he put his administrative resources into the great survey that became the Domesday Book, rather than new laws. His son, Henry I, however, ordered a work that he presented as the laws of the last recognized Saxon king, Edward the Confessor. His claim that it contained the laws that English nobles had expounded for William I was not remotely based on fact, but it did represent the idea that England was a unified kingdom, and that its laws were based on ancient tradition. Another author compiled a different set of local laws that he attributed to the same king, the *Leges Henrici Primi*. This text more closely reflected the reality by describing three distinct systems: the laws of Wessex, made by Alfred and his successors; the laws of Mercia, which applied in the north; and the laws of the Vikings, the

Danelaw. Someone also translated them into Latin, for the use of the Norman judges and administrators.[26]

By this time, the Normans had taken over most landed estates from the English nobility, and Henry I directed that the new landowners should periodically attend his royal courts. These were both political and social gatherings, where the king and his nobles would make collective decisions, seek and give advice, witness transactions, and enforce communal obligations as well as hearing legal cases. The Saxon kings had established courts in the shires and hundreds which followed a similar pattern, drawing together large numbers of men to debate and organize local affairs. Keen to extend his control over these forms of regional government, Henry gave directions as to how they should be organized. All important people should attend them, he said, including bishops, earls, sheriffs, hundredmen, aldermen, stewards, reeves, barons, vavassours, village reeves, and all landowners. He was paving the way for the centralization not just of law but also of justice.

Still very much a Norman, Henry spent a good deal of his time in France. But when in England, he travelled around to check on the work of the local courts and hear legal cases.[27] He took seriously his duty to mete out justice, having pledged, in his Coronation Charter, to 'place strong peace on all my kingdom'. When he was away he delegated this work to officials, some of whom gradually became specialists in law and legal procedures. Acting as judges, they heard the most important legal cases. In their role as administrators, they also had to unify the system of landholding, which was becoming increasingly complicated. The number of monasteries was expanding, along with the amount of land they owned, as wealthy men and women made donations or grants to them in their wills, and this inevitably led to legal arguments about ownership and the right to receive rents. The kings' officers had to consider their claims, classify their property, and specify their rights. The officials may have referred to the laws drafted for Henry, and they certainly seem to have had a sense that they were supposed to recognize English tradition. In this, their processes were quite different from those of the church courts convened by the bishops, which applied the canon law to ecclesiastic and family issues. The shire and hundred courts continued to hear local disputes, including allegations of homicide, theft, rape, forgery, and arson, using the traditional procedures of oaths, ordeals, and trial by battle to decide tricky questions of innocence and guilt.

After the chaos of Stephen's reign in the mid-twelfth century, the new king, Henry II, embarked upon a wave of political and legal reforms. He made regulations for debts, for the sale of wine and for other commercial affairs, and for the possession of arms. And he appointed a small number of his most trusted advisers to act as judges in his courts, introducing new rules to govern their procedures. These included the use of witnesses, the appointment of officials, and alternatives to trial by battle. The new judges toured the country holding *eyres*, large gatherings in which they reviewed recent events, investigated complaints against local officials, and heard legal cases. To guide their procedures, Henry introduced new writs. These specified the written forms in which legal claims had to be made, rather as the Roman formulae had done. In these ways, the king and his judges began to systematize legal practices and the principles they applied, gradually establishing a new 'common law'. About half of Henry's judges were clerics, who sat in ecclesiastic courts as well as the royal eyres, and so they were familiar with the canon law. In exceptional cases, such as the trial of the Archbishop of Canterbury Thomas Beckett in 1164, the lawyers might even use arguments based on Roman law. This case indirectly prompted Henry to introduce an important new writ, the action of *novel disseisin*, which governed the procedures for making claims to land.[28] In these ways, ideas and principles from the Roman civil law crept in to English practices. But their influence was limited. The new writs and procedures largely developed piecemeal, in response to immediate problems and practical needs, largely those of landowners in dispute about property, rents, and inheritance, and they reflected long-established customs and traditions.

Perhaps prompted by Henry's interest in the law, in the late twelfth century a young scholar produced a treatise on 'the laws and customs of the kingdom of England' which he named after his patron, the judge Ranulf de Glanvill. Clearly inspired by Justinian's *Corpus Iuris*, he intended that his work would explain the practices of the English royal courts to those who were more familiar with the civil law. Maybe he even hoped that it would be taught in the new university at Oxford.[29] He declared that he was describing the 'English law', which, although not written, was, as he explained, the law applied in the kings' courts. He insisted that the English common law constituted a system of its own, just like the civil law then being developed in Bologna and applied by the courts of Paris.

In practice, recognizing the new writs, Henry's judges developed standard approaches to land ownership, inheritance, wardship, the status of widows, and other concerns of the landowning classes. Gradually their work extended to the legal affairs of less wealthy citizens, including tenants, who might use the new writs to resist claims by their lords. In the early thirteenth century, a number of the kings' judges, led by Henry de Bracton, made a further attempt to consolidate and systematize this common English law, producing a lengthy treatise which described the law being applied in the kings' courts. But, although they declared that the king exercised complete jurisdiction over the law of the realm, none of Henry's successors attempted to produce a comprehensive code. Ignoring the example of the civil laws, they were content to let the English law develop through the system of writs. There was a strong sense that the English common law was based on ancient custom, and when the barons wanted to challenge the power of King John, they felt entitled to create a legal document to limit his powers, the Magna Carta.

The kings could nevertheless issue decrees to supplement the courts' practices. Major pieces of legislation, such as the Magna Carta, introduced legal reforms in all sorts of areas. In addition to the famous clauses that limited the powers of the Crown, the Magna Carta dealt with wardship and dowry, the regulation of moneylenders, weights and measures, and the management of royal forests, also setting out rules for foreign merchants, mercenaries, and hostages as well as numerous procedural measures designed to improve court processes. Some of these effectively gave people new rights—for example, in the case of unlawful dispossession of land. But for the most part, it was the judges of the kings' courts who developed the common law. Over the following centuries, they became more specialist, developing and refining the system of writs and gradually extending their jurisdiction to cases traditionally heard by local courts.

Scholars continued to teach Roman law in the English universities, where many of the judges trained, but unlike their counterparts in continental Europe, advocates learned about the law through practice and apprenticeship.[30] Initially, they gathered at the court of the Common Bench at Westminster, where they listened to cases, kept notes on the most interesting ones, studied statutes, and probably engaged in advocacy exercises. From around the 1340s, they began to move into the apartments of the Knights Templar on what is now Fleet Street, and they soon expanded into other inns in the area, conveniently close to the kings' courts. Before long they had established a society of expert lawyers, and eventually the new institutions introduced training programmes for aspiring advocates. At the same time, the judges began to consult and refer to records of previous cases. Gradually, they coordinated their approaches to legal problems, and their practices of consulting past cases eventually led to the system of precedent.

In substance, of course, much of the law applicable in England and Wales was not so different from the laws that emerged in continental European countries, and the legal scholars at the Universities of Oxford and Cambridge consolidated the reputation of the civil law as one of the most prestigious subjects. But in the precedents and procedures used by English advocates and the institutions in which they trained, the English common law followed a different path, and it remained distinct. When the movement for codification swept continental Europe in the eighteenth and nineteenth centuries, it had few influential advocates in England. Here the judges and lawyers continued to develop their own laws, relying on past cases.

THESE RELATIVELY UNGLAMOROUS events in Western Europe ultimately set the stage for the legal systems that now dominate the world. But there was nothing inevitable about it. Nor was there anything inherently rational, or superior, about the laws they produced. Most Germanic codes were haphazard lists of rules and judgements, customs were codified in random ways, and Roman laws and ideas were introduced into contexts in which they patently had no relevance. But kings throughout Western Europe were inspired by the grandeur and sophistication of the Roman tradition and they adopted its forms, aspiring to the authority of the historical emperors. Eventually the more ambitious expanded their laws to reflect the concerns of their developing administrations, creating rules with more pragmatic purposes. The main divergence between the civilian and common laws came after the rediscovery of the *Corpus Iuris Civilis*, which gave the civil law status and authority within the Holy

Roman Empire and the kingdoms of France and Spain. It also gave legal scholars renewed respect. In England, not for the last time, the rulers decided to follow a different path when they confirmed what they imagined were ancient English legal traditions, rather than adopting the civil law. Over time, English law developed, rather as Roman law had, from a combination of writs, decrees, and recorded cases.

These legal projects were a long way from those of the Mesopotamian kings, but, like them, the European rulers promised that their laws would bring peace and order to their people. There was also a sense that law represented a higher order, the order of God invoked in coronation oaths, the intellectual order of Roman law, and the order of justice. And this was an order that people considered the rulers should enact and respect. It laid the basis for ideas about the rule of law.

THE EARLIEST LAWMAKERS, who crafted the rules that developed into the great legal systems, were all trying to order the world around them. But they were pursuing very different visions. The Mesopotamian kings promised to bring justice to their people; the Hindu brahmins explained the principles of the dharma to guide a body of religious adherents; and Chinese rulers wanted to impose peace and order in unsettled times. These projects of justice, duty, and discipline emerged quite independently, and at first quite modestly. But the casuistic form of the Mesopotamian laws was adopted by both Israelite priests and Greek citizens; brahmins travelled with their texts throughout Southeast Asia, inspiring Buddhist as well as Hindu kings; and later Chinese rulers imposed their laws on the people of vast empires. Roman citizens had, meanwhile, followed their Athenian counterparts by formulating laws in their quest for justice, little knowing they were laying the foundations for one of the world's most influential legal systems. And the Jewish laws provided a model for the Islamic legal scholars, who founded a new legal tradition alongside their burgeoning religion.

The third part of this book asks how European monarchs eventually combined these different ambitions of justice, duty, and discipline to form the legal systems that now dominate the world. But in the intervening centuries, kings, emperors, scholars, and judges were all inspired to produce their own laws. In quite small communities and networks, too, clerics, councils, peasants, and tribesmen crafted rules for their own purposes. Some were elaborate sets of rules, others closely followed the forms of one of the great legal traditions, and still others made bold claims to autonomy. Meanwhile, judges and mediators everywhere developed complex procedures to establish the truth. Not all had ambitions to nation- or empire-building, or held visions of a cosmological order, but they all mapped out an idea of civilization. Ordinary people created laws to represent the contours of the social order they wished for themselves and their communities.

PART II

THE PROMISE OF CIVILIZATION

CHAPTER SEVEN

AT THE MARGINS

Lawmaking on the
Fringes of Christianity and Islam

K ings, priests, judges, and scholars crafted the rules that developed into the world's major legal systems, but people on the margins also grasped the possibilities that law offered. Tribesmen, villagers, and merchants, along with princes, clerics, and scribes, turned to law with their own projects and ambitions. They generally had far less grandiose aims than the founders of the major legal traditions, but they were all seeking new ways to order their worlds. On the western fringes of medieval Europe, scribes in the miniature kingdoms of early Ireland and in the commonwealth of medieval Iceland wrote pages of complex laws. To the east, European and Byzantine laws inspired bishops, princes, and merchants in the early Russian princedoms, while a priest in Armenia created his own laws under the threat of expanding Islam. Largely pragmatic, their laws were shaped by custom and tradition. They also enshrined visions of social justice, religious discipline, and a sense that law should constrain their rulers.

WHEN ROMAN SHIPS first sailed across the Irish sea in the early centuries of the common era, they found a land of green pastures and scattered woodlands in which farmers grew cereals and tended herds of cattle.[1] The wealthy lived in hilltop forts, where they patronized the druids and quickly realized the possibilities offered by new forms of trade. Soon they were buying wine, fine cloth, glassware, pottery, and jewellery from Britain and Gaul, sending hunting dogs, foodstuffs, and slaves in return. They adopted agricultural techniques from the Romans, built water mills, and planted new strains of cereal. Production improved, the population expanded, and the rich accumulated more wealth.

Traders and missionaries also brought the ideas of Christianity to Ireland. After the Romans retreated from Britain in the fifth century, Pope Celestine sent a bishop to minister to the Irish who 'believed in Christ'. Sometime later, slave traders captured the educated son of a British farmer and transported him to Ireland, where he was set to work as a shepherd. He eventually escaped, but later decided to return to Ireland to spread Christianity. St. Patrick, as he became, readily appealed to the poor, whose lives he understood. He also converted many of the elite, possibly encouraging them with Roman examples. The wealthy duly summoned churchmen, patronized bishops, and founded churches, while devout converts formed small communities to lead celibate lives and the intrepid set sail on perilous craft to take their religion to even remoter shores.

Irish clan leaders had by now established themselves as rulers, and in the sixth century there were about 150 'kings' on the island. Around them clustered groups of a few thousand 'clients', known as their *túatha*, to whom the kings granted livestock, land, and protection in return for produce, services, and loyalty. A few of the Irish kings established superiority over others, claiming tribute from lesser rulers and summoning their free-men to regional assemblies, and ultimately five set themselves up as superior kings in each of Ireland's provinces.[2] But none succeeded in claiming authority over all the island. For most people, it was their relationship with their immediate king that counted. All freemen were expected to enter into a client relationship with one of them and join his túatha. The kings consulted their freemen in public assemblies when they needed to form treaties, issue edicts, recruit soldiers, or resolve legal disputes. The 'half free' had less autonomy and were bound more closely to their kings, who granted them use of land and livestock. The wealth-iest also owned slaves, generally war captives, while the poor could descend into debt bondage, effectively slaves of the rich.[3]

The kings also patronized poets, lawyers, and clerics.[4] The poets, heirs to a long Irish tradition, recited songs, stories, and genealogies in which they glorified the kings and dramatized Irish history for their audiences. As professionals, they had to learn large numbers of texts before they could practise their craft. The lawyers specialized in reciting proverbs and maxims, passing on everyday wisdom about good and bad behaviour, morality, and social relations in memorable, often obscure sayings. Families of hereditary poets and lawyers now sent their sons to train in the new monastery schools. The growing community of clerics was meanwhile elbowing out the druids, who were eventually reduced to scapegoats in the crusade against paganism.

The poets and lawyers were both inspired and threatened by Christianity and its specialists, who had brought new techniques of literacy and learning to their land. They had a script, *ogam*, which they carved around the edges of standing stones to record genealogies and traditional wisdom. But literary Latin, inscribed on parchment, was far more useful, and poets and lawyers had adapted the script to their own vernacular by the seventh century. The resulting Old Irish was fearsomely complex, with fourteen noun declensions, conjugated prepositions,

infixed and suffixed pronouns, and a complicated system of initial mutations. The medieval poets and lawyers learnt and systematized its grammatical intricacies in the monastery schools,
where they also studied religious texts and the canon law. Then
they put their new expertise to work recording traditional Irish
wisdom. While the poets wrote genealogies, annals, and stories
of saints' lives, the lawyers developed Ireland's traditional proverbs and wisdom into sets of laws, possibly copying the form
of the Christian canon law.[5] Over roughly one hundred years,
from the mid-seventh to the mid-eighth centuries, they covered
quantities of parchment with dozens of texts, which run to six
volumes in the modern edition.[6]

Many of the Irish laws concerned the sorts of practical problems that arose among Ireland's farmers: how to divide land
among heirs, how much compensation should be paid for injuries, and which offences deserved punishment. Relations of honour and revenge still shaped the ways in which the Irish thought
about their social groups. As among the Germanic tribesmen,
payment of compensation was the basic way to resolve many
disputes. The Irish laws specified compensation payments for
murder and injury; penalized trespass, theft, and the felling of
trees; regulated legal procedures; and made rules for contracts,
loans, pledges, and sureties. Naturally, many laws concerned
farming and described different types of land, as well as regulating the maintenance of fences, roads, and tracks. They also
specified penalties for trespass by livestock and damage to trees.
The lawyers went into intricate detail on surprisingly mundane
topics, such as categories of dogs and cats, livestock values, the
treatment of fostered calves, and the qualities of horses.[7] Beekeeping presented one scribe with a uniquely challenging set of
problems. The Irish valued their bees, using the honey both as a
sweetener and a medicine, and catching swarms was one of the
few types of work allowed on a Sunday. But bees are difficult to
control and swarms regularly escape to neighbouring properties.

One lawyer tried to apply the rules on property ownership and liability for livestock to the practice of beekeeping. When this did not work, he looked for useful parallels in the laws on the management of mill-streams that crossed multiple properties and rules about the produce of trees that overhung a neighbour's land. Using these as precedents, he produced a text with complex rules for beekeepers. Its legal intricacies can hardly have helped farmers who had to rush off with baskets and smoking brands to chase down a swarm as it crossed fields and hedges. But the scribe obviously enjoyed the intellectual challenge of his task, just as the Roman jurists had done many centuries before him.[8]

Almost half the Irish laws concerned social status. All freemen had an honour price, and wrongdoers had to pay that price if they insulted, injured, or satirized anyone; if they stole someone's property, or that of his kin or dependents; if they refused anyone hospitality; or if they raided someone's house or molested his wife or daughters. One law even provided that if someone borrowed festival clothes and failed to return them promptly, he had to pay the honour price to compensate the lender for the embarrassment of being improperly dressed.[9] One's honour price also affected the quality of the oath one could swear in a legal case, with consequences for the proof of a claim. Honour prices marked out social status, that is. They distinguished three ranks of kingship, several classes of freemen, and the unfree. The laws also classified professional groups—the clergy, lawyers, and poets—specifying their skills and duties. They described physicians, smiths, carpenters, musicians, and entertainers, and one text talks of jugglers, jesters, acrobats, and professional farters.[10] Others discuss the social positions of wives, sons, foster children, more distant kin, tenants, and lunatics, and how they should be treated.

Although the Irish laws clearly demarcated social groups, many were inordinately complicated. The laws on the grades of kings specify the exact number of their clients, while the distinction between two classes of freemen is expressed in specific herd and house sizes. Reality cannot have been so precise. When the texts stipulated the qualities of different professionals in such great detail, requiring that judges had to be experts in Irish law, poetry, and canon law, their legalism was more scholastic than practical. They also specified fines and honour prices in terms of two abstract measures, the *sét* and the *cumal*. Sét originally meant 'wealth', later 'cattle', and cumal literally meant 'female slave', but both terms came to be understood as units of currency—one cumal, for example, might be considered equivalent to so many sét. In practice people would have worked out amounts in whatever items of value they had on hand, typically silver, cattle, or grain.[11] Like some of the Germanic legal codes, the Irish laws attempted to impose order on what must have been far less tidy and more varied social relations.

The legal texts go into great detail about the duties of judges, to whom parties could turn with really serious disputes.[12] Not only did a good judge need know Irish law, canon law, and poetry, but he had to be prepared to give a pledge in support of his judgement and to swear on the gospel that he would speak the truth. A judge was liable to pay a fine if he judged a case improperly—for example, by listening to only one party. The texts set out complicated rules for legal procedures and even for styles of reasoning. A judge had to state whether his decision was based on a 'legal verse', a maxim, a scriptural text, an analogy, or 'natural law'. There were also rules about oaths, ordeals, duels, and the use of witnesses and sureties. If facts were disputed, the judge needed witnesses of truth, who might have to undergo an ordeal to establish their veracity. If the case turned on an oral agreement, a surety would need to prove the making of the contract. Other cases, as one text explains, could concern 'justice', as, for example, when goods turned out to be less valuable than anyone had thought. This needed a different type of evidence.

Meanwhile, dependent people or those from the lowest classes needed to obtain guarantees from their kin or their king.[13]

Despite all this intricate legalism, the kings provided no means of enforcing the resulting judgements. A successful party not only had to pay the judge but also had to rely on family members to force wrongdoers to pay up. Quite distant kin were liable to account for the wrongs and debts of family members, who could also call upon them to help prosecute their own cases or give security. They were liable to be drawn in on both sides of a dispute. Successful parties might have to 'distrain' for what they were owed, that is, take it directly from a debtor or one of his sureties. The texts surround these practices with complex rules. A creditor could ritually enter a debtor's land in order to persuade him to accept the authority of a judgement, but if the debtor was of high status, the creditor had to give him notice and then fast for several days before he tried to distrain. This was effectively to force the debtor to pay up, or to offer security, or else to challenge the debt by starting his or her own fast. The texts probably make these procedures seem tidier and more rule-bound than they actually were, but it is clear that the Irish took their legal cases seriously and worried about the quality of the processes and the justice they produced.

Why did the Irish pour so much effort and resources into all this legalism? Some of the earliest Irish legal texts largely consist of maxims and verses, suggesting that the authors were recording the oral wisdom of their poets and lawyers. They later wrote in plainer prose and eventually developed a highly literary style. But many texts take the form of questions and answers, apparently modelled on the practices of teachers, who probably used them to train law students and aspiring judges. Lists of examples and discussions of etymologies suggest similar purposes.[14] One text on marriage disputes, for example, distinguishes the different circumstances that might lead to a divorce, with different consequences for the bride price, and goes into some detail about the evidence that would be needed to support a claim.[15] It then lists a number of practical problems that the judge might have to consider, including how a woman could prove that she was menstruating on a particular day. The text seems to reflect the sorts of examples a teacher might use to challenge his pupils in legal reasoning. The Irish laws recorded traditional wisdom and formalized the rules that judges could and should apply in court cases, then. But the writers were primarily thinking of their students, discussing the laws they should apply rather than setting them out in an authoritative way as a ruler or legislative assembly might do. In the end, the texts presented a complex web of laws, which made Irish society seem much more orderly than it actually was.

Still, the Irish lawyers made bold claims for the importance of their laws. One text maintains, implausibly, that the laws had introduced status distinctions into Ireland in defiance of the foreign canon law, which asserted equality between all men.[16] The scholars may well have started simply by recording the ideas already circulating in maxims and poetic verses, but they promoted the idea that judges needed to refer to the rules of their texts in order to establish truth and justice.[17] This also, of course, confirmed their own authority as legal experts and, at least in theory, limited the legal authority of the kings. Several texts emphasize the reciprocal relations that should exist between a king and his people. It is the people, they state, who appoint the king, and he, in turn, has to support and protect them and to act justly if he is to keep disasters and plagues from afflicting his realm.[18] He has to eat the right foods, maintain the right sorts of fortresses, and keep the right sorts of company. If he refuses hospitality, shelters a fugitive from justice, tolerates satire, eats stolen food, or betrays his honour, the king will lose his honour price, the text warns, effectively forfeiting his status. One text even describes how the king should spend his week: on Sunday he should drink ale, on Monday hear legal cases, on Tuesday play board games, on Wednesday go hunting, on Thursday have sex, on Friday go to the horse races, and on Saturday hear more legal cases.[19] This startlingly schematic text was probably grounded in old traditions—for example, that the king should provide ale for his people—and it was using these to illustrate the structure of the new Christian week (although, interestingly, it makes no mention of worship). But it also underlined the idea that the king was responsible to his people. He was bound by the laws, just as they were.

By inscribing ancient wisdom onto parchment, the lawmakers must have provided Irish people with a strong sense of their history and identity. The church and its clerics may have acquired land, patronage, and authority, but alongside the poets' genealogies and stories, the laws would have given people a sense that there was a proper way to live, one that was rooted in their land and their history. They were Irish laws for Irish people. It would be too much to credit the laws alone with the failure of any single king to consolidate power over the whole island. But they must have given articulate people greater confidence to stand up to authoritarian behaviour, and to insist on what they felt was proper conduct on the part of their kings. As well as guiding judicial practice, the texts constructed a legal edifice that could, at least at times, have provided checks on the exercise of power.

After around a century of intense legal activity, the Irish scholars seem to have considered that they had finished their task and practically ceased to write new texts. Instead, they continued to read and comment on the old laws, much like the medieval Italian scholars who wrote detailed glosses on Justinian's texts. The original authors had tried to address contemporary problems, but in later centuries it was the antiquity of the old Irish laws that gave them authority.[20] Meanwhile, the ruling dynasties of each province contended for power, although none succeeded in uniting Ireland before it was overrun by the Normans in the twelfth century. The invaders introduced the English common law into the areas they controlled, but their hold over many parts of Ireland was tenuous, and Irish judges continued to use their traditional texts. By the sixteenth century, they were quoting laws that were nearly nine hundred years old. But power and politics prevailed, and when the Irish were eventually brought under the jurisdiction of the English law, their texts finally disappeared into the libraries.

WHILE THEIR BISHOPS were founding monasteries, other Irish converts to Christianity sought more extreme modes of devotion and embarked in fragile coracles over the seas to the north and west. By the eighth century, a number of them had reached Iceland, where they established a tenuous foothold in a virtually empty land and lived ascetic lives. Three-quarters of the island was covered in volcanic ash and glaciers, and even the river valleys were too cold to grow anything other than barley and peas, but this unpromising environment attracted new settlers. A wave of Norwegian longships arrived on the island in the late ninth century. Despatching the Irish hermits, the Norsemen established themselves in turf houses, where they dug gardens and cultivated small fields. They did some fishing but also built up herds of sheep and soon came to depend upon meat, milk, and wool for subsistence. The settlers flourished, and over the next two hundred years the Icelandic population increased from a few thousand to something close to one hundred thousand. Scattered through the valleys and coastal lowlands, they formed a commonwealth and resisted any form of kingship for almost four centuries.[21]

The first wave of Norse settlers established an annual meeting, the *Althing*, which all adult men were supposed to attend. Here, the island's freemen gathered for two weeks every midsummer to hear public announcements, receive summonses, listen to speeches, and resolve disputes. As they spread farther around the coasts, the islanders established new 'quarters', each with its own *Thing*, and these were further divided into three local Things, which were convened annually by three local chieftains. The head of every household had to declare allegiance to one of these chieftains and attend their local Thing. They could also attend the Althing, and the wealthy had to contribute to its cost. It was, at least initially, a remarkably democratic form of government. The chieftains took responsibility for maintaining order in their regions, overseeing communal matters (such as allocating meadows), dealing with people who shirked communal duties, and organizing maintenance for the poor. They established courts to hear legal disputes, considered allegations of theft or sorcery, and were expected to confiscate the property of outlaws. They also had to attend the Althing and convene their local Thing, first purifying the ground on which it was to be held.

At the Althing, the Lawspeaker would recite the island's laws. This position had been established at the first meeting and it remained fundamental to Icelandic government. The Lawspeaker had to recite each of the island's laws at least once every three years, so that ordinary people could hear and remember them. He also trained young men to be legal experts. The Lawspeaker sat with forty-eight chieftains (and later two bishops) at a council, known as the *Logretta*, which made new laws, heard and answered queries about existing rules, and considered petitions for exceptions or exemptions from particular laws and obligations. But, as in Ireland, the Icelandic laws appear excessively complicated.

It was literacy that first prompted the Icelanders to write down their laws. After their initial rudeness to the Irish Christians, they listened more receptively to the teachings of missionaries who travelled to their island, and one hundred years later the Althing decided that all the Icelanders should adopt Christianity.

The missionaries had also brought literacy. The Althing commissioned a small group of scribes to write down the island's laws in 1117, and this set a precedent. At each Althing, the Logretta commissioned an exercise of review and revision to take place over the following winter months. A torrent of legal creativity ensued, and each year the Logretta approved new laws. By the end of the century they had made and amended so many laws that the three-year recitation rule had become unworkable. The Logretta had to make a citation law to tell people which of the rules, now written on vellum scrolls, were still in force. The legal texts were finally collected into a single lawbook a few decades later. It stretches to seven hundred densely printed pages in the modern edition.

Even if the lawbook included some laws that were already obsolete, the effort indicates that the Icelanders were enthusiastic legislators. They regulated farming practices in minute detail: farmers were required to make the most of their land and cultivate it to the maximum extent, presumably so that they could contribute to the costs of the Things, and they had to be scrupulously fair to their neighbours. One law demanded that they separate out any hay that had blown onto their land from a neighbour's field and return it.[22] The laws also gave detailed instructions for processes that could not have been at all common, including the way in which people should dig up and move old graves, in case they needed to transport them to a new site. This particular law specifies the number of neighbours who should be called upon to help, the tools they should use, and the time they should begin digging, and it directs that the men must search for bones as carefully as if they were looking for money.[23] Here, the law goes beyond a statement of basic rules that everyone might be expected to follow to describe ideal procedures.

Other laws do seem to have had more practical applications, including laws about maintaining family members and dependents. In some cases, a man might have to compel his relations to accept him into debt slavery in order to fulfil these obligations. There were different obligations concerning the maintenance of spouses and natural kin. The laws specified that members of a family had to apportion some of the liabilities among them. The great Icelandic sagas, written later, in the thirteenth century, often describe disputes arising from a failure to maintain kin, indicating that these were real and important issues for the Icelanders. Further complex rules governed the payment of blood money (compensation for a killing). They stipulated not just the total compensation but also how it should be divided among a wide circle of kin, down to fourth cousins. These minute fractions would have been unrealistically complicated to calculate; in many cases it was probably not even possible to divide a coin into small enough pieces. But the rules served to mark out membership of the wider kin group.

Family was important in Iceland. Poor people depended on their relations for economic support, and to bring an important legal case it was necessary to gather a crowd of supporters. So a wide circle of kin enhanced power and status. Blood money was not itself used to mark differences in status, as it did in Ireland and among many Germanic tribes, and as far as the laws were concerned, everyone was equal. But in practice wealth did bring status. The rich had obligations to contribute to the costs of the Althing and to maintain the poor. Having the resources to bring legal cases also established honour. The less powerful had to transfer their cases, for a share of the proceeds, to someone who had greater capacity. Status, then, could be acquired through wealth and family connections, although it could just as easily be lost.

The Icelanders' written laws indicate complex legal procedures. To hear serious cases, the chieftains were supposed to select thirty-six men to form a court. These were mostly farmers, so they gathered in a field, sitting on rocks as they considered the evidence and arguments. More complex cases might go to the court convened by the quarter, where they would be heard by thirty-six judges; the highest court, held at the annual Althing, included thirty-six of the judges nominated by each of the island's forty-eight chieftains. The lawbook contains almost one hundred pages of complex and formalistic procedural rules. It seems unlikely that they were always followed, especially since most judges were not specialists, just farmers gathering to do justice. But in difficult cases they could ask the legal experts who surrounded the Lawspeaker for guidance. Everyone clearly thought that legal cases should proceed properly.

Cases were also spectator sports. Large numbers of people gathered to hear the most interesting and salacious. Pauper children staged plays based on lawsuits, and even servants got together to hold mock trials.[24] And yet the chiefs provided no officials or other means to support the processes or enforce their judgements. The parties had to bring their own claims, secure the attendance of witnesses, organize the hearings, and ensure the judgement was respected, something that required both time and resources. But the islanders do seem to have respected the decisions of their courts. They commonly ordered payment of a 'three-mark' fine, and in really serious cases the judges could declare an offender to be an outlaw, banishing him from the island for three years. Records indicate that courts often had to make arrangements to support the dependents of an outlaw, implying that the islanders did collectively enforce these orders.

The sagas offer tales about feuding, violence, and bloodshed, which probably make Iceland society seem more violent than it actually was. In fact, many of their stories revolve around legal disputes and court cases. An ethos of competition, honour, and revenge pervades these stories, extending to dramas that unfolded at the Things. They give the impression that as well as fighting with fists and weapons, people competed in legal contests and fought out their rivalries in local and regional trials. The Things, councils, and courts may have provided ordinary

Icelanders with the opportunity to challenge others for status and power, but they also reinforced the idea that they were governed by a single law. *Vár lög*, 'our law', meant all of Iceland, and the islanders considered that their laws were as old as their community.[25] Some even claimed that the law had roots in an earlier civilization, even if it had not always been written. It confirmed that the Icelanders were a single people who resisted the domination of any king.

This was the society the Nordic settlers initially established and the one represented by their laws. But it did not last forever. Over time, some chieftains managed to acquire more power than others and to exercise more control over the people and activities within their areas. The democracy of household patriarchs and the inclusive structure of the local and regional Things gradually broke down. By the mid-thirteenth century, only twelve chieftains remained from the original thirty-six. This small elite, perhaps feeling that it would benefit them to enter into alliances with more powerful monarchs, ended up giving over sovereignty of their island to the Norwegian kings in 1260. This also meant submitting to Norwegian laws. But the Icelanders did not allow their own laws to disappear. Though they were still scattered among a profusion of different manuscripts, scribes gathered them into a single lawbook. Known as *Grágás* (Grey goose), the collection is a monumental record of the Icelanders' literary and legal activities. Some of its laws may already have been obsolete when the text was written, and others soon would be. But the Icelanders clearly thought it important to create a record of what their laws had been. It was a titanic project, and it stood as a testament to the autonomy and traditions they were about to lose.

WHILE THE REMOTE communities of Ireland and Iceland were writing their own laws, inspired by the now-faded Roman tradition, all had not been lost in the east. Here, the church was the guardian of Roman laws, supported by the Byzantine emperors.

In the late tenth century, the emperor Basil II faced a revolt from two of his generals, and, in need of military reinforcement, he turned to the ruler of a large territory to the north of Byzantine lands, Prince Vladimir of the Rurikids. In gratitude for the prince's help in quashing the rebels, Basil allowed Vladimir to marry his sister. He also arranged for Vladimir to be baptized. Returning to his capital at Kiev in 988, the prince ordered that his twelve sons, along with his nobles, adopt Christianity. Then he declared that all of the city's forty-five thousand inhabitants should congregate on the banks of the Dnieper, where Byzantine priests would baptize them. Most complied, probably fearing the consequences of refusal. As they made their way to the river, they were doubtless impressed by the shattered remnants of the wooden statues of Norse, Slav, Finnish, and Iranian gods, which Vladimir himself had erected just a few years earlier.

The prince next ordered that the governors of other Rus towns should convert their populations. He founded a church in Kiev and issued a short statute in which he declared that he was granting the new institution financial support from his own resources. He claimed that he was following Byzantine tradition by giving authority to the church's courts to hear legal cases. These courts, he said, should consider issues of divorce, rape, abduction, and other family matters; accusations of sorcery and magic; and improper behaviour around churches. The new bishops were to have jurisdiction over clerics and their families, over pilgrims and wanderers, and over physicians, the blind and the lame, and people in monasteries and hospitals. They were also to take charge of weights and measures.[26] These events laid a foundation for the creation of the first Russian laws.

Vladimir's family, the Rurikids, were relative newcomers to Kiev, descendants of Nordic traders and warriors who had moved into the lands of what are now Russia during the eighth and ninth centuries. Here, they harried and eventually dominated the Slavic tribes and, over time, settled in small towns, where they traded furs and slaves. By 907, they had established constructive relations with their Byzantine neighbours and entered into a series of written agreements. Under these agreements, the emperors granted Rus merchants permission to stay and trade in Constantinople.

For a while, Rus warlords competed with one another for power, but eventually the Rurikids defeated their rivals and Vladimir established his capital in Kiev. By 985 he was, at least notionally, ruling a vast territory.[27] Thinking of himself as a prince, if not a king, and probably aspiring to the sophistication of the Byzantine emperors to the south, as well as the Carolingians to the west, Vladimir was entirely amenable to Basil's suggestion that he adopt Christianity.

Vladimir's death in 1015 prompted succession contests between the numerous sons of his various marriages. This was to be a recurrent pattern over the next few centuries. Eventually, Iaroslav Vladimirovich emerged victorious, and, like his father, turned to Constantinople for inspiration. In Kiev, he built his own St. Sophia, a smaller version of the great Byzantine basilica; sponsored public inscriptions in Greek; and commissioned new books for his church. By now Constantinople had appointed a metropolitan for Kiev, a senior cleric answerable to the Byzantine patriarch, and Iaroslav established bishoprics in several Rus towns. He also founded the Monastery of the Caves near Kiev, whose monks ordered a monastic rulebook from Constantinople.

At some point, Iaroslav issued a brief set of laws, the *Russkaia Pravda*.[28] Apparently designed to address cases of conflict among the Rus people, the first law specified who could take revenge for a killing, limiting it to close relations, with compensation due in other cases. The next rules specified compensation

for different sorts of injuries and theft, for insults, and for har-
bouring a slave, and gave directions about the sorts of evidence
a complainant needed to bring. These rather basic laws probably
reflected the sorts of problems that arose among the Rus nobility
in a society still shaped by tribal loyalties. It may be that Iaroslav
was motivated by the example of the Byzantine and Carolingian
kings, who counted lawmaking among the attributes of a Christian ruler. But, unlike his Germanic counterparts, he ordered the
scribes to write in the language of the people, Eastern Slavonic,
not the church's literary language, nor, indeed, Byzantine Greek.
His rules also show no trace of Roman influence. Iaroslav possibly created the *Russkaia Pravda* following a disturbance in the
city of Novgorod, as a means of asserting authority over this
distant and potentially rival town, but he cannot have expected
that the officials he sent to govern major towns, which included
several of his sons, would enforce the laws in any detail.[29] They
were, at best, guides.

For the most part, Rus farmers, merchants, and artisans followed their own customs and settled disputes locally. But, probably encouraged by the example of the laws and the documents
used by their clerics, Rus people began to write.[30] They found
that the peeling bark of their birch trees offered a perfectly good,
if smaller, alternative to parchment, and used pointed sticks to
scratch letters on the soft inner surface. The resulting feather-
weight curls could easily be carried over long distances. Soon
merchants were using them to record prices and give instructions to partners in distant cities. They requested assistance, sent
strongly worded complaints to those who had not paid them, and
threatened to take debtors to 'the town', that is, to the prince's
officials. Literacy soon spread beyond the mercantile classes.
Children learned to write and drew pictures on pieces of bark.
An icon-painter noted his commissions. A woman complained to
her brother that she had been slandered. Another woman offered
advice on running a household. A young woman complained

that her boyfriend was ignoring her, while yet another received a proposal of marriage, all on birch tree curls. Meanwhile, the parents of a young man consulted a matchmaker, a monk made excuses for having missed an appointment, nuns sent notes about the management of their convent, an official apologized that he could not supply fish, and someone wrote out an incantation and lines from a sermon.[31] Some people asked scribes to write out their words, but many were literate. Their missives contained instructions and records, rather than legal agreements, but they paved the way for more formal legal practices.

IAROSLAV ISSUED FURTHER statutes granting financial support to new churches and increased the powers of their courts. Merchants found they could sometimes obtain justice from bishops and senior clerics, who might persuade a recalcitrant debtor to pay up, but the courts were as much a threat as a practical resource. The widow of one merchant wrote to demand payment for a boat, pointing out that her husband had specified this debt before he died and that the priest had recorded it. So, she warned, 'give them to Lukas; if you do not, then I will fetch an officer from the prince and it will cost you even more'.[32]

Iaroslav's death in 1054 prompted another series of succession contests, but at some point, three of his more influential sons reached a compromise. They may have commissioned the expanded version of the *Russkaia Pravda*, a code with forty-three articles.[33] It now included rules on the compensation to be paid for killing men in the prince's entourage—the stable master, the field supervisor, contract labourers and peasants, wet nurses, and tutors—as well as fines for killing the princes' horses or livestock. The laws also specified penalties for theft—of boats, doves, chicken or other fowl, dogs, hawks, and hay or firewood. They forbade people to plough over border markings, and they distinguished between thieves killed by day and by night, effectively excusing those who surprised a thief during the hours of darkness. And they carefully specified different penalties for stealing beehives, bees, and their honey. These apparently random laws probably had the princes' immediate entourages in mind, and some may have reflected cases that their judges had decided. But there is no evidence that the princes distributed their laws widely or that any administrator applied them among the general population. Their officials collected tithes and raised taxes, but they exercised little administrative control over farming, herding, family relations, or artisanal activities in the towns and villages. The laws symbolized, rather than directly implemented, the authority of the Rurikid princes.

For most of the Rus people, custom (*obichay*) was more important than the laws of their rulers (*pravda*) or the moral directions of their priests. But the clergy continued their efforts to spread the practices of Christianity and stamp out pagan 'customs', appealing to a sense of *zakon*, a higher Christian law. Writing in the early twelfth century, the author of the Primary Chronicle, a history of Kievan Rus, declared that 'we Christians, of whatever land, who believe in the Holy Trinity, in one baptism, and in one faith, have one law [zakon]', and he criticized those who continued to think that ancestral custom was law.[34] The Byzantine church had drawn up several sets of rules to help priests guide their people towards Christian practices, which specified the penances for a host of different sins. Senior Rus clerics also encouraged priests to turn to them with queries. In around 1080, the Kievan metropolitan Ioann II published guidance he had given on assorted problems: whether a priest should baptize a baby too weak to suckle, for example, or an unclean mother should be allowed to feed her child. Could people ever eat carrion? How should the priests deal with those who ignored fasts, with adulterers, and with those who practised magic or sorcery? When should laypeople sit and stand during a service, what should be done with damaged icons, and what penance should be issued to separated couples, or to those who sold baptized slaves? The Rus clergy took their duties seriously in applying the church's rules.[35]

Some decades later, a monk from Novgorod recorded some robust answers he had received from a bishop on matters of discipline and ritual practice. He recounted how someone had brought the bishop a grouse during a feast only to receive an order from the cleric to throw it over the fence, since 'it would not be right to receive communion after eating that'. The monk also described how he had read the bishop a popular text claiming that a child conceived on a Friday, Saturday, or Sunday would become a robber, a fornicator, or a coward. The bishop had simply retorted, 'Those books of yours should be burned.'[36] And yet the bishop could be lenient: for example, he advised against disciplining a young priest who could not restrain himself from having intercourse with his wife on a Monday, in the prohibited period between the Sunday and Tuesday services.

By the early twelfth century, senior clerics were copying versions of Byzantine *nomokanon*s, compendiums of canon law and church pronouncements.[37] Monks drew up constitutions for their monasteries based on Byzantine models, which told their members how to sing monastic offices, make prostrations, read lessons, stand in church, and sit at table, as well as what to eat on which days, even though many of their rules, particularly on food and clothing, were inappropriate for the colder climate of northern Rus.[38] Soon, the clerics were debating what all these laws meant and how they should apply them.

The Rurikid princes continued to support the church, confirming the jurisdiction of the church courts. Meanwhile, the princes were adding to Iaroslav's laws. By the end of the century they had issued an expanded version of the *Russkaia Pravda* in 121 articles. They added rules on debt and interest rates, liability for goods lost in storage, protection for those who lost possessions in a shipwreck; rules on how to manage indentured labourers and slaves and how to deal with offences committed by them; laws on inheritance, on different types of slavery, and on how to deal with runaways; and more rules on beehives and a community's duty to track down stolen swarms. There were also rules for evidence and the witnesses needed by merchants when they claimed payment of debts or the ownership of stolen goods sold at a market.[39] The princes were now looking beyond matters that concerned their immediate circle and trying to regulate economic activities among the wider population.

A significant proportion of the urban population was by now literate, and they continued to write short letters to each other on birch bark. By the thirteenth and fourteenth centuries, people were writing instructions about unfinished business if they feared they were close to death, creating a form of will. As they pursued their business transactions, they began to issue receipts for purchases and to rely on written documents as proof of land ownership, which they could show to officials when there were disputes.[40] They were developing their own legal practices in ways that expanded the possibilities and certainties of their commercial relations. In the flourishing towns on the Baltic coasts, the Hanseatic League, an early trade association, linked traders in German and Scandinavian towns, and the most successful Rus merchants entered their networks. Merchants in Novgorod were particularly active in this trade, profitably exporting hundreds of squirrel pelts to foreign merchants. Eventually, in 1229, the city of Smolensk entered into a treaty with Riga to regulate the conduct of Rus traders in other Baltic cities, one of the agreements that laid the basis for the more systematic trade rules that eventually regulated relations within the league.[41]

THE TWELFTH CENTURY had seen further struggles for succession among the Rurikid princes, and the Rus were ill-prepared to resist the onslaught of the Mongol armies, who arrived in 1237. The invaders sacked Kiev and devastated the surrounding farmlands, but they did not stay, soon moving on to the west and leaving many of the governmental structures in Kiev intact. The Rurikid princes gradually restored order, although the Mongols of the Golden Horde insisted they should be able to approve, or reject, the Rus princes.

The metropolitan retained his seat in Kiev, and religious scholars continued their work translating and copying new ecclesiastic and legal texts, including a new nomokanon commissioned by Metropolitan Kirill.[42] The Rus scribes sometimes added notes on local customs; one even wrote out the rules of the *Russkaia Pravda*, bringing together the ecclesiastic and royal laws in a single document. Senior clerics remained concerned about discipline among their juniors, and at one synod Kirill bemoaned the country's woes. People had been scattered, cities taken, strong princes had fallen to the sword, and churches had been desecrated at the hands of godless and unclean pagans, and almost all of this happened, he said, because church canons had been ignored. He presented the synod with a new set of rules and made a rousing call for everyone, led by the clergy, to return to a more disciplined way of life. But however successful Kirill's call for discipline among churchmen may have been, further struggles for succession arose among the Rurikid ruling families. By the end of the thirteenth century, ascendant rulers in Poland and Lithuania had overrun parts of Rus's western territories, and Kirill's successor moved out of Kiev. Eventually, the princes of Moscow refused to recognize the Kievan rulers, paving the way for what was to become the Grand Duchy of Moscow.

An untidy assemblage of texts and rules regulated the lives of the Rus throughout this period. The *Russkaia Pravda* told the wealthy how to manage their labourers and slaves, but it hardly regulated property ownership or everyday farming activities. In the countryside, people largely followed their own customs, their obichay, and in the towns the authorities managed urban problems. Traders used birch bark to send instructions and developed standard forms and practices, some of which were recognized in the later version of the *Russkaia Pravda*. Those who engaged in Baltic trade relied upon international treaties and the rules of the Hanseatic League. Meanwhile, senior clerics urged all to follow the Christian zakon, and monastic communities followed their own constitutions and the detailed regulations of canon law.

Rus society was more complex and heterogeneous than that of the Irish and Icelanders. The Rus people looked to multiple sources of law, with different aims and ambitions, depending on who they were and what they were doing. The princes were inspired by grand lawmaking emperors, although they based their laws on practical issues; the church had penance and discipline firmly in mind; and ordinary people relied on custom and their own written documents, developing the beginning of legal forms to regularize their own commercial relations.

MEANWHILE, ON THE southern fringes of Rus and forming the easternmost lands of the Byzantine Empire, a mountainous territory between the Black and Caspian Seas was home to the Armenians. Even before the Byzantine conquest, Greeks, Parthians, Romans, and Sassanians had overrun their country, but these invasions were punctuated by periods of autonomy when Armenian kings united their people. They also adopted Christianity in the year 301, even before Constantine ended the persecution of Christians, and founded one of the earliest cathedrals in Christendom. From then on, Armenians retained their faith, even when their country was conquered by the Sassanians and incorporated into the Umayyad and Abbasid caliphates. Later freeing itself from the caliphates, Armenia became relatively independent, but by the eleventh century it had fractured into a number of small states, which were conquered by the Byzantines in 1045. By this point, the Muslim Seljuks were already threatening the eastern territories of Byzantium, and as they moved westwards they overran Armenia in 1071. The Muslim emirs deposed the Armenian kings and lords, but some of them managed to escape. Fleeing south and west to the shores of the Mediterranean, they established the Armenian kingdom of Cilicia, which flourished from 1198 to 1375.

Throughout these upheavals, the Armenians remained resolutely Christian. Priests and bishops continued to minister to their people, founding churches and monasteries, many perched spectacularly on rocky outcrops in remote gorges. And they translated the pronouncements of the major Christian councils held from the fourth century onwards. Gradually, they expanded the Armenian canon of ecclesiastical literature. Defying the Seljuks, one cleric created a manual for priests, a 'penitential', in the early twelfth century, in which he advised Armenian priests how to hear confessions and apportion penance, basing his work on the Book of Leviticus. But the bishops were understandably concerned about the effects of the Muslim occupation on the faith of their people, and it troubled them that the Seljuks did not accept Armenian forms of justice, insisting that all disputes should go to their own courts, where Armenians would be subjected to Islamic law. So the bishops encouraged their scholars to create an Armenian law code, and several rose to the challenge. Some translated the Syrio-Roman law code, while others turned to codes of the Byzantine emperors Constantine and Leo, along with military regulations made by the Greeks. But it was a respected priest and teacher, a *vardapet*, named Mxit'ar Goš, who put together the most successful and enduring manual. Beginning his work in 1184, he created the text that Armenians thought of as their law into the sixteenth century.

Mxit'ar Goš based his text on material from the Old Testament along with the Armenian canons and the penitential recently created by his compatriot.[43] He started with the roles of judges, secular leaders, and ecclesiastics and then went on to marriage, divorce, and children. He interspersed these sections with laws on princes and peasants, and the majority of the 251 clauses appear somewhat random. Careful scholarship has revealed that Mxit'ar simply took extracts from his different sources, transcribing rules and commentaries from parts of each in turn, so that the provisions on marriage, for example, are scattered throughout several different sections. Many of the laws concern church matters and the work and authority of the vardapets, but others deal with secular issues, taking laws on farming from the Books of Exodus, Leviticus, and Numbers, and adding rules that probably reflected Armenian custom on farm animals, the wrongful cutting of crops, arson, mills, and livestock sales. Mxit'ar occasionally acknowledged that he was drawing on oral sources, particularly in his discussion of divorce, defences to homicide, and marriage between kin. And scattered throughout are pejorative references to Muslim customs. He directed that Armenians should engage with them, if at all, in ways that avoided adopting their most problematic rules.

In a lengthy introduction to the laws, Mxit'ar explained that by having their own law code Armenians would be able to avoid the infidels' courts. The book, he declared, would enable them to recall the right law for any particular situation. Just as important, it would indicate to foreigners 'that we live by a code, so they will no longer reproach us'.[44] He clearly hoped that Muslim officials, used to dealing with literate qadis and scholarly muftis, would be impressed by his code and more willing to allow Armenians to run their own courts. But Mxit'ar also explained that, as well as laying down penalties to be meted out by courts and enforced by rulers, he was offering religious guidance and discussing appropriate forms of penance. In all likelihood inspired by Islamic law, with which his own religion was now in competition, he set out to create rules for conduct with moral and spiritual aims as much as laws designed to be applied in practical situations. Spiritual concerns, he emphasized, should always take precedence over written codes. Mxit'ar did not, that is, present his text as a definitive law code, and he described its rules as neither the redaction of ancient custom nor a comprehensive guide to practice. Nevertheless, he was confident that it would allow the Armenians to avoid being drawn into the Muslims' courts.

Armenians embraced the code despite its rather provisional and unsystematic nature and its very tentative introduction, and over the next century different scholars produced two revisions. While Mxit'ar had assumed that only bishops would administer justice, for example, the later authors extended legal jurisdiction to local princes. They also tried to separate out the religious and secular material. A third revision added more customary rules on practical and nonecclesiastical subjects.[45]

Meanwhile, the Armenian kingdom in Cilicia prospered. Its kings hosted many of the European crusaders and established a base for the head of the Armenian church. In 1265, the brother of the king, also one of his senior officials, undertook a further revision of Mxit'ar's code. He wrote in the Cilician vernacular, the language spoken by the people of the region, and reordered the subject matter, presumably to make the code more practical. His text started with articles concerning the king and the nobility, continued with military and ecclesiastic affairs, moved on to marriage and inheritance, and then set out regulations for mercantile activities, the position and management of serfs, and rules for compensation. From its rather hesitant beginnings, Mxit'ar's text had now become a practical set of rules for people trying to maintain their autonomy against the imperial ambitions of far more powerful neighbours.[46]

Armenian Cilicia eventually fell to the Muslim Mamluks in 1375, but this did not spell the end of Mxit'ar's law code. Under the Seljuk onslaught three centuries earlier, many Armenians had fled northwards into what is now Ukraine. The Mongols captured Kiev in 1240 and many Armenians moved on again, this time westwards to Galicia and Volkynia, where they clustered in the larger towns. Here they established their own quarters, where they worked as goldsmiths and silversmiths, painters, and weavers and built their own churches. Their numbers increased in later waves of migration, and many merchants built up successful businesses and trading houses. When the Polish king Casimir III occupied the region in 1340, he recognized their economic importance and granted the Armenians, along with Jews and Ukrainians, the right to maintain their own traditions. He also declared that they could practise their own laws. In the larger towns, such as Lvov, the Armenians now established their own courts, where elected elders sat with judges to hear legal cases. At least nominally, they applied the laws of Mxit'ar Goš. They created a new edition of the code, which they translated into Latin so that the Polish king, Sigmund I, could read it. The king approved its use in 1519, although he insisted that cases involving murder, physical injury, damage to property, and theft should be tried in the city's tribunal.[47] The style of justice meted out in each court may not have been very different, but it was important to the Armenians that they maintained their own traditions and their own laws.

Over the following centuries, Armenians played a major role in networks of eastern trade, travelling through Russia, the Crimea, the Ottoman Empire, Persia, India, and beyond. They established numerous small colonies in distant lands, where they continued to consult Mxit'ar's code. Rules extracted from the Bible and the Christian canons in the twelfth century may not have been of great practical use to Armenian traders living in the ports of Bombay and Calcutta, but their code was their own. It represented the fact that they were maintaining their laws and customs. Rules rather tentatively drawn up by a pious vardapet, with symbolic as much as practical aims, had become the law of a dispersed people and a long-standing marker of nationhood.

THE CIVIL AND common law systems were still tentatively taking shape in Europe when the princes, scholars, councils, and priests of Ireland, Iceland, Rus, and Armenia wrote down their laws. They largely adopted the casuistic form of the Roman tradition, but most had pragmatic purposes. Their laws reflected local customs and social problems and offered rules for evidence and the resolution of disputes. But there was almost always a sense that the laws represented higher principles, a vision of how the world ought to be. The Russian princes aspired to the law-making practices of their Byzantine and Germanic counterparts, and their bishops ordered texts from Constantinople and adopted the disciplinary forms of the Christian penitentials. Mxit'ar Goš wanted to demonstrate the Christian commitment of his people, probably inspired by the laws of Seljuks, and his law code came to stand for the nationhood of a dispersed people. The more pragmatic Irish and Icelandic laws also had higher purposes. Their complexity suggests a social vision, a higher intellectual order. They were the laws of independent and fair-minded people, who knew how to govern themselves and could control the power of anyone who might impose on them.

CHAPTER EIGHT

EMBRACING THE LAWS OF RELIGION
The Hindu, Jewish, and Muslim Worlds

The great religious systems of the Hindus, Jews, and Muslims concentrated on duties more than rights. They created rules to guide individuals in their daily lives, spelling out how they should act in accordance with their dharma or by following God's path for the world. Eventually, millions of people lived under the directions of the Hindu Dharmashastras, according to the laws of the Torah, or by the rules of Islamic legal texts, at least in principle. But these religious rules impinged on people's lives in very different ways, mediated by priests, scholars, local councils, and community pressure. Many also tried to adapt them to local circumstances, using rules and techniques developed in distant times and places to address their own pragmatic social concerns.

MEDIEVAL INDIAN PEASANTS took most of their legal disputes to village councils and local mediators. These people were familiar

205

with regional customs and practices. But medieval Indian society was also shaped by the ideas of the Hindu brahmins and their legal texts. The oldest of the Hindu laws, Manu's Dharmashastra, written in around the second century of the common era, had inspired an outpouring of writing on dharma. Over the next few centuries, the Indian scholars affirmed and elaborated the hierarchy of social status that put the brahmins and ruling classes above the castes of commoners and servants. The religious specialists established a system of religious authority that was largely independent of any ruler's political power, and gradually, they exported this system to much of the subcontinent.

In most of southern India, herdsmen and farmers formed tribal groups until the fifth and sixth centuries, when they developed more intensive agricultural systems and diversified their activities.[1] Tribes gradually gave way to villages, towns, and market centres; people took on more specialist occupations; and local leaders increased their power, eventually assuming the status of kings. Many of these rulers welcomed the brahmins who migrated from the north. In exchange for ritual services, they granted them land, protection, and relief from taxes. As brahmin families acquired land, they continued to work as religious specialists, and both rulers and ordinary people sought their advice on ritual and legal issues.[2] The brahmins' ideas about ritual practice, purity, and hierarchy, along with the social rules expounded in their texts, gradually spread throughout the subcontinent.

In practice, issues of caste status and occupation demanded much legal attention from the brahmins. But they generally did not trouble themselves with minor quarrels, and peasants and artisans were uninterested in learned opinions on matters of trade practice and agricultural custom. All Indian people were rooted in social groups, generally more than one, which defined their social obligations to their neighbours, families, partners, and associates. The Dharmashastras made it clear that kings should recognize these customs and laws. The Arthashastra, the guide for kings completed at around the same time, directed that the royal bureaucracy should record the laws, transactions, customs, and rules of regions, villages, castes, families, and corporations.[3] A twelfth-century commentary on Dharmashastra refers to the agreements that could be made on important matters not only by groups of brahmins but also by guilds, itinerant traders, merchants, military units, castes, cow herders, regions, towns, villages, and families. Each of these, the text directed, was to recognize its own dharma, its own practices, and its own duties. An inscription from southern India recognizes the jurisdiction of merchants' groups to regulate the activities of their artisans and punish offenders who breached their rules. Even 'heretical' sectarian groups, Buddhists and Jains, were allowed to make their own rules.[4] Without doubt, most rulers found it expedient to allow them to do precisely this.

In reality, many of the groups overlapped, and people were often governed by multiple directives simultaneously. An individual weaver might have to recognize the rules of his guild, the directions of his village council, and the orders of the temple that owned the village land, as well as the obligations of his caste, as directed by the shastras.[5] Guilds agreed upon rules to regulate their working practices, including sanctions for anyone who breached them; groups of potters and weavers regulated the materials, quality, and styles of their products; and merchants got together to set prices and fix standards for quality and weights. An inscription from Karnataka in southern India refers to groups of tradesmen, including betel-leaf sellers, oilmen, sealers of flour, and other merchants, who would punish assaults, theft, tax evasion, looting, and breaches of contract by their members, as well as any failure to contribute to the local temple. Herders and soldiers also formed groups, and caste groups demanded that their members participate in ritual performances and controlled practices of marriage, diet, and dress. Buddhist monasteries drew up rules to tell their members how to eat, beg, and interact with the laity.

Most groups did not reduce their rules to writing except when a dispute arose and they felt it would be prudent to record a settlement. These were hardly laws. But occasionally, powerful individuals and local groups got together to draw up an agreement on how to manage communal affairs. Maybe the temple was in need of extension, or the water reservoir, a communal pond, or garden had fallen into disrepair, or a natural disaster had brought vulnerable families to the edge of starvation. They might also arrange to manage and finance rituals, including rites of passage for destitute orphans or for migrating groups.

For the most part, the rules of local groups were much more present in people's everyday lives than the laws of the Dharmashastra or the commands of their king. But occasionally groups did present rules to their king and ask him to disseminate and guarantee them. And while elders or members of a caste council could confirm ritual duties and expectations, they might ask a brahmin to advise in tricky cases of marriage or inheritance arrangements. Could a father marry his daughter to his wife's widowed brother-in-law? Apparently not, according to one brahmin's response. They might also consult the specialists if they were unsure whether a crime had been committed, particularly slander or assault.[6] The brahmins' advice barely distinguished law from ritual practices.

When the Muslim Mughals swept onto the Indian plains in the sixteenth century, they introduced systems of Islamic law and reduced most of the Hindu kings to vassals. But the sultans allowed the existing rulers to continue their religious practices and to follow the ancient legal texts as they managed their people and resolved their disputes. The basic ideas in the Dharmashastras, particularly the hierarchy of caste, continued to shape people's lives. At times, so did the more technical rules about property transactions, inheritance, and evidence. But the brahmins' texts were never supposed to regulate the lives of the lower castes in any detail. Left to their own devices, most social groups made their own rules, often adopting the legal forms they learned about from the more literary practices of their kings and priests.

★

MANY MEDIEVAL JEWS felt equally distant from the Geonim, the highest scholars. But from Roman times, most lived in close-knit communities, dispersed around lands that were soon occupied by Muslims, and they were conscious of the rituals and traditions that distinguished them from surrounding populations. This meant that Jewish laws usually played a prominent role in their lives.

Beginning in the seventh century, when the Umayyads conquered Palestine along with most of the rest of the Middle East, many Jews came to speak a version of Arabic, although they wrote it in Hebrew characters, and they adapted their lives and activities to the customs of the towns and cities where they settled. When the Abbasids established their capital in Baghdad in the mid-eighth century, the Geonim continued their work, but by now the Jewish diaspora had established other centres of learning, not least in North Africa and Spain, and they continued to respect the authority of their rabbis and the laws of the Torah.

Many new commercial opportunities arose at this time, as valuable goods flowed in from the east, and through much of the Middle Ages Jewish merchants participated in a lively trade around the Mediterranean. In the tenth century, the Fatimids rose to power in North Africa, expelling the Abbasids from Egypt. This was a turbulent time in the Middle East, with the arrival of the Seljuks in the late eleventh century, the launch of the Christian crusades, and the onslaught of the Mamluks in the mid-twelfth century. Even before the Mamluks conquered Syria and Egypt, in 1250, there were plenty of hostile forces to trouble the Fatimid armies, but their rulers hung on to power for two centuries. Egypt was an extraordinarily fertile region—it had long supplied the Roman Empire with wheat and was now exporting flax in large quantities—and the Fatimids established their capital in a new city at Cairo.[7]

Cairo replaced the old capital at Fustat, just two miles to the south, but Fustat remained an important commercial centre and was home to many Jews. Everyone, caliphs and warlords alike, recognized the importance of the merchant vessels that plied Mediterranean waters and the caravans that brought valuable goods from the east. So despite the conflicts, most people respected the merchants, who travelled between Constantinople, Sicily, and the maritime cities around the Mediterranean. Egypt received goods from ships that arrived in the Red Sea after long journeys from India and the far east, and Fustat was the emporium into which foreign goods initially flowed, and where customs dues had to be paid on consignments intended for foreign lands. It was the merchants of Fustat who supplied the rest of Egypt with foreign currency and commodities—including shoes, clothing, tools, parchment, and ink.

Many of the Fustat merchants were Jews. Their communities blossomed under the Fatimid caliphs, who largely left them, along with the Christians, to organize their own affairs. As long as they paid a poll tax to the government and complied with its regulations, Jews were both welcome and protected. For the most part, they clustered in the urban centres, particularly Fustat and Alexandria, where many amassed considerable wealth. A number owned vineyards, orchards, and fields, while some worked as artisans or physicians, and a few even took positions at the royal court. But in the main cities they were overwhelmingly merchants. Here, they lived in neighbourhoods clustered around a synagogue, to which they could walk on the Sabbath. But the Fatimids did not establish ghettos, and Jewish families took apartments in blocks alongside Muslims and Christians.

They also established hostels where foreign merchants could stay, stable their pack animals, and store their goods. Like the caravanserai on the silk roads, their courtyards were always piled high with sacks of raisins, barrels of honey, and packs of hides or mats, and the Jewish quarters of Cairo thronged with travellers from Sicily, Pisa, Genoa, Seville, and Palestine. They did business with Muslim and Christian traders as well as fellow Jews.

It was the synagogues that anchored the Jewish communities. There were two Jewish congregations in Fustat and one in new Cairo, each with its own synagogue and rabbis. Originally made up of immigrants from Babylon and Palestine, by the eleventh century the two at Fustat were competing with each other for members, offering honorary titles, and boasting of their magnificent Torah scrolls, fine carpets, and superior services. But relations between them were normally good. Each synagogue's main building and courtyards were big enough to hold all the men of the area, who gathered to hear the Torah, religious teachings, and public announcements and to discuss public affairs. The assemblies would also make decisions about the maintenance of the synagogue, the appointment of its officials and committees, the provision of education for poor children, support for widows, care of the ill and disabled, and ransoms for captives. The assemblies could not officially make rules that would bind the whole population, so the documents recording their decisions were often signed by everyone present. But, in practice, their decisions were respected by the community as a whole.

The local Jewish leaders (often known by the Arabic title of *muqaddam*), performed both religious and legal duties. They maintained peace and unity within their communities, decided questions of religious law and ritual, gave religious teachings, and supervised the education of children. Assisted by a board of elders, they signed contracts, issued rules, and represented their communities in negotiations with government officials. Most importantly, they had to authorize marriages and divorces and hear legal cases. Over time, the influence of scholars back in Palestine on the Egyptian Jews faded, and a secular leader for all the Jewish congregations emerged in Cairo.[8] From 1065, the Fatimid authorities recognized this leader as a prince, the Jewish *nagid*, or *rayyis*. The nagid, if he had sufficient support, would hold office for life. His most important role was to act as an intermediary with the government and its officials. When pirates from Tripoli captured a ship containing one of the Geonim and his family, for example, the nagid approached the commander of the caliph's fleet to rescue the captives.[9] In turn, the Fatimid authorities would go to the nagid if they needed assistance in assessing and collecting taxes from the Jewish population, although the nagid did not himself raise taxes, and collecting funds for charitable purposes remained the responsibility of the synagogue committees.

As far as the Cairo Jews were concerned, they lived by the Torah. This was the source of the laws the rabbis explained in their synagogues and which men taught to their sons. And it was what set them apart from their Muslim and Christian neighbours. Even if their customs, clothes, and food were not so different, they worshipped in their own religious houses and took advice from their own scholars on how to conduct their personal and religious lives. Most were probably aware that their rabbis and judges sometimes consulted even higher authorities in Jerusalem and Baghdad, scholars whose names their rabbis pronounced respectfully during prayers.

In 1896, two Scottish women travelling in Cairo came across a rare Hebrew text, which a merchant told them had come from a *geniza*. This was the storeroom of a medieval synagogue in which the congregation had deposited its old texts, not wishing to destroy anything that bore the name of God. Like the Chinese grave texts and the Dunhuang scrolls, many of them were legal documents, largely dating from the eleventh and twelfth centuries.[10] It is evident from these geniza documents that each synagogue employed a small group of scribes, members of a tiny literate elite, who recorded the decisions of judges and committees and drew up the documents that individual Jews and their families needed in their personal and commercial lives.[11] They drafted marriage contracts, bills of divorce, and deeds of manumission, all of which usually stated that they were made according to 'the law of the Jews', 'Moses and the Jews', or 'Moses and Israel'. Court documents bore the same notation. When a judge issued a summons to the husband of a woman who had threatened another with 'necromancy and bone-rattling', for example, it stated that if the husband delayed attending court, the judge would take action 'according to the law of Moses'.[12]

In theory, it was the community that remained the final legal authority, and sometimes petitions or agreements were addressed to 'the elders and congregation' or 'the children of Israel'. In fact, according to tradition, individuals who felt they had been wronged could interrupt public prayer in the synagogue 'to call on the Jews for help', and the petitioner would stand on the reader's platform to prevent the reading of the Torah. In one incident, an angry congregant even tried to lock the Torah shrine. Women with a complaint had to find a male friend or relative to do this for them. The elder sisters of two orphan girls, for example, had apparently seized the family home while their brothers were away, and the wronged girls persuaded a friend to raise their case publicly the very next day.[13]

Each of the three major congregations had its own chief justice appointed by the nagid, and in really important cases they would form a court together.[14] But more often, they sat alone or delegated cases to other judges they appointed. They also recognized and approved decisions made by more informal tribunals. Groups of elders or merchants would get together to settle a

dispute, perhaps calling on a trained scribe to draw up an agreement in proper legal form, but they could act in more pragmatic
ways than judges. In one case, a merchant sold some substan-
dard wine shortly before he set off for Athens. By the time the
buyer discovered the problem, the seller had disappeared, so he
brought a case against the merchant's father. A judge refused
to hear the petition, on the basis that the father was not legally
responsible for the commercial activities of his son. But a group
of 'upright elders' successfully pressured the father to pay compensation, and the written agreement records that he eventually
paid every instalment.[15]

The Cairo judges would hold their courts on Mondays and
Thursdays, continuing a tradition from Palestine, where courts
were held to coincide with markets.[16] In these sessions, they
heard depositions, examined witnesses, and studied relevant documents. A large case might require a dozen court sessions over
as many months, particularly when the judges faced loquacious
litigants. 'They made many statements which, to report, would
lead us far afield', one scribe complained.[17] When the evidence
was disputed, the judges would, as a last resort, require the parties to swear an oath as to the truth of their testimony. This
was done in a ceremony designed to impress and terrify. The
judge removed a Torah scroll from its ark, draped it in black,
and placed it on the communal bier, where the ceremonial trum-
pet, the *shofar*, was a reminder of death and the last judgement.
Then the witness made his oath, which often included awesome
curses, in the name of God and the Ten Commandments. Even
women had to enter the men's section of the synagogue to hold
the Torah when they took the oath. If two merchants disagreed
about a contract, the accuser took the oath, after which the accused answered 'Amen', to take the consequences on himself. In
practice, as was the point, the elders were often able to negotiate a settlement just before the parties were due to undergo this
fear-inducing process.

In the absence of an immediate settlement, the judge investigated and decided on the central facts of the case, and then the parties, or the judge himself, presented it to one or more experts for a legal opinion. Sometimes the scholar in question would refer it on to someone even more senior, and in a really important case the parties might request advice from the Geonim in Jerusalem or Baghdad. On receiving the opinion, the judge would again encourage the parties to settle, which they often did. Indeed, judges would try hard to achieve this and avoid having to judge the case, because giving an erroneous judgement amounted to applying the law of the Torah incorrectly. If further attempts to settle failed, and the judge still harboured doubts, he could refer to his superiors, or the parties themselves might approach the nagid and ask him to instruct the judge how to decide, in a sort of reverse appeal. To exert pressure on their opponents, merchants might also threaten to apply to a Muslim court, which could entertain cases involving Jews, particularly if one of the parties was a Muslim. Jewish leaders, however, strongly disapproved of this route.

If they decided that a wrong had been committed, Jewish judges could order payment of a fine. In serious cases, the death penalty was also a possibility. One accused declared that he was prepared to suffer execution if it was proved that he had cursed the head of the Jerusalem academy. But flogging and banishment were more common. Case records from the eleventh century indicate that a careless religious butcher was flogged and forced to make a confession, as was a carpenter who had let his gentile employees work on a Saturday. Expulsion from the Jewish community was more serious. No Jew was supposed to have any dealing with someone who had been expelled, even to the extent of talking or shaking hands, let alone offering food or shelter or entering into business transactions. Nor could the outlaw be admitted to a synagogue or allowed a burial. The Cairo judges threatened to expel one insolvent debtor who had broken a solemn promise to pay his creditors a percentage of their debts; they did the same to a woman who had brought her brother before a Muslim court using false documents.[18] According to one legal document, horrible curses accompanied an order for expulsion. But once it had been made, the person had a certain time within which to 'clean himself', which generally meant accepting the court's judgement.

Expulsion was also a sanction that could work across borders. The Cairo documents include an expulsion order made by a court in Aden after it heard that a Jewish merchant from Baghdad, then living in India, intended to abscond to Sri Lanka and avoid his obligations.[19] In these cases, the judges could send orders to their counterparts in distant lands. Equally, the Cairo judges might have to act on orders made elsewhere or consider the validity of a commercial agreement drawn up in Spain or Sicily. But it was a small world, and they would often recognize the signatures of the judges who had authorized the documents in distant places.

The Jewish judges applied some laws strictly, including those on inheritance. They even felt obliged to apply the laws on levirate marriage, whereby a brother might marry the widow of his deceased sibling in order to continue the family line, even though the original rationale for the rule hardly applied in urban Fustat.[20] But over the centuries, they had to adapt some of their laws to new economic conditions, and their contracts often concluded that they were written in a form 'instituted by our scholars and used in the world', meaning mercantile custom. The Jewish legal scholars also adopted pragmatic attitudes. When a trader consulted one of the Geonim about the validity of bills of exchange, which were not traditionally enforceable in Jewish law, for example, the scholar declared, 'Our scholars have said that one should not send bills of exchange, but we see that people actually use them; therefore, we admit them in court, since otherwise commerce would come to a standstill. We are giving judgement in accordance with the laws of the merchants.'[21]

The most famous of Cairo's Jewish scholars was Maimonides, who had fled Almoravid Iberia in 1148 and made his way to the Fatimid court. He was appointed as a physician to the sultan and soon established a reputation as a respected scholar. He, too, allowed compromises in his work on commercial law. His *Book of Acquisition* describes the traditional Jewish law on contracts, which held that an oral agreement was not binding. In sixty-six long paragraphs, he explained how different types of objects should be acquired, but he then conceded that 'land, slaves, cattle, and other movables', in effect anything, 'may be acquired by symbolic barter'. The purchaser, he explained, merely had to hand over some article, of however small a value, in exchange for 'the yard, wine, cattle, or slave', which then became his, even before he had paid the purchase price. This was, in effect, to sanction oral agreements. He recognized that they were essential to the smooth running of Mediterranean trade.

Egyptian merchants of all confessions entered into partnerships and agency agreements and drew up contracts about the division of profits and losses. They also made arrangements for bailment, whereby they held goods for others or deposited their own with someone else, using careful language to specify their arrangements. Most only lasted a number of months, after which the parties would take an account of their business and divide the remaining goods and money, but if a venture was successful, they might renew the arrangement. They were generally careful to document all these transactions using proper Jewish forms.[22] The laws of the Torah, drawn up several centuries earlier in the largely agricultural lands of Palestine, were hardly sophisticated enough for these complex legal arrangements, but merchants and their scribes continued to follow them as far as they could.

THE CAIRO MERCHANTS often entered into commercial relations with partners from overseas, and international trade presented its own legal difficulties. The widely spread Qaraite minority, who did not recognize the Torah, developed different legal forms for contractual arrangements, which were different again among the Muslims. In one case, a scribe at the rabbis' court in Acre had to authorize the sale of cheese by a Qaraite merchant to Rabbanite purchasers in Cairo. Sheep's cheese was a staple of the Middle Eastern diet and many merchants made handsome profits buying up supplies in Sicily, Crete, and Palestine and shipping them to Egypt and India. In this case, the scribe certified the quality of the merchant's consignment and its suitability for Jewish consumption, but he had to resort to clever legal technicalities to satisfy both the Rabbanite and Qaraite traders, who recognized different rules for oral contracts.[23] Marriage arrangements also differed between Jewish communities, and scribes would have to use formulae from both when drawing up a betrothal agreement between a Rabbanite and Qaraite, which did sometimes happen. Some eleventh-century contracts stated that they had been made 'according to the statutes of our scholars and the laws of the state' or 'the laws of the gentiles', followed by both Aramaic and Greek formulae.[24]

When they drew up marriage agreements, scribes sometimes resorted to the legal formulae they used in commercial arrangements. But in the twelfth century, they began to set out the parties' duties and expectations in much more detail, generally giving more rights to women than before. Some agreements forbade a husband to force his wife to move to a new home, for example, or forbade him to take another wife or acquire female slaves without her permission. One scribe sought approval from the nagid for a new set of phrases, asking him to translate Muslim precedents into Arabic. Changes in Muslim practices had encouraged Jewish women and their families to ask for the new protections, which the scribe wanted to incorporate into a traditional Jewish contract.[25]

The Cairo Jews of the eleventh and twelfth centuries were more fortunate than some of their contemporaries. In Yemen, Muslim rulers threatened Jews with apostasy, which moved Maimonides to write his famous text in their defence, the *Epistle to Yemen*, in 1172.[26] But for long periods in the Middle Ages, the ruling classes in Spain, Italy, and much of northern and eastern Europe valued their Jewish communities. The Jews, in turn, adapted to local circumstances, which enabled them to flourish in different contexts. Their leaders, judges, and scholars generally recognized the needs of merchants to adapt to local commercial contexts and enter constructive relations with partners from different backgrounds. But scholars continued to consult the Torah and the texts of the halakha. And like the Hindu landowners, who used *shastric* forms for their transactions, they insisted on technical legal rules and forms to make commercial agreements dependable, marriages valid, and claims coherent, and judges followed the procedures prescribed by their traditional texts. These rules and requirements connected them to a wider religious world. Based on the sacred texts of the Torah and often the subject of rabbis' sermons, their laws distinguished them from both their Muslim and Christian neighbours.

ALONGSIDE THE JEWS, most of the populations that lived around the southern shores of the Mediterranean, in the Maghreb, were Muslims, and they respected their own texts and legal traditions.[27] All knew that the shari'a laid out a path for right conduct and that there were correct and incorrect ways of saying prayers, performing ablutions, donating to religious foundations, and dividing property. As among the Jews, they generally did not see any hard and fast distinction between the rules that governed social relations and those that concerned moral conduct. Nor did their legal specialists insist upon one. Islamic law was part of a wider set of moral norms that sought to promote an ideal society by regulating the moral and ethical conduct of believers.

In practice, ordinary people would consult their muftis, local legal scholars, when uncertain about the small rituals of daily life. But they also turned to them to resolve the sorts of arguments that people have everywhere, about buying and selling property, access to water and other resources, marriage and divorce, the status of illegitimate children, and so on. In these cases, both the mufti and the local judge, the qadi, might be called upon to help resolve a dispute. The qadi took primary responsibility for legal cases, but he might well turn to a mufti to advise on uncertain points of law. And it is from the records of these legal specialists that we know much about how medieval Muslims lived and the legal troubles they faced.

By the twelfth century, Fez, in modern-day Morocco, had become one of the largest cities in the world. The Marinids, tribal Berbers, had migrated northwards to take advantage of the faltering Almohad regime and eventually took over most of the Maghreb region, distributing its lands among their kinsmen and loyal soldiers. But the new sultans faced a number of rebellions by the urban populations, not least in Fez, and realized they needed to control the local elite. So they embarked upon a religious programme, building and supporting mosques and religious schools and establishing the first madrasa in North Africa. Their orthodox version of Islam attracted large numbers of students. By the fifteenth century, Marinid power was waning, but Fez remained an important centre for scholarship. And in 1469 it provided a refuge for an important legal scholar, Ahmad al-Wansharisi.

Wansharisi had fled Algeria after incurring the wrath of the Zayyanid sultan, and in exile in Fez he was delighted to run into one of his former students. This member of an important local family invited the teacher to his house and showed him the magnificent collection of manuscripts his family had gathered over many years. It included thousands of judicial documents and fatwas, which they invited Wansharisi to study. The scholar hired two donkeys and loaded them up with the most interesting documents. After carefully guiding them back through the narrow streets, he arranged two huge piles of documents in his courtyard. They provided work for the next eleven years, during which he copied out around six thousand of them into a text known as the *Kitāb al-Mi'yār*. His text documents brought together legal opinions issued by Maliki muftis over a period of five hundred years.[28]

The chief qadi in Fez took responsibility for resolving most disputes, although the Marinid sultans also held councils, while regional qadis dealt with local affairs. Most held court at the Friday mosque or in their homes, where citizens asked them to certify legal transactions, authenticate witness statements, and confirm the authenticity of previous fatwas, as well as to consider legal disputes. The qadis had to assess the evidence carefully and hear both parties, and they could only pass judgement if the witnesses' testimony was reliable according to Maliki rules. If it was not, but the qadi felt that there was still a case to answer, he could instead act as a mediator. And in either case he could call for a legal opinion, a fatwa, from a respected scholar. This would often help him persuade the parties to accept an outcome. In a straightforward case, he might simply need confirmation of legal doctrine, which he could obtain from an ordinary mufti. On a complex point of law, the qadi would consult one of the most distinguished jurists.

These were the legal opinions that formed the thousands of fatwas in Wansharisi's collection. In the legalistic medieval Islamic world, maritime commerce, the status of non-Muslims, religious endowments, and even Christian festivals raised difficult issues, which people took to their muftis. A large proportion of the fatwas concern inheritance, probably reflecting a common source of disputes. Islamic law provided that property-owners had to leave the majority of their property to their children, with sons receiving twice as much as daughters. But the rules often gave rise to arguments, particularly when a property-owner tried to circumvent the rules—for example, by putting some of his property into a family endowment. This action required documents to be in the correct legal form and properly witnessed. Disgruntled relatives who otherwise stood to inherit would often challenge their validity. Detailed arguments over the words and how they should be interpreted might follow. The qadi might invite both parties to swear an oath as to the validity of the document. A 'complete, binding, legally valid oath' would confirm it, while refusal would not.

Many of the fatwas concern other types of family relations. In one case, a young man named Salim claimed to be the natural child of one Ali, head of a leading family in Fez. Ali had recently died, and Salim made a claim on his property, which his other children contested.[29] Salim had been born to a slave who belonged to Ali's daughter, who was then living in her father's house, where Salim was raised. The main question for the qadi was a simple one: was Salim Ali's son? In the absence of direct evidence, Salim gathered no less than ninety witnesses—relatives, neighbours, friends, and professional witnesses—to testify that they had heard Ali refer to Salim as his son, that Ali's other children had referred to him as their brother, and that townspeople regarded Salim as Ali's son. The qadi questioned them carefully to make sure, in particular, that when Ali's children had referred to Salim as 'our brother', they meant it literally, not just as a figurative reference to common humanity. Ali's other surviving son had gathered contrary statements, but the qadi largely rejected them on cross-examination because, as he pointed out in the documents he later sent to the mufti, they did not deny that Salim had been raised in Ali's household. The qadi also considered that Ali's failure to acknowledge Salim publicly could have stemmed from a fear, reported by one of the witnesses, that sexual relations with the slave of his daughter were illegal, something that was not, in fact, the case. Still, the qadi was troubled by the fact that Salim, in his original statement, had denied that his mother belonged to Ali's daughter, which obviously undermined his credibility. So the judge sought the opinion of several local jurists, who confirmed his inclination to accept Salim's claims. But, presumably because the case had attracted considerable attention, the qadi still felt the need for caution, so he sought an opinion from a very eminent mufti. This fatwa confirmed the qadi's assessment of the evidence and commended his exemplary attention to detail.

Many other fatwas in Wansharisi's collection concern issues of legal procedure and the quality of evidence, including the probative value of a rumour, the status of evidence given by nonprofessional witnesses, and the admissibility of second- or thirdhand evidence. Property ownership caused numerous disputes among the Maghrebi populations, and one set of fatwas concerns a long-running dispute between two villages over a river in the Atlas Mountains.[30] This rather barren area had been settled several hundred years previously by enterprising farmers, who had constructed dams, canals, and water-lifting devices which allowed them to irrigate the surrounding area and plant fields of barley, flax, and hemp as well as olive groves and orchards of fig and mulberry trees. The dispute between the villages was caused by a series of droughts from 1284 onwards. The lower village, Mazdgha, complained that the higher one, Zgane, was taking so much water that their own lands and orchards were parched. They had a right, they claimed, to a fair share of water in a year of scarcity. The qadi asked a mufti for an opinion, and the mufti declared that according to legal principle the first village to have established its mills, gardens, and settlement should take precedence. Since both villages were ancient, however, there was no satisfactory evidence one way or the other; thus, the water should continue to be shared between them. He seems to have left it to the qadi to specify how the shares should be worked out. A second mufti confirmed his opinion, and a third, consulted a short while later, expressed the view that the issue was whether one or other of the villages had 'appropriated' the water, by, for example, channelling it into dams and canals. But, again, the lack of evidence did not allow for any definite decision.

Another drought, thirty-seven years later, in 1321, prompted further argument between the two villages. The chief qadi in Fez now sent investigators to map out the area, including all the water sources, dams, and canals. They produced a meticulous report, but again, it did not prove the rights claimed by Mazdgha. Twenty years later, Mazdgha again went to a qadi, who sought two further fatwas. Both muftis now expressed the view that Zgane, the upstream village, owned all the water, so that Mazdgha was only entitled to use what Zgane did not need. Although this was certainly problematic for Mazdgha, it clearly did not make their situation impossible, for the village was still there in 1421, when another drought prompted the residents to return to court. This time the qadi sent the case to the most distinguished mufti in the region, who wrote an extensive fatwa in which he reviewed all the evidence, reports, and previous opinions. The mufti carefully combed through all the possible circumstances in which Mazdgha might have established a right to water: the villagers had claimed that they had been the first to construct canals and fields, for example, that they had received an express or implied gift from Zgane, and that they had a legitimate claim through express or implied use rights. The mufti concluded that there was no evidence for any of these claims. He referred to a record of the Prophet's life, which briefly described an instance in which Muhammad had given priority to an upstream community. On this basis, the mufti declared that Zgane owned the water. This citation of an original Islamic source seems to have resolved the issue once and for all, albeit disastrously for the inhabitants of Mazdgha. The documents do not relate how the two villages fared over the next decades and centuries.

Over the 150 years or so during which their dispute had simmered, the villagers' economies and livelihoods must have fluctuated greatly, with droughts, floods, demographic changes, and technological developments. Yet throughout, the law itself did not change. Even if the muftis finally adapted it to new circumstances, no one seems to have doubted that it remained a fixed element within the flux of environmental events and human fortunes.[31]

FOR ORDINARY MUSLIMS, then, Islamic law, the fiqh, offered a sense of stability, as did the legal forms developed by their scholars for property transactions. In the Touat, a desert region of Algeria, for long on the fringes of the Islamic world, farmers and traders settled in tiny groups around small oases. Here, they constructed communal irrigation systems to feed the fields and date plantations from which they eked out a living.[32] In the fifteenth century, Muslim qadis arrived to guide local populations towards more Islamic ways of life, establishing themselves as religious authorities. They advised local councils on how to record property arrangements and irrigation agreements, and soon the local populations were employing scribes to write out documents for the most mundane transactions, which they carefully preserved in their archives. Conducting research in the twenty-first century, an anthropologist discovered hundreds of slips of paper that the local populations had rolled up and crammed into hanging baskets in complete disorder. Deciphering the faded and cramped writing, she found that the Touati scribes had used Islamic legal forms to record quite mundane arrangements, often in ways that made no obvious practical sense. They had adopted traditional

Islamic formulae to declare a grant of land or water to be 'total, irrevocable, and permanent', for example, even if it was obvious that the fields in an oasis often reverted to desert and irrigation channels silted up. Several documents parcelled out shares of water using confusing and unworkable measurements. Even more puzzling, some divided up and sold property in precise fractions, including donkeys, courtyards, and, in one case, a toilet. It was apparent that the scribes had used legal forms devised long ago for land transactions in Arabia to distribute property that could not sensibly be divided.

So why had it seemed so important to these remote Touati farmers that they should use precise measurements and standard Islamic categories? The Islamic legal forms must have represented the civilization of a larger world to people leading fragile lives in a remote Saharan oasis. Scratching out a living on the edge of a desert, the Touatis must have constantly felt threatened by the encroaching wilderness. But, as Muslims, they could turn to the divine for protection. This meant following the shari'a, God's path. By using Islamic legal forms and language, they transformed local transactions into elements of a larger Islamic civilization, one that promised them a degree of permanence. This was what the shari'a and its scholars also represented for the people of Fez.

NOT ALL MUSLIMS were so keen to incorporate Islamic legal forms into their daily lives, however, and some instead created their own legal texts as markers of independence. This was the case for the Daghestani people, who lived in the dry and mountainous region that lies to the east of the Caspian Sea. Several ethnically distinct groups inhabited this precipitous terrain for many centuries, constructing intricate irrigation systems to bring water to small areas of flat land and tending cattle, sheep, and goats on the high pastures. Fought over by Romans and Sassanians, the region was absorbed into the early Arab caliphates, and in the tenth century most of the population adopted Sunni Islam. The Seljuks barely ventured north of Armenia, but the populations remained Muslim while Mongol horsemen swept through, before the region again became subject to Muslim rulers in the form of the Persian Safavids. These were challenged, in turn, by the ascendant Russians, who tried hard to annex the territory several times over the next three centuries, finally expelling the Persians in the early nineteenth century.

Throughout these unsettled times, most of the Daghestani population took advantage of the difficult terrain to pursue largely autonomous livelihoods.[33] Thinly populated mountainous regions are notoriously difficult to govern compared to lowlands where agriculture produces surpluses, rulers amass wealth, and towns can be established. The Daghestanis mostly formed village communities, which in turn united as confederacies, in a pattern that endured into the nineteenth century. A number of prominent families set themselves up as lords, *khans*, and in theory owned the pastures in their regions, which they rented to local families in return for military assistance. The most powerful khans persuaded local confederacies to pay them tribute and provide troops for raids or defence, but most were only able to control the villages that lay closest to them. Especially in the mountains, the majority of communities acted independently. In 1830, as Russian forces penetrated more deeply into the region and took the measure of their new subjects, one of the generals declared contemptuously that the local khan was unable to do anything without calling an assembly, and that his people offered him food and livestock 'as if by charity'.[34]

The Daghestani people thought of themselves as forming clans, united by extended family ties, but for all practical purposes they formed villages, centred on groups of fields and pastures which included members of several clans. Meetings of the adult men took charge of village affairs and resources, selecting three or four leaders to manage day-to-day matters. These leaders, in turn, appointed assistants to help them supervise agricultural and herding activities, decide when the farmers should start sowing or harvesting, and oversee the systems of rotation by which the villagers protected their crops from the communal herds of livestock during the summer months. The leaders also organized village meetings, summoned people in dispute to the village court, and levied fines on anyone who breached village rules. At the end of a year of office, all had to swear an oath on the Quran that they had performed their duties correctly and collected all due fines. If they failed to do this, they were themselves liable to pay a fine. Alongside these leaders, the village elected legal experts, maybe twelve at a time, to whom anyone with a legal dispute had to take his or her case. These experts were responsible for announcing legal decisions, both judgements in individual cases and new village laws. They would ask for witnesses to support disputed claims, and someone accused of wrongdoing might have to call family members to support his or her innocence by swearing an oath—the graver the charge, the larger the number of oath-takers. There is little evidence of the ways in which cases were heard or judgements enforced, but securing payment of fines, generally expressed in head of cattle or measures of grain, would not have been difficult in a small community.

Most Daghestani villages developed similar methods to coordinate their agricultural and herding activities and similar systems of property ownership and conflict resolution. Fields and buildings could be privately owned, in which case villagers were not allowed to sell them to outsiders. Some fields belonged to the mosque, which it leased out for its support. The leaders ensured that the villagers ground the corn harvested from the mosque's fields and baked bread for the Ramadan feast. There were also communally owned fields, pastures, and woods, and the leaders carefully controlled how the villagers used these common lands and their produce. They protected public wells and pools, specifying fines for anyone caught polluting them, and they required villagers to form work parties to maintain roads, bridges, and gates. Each village jealously guarded its autonomy and its property and prevented its members from allowing the cattle of other villages onto their pastures, or even giving hospitality to strangers for too long.

Historically, Daghestani people had always raided each other's livestock, sometimes initiating long-running blood feuds, and in order to secure more widespread peace, they often entered into agreements to limit attacks and retaliation. Over time, a number of villages might combine into a confederacy. These confederacies could unite anything from a group of small settlements, functioning almost like a single community, to a group of twenty major villages spread over a vast territory. Their leaders would establish an organizational structure by holding general meetings, electing leaders, and hearing legal cases. Although it was much more difficult to exercise control over a fragmented group than over a single village, many confederacies were established by legal documents. The villages used treaties and agreements to regulate relations between them as well as between villages and confederacies, or with their khans. For the most part, the communities used their documents to try to limit violence and antagonism, especially by forbidding or limiting individual acts of retaliation and confiscation. These were the same problems that the early Germanic kings had faced. In other documents, the Daghestanis specified the right of a khan to receive taxes, or the fines from legal cases or services, from his people. Like the Irish, many Daghestani communities felt entitled to specify and limit the rights and powers of their lords.[35]

These written agreements began to appear in the eighteenth century. There had always been unrest in Daghestan. Inter-village raids, environmental disasters, attempts by khans to assert control over their villages, battles between Russian and

Persian forces, and ultimately Russian attempts to control the region all generated conflict and even outright violence. And this may have convinced some of the more literate villagers that it would be prudent to cement alliances in written treaties. This realization may, in turn, have encouraged them to think they should use written agreements to preserve order in their own communities. In any event, from the eighteenth century, several villages started to write down important decisions taken at their meetings, and these included the judgements made in legal cases.

The villagers presumably intended that these decisions should act as precedents in future cases. To begin with, they simply recorded their decisions on pieces of paper, or even on the cover of their village Quran. Most reflected agreements that the villagers had recently made, rather than matters of ancient custom, in contrast to the Irish and Icelandic laws. Some of the simplest recorded the fines that had to be paid for basic offences. One might begin, for example, with, 'The people of the village of Asab have agreed that he who steals a cow has to give . . .', or record a fine given to someone who allowed livestock to walk across a graveyard.[36] Others dealt with the offences of murder and manslaughter, injury, theft, arson, other damage to property, family matters, slander, debts, and fraud. Some villages eventually gathered their records together in more or less systematic ways. The more substantial collections also described the political organization of the village, including rules for the use and protection of communal resources and the consequences of negligence by shepherds. Others sought to enforce religious duties. Over time, the Daghestani villagers came to think of their rules as *'adat*, the Arabic term for customary law.

Confederacies, too, bound treaties and agreements together in lawbooks, which might present narratives on the history and geography of the region alongside an overview of the agreements made between its villages and settlements. These often concerned the handling of offences, or records of agreements between different villages not to help each other's enemies. Some also provided for military defence and the protection of the community. But several recognized the autonomy of each village over the affairs of its members and even penalized individuals who appealed to the confederacy court without permission.

Recording agreements and rules on paper seems a sensible way to manage local affairs, at least to modern eyes, but in these relatively small villages most people must have known each other, and social pressure was probably an effective means of enforcing good behaviour. Many communities do perfectly well without codes of laws, and written rules can less easily be changed and adapted to new circumstances. So why did the Daghestani villagers think it was useful to put time and effort into writing down their laws? And why did they record them in Arabic, rather than in the local language, which would have made them more accessible to the general population? Maybe they were inspired by the literate practices of their religion and the example of the shari'a. Complicated relations between villages and confederacies and the need to create secure alliances may also have prompted written agreements. Regardless, the texts must have reinforced a sense of village community and confederacy solidarity in the face of external forces. They represented them as a single community, which could combine to resist the aggression of other villages, ambitious khans, and even Islamic clerics.

By 1828, the Russians had concluded peace treaties with the Persian Qajars and the Ottomans which confirmed their possession of the Caucasus.[37] But they found it difficult to assert control over the mountainous regions. The Daghestanis were independent people, ready to fight outsiders and resist the advances of the cumbersome Russian army. In the face of continuing Russian aggression, a number of charismatic Islamic leaders were able to unite both the Daghestanis and the neighbouring Chechens in a fierce and prolonged military resistance. Launching a *jihad* movement that lasted for three decades, the Imam

Shamil effectively established an Islamic state in the region in the 1850s, with councils and deputies who could transmit his commands and raise taxes and troops. He also attempted to enforce an orthodox form of shari'a among the people, appointing qadis to hear legal cases and pass judgements, and he described the local 'adat as 'un-Islamic, heretical, and Satanic'.[38] And yet, although keen to resist Russian incursions, most Daghestani villagers were not impressed by the tactics of these imams and distanced themselves from their religious conservatism. Some of the village rules made during this period recognized, or even required, that the village should have a qadi to administer religious endowments, collect and distribute the Islamic tax, recognize and dissolve marriages, and settle inheritance disputes. But many village lawbooks only paid lip service to the shari'a.[39]

Rather than reflecting a higher religious order or the wisdom of ancient scholars, the Daghestanis' 'adat agreements and lawbooks represented their own collective decisions. They were practical rules and documents, intended to maintain order in and between villages and confederacies and to help litigious people resolve their disputes. But they were also a confident assertion of autonomy in the face of competing claims to power and authority. The leaders of the Daghestani confederacies were inspired by distant legal traditions to make laws that asserted the importance of their own customs and history.

MEDIEVAL INDIAN PEASANTS, Mediterranean merchants and townsmen, Saharan villagers, and Daghestani tribesmen all tried to live according to the rules of their religion, respecting its laws and the obligations they imposed. The laws gave them directions for daily life, specified forms for commercial transactions, and allowed judges to resolve disputes, and they were respected as much as enforced. And they shaped the lives of ordinary people in very different ways. For most Indian peasants, like the Daghestani tribesmen, religious rules and experts were relatively distant. The scribes adopted basic legal forms, instead, to make their own laws, which addressed pragmatic concerns and confirmed their own customs and history. A sense of communal agreement gave these laws their force. Religious legal specialists and their texts were far more present in the lives of Jewish and Muslim merchants and townspeople. Their laws offered people a sense of identity, a means to distinguish themselves and their communities from the surrounding populations. They represented a religious order, an order of duties and obligations, which transcended the pragmatic concerns of daily life. But all seem to have offered a sense of stability amidst the uncertainties and flux of daily life.

CHAPTER NINE

IMPERIAL LAW AND DIVINE JUSTICE
IN MEDIEVAL CHINA

The disciplinary legal systems of the Chinese emperors
created a highly legalistic world for the citizens of their
empire. Already under the Tang and Song dynasties of
the sixth to thirteenth centuries of the common era, China's rulers established courts in the remotest corners of their empire.
Here, ordinary people were expected to seek justice and magistrates tried to discipline them into acting as good imperial subjects. The law prescribed harsh punishments, especially for the
lowest classes, and reached far into the daily lives of ordinary
people. It imposed, quite successfully, an order of discipline on
a huge population.

Contemporary reports talk of gruesome punishments, bribery, and corruption, but the image of heavy-handed discipline
was probably more dramatic than the reality. In practice, Chinese litigants and magistrates wrestled with bureaucratic forms,
laws that didn't quite fit the case at hand, the difficulty of establishing the truth, intractable litigants bearing pointless grudges,
and the delays and defects of a bureaucratic system of justice.
Even illiterate peasants and herdsmen, who generally did their

235

best to avoid local courts and officials, became used to dealing with legal forms and bureaucratic requirements.

BY THE TURN of the first millennium, Chinese rulers had established the most extensive and legalistic administrative structures to be found anywhere in the world. And legalism had seeped into the lives of most ordinary Chinese people, including their relations with the afterlife. Documents recovered from a grave dating to the fourth century BCE include legal petitions that people had presented to their deities.[1] They indicated that a bureaucratic pantheon of spirits, headed by a supreme deity, managed a realm of troublesome ghosts, officious spirits, and deceased souls. One deity, the Director of Fate, calculated mortal life spans, and if someone seemed close to death, relatives would petition the deity in a desperate attempt to secure a reprieve. A bamboo slip from this period recounts how a dead man rose from his tomb after family members beseeched the deity to reexamine his records. After considering their petition, the Director of Fate agreed to issue an instrument of resurrection.[2]

These practices continued over the following centuries. Documents from the late Han period, in the second century CE, include memoranda by which people informed the deity about the arrival of a newly deceased, using forms required by their government when they travelled between districts.[3] They buried their dead with lists of grave goods, so that underworld deities could check them, along with contracts to prove ownership of their grave plots.[4] Family members petitioned underworld judges to declare the deceased not guilty of any crimes, fearing the activities of the spiritual prison scribes, messengers, and police, and the punishments they could mete out. And Daoist priests, whose religion flourished under the Han, assisted petitioners by drawing up documents to respond to the legal activities of a discontented ghost who might have issued proceedings against them in the underworld.

In the world of the living, local magistrates sitting in the *yamen* of the Qin (221–206 BCE) and Han (206 BCE–220 CE) dynasties heard hundreds of cases each year. They consulted dozens of legal texts and meted out an array of punishments, all carefully calculated to match the rank and status of the parties. Officials used legal documents to manage agriculture and commerce, control their subordinates, maintain flows of information, requisition labour, control religious practices, monitor family structures, and manage property. And the legalism of the Chinese bureaucracy impressed surrounding rulers. In Turfan, far to the west of central China, the leaders of Turkic tribes copied Chinese techniques of government. Grave sites in these regions have yielded quantities of paper, much of which had been recycled to make shoes for the dead or papier-mâché coffins, and patient scholars have been able to piece together thousands of ancient documents.[5] They indicate that Turkic scribes were borrowing Chinese legal phrases to create contracts to purchase land, houses, and slaves; to borrow grain, cloth, and money; to rent land; and to hire labour long before the Tang armies arrived in 640 CE.

FOLLOWING THE FALL of the Han dynasty in the third century CE and a period of political confusion, the Sui and Tang dynasties reunited central China and created a spectacular capital at Chang'an.[6] The first Sui emperor created a legal code which combined and adapted laws made during earlier periods, and the first Tang rulers commissioned a team of legal experts to expand and improve it.[7] The Tang code, published in 653 CE, opened by outlining a hierarchy of five punishments: least serious was a beating with a light bamboo stick, next was a beating with a .

heavy bamboo stick, then there was penal labour for one to three years, then life exile, and finally the death penalty. The following five hundred articles set out a long series of official duties, crimes, and penalties. These largely depended on the status of the offender, whether lay or official, reinforcing the social and political hierarchy. It was a carefully controlled legal regime in which an extensive range of crimes merited physical punishment, including the sorts of behaviour that, in other contexts, would lead to civil claims.

Stories, pictures, and official accounts from this period confirm the use of torture, mutilation, and execution. Magistrates had to secure a confession before an offender could be punished, even if the evidence was overwhelming, and they regularly resorted to torture, starting with beatings, for the most recalcitrant. Even a single stroke could draw blood, and a full beating left the victim temporarily unable to walk and at risk of infection. The scholar-officials at the higher levels of the administration did debate the purposes and principles of the law, turning to Confucian ideals to justify the use of punishment. They needed, they felt, to maintain order through discipline, and the law was supposed to reform and educate. Punishment, and the threat of it, was meant to encourage good behaviour and deter crime. They also considered that rulers should be merciful and periodically declare amnesties, under which criminals would have their sentences commuted, prisoners would be released, and criminal proceedings discontinued.[8]

The Tang emperors declared a great amnesty every few years, first when they took the throne and then on other auspicious days, including their birthdays. On these occasions, they would announce measures for tax relief, rewards for the 'virtuous', promotions for officials, ceremonies for the dead, gifts for princes, and aid to families who had lost members in military campaigns. Sometimes they also announced that debts would be forgiven, providing some relief to impoverished peasants. A natural sign, such as an earthquake, might call for an amnesty, as would a period of civil unrest, when the emperors would pardon those who had become outlaws, release criminals to serve in the army, give relief from famine, and hope to pacify a rebellious region. A great amnesty was a grand gesture. It would be announced at sunrise, after the emperor had made sacrifices at a shrine outside the city walls. He then climbed to the top of a grand gate, where he stood flanked by a pole holding a golden cockerel, looking down on the crowd. Officials, members of the imperial guard, ordinary people, and prisoners all listened as a drum was struck one thousand times. Then the prisoners were free. In the provinces, local officials held similar, if less spectacular, ceremonies when they read out the text of an amnesty sent from Chang'an. As with all imperial edicts, they set up a stand covered by a purple cloth in front of a crowd of officials, ordinary people, Buddhist monks, and Daoist priests. An amnesty, they declared, would give the empire a new beginning and offer people the chance to reform themselves.

By the middle of the eighth century, the Tang armies controlled a vast area, extending to Turfan in the far west.[9] The administration had introduced a system of land registration and required that people draw up certificates to record the sale of all livestock and slaves, which government officials would check at border posts. In the grave of one moneylender from Turfan, archaeologists found fifteen contracts he had drawn up or signed. Some involved loans of money or silk cloth (an alternative currency), one the acquisition of ninety bundles of hay, presumably for his herds of sheep and camels, and another the purchase of a fifteen-year-old slave. Chinese subjects on the fringes of the vast empire were using sophisticated legal agreements at a time when the Anglo-Saxon and Germanic kings of medieval Europe barely knew how to write.

Although the Chinese political and military control over these areas was relatively weak, interrupted by both Tibetans and local warlords over the following centuries, the local populations continued to use Chinese administrative forms and legal phrases when they bought and sold goods and land. So did the inhabitants of Dunhuang, the oasis farther to the east, where the silk roads branched out across the Taklamakan Desert. Documents found in the library cave at Dunhuang dating from the Tang era include some of the earliest examples of Chinese block printing, and this technique was probably responsible for an expansion in literacy. Fragments of school books indicate that children studied Confucian ethics, mathematics, vocabulary, and the complicated rules of social etiquette. Meanwhile, officials allocated land to peasants and controlled markets, enforcing standard prices for basic goods. The perils of long-distance trade presented particular problems, and the owners of pack camels drew up detailed rental agreements. These often stipulated, for example, that if a camel died, became ill, ran away, or was stolen by thieves, the renter had to bear the loss.

Even if they spoke different languages, followed different customs, and never even dreamt of visiting Chang'an, herdsmen and traders in the far reaches of the Chinese Empire learned the same subjects, used the same contracts, and followed the same property rules as merchants in the capital and fishermen on the Pacific shores. By the tenth century, quite ordinary people were creating their own wills and using contracts to adopt children, divide property, sell land, free slaves, and hire labour. The barely literate copied out models for these sorts of transactions into cheap brown paper booklets. Meanwhile, the more prosperous would persuade local officials to help them draw up documents for land transactions, in which they inserted clauses to take advantage of new Tang laws, which might allow them to charge interest or rely on guarantors. Many of these contracts also denied the applicability of future imperial amnesties, stipulating that debts were to be paid regardless. They were confident in the power of their written documents.

But there were obviously limits to the effects of the imperial laws, as well as the amnesties, in the remoter areas, including those that forbade the sale of commoners into slavery. When one official conducted an investigation in Turfan, he found that 731 people impoverished by floods, droughts, or interest payments were languishing in debt bondage.[10] Creditors could take their debtors to court, where the magistrate might order punishment for nonpayment, but many clearly found it more convenient to persuade debtors to sell their children, or themselves, into slavery.

Meanwhile, the wealthy benefitted from a flourishing economy, and the Tang rulers created a spectacular court at Chang'an. The emperor Xuanzong staged elaborate ceremonies, hosted Daoist and Buddhist clerics, established a poetry academy, and promoted music and dancing, all while keeping a close eye on his administration and the defence of China's complicated borders. But in 755, as Xuanzong aged, an ambitious military governor was able to take advantage of his relationship with a young courtesan to amass power and stage a rebellion. Over the next century, the emperors who succeeded Xuanzong had to allow military leaders even more power, and the central government lost its grip on much of the country's administration, including the system of land ownership and regulation of trade. And it retreated from large areas, including Dunhuang. The regime limped on until 907, introducing new taxes on sales of salt, wine, and tea, but softened its control over most commerce. Ironically, this indirectly benefitted the economy, encouraging new markets and regional trade, laying the groundwork for commercial developments under the Song.

The Tang regime finally gave way to a period of political confusion during which a number of kings and generals vied for power. A military commander known as Taizu eventually overcame his rivals, and in a campaign that lasted practically throughout the sixteen years of his reign (960–976 CE), he united most of the territories formerly controlled by the Tang.[11] Taizu established a new capital at Kaifeng, in modern-day Henan, where he pursued diplomatic relations with the Indian Chola Empire, the Fatimid caliphate in Egypt, and Central Asian rulers, and he even received a diplomatic mission from the Byzantine court.

Taizu was keen to restrict the local power of army leaders in order to avoid the problems that had plagued his predecessors. But both he and his successors in the Song dynasty faced threats from powerful groups to the north and west. The Tangut Xi Xia had moved into parts of western China after the fall of the Tang, and the Mongol Khitans established their Liao dynasty in an extensive area to the north, around modern-day Beijing. The Song emperors had to maintain a sizeable army to resist their incursions, and the ongoing warfare prompted innovations in military technology, including the use of gunpowder. Inevitably, the northerners quickly adopted these new techniques, and the Song had to sign conciliatory peace treaties with both groups. Then, in 1115, the Jurchen, a Tangusic-speaking people, erupted from Manchuria and overwhelmed the Khitans, going on to attack Kaifeng. By 1127, they had driven the Song out of northern China. But despite this defeat, the Song regrouped and established a new capital at Hangzhou, consolidating control over their southern territories. And until 1279, the 'Southern Song' emperors presided over a largely peaceful and stable regime.

THE SONG RULERS built upon many of the advances and institutions of their predecessors. They promoted new and more productive methods of rice cultivation, using species imported from southern Asia, along with innovative technologies for irrigating paddy fields and terracing the uplands. Rice farming produced substantial surpluses and the population doubled, reaching one hundred million by the twelfth century. The government promoted liberal commerce, and maritime trade expanded into South Asia, impressing both Moroccan merchants and a Venetian explorer, who arrived in the last years of the regime. In his vivid account, Marco Polo declared that the Yangzi River carried more traffic than all the rivers and seas of the Christians put together.[12] In the cities, Chinese merchants established guilds to organize wholesale trade, set prices, and negotiate with the government. Tired of using iron coins, which they carried on heavy strings, some created notes to record debts and the goods they entrusted to shopkeepers. When they began to exchange these notes with other traders, who recognized the right of the bearer to collect the debt or goods, the system of paper money was born. The government soon appreciated the possibilities this offered, authorized a small number of shops to issue the notes, and then took over the whole system.

The government's postal stations further facilitated the expansion of trade, which spread throughout the rural areas. Farmers began to diversify, producing wine, charcoal, paper, and textiles, which they sold to brokers, and some specialized in crops such as sugarcane, tea, oranges, bamboo, oilseeds, and hemp. Others cultivated the mulberry trees needed for the production of silk, building up businesses in which they employed teams of labourers to tend the plants, pick and sort the leaves, care for the silkworms, and harvest their cocoons. Specialist producers could sell their wares to merchants and brokers and buy staple foods and household goods in the new markets established in towns throughout China. In some areas, mines and ironworks employed large numbers of labourers and developed new technologies, including hydraulic systems to drive bellows and explosives for excavation. These new techniques in turn fuelled the ship- and roadbuilding industries, as well as providing useful tools for farmers and artisans.

Hangzhou soon attracted a population of over one million, astounding Marco Polo, who described it as the finest and most splendid city in the world. He marvelled at the systems that brought in enough food to supply the inhabitants.[13] Guides eagerly showed him where to buy the best painted fans, ivory combs, wicker cages, literary texts, turbans, and rhinoceros skins.[14] Silversmiths, silk weavers, and the makers of ceramics and lacquerware had developed and adopted techniques that flowed into China from elsewhere. The houses of the wealthy attracted courtiers, artists, tutors, and entertainers, while public festivals and banquets drew huge crowds of people, who thronged to the teahouses and restaurants. In the entertainment quarters of the major cities, visitors and residents could enjoy the performances of puppeteers, acrobats, actors, sword swallowers, snake charmers, storytellers, singers, and musicians, along with plentiful refreshments and the services of prostitutes. Meanwhile, scholars pursued their studies, enjoying the new editions of classic texts made available by woodblock printing and, from the eleventh century, movable type. While they studied philosophy, mathematics, science, and technology, ordinary people read handbooks on agriculture, childbirth, pharmacy, divination, and Daoist rituals.

In the early decades of the Song, the emperor Taizu expanded the civil service, and his successors were acclaimed for their considerate government, during which they deferred to the wisest ministers. Elevating civilian over military leaders, they strengthened the Tang system of examination as the main route into the civil service, and this in turn prompted an expansion in education, helped by the circulation of newly printed texts. The number of hopefuls sitting for the examinations increased from thirty thousand to four hundred thousand, and the civil service itself expanded to twenty thousand officials. The aristocratic elite retained much of its wealth and influence, but government positions were officially open to ambitious and capable students from any background, in any part of China, and the sons of successful merchants were often able to join the civil service's higher ranks. This status allowed them to pursue a range of intellectual interests alongside their administrative duties. They promoted new agricultural techniques, supervised military defence, and wrote works on history, geography, ritual, music, poetry, and mathematics. Many officials were conscientious and committed. They believed it was their duty to be the first to worry about the world's troubles and the last to enjoy its pleasures, and they pursued serious debates about principles of government and law. Many advocated ambitious reforms, sometimes dividing into factions, which engaged in wastefully antagonistic arguments. But they all emphasized the need for loyalty to the emperor, to China, and to its culture while lamenting political fragmentation. Particularly after the loss of the northern territories, many scholars took a new interest in Confucianism. They debated human nature and the possibilities of goodness, and discussed with their disciples such things as how to sit quietly, how to evaluate what they read, what to make of ghost stories, and how to rid themselves of selfish thoughts. And they all agreed that Chinese society should be reformed from the bottom up, through education.

The scholars who dominated the upper levels of the imperial bureaucracy regarded the law as a means of maintaining the social order exemplified by the emperor.[15] A system of rewards and punishments, they all agreed, was fundamental if they were to reform individual behaviour. Taizu had issued a new code, virtually unchanged from Tang times, but successive emperors issued further edicts, and their civil servants drew up supplementary sets of rules. They responded to the needs of expanding commercial activities and tried to regulate government officials, setting standards for weights and measures, prison instruments, tax quotas, the numbers of recognized scholars, and their salaries. But their scribes turned many sets of rules into works of baroque complexity, especially those that regulated conduct at the court or within the imperial household. Detailed ordinances known as *shi* regulated the work of the finance commission, the directorate of education, the ministry of personnel, the office of academicians, the civil service examinations, official salaries, and the ceremonies to be carried out in the most important ritual temples. Some specified the forms to be used by government officials when writing reports on their subordinates, the terms to be written above the line as a mark of respect, and a list of characters not to be used because of their resemblance to words associated with the imperial family. Other shi contained rules for archery tests, the flags to be awarded to people of rank, the hearses that should carry the coffins of officials, according to their rank, as well as their grave mounds, and the rods to be used to punish offenders. Others contained detailed specifications, with precise measurements, for palace architecture, official storehouses, the ingredients to be used in the imperial kitchens, and the fodder to be provided for official horses. Practically all activities that concerned the emperor and his court were subject to shi, from the gifts presented to empresses to the details of their chariots, the tea system, and the administration of the inner palace. Others specified the libations to be made during Daoist ceremonies and gifts for Daoist nuns.

Taking advantage of printing, civil servants collected many of these new rules and regulations into compendia, which soon expanded to fill long shelves in their libraries. The rules they created for the use of one of the emperor's ritual halls were published in 1,200 volumes, and the scribes who compiled regulations for the reception of envoys from Korea filled 1,500 volumes. Excessive as they were, and unlikely as it is that they could all have been enforced with any precision, the shi must have imparted a sense of order, almost a geometry, to the running of the Chinese state. Everything and everyone had its place, and the most minute processes were carefully mapped out. And the closer you were to the emperor, the more regulated the world in which you moved.

OUTSIDE THE GLAMOUR, wealth, and intrigues of the imperial court and the bustle and commercial whirl of the capital, provincial China was governed by an extensive bureaucracy.[16] The smallest official unit was the district, the *xian*, headed by a magistrate, who was supposed to serve as a moral exemplar for the people. One xian might comprise 2,500 to 3,000 households, and there were 1,300 of them in Song China. The magistrates employed sheriffs, registrars, and clerks to work in their offices, the yamen, where they helped him to collect taxes; manage a network of roads, transport, schools, and shrines; organize staff and archives; carry out imperial commands; and keep the peace, as well as deciding legal cases. Ten to twelve xian formed a prefecture, which had a similar bureaucratic structure. The prefects were responsible directly to the emperor, but supervising them was another layer, commonly known as a 'circuit', in size roughly equivalent to the modern-day province. This was staffed by commissioners, who oversaw the finances, military, agriculture, and judicial systems in their regions.

Officials were supposed to implement the Confucian ideals of morality, loyalty, respect, and restraint. Practical though most of their tasks may have been, they had all studied the Confucian classics, and commissioners often issued directions about the qualities of good officials, the problems of corruption, and the social and family relations they should promote. But none of the officials had received specialist training, and newly appointed magistrates relied on their clerks to guide them through the morass of laws and regulations that impinged upon their duties. They could also turn to the many handbooks of advice and records of legal decisions compiled by their colleagues, such as the *Collected Models of Clarity and Lucidity*, put together by a diligent official in the mid-thirteenth century.[17] This text starts with a set of admonitions, commendations, and warnings. It records the statement issued by a newly appointed commissioner about his goals and priorities in which he explains the behaviour he expects of his staff: they must not act with disdain towards their subordinates, and they must not be impatient or lazy, act with bias or inattention, fail to show kindness and sympathy, or take advantage of their positions for personal gain. He expresses distinctly Confucian views: that human nature is unchanging, that leadership must be exercised through example, and that proper administration depends upon open and honest communication.[18] Another commissioner criticized his judicial staff for entertaining requests and pleas directly from litigants, rather than demanding that they go through official channels, thus laying themselves open to bribery. Yet another admonished prefectural and district officials for meting out excessive beatings, reminding them that a sentence of twenty blows in practice meant ten. This 'defect', he said, stemmed from lack of discipline; they must remember that the imperial law is intended to be merciful. Others condemned careless reports, rewarded a tax supervisor for refusing bribery, meted out punishment on a lowly clerk who used deception to attain a higher rank, chided officials who refused to discipline a corrupt officer, and demoted an incompetent magistrate.

The magistrates often used distinctly moralizing language in their directions and judgements. In line with the official purpose of rewards and punishments, they often explained their legal decisions in terms of deterring others or encouraging wrongdoers to reform. One railed against the condition of the local jail, which he had just visited, because prisoners were suffering. Ordering his subordinates to correct the problem, he declared that jails were meant to be places of reform: 'The intent of the ancient kings was to cause the guilty to be imprisoned in order to make firm their hearts and minds, having them do hard physical labour and endure deprivations, so as to motivate them to control their emotions.'[19] In setting out the reasons for their decisions, magistrates often commented on the morality of the litigants' behaviour, freely criticizing unvirtuous conduct and often echoing the attitudes about human nature instilled during their Confucian training. In a dispute over the sale of land, one declared, 'Originally [the claimant] got his property through un-righteous means. Now it has been lost in much the same way. This is what usually happens. . . . [The claimant] has tried to imitate this way of behaving. In the future when we look back on what has happened, it will seem much as what happened in the past.'[20]

But punishment was still the answer to deliberate criminal behaviour. Criticizing a clever tenant who had refused to pay his rent, assaulted the landlord's servant, and raised unjustified legal arguments 'in a stupid and reckless way', one magistrate declared, 'If others should imitate this bad example and behave like beasts, then all those who have houses and stores to rent would suffer through their tricks. To prevent such deterioration in social customs, the crime has to be properly punished.'[21]

MOST OF THE legal cases that came to the yamen were initiated by members of the local population. Complaints about petty crime occupied many magistrates, particularly in the urban ar-eas.[22] Flooding, droughts, and earthquakes sometimes caused mass migrations, and many of the displaced ended up on the outskirts of the towns, trying to make a living as porters and labourers. Without the support of kin networks and community groups, they could easily descend into patterns of petty crime. But for the majority of peasants, who were relatively secure in their livelihoods, daily life was taken up with ploughing, weed-ing, irrigating, and harvesting their grains, rice, and vegetables and tending their animals. They attended markets, cared for the young and elderly, arranged and celebrated marriages, and wor-shipped at local temples. They had to pay rents and taxes, defend their lands and houses against bandits, and try to avoid offi-cials. Most peasants tilled their own holdings, particularly in the central rice-growing regions, and many found themselves drawn into disputes over property transactions. The more prosperous might also pursue cases about land division and inheritance, often against a background of family disharmony.

Magistrates heard their petitions, but tried to discourage litigation, and were quick to criticize those they thought responsible for disunity. In one property dispute between a stepson and stepmother, the magistrate ruled on the legal issue but also declared that the son should now 'purify his heart, rectify his bad behaviour', and be more helpful and patient with the widow. And she, in turn, should be kind and caring for him.[23] Another criticized a son for misusing family funds, as well as his mother for suing him. The magistrate required both of them to file statements acknowledging his admonition and saying they understood that they would be liable to punishment if they continued to quarrel.[24] The magistrates took the duties of children towards their parents seriously and were prepared to punish them when they shirked those duties—for example, by making an unfilial son wear a *cangue*, a heavy board fastened to the neck, and perform daily greetings to his father.[25]

The courts entertained complaints about crimes of all sorts, from theft of a piece of silk or a bunch of onions to assaults and abductions, rape, murder, and arson. Magistrates often complained about the difficulty of controlling bandits.[26] Any individual could bring a criminal complaint, and if they caught someone in the act they could claim a reward. But the magistrates also took what we might call social crimes seriously. These included selling fake medicines, gambling, practising forbidden rituals and witchcraft, and trafficking in people. Irritated individuals even complained about bad behaviour by fellow spectators at a boat race, and the abusive language used by a public ferryman. The vindictive could persecute their enemies with legal complaints, but anyone who made a false accusation of criminal behaviour faced the same sentence as the one that the crime itself carried. The collected cases contain many examples of magistrates convicting those who maliciously tried to take advantage of the court system by making wrongful accusations.

The Chinese legal system was highly formalistic, with elaborate rules for petitions, evidence-gathering, confessions, decisions, and judgements.[27] Illiterate people were supposed to go to licensed clerks, who would write out their documents in proper form. When they got to the yamen, they found a courtroom arranged to impress. The magistrate sat on a dais at a high bench covered with a red cloth, on which his clerks had arranged the symbols of his authority: the square seal of the tribunal, wrapped in brocade; a gavel; two writing brushes, one for red and one for black ink; and an ink slab. He was flanked by scribes and other officials seated at lower desks. The accused had to kneel on the bare floor below the judge, next to court runners, who might be holding manacles, fetters, and a cangue, along with the flat bamboo staves used for beating. The less scrupulous magistrates, hoping to obtain a confession and bring the case to a speedy conclusion, would be tempted to order a quick beating. All they needed was the consent of their assistant and the legal clerk, and many of those convicted claimed, on appeal, that they had wrongly confessed because they could not stand the pain of the blows. The more conscientious magistrates would do their best to uncover the truth, trying to assess the reliability of a witness's statement from his or her demeanour and using innovative methods of investigation, even going out in disguise to investigate the facts of a case. In contemporary detective stories magistrates often featured as heroes who invented ingenious means to catch clever criminals and mete out justice. Having established the facts, the magistrate then had to apply the law. This was a process made more complex by the mass of legal rules and collections of precedents they were supposed to consult. The legal clerks assisted by searching the archives to assemble the relevant legal provisions, which might not be consistent. In such a case the magistrate was supposed to apply the most recent expression of imperial will. He then issued a judgement, giving directions about any property in issue and determining the punishment.

The magistrates had to make sure they followed the law and the evidence in order to avoid criticism by their superiors. They were expected to insist upon proper evidence, including written documents in land transactions, and to enforce the laws on limitations, the time during which a case had to be brought. It was twenty years for a complaint about the inequity of a conditional sale, while a dispute over the division of property had to be brought within three years. Still, within limits, the magistrates could waive the rules when they felt they should be merciful. In an inheritance dispute, one declared, 'The government does not wish to follow the usual precedent of taking over the estate [of someone who died without children]. It orders that [one part] should be set aside for the burial of the deceased and the remainder should be equitably divided. . . . This is not in accord with the legislative intention, but the government prefers to be kind.'[28] In another case, the magistrate acknowledged that a man who had made wholly unbelievable and very serious accusations against his nephew ought to be referred to a higher level for punishment. But he went on to explain that he had decided to be lenient and would only sentence him to a beating.[29] Magistrates often acknowledged the difficulty of reconciling the intent of the law with 'human feelings' and their sense of what was right.[30]

Faced with a mountain of legal complexities and fearing criticism for mistakes, many magistrates referred tricky cases to their superiors in the prefectures.[31] Allegations of more serious crimes had, in any case, to be recorded in detail and referred upwards. A litigant could also appeal if he or she thought a magistrate had committed a serious error. If an accused repudiated his confession, the district officials were supposed to refer the case to the prefecture. The case would then follow an even more elaborate process, considered separately by one of two inquiring offices, which investigated facts, while another, the law office, reviewed the law. An accused had to repeat a confession on more than one occasion, and if he or she refused, the case would be sent to the other inquiring office for review.

The rules were designed to give litigants considerable protection in a system that used torture to extract confessions. But even these procedures could obviously be abused. Some officials would stuff an accused person's mouth with rags to prevent him from denying a confession, or read his statement so fast that he did not understand it. In any case, the inquiring and law offices would send their reports to the prefect, who would give a judgement. The legal officials all had to concur in his decision. If they decided on a sentence of capital punishment or exile, the prefect had to submit the case upwards again, to the circuit. At this point, the commissioners could confirm the sentence, or, if they had any doubts, refer it on to the emperor. A convict also had a final chance to protest his innocence and demand a retrial at the gate of the city before he departed into exile, or at the marketplace where he was to be executed. Taizu, founder of the Song dynasty, announced that all those who were sentenced to death should be able to come to him for a review, and he did regularly spare lives. By the middle of the eleventh century, the prefectures were handing down around 2,000 death sentences annually, but of the 264 reviewed by the central government in one year, only 25 were confirmed.

The system of imperial amnesties also meant that many convicts were spared. The Song continued the Tang practice of making great declarations, supposedly to reform wrongdoers and reintegrate them into society. One government official declared that if the magistrate displayed notices of an amnesty in an area notorious for its violent gangs, 'the bandits' feelings [would] be moved and they [would] surrender', although their leaders should still be suppressed 'without mercy'.[32] But the frequent amnesties led some to complain. In one notorious case, a tenant farmer killed his landlord when he tried to collect the rent; after being freed, he went to call on the landlord's family. Here, as they later reported, he boasted of his good health and asked why the master had not recently come to visit.[33]

For all its safeguards and the underlying ideal of mercy, the Chinese legal system was easily abused, especially at the lowest levels. Clerks regularly extorted bribes from defenceless litigants, leading both magistrates and higher officials to rail against their corruption and try to deter litigation. Bringing a case to court, as one put it, 'merely fattens the clerical personnel'.[34] The magistrates warned repeatedly that going to court meant laying oneself open to demands for bribes, not to mention the likelihood of a beating, or worse. And they criticized those who encouraged litigation by acting for others, 'those with brushes in their hats'.[35] Going to court, one declared, would lead to neglect of one's occupation, damage to family property, humiliation at the hands of guards, tiring journeys, and possibly confinement in prison. Internal litigation also hurt a kinship group and injured a community, he pointed out. It should only be initiated by those with long-standing grievances, the poor or weak who had been oppressed by the rich and powerful, or the uneducated who had been victimized by the clever. It was for 'someone with his back to the wall who has no option but to cry out against injustice'.[36]

Ultimately, the courts could do justice. Local strongmen would sometimes find themselves facing the discipline of law, as would corrupt officials. In at least one case, a group of local people came together to complain about a local tyrant who was fraudulently claiming to have official status, extorting money, diverting tax revenues, and sheltering fugitives so as to be able to demand money from the local sheriffs.[37] And although many magistrates had a reputation for meting out harsh justice, they were themselves subject to scrutiny by their superiors. During a process of appeal, they could be disciplined for errors, as could a prefect who was adjudged to have handed down the wrong sentence. Equally, a magistrate who cleared an innocent person of a grave charge would be publicly rewarded. One described himself as 'a humble district magistrate with little prestige' who had had to stand up to the overbearing behaviour of a former official when he tried to intervene in a legal case.[38] Most regarded themselves as upholders of justice, sometimes against the odds.

Most disputes, of course, never reached the courts. As in later periods, people turned to community leaders, local policing groups, and ritual associations to mediate common problems.[39] New ideas about genealogy spread under the Song, encouraging the establishment of lineage organizations, which could step in to resolve family conflicts. Evidence from later periods indicates that court officials would often send litigants away to mediate, and the Song compilations record magistrates making strenuous efforts to bring conflict to an end once and for all, sometimes going beyond the letter of the law, or asking litigants to sign a declaration that they had brought a much larger family quarrel to an end. The Confucian emphasis on stable social hierarchies, filial piety, and loyalty to one's superiors encouraged informal peace-making. One magistrate criticized a man who had brought a petition to dispute the inheritance of his nephews, expressing surprise that the uncle was a Confucian scholar: 'I have always instructed people about what would be proper and reasonable. Even lowly and inferior people feel remorseful and regret their errors, returning to the good natures with which they were endowed by Heaven. . . . What is needed is the restoration of a harmonious atmosphere, without violating the principles of the law, the destruction of blood relations, and the squandering of family wealth.'[40]

OUTSIDE THE COURTS, peasants had long been used to creating documents to deal with their property, and magistrates everywhere insisted upon them as evidence of ownership. In the farther reaches of the empire, under less scrutiny from the central administration, the Song administrators exercised less control over their populations, and they barely enforced the system of land registration. But, as one commented, 'It is true that country people sometimes use property in ways that are not in accordance with the law. However, they all have written contracts of conditional sale.'[41]

Chinese people also used contracts to sell themselves. Under the Song it remained illegal to buy and sell freemen and women, but poverty and disaster led the most unfortunate to exchange their wives and daughters for money.[42] It was a survival strategy, and many popular tales record their stories. One recounts that a travelling merchant heard a man sobbing at an inn in Kaifeng and discovered that he had sold his daughter to pay back money he had stolen. The merchant offered to buy the girl and gave the father money to repay the price, advising him to threaten to sue if the purchaser did not agree to return her. The strategy worked, presumably because the purchaser was afraid of the consequences of his illegal contract. But when the father and daughter arrived to meet and thank the merchant, he had already left, his good deed done. Another story describes a woman who sold herself, while starving, to a broker. When the husband tracked her down, he sued for her return, and the court ordered him to pay the sale price as compensation. But before he could do so, the woman again disappeared. Maybe she was trying to escape an abusive husband. A doubtless apocryphal tale recounts how a woman abducted by a broker was discovered years later by her husband, who complimented his dinner-party host on the quality of a special dish, which moved him to tears by its similarity to his wife's cooking. He was then overcome with emotion when he discovered that the talented cook was, in fact, his former wife.

Chinese people also continued to turn to legalistic documents in their interactions with the underworld. Under the Song, new cults and temples for 'city gods' spread throughout China—that is, local deities who were supposed to protect the inhabitants—and Daoist priests often decked their shrines with statues of judges and legal officers, surrounded by all their legal paraphernalia.[43] Devotees would ask the priests to issue legal proceedings to exorcise troublesome spirits, using forms for accusation, investigation, and interrogation that closely followed the documents required by district magistrates. In later periods, Chinese writers referred to the demonic and celestial legal codes that the underworld judges had to apply. They apparently followed even more extensive rules than their earthly counterparts in courts staffed by an even more elaborate bureaucracy. In the underworld, they judged the deceased and entertained petitions from both unavenged ghosts and living petitioners. They could also help magistrates in this world identify guilty parties and punish corrupt officials. Popular writers published exciting tales of divine intervention in legal cases which enabled resourceful magistrates to do justice against the odds, often saving an innocent prisoner in the nick of time. Although these were works of fiction, people do seem to have taken the possibility of divine influence on legal cases, as well as punishment in the underworld, seriously. Officials sometimes interrogated suspects before judicial deities, and on occasion they even held trials in Daoist temples.

THE SONG REGIME lasted until Mongols rode in from the steppes in the thirteenth century. After conquering the northern areas, they established their own dynasty, known as the Yuan, with its centre at Beijing. This fell in 1368, to be replaced by the Ming. The Ming emperors built the splendid palaces known as the 'Forbidden City' and exercised relatively light administrative control. They instituted a principle that the law should be known to all and made legal texts widely available. But people continued to put faith in the power of the deities to assist with legal cases. The compiler of a set of legal judgements from this period refers casually to the intervention of spirits and ghosts in many of the cases he describes.[44]

In the mid-seventeenth century, the Ming dynasty gave way to the Qing, whose rulers created their own legal code. But they largely maintained traditional legal structures and forms, basing large parts of their code on the Tang laws. During the next three centuries, they introduced a mass of new rules and regulations. With population growth, district magistrates had to take charge of new villages, overseeing up to a quarter of a million people, and they recruited large teams of unofficial clerks and 'runners'. But, with official approval, people continued to turn to local mediators and lineage associations to help resolve their disputes. Qing villages also elected their own representatives, largely to collect taxes, and any of these local officials, along with elders and lineage heads, could act as mediators in local disputes.[45] While trying to avoid the yamen and the interference of local officials, peasants still used documents to formalize all sorts of local transactions, including sales of wives, children, and themselves at times of extreme poverty.[46] In desperate circumstances, an impoverished household might incorporate an unmarried man, who would contribute his labour to the household resources in return for a share of the wife's bed. Like debt bondage, this system of polyandry was illegal, and magistrates were supposed to punish such arrangements. But they often bowed to reality and acknowledged the importance of the practice as a survival strategy. Chinese peasants continued to record their agreements in writing, valuing the certainty they provided, even if the law forbade what they were doing.

Chinese legal practices, including the use of documents in everyday life and petitions to deities of the underworld, continued to follow similar patterns into the twentieth century. It was only the rise of the Nationalist government in 1928 that finally brought an end to the laws, legal forms, and elaborate system of crimes and punishments that the Chinese emperors, their scholars, officials, and ordinary people had developed over a period of two thousand years.

★

ORIGINALLY CREATED FOR ambitious rulers several centuries before the common era, Chinese systems of crime and punishment were developed over two millennia by emperors who placed their faith in the power of punishment to control their people and manage their territories. Their laws promised an order of discipline. So did the legalistic practices that reached to the farthest corners of their empire. Scholar-officials required people to use the correct legal forms for numerous transactions and follow detailed rules for court procedures. Peasants, herdsmen, and traders all managed their land, commercial relations, and family arrangements in legalistic ways. Courtiers and officials had, meanwhile, surrounded the imperial court with unimaginably complex legal rules. The idea of a rule-based and geometric order also seems to have provided the model for a hyper-bureaucratic court in the underworld, to whose deities quite ordinary people presented legal petitions.

The emperors associated themselves with both law and divinity, so it was natural that Chinese people should come to see their deities as part of an elaborate administration subject to extensive regulations and bureaucratic requirements. Legalism came to seem like the natural order of things. It is not so different in the modern world, where Western legal systems have expanded, bringing legalistic rules to bear on all corners of daily life.

CHAPTER TEN

COURTS AND CUSTOMS IN THE EUROPEAN MIDDLE AGES

T hroughout much of the Middle Ages, European kings and emperors struggled to assert their authority and apply their laws among diverse populations. They promised peace and justice in coronation oaths, patronized legal scholars, established courts, codified customs, and issued their own laws. But the separation between church and state had left the kings' laws without the sanction of religion. Nor were medieval governments strong enough to impose an order of discipline on their populations in the way that the Chinese did. Few ordinary people had confidence in the judges and laws of their rulers; in any event, going to court was time consuming and expensive. Still, many grasped the pragmatic possibilities of legal forms.

Most people associated more closely with their villages, local lords, urban quarters, or trading networks than with any king or bishop, and many of these entities made their own rules. Legal techniques filtered into their thinking and practices, and people adapted external laws to their own pragmatic purposes. In France, the rediscovery of Roman law alongside the kings' projects of centralization prompted a turn to legalistic practices of justice, even at local levels. In England, too, local tribunals gradually adopted more legalistic forms, although it was still several centuries before the kings' courts absorbed all their work.

IN CONTINENTAL EUROPE, a wave of lawmaking followed the 'rediscovery' of Roman law in the twelfth and thirteenth centuries.[1] The Lombards, who had already collected their laws into the *Liber Legis Langobardorum*, now wrote down feudal customs as laws in their *Libri Feudorum*. This book became widely accepted as authoritative on relations between lords and vassals throughout much of Europe, including in the Holy Roman Empire.[2] Frederick II of Sicily, who went on to become Holy Roman Emperor in 1220, commissioned a lawbook that used the language, categories, and reasoning of Roman law, his *Liber Augustalis*. In the loose confederation of Germanic principalities and free cities that made up the Holy Roman Empire, civil legal scholars brought new laws together in further collections.[3] The most famous of these, the *Sachsenspiegel* (Mirror of Saxony), combined the *Lehnrecht*, principles of feudal law drawn from the Lombards' *Libri Feudorum*, with the *Landrecht*, records of custom. The text was translated into several different Germanic dialects and influenced legal practices well beyond the borders of Saxony. In order to discover and declare what the law was in any particular case, larger towns appointed groups of citizens, the *Schöffen*, to examine their ordinances, customs, and any relevant text. Eventually, keen to unify their heterogeneous empire, the Holy Roman Emperors encouraged the use of the civil law and demanded that all senior judges should train as jurists. But although some scholars argued that the civil law represented a common European culture, the idea took several centuries to crystallise.

The Castilian kings had also ordered an ambitious set of laws in the thirteenth century. They modelled their *Siete Partidas* explicitly on Justinian's Digest in an attempt to assert their supremacy among Spain's independent kingdoms. But Spanish judges still thought they should be applying the laws and customs of their own lands, and Spanish officials commissioned local codes, known as *fueros*. In France, too, both government officials and regional lords asked scribes to record local laws in collections; these *custumals* were intended to assist lords and judges in the administration of justice.[4] Once they were published, people began to quote them directly to support their cases, with some success. Judges and lawyers, however, had become convinced of the superiority of the emerging civil law in which they had trained. And the scribes, although they made genuine attempts to record customs, inevitably translated much of what people told them into the existing categories of Roman law. They adopted concepts and ideas from Justinian's Institutes and sometimes copied the organizational structure of the Digest. This all reinforced the idea that the civil law was the ultimate model.

For some time, local judges and mediators continued to approach disputes in traditional ways, seeking to broker compromises between parties at odds. But the idea that litigants could refer to an objective, impersonal set of rules to pursue their interests gradually took hold. Records from Septimania, in the south of France, indicate that in the twelfth century most people sought out 'good men', that is, arbitrators, to help with their disputes. In serious cases, generally those involving large landholdings, the parties might turn to the abbot of the nearest monastery or the local viscount to mediate.[5] Monasteries were now substantial landowners, with complicated rights to rents and other dues, and their abbots would often find themselves in dispute with the local nobility about their land rights and entitlements. Cases could drag on for years as different prelates and nobles tried to mediate between them. The arbiters might apply pressure to the parties, but they could not force them to accept a decision, or even to abide by the terms of a compromise. Occasionally they could refer to a charter, which might indicate who had legal rights, but the precise Roman categories of land ownership had largely been forgotten, and without them it was difficult to hand down an authoritative judgement. More often they simply compromised by dividing up the property in dispute. Even when they negotiated an agreement, mediators had to ask the parties to swear an oath to abide by its terms. They were dealing with sentiments of honour and shame, particularly among members of the upper classes, whose pride had to be soothed. The arbiters persuaded them to compromise by referring to respected wisdom and threatening public condemnation.

Gradually things changed. During the thirteenth century, the French kings began to assert more authority over the provinces that they nominally controlled, sending agents to collect rents and demand service from landowners. With the support of the church, they could confiscate property from 'heretics', a tactic they could use, in extremis, to subdue a defiant nobleman. In less extreme circumstances, they could call on papal delegates to threaten a citizen who refused to accept a judge's order with excommunication. The French kings also drew the nobility into the circles around them. Keen to establish a more centralized judicial structure, they instituted a system of appeals to new courts in Paris.[6] Now a landowner in Septimania might find that a nobleman was making a claim to his farms in a court hundreds of miles away, or that he faced demands for military service by the agents of a distant government. Gradually, the pressure to compromise within a close social circle disappeared and the arbiters started to act like judges, making definite decisions, which they expected the parties to obey. At the same time, they began to record the decisions they made in their new courts more systematically, using Roman words and phrases, indicating that they had 'inquired about the truth' and used 'witnesses and instruments'. Whether or not they actually had, these phrases created a sense that there was a proper way of meting out justice, one that resembled the legalistic practices of the Roman civil law.

As the judges and mediators tried to apply consistent rules in their courts and people accepted authoritative decisions, the old systems of mediation and compromise began to break down at all levels. The new laws provided people of all ranks with a machinery that was impersonal, but which also offered them a language by which to challenge others, even those of higher status. In the courts, city consuls found they could resist the claims of a viscount, the viscount could respond to the arguments of an archbishop, the archbishop could take on the consuls, and all of them could stand up to the king. They could cite the law in arguments against people who were both distant and more powerful. It was not, of course, a perfect system, and the legal arguments did not always work, but they gave people a way to take on those who tried to dominate them. Law now supplemented the moral and religious arguments people had always used in front of arbitrators, and its ideas and techniques filtered into local contexts. The lords imitated the king and hired trained lawyers to be their judges, while both villagers and city dwellers discovered that the new courts were places where they could assert some rights. Law now held the promise of justice.

Over the next centuries, law developed in different ways in different parts of Europe. Kings and their governments, bishops and churchmen, lawyers and law schools, lords and scribes, all played their part, not to mention the upheavals of wars, crusades, and campaigns against heresy. New and reforming rulers often created or amended their laws and adopted styles of Roman legal procedure. Even the Scots, in defiance of their southern English neighbours, sent young men to study the civil law in France and Italy. The influence of Roman law hovered over the more ambitious laws produced in the movements for codification that eventually swept Europe. But it was not until the nineteenth century that Europe's rulers produced the laws that would eventually inspire people in distant parts of the globe.

★

CHANGE WAS EVEN more gradual in England. Not long after the Norman conquest, an English scribe compiled a set of Anglo-Saxon laws that he attributed to King Henry I. He introduced his collection with the statement 'Agreement prevails over law and love over judgement.'[7] He was referring to the 'lovedays', where people would gather to resolve conflicts and make public declarations of affection. Bonds of love were supposed to bring about peace and security, and even lords and their vassals were supposed to feel love and affection for one another.

The legal reforms introduced by Henry II in the late twelfth century put the power to declare what the 'common law' was in the hands of the judiciary. Royal judges travelled around the country to hold eyres, courts in which they adjudicated on disputes among landowners, generally arguments over property and succession, and it became an insult to the king to compromise after a writ had been issued. They also sat in judgement on those accused of serious crimes, rather than allowing vengeance to run its course. Meanwhile, English scholars, inspired by the example of Rome, wrote treatises on the 'unwritten law' of England. Their texts marked the beginnings of the legal system that eventually extended throughout England and Wales, but it was several hundred years before this system superseded local and specialized laws and courts.

Although the lovedays lingered through the following centuries, for most of the Middle Ages and into the early modern period peasants, artisans, churchmen, and merchants all turned to local courts, which were often sanctioned by the Crown to resolve disputes. They cited custom as well as law to local judges and expected a jury of their peers to consider charges against them. The Anglo-Saxons had established courts in the shires and hundreds, the smaller divisions of the counties, where knights, landowners, and freehold tenants gathered periodically to debate and manage local affairs. The Normans continued this system, and Henry II appointed a sheriff to each shire and hundred. The sheriffs would summon a jury of twelve freemen to each *tourn*, the court they held every six months or so, where they considered allegations of crimes, including robbery, murder, and theft.[8] Occasionally, the king's eyre would descend upon the shire, where it would sit for several months to review the activities of the local courts and hear the most complex legal cases, generally disputes over the ownership and inheritance of great estates along with allegations of the most serious crimes.

During the thirteenth century, the eyres were eclipsed by the *assizes*, royal courts that toured distinct parts of the country 'on circuit' and took over the work of the hundred courts.[9] Along with local justices of the peace, who eventually superseded the sheriffs, they heard allegations of 'felony', that is, serious crimes such as homicide, robbery, and arson, breaches of various regulations, and disputes between individual citizens. Although private prosecutions alleging felonies framed them as crimes, people were generally seeking the sorts of compensation that would today be granted by civil courts. And they could also complain about officials. Eventually the courts developed new writs by which people could allege negligence by those giving medical treatment, shoeing horses, or transporting goods, or anyone who had failed to control animals or fire.[10] Local juries had to investigate the allegations, whether they concerned property or shipwrecks, trespass or water, the discovery of treasure or the activities of outlaws, fugitives, or poachers, or an issue such as when markets could be held. At times of unrest, they had to investigate organized violence, abuses of legal procedures, and conspiracies. By the late fourteenth century, they were also overseeing the use of weights and measures and investigating the forging and clipping of currency (that is, shaving off the edges of valuable coins), demands for excess wages, and sales of inferior goods.

But seeking justice in the assizes was complicated and expensive, and for most peasants it was in their manor that disputes were resolved, local affairs were managed, and justice had to be sought. Medieval English peasants lived in villages, hamlets, or farmsteads, but in legal terms they belonged to manors. The lord of the manor, for whom they tilled the fields, may have been a Norman lord, an abbey, a priory, or the Crown itself, and the larger estates included land scattered throughout several different parishes and shires. So near neighbours in some villages might belong to different manors. Most peasants were vassals, known as *villeins*. The lord granted them the right to work a few fields and feed their livestock on common pastures in return for a share of their produce and services. Villeins also had to work on their lord's fields, grind his corn, transport his timber, and tend his animals. Only some peasants were freeholders, who held their fields without all these obligations, and even they still had to attend the lord's courts.

When the Norman kings parcelled out these estates, they also granted the new owners the right to hold courts.[11] The lord's bailiffs, reeves, and stewards, the officials responsible for the management of the estate, would summon all the (male) tenants, that is, the villeins and freemen of the estate, to act as 'suitors' every three weeks. At these courts, the suitors would review rules for the use of common pastures, woods, rivers, and ponds, deciding who could let their cattle and sheep onto the pastures, who should guard them from the fields, in which parts of the woods the villagers could let their pigs root for acorns and beechnuts, and who could keep geese on the village pond. They collected taxes and dues, recorded the work carried out by the villeins, investigated disturbances and rumours of quarrels and fights, and recorded the names of those who had left the manor. The suitors would also have to consider any charges the officials brought against tenants who had breached the rules. Maybe a tenant had failed to attend the court or perform his duties in the lord's fields or mill; a woman had let her animals into the lord's corn, or had married without his leave; or a freeman had refused to sell ale to the lord's servants. They heard allegations that someone had not paid all his rent, or had tried to lease out his fields without permission; others may have been seen taking fruit, destroying corn, poaching, or encroaching on a neighbour's land. The suitors would normally fine offenders, but after a fourth offence someone could be sent to the pillory or paraded around the village on a tumbrel.

Peasants would also bring their own grievances to the court. In one case, a careless dog owner had let his animal kill twenty-four of the complainant's geese; in another, a devious farmer had created a path across his neighbour's land. Villagers might make complaints about the quality of the ale and bread brewed and baked on the manor. In the thirteenth century, the kings granted special jurisdiction to some lords to travel around the country and hold 'assizes of bread and beer', to enforce national standards of quality and price. The suitors might also have to decide on local customs—for example, which of two sons should inherit his father's lands or whether it should be divided between them. Villagers could be harsh with one another. Douce, the daughter of a tenant at Cranfield in Bedfordshire, claimed the right to inherit his lands, something initially confirmed by the suitors in the manor court. Later, however, someone discovered that Douce had borne a child out of wedlock, and the suitors felt obliged to follow earlier cases in which the court had declared that a daughter who 'trespassed' in this way lost her right to inherit. They denied the unfortunate Douce her land.[12]

For most English peasants, the manorial courts were the places they could air grievances, register land transactions, and

debate matters of common interest. Tenants could also get together to make a request to their lord about the management of
common resources or the activities of outsiders. If the tenants
of another manor had encroached onto their lands, they could
try to persuade their own lord to investigate and, if necessary,
bring a case in the higher courts of the hundred or shire. As one
scholar has put it, most people probably thought of the manor
court as 'theirs', a place in which they might be listened to and
judged by their friends and neighbours and where they might get
a more sympathetic hearing than in the royal courts.[13]

If a peasant persisted in refusing to pay his taxes or was
caught in an act of theft, the manorial court could 'put him
out' of the village and prevent him from having fire and water,
effectively making him an outlaw.[14] The villagers had to 'raise
the hue' if they discovered any wrongdoing, which meant that all
those in earshot had to search for the suspect. A criminal could
take sanctuary in a church, which the local villagers then had to
guard, or he could 'abjure the realm', that is, promise to leave
the country, something that had to be policed by the villagers. If
a body was found, a coroner would summon all the men from
the four nearest villages to an inquest, something that could be
highly inconvenient if it happened during harvest. In all these
cases, the county sheriffs would check that the villagers and manorial officers had acted properly.

In a system inherited from Anglo-Saxon times, all unfree men
were supposed to belong to a tithing, a group of ten or more,
which took responsibility for the good behaviour of its members.
If someone committed a serious crime, the sheriff could summon
a representative of his or her tithing to the county court. He
could also summon a sworn deputation from the hundred to
'present' cases of treason, homicide, theft, arson, rape, poaching, and any shedding of blood reported from the manors, as
well as every raising of the hue. The sheriffs could mete out fines
and hangings, and the more authoritarian ones would browbeat

villagers into informing on friends and acquaintances. Vengeful peasants could cause anxiety and expense to their enemies by alleging a serious wrongdoing, but they could also close ranks to hide one of their own, blaming unknown 'vagrants' for an unsolved crime. Peasants found it a burden to sit in the sheriffs' courts, but it did give them the chance to participate in the administration of justice, in a small way deciding what the law was and should be. And they brought ideas back to the manor courts: that grants of land gave them rights, that certain people were entitled to inherit from others, and that they could argue self-defence or accident to a charge of homicide or wounding.

In this way, rules, practices, and principles developed within the royal system of courts filtered down to the manors. A principle dating back to the laws of Henry I provided that no one should be judged by men of lesser status than him. This meant that if a freeman was accused in the manor courts, a jury of freemen had to be convened to hear his case. And the nobility would have been aware of the Magna Carta, signed in the thirteenth century, which declared that no bailiff should accuse a man in court without the production of reliable witnesses: 'No freeman shall be taken or imprisoned or disseised or exiled or in any way destroyed . . . except by the lawful judgment of his peers or by the law of the land.'[15]

As literacy became more common in the thirteenth century, the lords began to employ clerks to keep records and accounts, inscribing notes about legal cases in the manorial court rolls.[16] As the population increased, they started to select a jury of twelve men to sit in their courts, rather than summoning all their tenants as suitors. Copying the practices of the sheriffs, who required local juries to present cases to them, the lords now required their juries to investigate and present cases, not just decide on charges brought by their stewards. The kings also granted some lords the right to hold *courts leet*, which would consider and punish more serious cases of injury and assault, effectively taking over the jurisdiction of the sheriffs' courts. In the courts leet, the juries would hear several cases at once. The process was much quicker than hearing them singly, but probably less just. Most jurors resented the time and effort this required, and no doubt they hated having to investigate and inform on their neighbours. But they were probably also keen to see offenders punished.

The cases that came to the manor courts generally involved simple issues of fact or questions about appropriate penalties, but the juries did sometimes have to decide on local custom, as in Douce's unfortunate inheritance case. Over the course of the thirteenth century, the manor courts began to make clearer distinctions between the rights and obligations of freemen and villeins. These were recorded on the court rolls, so that people could refer to the records if they thought their lord was unfairly depriving them of land or their fellow villeins were encroaching on it. As the royal courts developed more complex writs for disputes about landholding, some of the new categories found their way into the manor courts. People began to use standard documents to record sales and transfers, property settlements, and joint tenancies. The manor courts adopted forms of action from the royal courts, such as *novel disseisin*, a means of claiming land, and *mort d'ancestor*, used in disputed inheritance cases, although they did not always use these complex forms correctly. The courts also had to decide on *heriots* (death duties), wardships (responsibility for orphans), and marriage relief as well as issues concerning inheritance (such as entails, remainders, and reversions and customary practices such as the deathbed transfer). They heard cases about *merchet* (a fine paid on marriage), *leyrwite* (a fine for fornication), franchise of waif and stray (the right to claim ownership of abandoned property and animals), *purpresture* (encroachment on another's land), and waste of villeinage tenements. Local customs survived for centuries, but more uniform rules and categories emerged over time. The uneven map of legal processes gradually developed clearer contours.

In the middle of the fourteenth century the Black Death swept England, devastating both populations and agriculture. In the Peasants' Rebellion, which followed in 1381, rebels destroyed or burnt many manorial rolls in a gesture of defiance towards their lords. But these events, dramatic though they were, did not undermine the manorial system. Over the following decades, lords reestablished records and peasants continued to turn to their courts for cheap and relatively effective justice.[17] Gradually, the lords rented out more of their land, rather than having villeins farm it directly for them, and took less interest in the management of their estates, which they more freely bought and sold. So they allowed juries to take charge of administrative matters, such as confirming boundaries, apportioning liability for rents and services, electing manorial officers, and selecting tenants for vacant tenements. The courts also sat less often. But people pursued justice in the manorial system into the sixteenth century, bringing charges against suspected thieves, against officers who tried to extract excessive dues, against brewers of bad beer, and against lepers whom they felt should be removed from their areas.

IMPORTANT THOUGH THEY remained, the manor courts were not the only places in which peasants could seek justice, or in which they might be charged with crimes. Issues about marriage, divorce, the legitimacy of children, and sexual crimes were all supposed to go to the church courts. Here, in the *rural chapters*, prelates, deans, and archdeacons heard disputes about the validity of a will or the lawfulness of a marriage, claims for goods or money based on marriage agreements, disputes over the inheritance of personal property, and allegations of fornication, adultery, incest, and bigamy, along with allegations of heresy and sorcery.[18] Churchwardens and other church officials would

summon people who failed to attend church on a Sunday or refused to baptize a child, misdemeanours which generally merited
a penance, rather than a punishment. Rectors and vicars might
also enquire into the payment of tithes. Peasants were supposed
to give every tenth sheaf of grain and one-tenth of their garden
produce, wool, milk, and newly born livestock to the church.
Spiritual concerns could also creep into practical arrangements.
Peasants might offer a pledge of faith to seal a contract; and if
someone later alleged a breach of the agreement, they had to go
for judgement to the rural chapter. The clerics were supposed
to apply the church's canon law, which had its roots in Roman
civil procedure, although there was rarely much dispute over
the crimes in question. What presented more difficulty was the
problem of how to assess circumstantial evidence of adultery or
fornication. One solution was to allow defendants to assemble a
group of friends and neighbours to swear to their good character, in an act of *compurgation*.[19]

The church was, at least in theory, concerned with the state
of men's souls rather than the regulation of their agriculture or
social lives, but medieval English men and women cared deeply
about their honour and often turned to the church courts to
defend their reputations. Insults, particularly those with sexual
innuendos bandied around in the heat of an argument, could
cause great offence, and, at the risk of republicizing the insult,
many sought public exoneration in the courts. Records from the
fifteenth century indicate that hundreds of people, many of them
women, complained that they had been defamed as 'whores' and
'strumpets', or sons and daughters of the same, along with an
array of other colourful insults. The deacons in Wisbech had
to consider insults of 'londleper' (vagabond) and 'hormonger',
along with people called 'horys, strumppetts, and fyssenaggs'
(whatever those were). And the insults could take a nationalistic
flavour. A witness in a Norwich court reported hearing 'thou
are a false flemming and a false stynkyng cokald', while servants

in Middlesex traded insults by calling each other a 'Skottishe prestes whore' or a 'Walsche prestes son'.

IN THE CENTURY or so before the Black Death, the wool trade had brought new wealth to the English populations, which increased markedly. New towns were formed, granted charters by the kings, where merchants established guilds to promote trade in wool, sheepskins, leather, lead, and tin, the five 'staples' of medieval commerce. Towns established borough courts, where local officials heard cases concerning credit and debts, trade disputes, allegations of minor violence, damage to property, and infringements of urban regulations.[20] Urban prosperity depended on courts that could resolve commercial disputes effectively and cheaply, and local officials exercised tight control over their courts. The fines also generated income for their coffers. But the jurisdiction and procedures of the borough courts varied enormously, and some towns had a variety of them, which could compete with one another for cases. Meanwhile, courts leet monitored the responsibilities of the tithings, coroners investigated causes of death, and staple courts monitored essential goods.[21]

Favoured elites, such as the Abbot of Ramsey, were also granted permission to hold fairs, which created their own 'pie-powder' courts. The fair of St. Ives, a small vill near Cambridge, soon attracted international merchants, while manorial lords held more local markets. In their courts, named after the dusty feet, the *pieds poudrés*, of travelling merchants, mayors, bailiffs, and stewards would hear claims of misconduct. They had to mete out justice swiftly, before traders moved on, and they might send the constables to seize goods or shame culprits by tying them to the pillory or tumbrel. As the wool trade expanded and the English economy diversified, so did the fairs, and eventually the Crown directed that in every town with a market for one of the staples the merchants should elect officials to arrest, try, imprison, and punish delinquent merchants. Most wrongs concerned debts, breaches of agreement, and the quality of goods. In 1275, for example, a baker at St. Ives accused a woman of breaking into his house, abusing his wife, and pouring yeast over his white flour.[22] This, he said, had cost him three pence, and he also wanted half a mark for the 'shame'. The bailiffs allowed the woman to bring witnesses to swear to her good character as a defence to the charge of abuse and damage, but *hamsoken* (house-breaking) was a serious charge, so they called for a jury of merchants and townsmen to hear the case. They were following the procedures of the manor and borough courts, to ensure that merchants were tried by a jury of their peers.

THE PRACTICE OF convening local juries to try disputes spread throughout most of England during the thirteenth and fourteenth centuries. It extended to Devon and Cornwall, where people followed the ancient practice of tin mining. During Roman times, tinners had extracted deposits from the fine-grained sand in Cornwall's rivers and streams, smelting it in small granite blowing houses, which dotted the moors and waste lands between farming villages.[23] The tinners were free to set up their 'bounds' anywhere, placing rocks or turves at the corners of an area, which they could claim as their own for as long as they continued to work it. Local sheriffs were collecting *tin coinage*, a tax on smelted tin, by the middle of the eleventh century, and in 1198 Richard I's chief minister convened courts in Exeter and Launceston where juries of miners decided on the law and practice relating to coinage. He also appointed a chief warden for the *stannaries*, as the mining areas were known, to oversee and enforce their 'ancient customs and liberties' and prevent tinners from selling their wares outside authorized markets. In 1201,

King John confirmed the customary rights of the tinners to mine and dig turves anywhere, including on the lands of bishops, abbots, or lords, 'as they have been accustomed to do'. Only churches and churchyards were immune, although the tinners had to pay a share of their profits as a 'toll' to the landowner. The king also granted free status to the tin miners, which meant they did not have to pay dues to the lords of their manors, tolls on roads and bridges, or charges at the markets. The chief warden, he declared, had to 'do justice and right' to the tinners, which could include imprisoning them in the stannary gaol or seizing the possessions of any they outlawed.

The practice of tinning presented unique issues for the law to resolve. The warden established eight courts over the next century, one in each of the mining districts of the two counties. Tinners charged with murder, manslaughter, 'mayhem', or other serious offences had to go to the royal courts, but lesser cases were heard by local jurors. Working tinners and blowers, the owners of blowing houses, the adventurers who funded new enterprises, smiths, colliers, and the makers of mining utensils all used the stannary courts. They also heard disputes between tinners and people not involved in the industry, although in this case, half the jury would be non-tinners. A landowner could complain if miners destroyed his crops, and a parson might report people he had caught digging in his churchyard. One tinner accused the local lord of evicting him from his rightful stream-works; another claimed he had been wrongly imprisoned by the mayor of Fowey for allowing the waste from his works to silt up the harbour. If the jury did not do justice, they could appeal directly to the warden.

The industry developed specialist procedures for assessing and marketing its products. Having smelted the tin, the tinners would stamp it with the owner's mark, a process regulated by the stannary courts, and take it for coinage to one of the tin towns. Loading their tin onto carts and packhorses, they arrived to meet the controller, with his stamping hammer, weights, and scales, who weighed and marked each piece of smelted tin. These he then passed to the assayer, who assessed the quality and determined the coinage. This the owner would have to pay before he could sell the tin to one of the London dealers or pewterers' factors who crowded the town. Merchants travelled from as far as Italy and Flanders to secure the best Cornish tin. The stannary courts regulated these processes into the sixteenth century. In 1508, Henry VIII established a Convocation of twenty-four men for Cornwall, six from each of the county's stannaries, to approve all 'statutes, acts, ordinances, and proclamations' relating to tin. Devon already had its own Convocation, effectively an independent parliament, to regulate its tin trade. These continued their work alongside the stannary courts into the eighteenth and nineteenth centuries.

THE ENGLISH CROWN granted charters for numerous other courts in the Middle Ages. Woodland, heath, and moor in many parts of the country were claimed by the kings as hunting grounds. The Saxon kings had enjoyed the sport, and William the Conqueror extended the lands reserved for the hunt.[24] By the thirteenth century these forests provided food for the king's table, timber for his building projects, and an income from fines and rents as well as sport for the king's retinue. Ignoring objections from his barons, Henry III passed the Charter of the Forest in 1217, which confirmed the status of these lands. But it also provided that no one should lose life or limb 'for the sake of our venison', that is, for poaching, and it confirmed the privileges held by local people to make ponds, take fowl and wild honey, collect timber and firewood (*estovers*), graze their cattle and pigs (*pannage*), and undertake a certain amount of mining. Sixty years later, Edward I passed another act to reinforce the offences of 'trespass in the vert' and 'trespass on venison', which covered all sorts of improper use of the forests.

Edward's act solidified a complicated structure of official over-sight and specialist courts for the forests. Wardens and foresters managed the land, took charge of slain beasts, checked for ille-gal activity, and caught, killed, and salted the venison required by the king. Bishops, sheriffs, and constables had to produce offenders before judges sitting in the eyres, and could even sum-mon earls and barons to answer for activities on their estates. Meanwhile, local communities elected their own *verderers*, who were directly responsible to the Crown for enforcing the forest rules. Just as coroners would investigate the suspicious deaths of humans, verderers could hold inquests into the deaths of slain beasts, and they could mete out small fines for minor offences. They supervised the taking of estovers and pannage, the felling of trees for the king, mining, and charcoal burning. Needy vil-lagers were tempted to allow their pigs to wander onto the forest to eat acorns and beechnuts, or to let them stay longer and roam farther than was allowed, and they crept in by night to collect brush and firewood or iron ore. Some took wild honey and cap-tured hawks, while the more ambitious felled trees, trapped deer, or surreptitiously cleared and incorporated forest lands into their fields. Most were fined when caught, although many were ex-empt because they were considered too poor. But if the verderers suspected poaching, they had to summon twelve jurors to hold an inquest, sending suspected offenders to the warden for impris-onment until the next eyre.

Forest eyres were normally held every two to three years, al-though when Edward I ordered the sheriff of the Forest of Dean to appoint four justices for an eyre in 1282, it was the first in twelve years. The hearings in Gloucester lasted for ten weeks and were still not finished when the king was called away to fight the Welsh. By then, a thousand people had attended, all those charged with offences since the last eyre, and many of them had

had to make an arduous journey to await trial and judgement. On the first day the judges considered fifty-eight cases of stealing and interfering with deer, two cases of people who had burned the heath, and seventy-two who had either failed to appear or given guarantees for others. The verderers had already dealt with minor offences, but the judges still had to consider the cases of over four hundred people accused of vert offences, including taking and selling oak, burning charcoal, cutting branches and brushwood, and grazing animals in the forest. Although the verderers issued fines and confiscated wagons, boats, and oxen from peasants who had stolen forest produce, they themselves later received fines for failing to prosecute all offences.

During the chaos of the Wars of the Roses, the Crown relaxed its oversight of these courts, but the system of forest management continued. When Elizabeth I needed large quantities of timber for her naval fleet in the sixteenth century, she reviewed and revived the system. It continued into the following centuries, only gradually subsumed by the work of the kings' courts.

Meanwhile, peasants and artisans who lived near seas and major rivers developed skills as fishermen, sailors, chandlers, and wherrymen. Their activities were all liable to present particular legal issues, which they took to the admiralty courts.[25] Someone who came across valuable goods washed up from a shipwreck might also find themselves defending their right to keep it in front of an admiralty judge. When Edward III turned his navy into a private enterprise in the mid-fourteenth century, he gave his lord admiral power to hear legal disputes. To guide the court's activities, the king put together a collection of documents that included the *Rolls of Oléron*, a set of laws and judgements for maritime trade that Eleanor of Aquitaine had drawn up some two hundred years earlier based on Byzantine mercantile laws. At least officially, the admirals were supposed to apply this civil law along with the 'ancient customs of the sea', even when they heard claims for mariners' wages, or disputes about the loss or delivery of freight. And, like the pie-powder courts, they had to mete out swift justice to sailors and merchants who would soon again put to sea.

The judges of the common law courts sometimes objected to the powers of the admirals, but in the sixteenth century Henry VIII confirmed their jurisdiction over all bays, harbours, rivers, and streams as far as the first bridge. He declared that they could hear cases of maritime trespass, riots, routs, unlawful assemblies, extortions, oppressions, contempts, concealments, misprisons, conspiracies, and other 'outrages'. These included crimes against the laws of the realm as well as the laws, customs, and maritime ordinances of the court of the admiralty.[26] The admirals and their deputies regulated the sale of boats, took charge of goods found in the rivers or on the shores, and registered merchant ventures, granting letters of safe conduct to foreign merchants who loaded their goods onto boats registered in English ports. Merchants, including clothworkers, leather sellers, tailors, and drapers, along with fishmongers, vintners, brewers, and grocers, would typically come to their courts with claims for loss of goods. When the *Edward* sank between Greenwich and Blackwall, a haberdasher brought a claim against the ship's owner for loss of his pack of felt hats and other valuable fashion items. Like other medieval courts, the admirals would convene a jury, largely made up of mariners, and they would include foreigners if the dispute involved a foreign party. Dutch and French merchants and sailors all came to the English courts along with Germans and a handful of Italians, Scots, Spaniards, Danes, Swedes, and Greeks, and many of them needed interpreters. In a complicated case the admiral might have to send deputies to take statements from crucial witnesses in other parts of Europe.

The admirals' courts also kept an eye on maritime regulations and punished minor misdemeanours. In London, a fisherman was convicted of 'forestalling fish' by selling it outside the official market at Billingsgate; he was sentenced to two months in prison, as well as the hefty fine of £4. Another was given two hours in the pillory for fraudulent begging with a counterfeit licence. A sailor was flogged when he deserted after taking his 'press money' and dragged through the water to the nearest shore, while a man who cut off a piece of rope on board a ship was ducked in the Thames. A shipmaster was, bizarrely, sentenced to a year in prison for carrying 'his majesty's subjects' to be educated abroad.[27] The use of riverways also caused problems. One man brought a claim against another who had prevented him from using the ford on a public right of way, forcing him to use a more dangerous crossing, where his pack animals had foundered. And a farmer claimed that his neighbour had cut the rope of the boat he used to reach his fields, letting it float away down the river Arundel.[28] But most cases concerned those with maritime occupations—sailors, masters of vessels, fishermen, sailmakers, and ships' carpenters, along with lightermen, owners of wharves, ballesters, and watermen.

Their quarrels did not always call for maritime expertise. One day, a waterman named Style was rowing a wherry near Greenwich Stairs when he noticed a boat rowed by another waterman, Tucker. Someone in Style's boat shouted 'lubberly knaves' at Tucker's craft, though 'only in jesting sort', as witnesses later claimed. But Tucker took offence and uttered 'lewd and ill speeches', going on to shout 'vile and irreverent' words to Captain Hammades, who was steering Style's wherry. The insults were returned, missiles thrown, and Style's head was cut open. Witnesses claimed they heard Tucker saying he 'cared not a straw if he had killed Style'. The next day Style was recovering in his local inn, the Cardinal's Hat, his head 'swathed in a kercher', when an apologetic Tucker appeared, saying he was 'sorry as for his own brother' and would make good (pay compensation), if honest men decided the matter. Style retorted that it was not just a matter of his own injury and loss of income; the matter touched the honour of Captain Hammades and required due process of law. He took the case to the admiral's court, which awarded him compensation for the three weeks he 'lay at expenses' and had to call upon a surgeon.[29]

Outside London, vice admirals toured the ports, summoning juries to present and hear cases. They considered claims that a shipmaster had abandoned sick mariners in Iceland along with allegations of unsafe pilotage and claims for nondelivery of fish, for maritime wages, and for breaches of hiring agreements, while vicars claimed tithes of fish. The courts took censuses of ships and mariners, held inquests into the grounding or loss of vessels, and took charge of findings on the seashore. But they depended on the knowledge and cooperation of local people. When Lord Admiral Sir Julius Caesar rode down to the West Country and tried to tell the local mariners what to do, his circuit ended in failure.[30] He was more successful in the many cases that resulted from hostilities between England and Spain, during which Elizabeth declared that all Spanish ships could legitimately be raided. Sir Francis Drake's fleet seized a ship riding at anchor in the heavily guarded port of Cadiz because it was loaded with Spanish wine, wool, and ducats, even though the ship's owners were neutral in the conflict. And English ships would harass any French vessels they encountered during later tensions between the two countries. Ambassadors, of course, intervened, peppering the lord admiral, the Privy Council, and even the queen with complaints and petitions.[31] This was the heyday of the admiralty courts.

WHEN HENRY VIII dissolved the monasteries, he distributed their lands among his most favoured supporters. Landowners were now extracting taxes in money or as payments in kind, but they could still enforce labour obligations. Tenants continued to grind their corn, reap their fields, dig and transport peat, and even accompany their lords on military expeditions. At the same time, the population was rapidly increasing, practically doubling between 1520 and 1600. The king introduced many new laws and statutory offences, and litigation increased, reaching staggering levels under Elizabeth around the turn of the century. One notorious local bully in Shrewsbury brought sixteen actions against his neighbours in the course of a year.[32] Scholars are unsure about how to account for this turn to the courts, but it may be that legal innovations and new ways of making claims encouraged those with grievances to try litigation. The central courts saw a huge rise in cases, as did the borough courts, and the manor courts remained important.

But the central common law courts gradually extended their capacity and their remit. Over the following decades, they took over the work of the forest courts, although the verderers continued their regulatory duties into the nineteenth century, and they absorbed the work of the pie-powder, stannary, and admiralty courts. Enclosures and other land reforms decreased the work of the manor courts, although, when industrialization led to population growth in areas without borough courts, disputants had to use the manorial courts for all sorts of civil disputes. The manor courts were only abolished in the land reforms of 1925.

DURING THE MIDDLE Ages, legal scholars everywhere studied the rules, principles, exceptions, and distinctions of the civil (Roman) law, and the church courts applied canon law. French judges borrowed their legal forms to create laws with general application, while English judges developed technical forms of landholding and succession in their system of writs. But most people, even the judges in the highest courts, had a sense that custom was important and ought to be respected. And the kings repeatedly confirmed this when they recognized the authority of regional courts, ordered that customs be recorded, and directed that wardens, verderers, and admirals should respect tradition. In their local courts, people could feel that law was rooted in custom.

Gradually, more centralized government, along with the techniques of legal professionals, drew people into the royal and imperial courts, where judges applied laws to make authoritative decisions. But, particularly in England, it was centuries before these formed anything like a single system or superseded the authority of local tribunals. Roman law might have provided the inspiration for much of this lawmaking, along with the writs of the English kings and judges, but the substance of the law was also developed bottom up, by local people addressing local problems.

CHAPTER ELEVEN

THE PROBLEM OF JUDGEMENT
Oaths, Ordeals, and Evidence

T
he legal systems that developed in Mesopotamia, India, and China promised justice, cosmological order,
and religious guidance. Disputes were often brought to
courts and judges for resolution, but they were also brought to
mediators, whether or not they had laws to refer to. Peasants
and herders argued about fields and livestock, townsmen complained about disruptive neighbours, dangerous buildings, and
dirty sewers, merchants argued over prices, landowners developed complex property arrangements, officials extorted money,
and people everywhere insulted one another and got into fights.
In an attempt to restore order, juries delivered verdicts, judges
gave judgements, officials meted out punishment, mediators promoted conciliation, elders gave practical advice, priests referred
to moral rules, and scholars crafted learned opinions.

The variety of the world's legal processes is almost as great
as the variety of its societies. But a problem every society has
faced is how to determine the truth. If a man claims that another has killed his son, the accused may protest that he did it in
self-defence. If a woman complains that she has been slandered

by someone, that person may swear she misheard what was said. A merchant may deny that he signed an agreement that his trading partner is trying to enforce. A shepherd may claim it was a lion who killed the sheep, while the owner of the sheep accuses him of carelessness. Who is to be believed? For all the differences in their laws, in premodern societies people everywhere came up with similar solutions to this most intractable of problems.

Oaths and ordeals might seem exotic to us now, even barbaric, but premodern societies the world over invoked the divine to determine whether someone was guilty of a crime. Sometimes people had to prove their innocence—or the truth of an accusation—by swearing an oath. In imperial Tibet, people made dramatic oaths in front of divine images, while tribesmen in the Middle East could gather dozens of people, *compurgators*, to swear oaths confirming their innocence. People in other places might have to undergo an ordeal, a physical test that would prove their guilt or innocence: ancient texts from Vedic India describe how priests should prepare for this procedure, and in Africa, the Caucasus, and pre-Christian Iceland, ritual specialists conducted alarming and painful tests. Oaths and ordeals come closer to a set of universal legal practices than anything else did, before the forces of colonialism and modernity spread European laws throughout the world. Eventually, laws of evidence superseded accusations made on oath and the proof offered by an ordeal, but it was a long time before these rules transformed criminal trials into the processes we know today. In the meantime, judges had to work out how to determine when an accused was guilty and ought to be punished. And this was not just a problem for the accused. Christianity, Hinduism, Buddhism, and Islam threatened divine retribution, the fires of hell, and a miserable rebirth for any judge who punished someone unjustly. The stakes could not have been higher.

★

IN THE SEVENTH to ninth centuries CE, a line of kings on the Tibetan Plateau transformed a loose coalition of nomadic tribes into a centrally controlled empire. As part of their project to turn potential rivals into loyal subjects, they staged elaborate ceremonies where the leaders of outlying regions would swear oaths of loyalty. These dramatic events were conducted in front of powerful local deities and probably involved animal sacrifices.[1] At the same time, the kings made strenuous efforts to regulate and control the blood feuds that regularly erupted between their tribes. The nomads had long competed with one another for pastures and raided their neighbours' animals, as their successors still do today. But now, probably emulating the legal practices of their Chinese neighbours, the Tibetan kings created sets of laws to govern the payment of compensation for murder or injury and to punish those who deliberately caused trouble.

One event that could generate conflict was the royal hunt, when the kings invited members of their court to chase wild yak in the high Himalayan valleys.[2] Although the ministers now formed a status hierarchy, rivalries lingered among them, and on the hunting field latent antagonism could easily erupt into a violent dispute. Whose arrow had killed the prize quarry, and whose dog had startled the horse that had thrown its rider? And if an arrow missed its target and hit a person, those nearby might easily suspect foul play. The kings created two sets of rules to deal with the consequences. They specified the amount of compensation to be paid after a killing or injury, which largely depended on the status of the wrongdoer and the victim, reinforcing the social hierarchy. But the laws also directed that someone accused of a deliberate killing had to gather twelve people to swear an oath testifying to his innocence. If he could accomplish that, he was simply liable to pay the blood money or wound price of his victim. If he failed to gather a sufficient number of people for the oath, he would suffer punishment for murder. Thus he could be exiled, lose his lands, his wealth, and possibly his life, and see his family taken into slavery.[3] The process of oath-taking determined whether a death was an accident or murder. The accused could also ask his oath-helpers to swear that he was not responsible at all—'It was not my arrow', as the text puts it. In this case, the accuser would suffer punishment instead. Slander was as serious as homicide.

Under these rules, the oath-takers would provide evidence that the accused had not intended to kill or injure his victim. But how were they able to testify as to his state of mind? On the hunting field, a high-ranking minister would be surrounded by a retinue of family, followers, and servants, but his thoughts were his own. And no Tibetan would have taken an oath lightly. Swearing an oath meant invoking one of the fierce protector deities who could mete out hideous retribution on anyone who invoked his or her name in vain. The process only makes sense if we understand that the accused was asking his compatriots to swear an oath of compurgation. Rather than giving direct evidence about his state of mind, they were affirming his *probity*, his integrity; they were saying that he could be trusted to tell the truth. They were affirming that this was not the sort of person who would have engaged in a dishonourable attempt to injure or murder a rival. A collective oath expressed the oath-takers' loyalty. It affirmed the honour of the accused, which proved that the incident must have been an accident, not a crime.

Similar practices were taking place in medieval Europe during exactly the same period.[4] The inhabitants of the British Isles still formed tribal groups which engaged in blood feuds, but by the tenth century, King Edmund I, in an attempt to restrain and regulate the associated violence, had issued a law saying that a victim's family could only take revenge on the slayer himself, not on the slayer's wider family. The Norman kings went further, banning direct retribution altogether. A killer now had to pay compensation to both his lord and his king, as well as to the victim's family. The monarchs were beginning to punish crimes directly. But this also meant distinguishing between a murder, an accident, and a killing in self-defence. And as in Tibet, the English kings expected an accused to bring compurgators to swear that the incident was not intentional. One self-important aristocrat brought fifty witnesses to swear that he had killed a rival in self-defence rather than in an act of premeditated murder.[5]

Before they entertained a criminal case, however, the English judges needed an accusation, and for a serious crime the accuser had to bring witnesses to swear oaths of confirmation. The accuser's word alone was insufficient. Like the Tibetan procedures, English oath-taking was done in public. It required careful preparation and culminated in the dramatic invocation of the Almighty. These elaborate processes were supposed to ensure that people did not make frivolous accusations. By the time of Henry I in the early twelfth century, the kings had formalized rules for oath-taking, and the law provided that if a royal judge entertained a charge brought by a single person, without other witnesses, and without the culprit having been caught in the act, then the accused could clear himself by his own oath and that of two neighbours. If, by contrast, an accuser brought good evidence before the court, the judges might expect the accused to rally as many as thirty-six compurgators.[6]

In medieval Cairo, the Jewish courts also expected witnesses to give their evidence on oath if the allegations were serious. The geniza documents describe parties assembling in the synagogue, where the witness held the Torah, draped in black cloth, while giving evidence. They sometimes read aloud the Ten Commandments, including the solemn statement that 'the Lord does not hold him guiltless that takes his name in vain'. There would have been no doubt in the oath-taker's mind that he or she was invoking God directly and that a false oath was a sin that would lead to punishment in the afterlife, and possibly also negative consequences in this one. The documents indicate that when all the preparations had been made, community elders were often able to intervene and persuade a trembling witness to agree to a compromise.[7]

Tribesmen in the Middle East also developed practices of oath-taking.[8] If there was good evidence of a murder—a corpse had been found in a hostile village, say, or had been discovered shortly after a group of people had left a place, or a person was found with blood on his clothes—then the victim's relatives could gather fifty men to swear an oath to confirm their suspicions. After this, they could either take direct revenge or demand blood money from the killer's family. These were oaths of accusation. Islamic scholars also advocated oaths of compurgation. If a corpse was found bearing traces of violence, then the victim's family could bring an accusation against all the members of the city quarter or village in which it had been found, which encompassed anyone within shouting distance. If the residents refused to take responsibility for the death, fifty of them had to swear an oath to deny their involvement, and any who refused would be imprisoned until they swore or confessed. Even if they all denied responsibility, unless they could convincingly blame someone else they were still liable for the victim's blood price. In other contexts, the tribe of a murderer had to gather a sufficient number of people to swear that they had outlawed the attacker from their tribe, in order to prevent a revenge attack. Islamic jurists formalized many of these traditional practices into law, although they also expressed disapproval of the way in which witnesses freely invoked the divine, and they directed that people should not swear oaths about crimes they had not witnessed. Still, particularly among the nomadic tribes of the Middle East, oath-taking continued for centuries. Legal documents drawn up by Yemeni groups as late as the eighteenth century describe compurgators gathering to prove that a killing was not intentional.[9]

Oath-taking was a near-universal means to justify an accusation or deny guilt. But it was everywhere a serious and elaborate process which imposed an intense moral burden on the oath-taker. Christian writers noted the 'extreme peril' involved in invoking God. Declaring a falsehood, even if accidentally, would amount to taking God's name in vain and incurring his wrath, with almost certain repercussions in the afterlife. Witnesses brought into church were expected to quake when the priest revealed the relics of a saint as part of the process. They knew they were putting their souls in peril.[10] One Bedouin tribesman in the Middle East was so incensed that he had to swear an oath to prove his innocence that he turned on his accuser threatening violence and had to be restrained by his kin.[11] People took oaths to avoid direct revenge, but in the highly charged atmosphere of tribal antagonism, the process itself could inflame tempers.

IT WAS AN honour and privilege to be able to swear an oath in self-defence, and only those with sufficient status possessed that option. Throughout the Middle Ages, the legal systems of Europe continued to rely on the process of oath-taking to prove innocence or guilt, and many English subjects insisted on their right to 'wage their law', that is, to take an oath to demonstrate their innocence.[12] But the lowest classes could not swear probative oaths. Vagrants and slaves were not 'oath-worthy'; nor was anyone who had already committed perjury. The Tibetans did not let the poor and indigent swear, either, on the basis that they could be too easily bribed, and it was thought that women's loyalty to their menfolk, and children's unformed minds, might lead them to lie. Ritual practitioners might be able to subvert the consequences of an oath and Buddhist lamas were also excused from having to invoke the deities.[13] In most contexts, those who did not have the family networks to gather sufficient oath-helpers were also at a disadvantage in processes that depended upon compurgation.

So how were these people to prove their innocence, or the truth of their accusations? English courts, Tibetan officials, and judges throughout the world turned to the ordeal as a solution. In a typical ordeal, the accused would have to take a hot iron bar or stone in their hand and walk a few paces. After this, the hand would be bound. If it was already healing when the judge or priest inspected it a few days later, it was a sign of innocence. Witnesses who took an oath invoked the divine, signalling that they were aware of the possibility of spiritual retribution if their evidence was false, while those who underwent an ordeal invited direct intervention from God or other spirits. The process itself indicated the truth.

Some of the earliest evidence of ordeals comes from India, in texts that date to the seventh century BCE.[14] The writer of one of the Vedas, the Vajñavalkya, described elaborate processes, indicating a well-established tradition. Four priests needed to sanctify the ground and purify the *proband*, the person undertaking the ordeal, who then had to recite the correct form of words and make offerings to the deities before undergoing the test. The text provides no details of what the ordeal itself involved, but it lists the types of people who should not be allowed to undergo this process. These included anyone who would be at a disadvantage, such as the ill, and anyone who had spiritual powers, which might enable them to manipulate the results. In medieval Tibet, judges and mediators also used ordeals when they needed to determine the truthfulness of contested allegations, particularly in cases of suspected theft.[15] A Tibetan legal treatise on oaths and ordeals starts, like the Indian text, with a list of those who should not be allowed to swear an oath. It continues by directing that mediators must take great care to ensure that the proband uses the right words and that the process is carried out correctly. The author was particularly concerned that the words should be clear, so that the proband could not subvert the process by carefully selecting words that would 'prove' his or her innocence without perjury.

French romances from the same period describe clever protagonists indulging in just these tactics.[16] By now, ordeals were well established in Europe.[17] The earliest Frankish laws, written in the sixth century CE, refer to 'the cauldron' used to test allegations of theft, false witness, and contempt of court. In this version of the ordeal, the proband had to draw a stone or ring from a pot of boiling water, after which the hand would be bound, as in the ordeal with the hot iron. Irish legal treatises written in the seventh and eighth centuries refer to 'the truth of the cauldron', sometimes to 'the truth of god', and one attributes the introduction of this practice, somewhat implausibly, to St. Patrick.[18] In England, King Ine of Wessex, in the late seventh century, refers to someone proved guilty of theft 'by a cauldron', and the laws of Aethelstan, three centuries later, give directions as to how ordeals should be conducted.[19] The test could involve hot iron or immersion in cold water. In the latter case, the witness would be undressed, bound into a foetal position, and lowered into consecrated water. The idea was that the water would reject the impure, so the guilty would float. Aethelstan's laws directed that before the test the proband had to stay with the officiating priest for three days, eating nothing but bread, water, salt, and herbs, and attending Mass every day. No more than twelve observers should attend the test on each side, each of whom must also have fasted for three days. Everyone, that is, had to recognize the seriousness of the occasion and the solemnity of a process that invoked a sign from God.

Medieval stories and other written accounts present lurid descriptions of ordeals, but scholars suspect that the practice was much less common than these accounts would suggest. The idea behind the process was to intimidate a witness into confessing. French and English sources are full of brave women who voluntarily undergo an ordeal to prove their fidelity or chastity, but, although priests may often have made all the preparations, at the last moment, faced with the horror and drama of the impending test, many probands probably gave in. By the ninth century, European practices involved a ceremony that was carefully prepared to put psychological pressure on the proband. He or she would be cloistered away for several days, dressed as a penitent, and tended by the priest who was going to administer the ordeal. The priest during this time would doubtless apply intense pressure on the proband to confess if he thought he or she was lying. The ordeal itself took place in a church or at some other holy site. After hearing Mass, the proband would invoke God and repeat his or her evidence, and the priest called on God, 'the just judge', to chase away the devil who had 'hardened [the proband's] heart'. Or he might invoke the biblical story of Susanna, who was falsely accused of sexual misconduct, and ask God to protect the proband if he or she was innocent.[20] Meanwhile, a blacksmith might be heating the iron bar that the proband would have to hold. Or people might be placing boards and ropes over a river or pit of water, into which the proband would be lowered. This extensive process would weigh heavily on a guilty conscience. If the accused held fast to his or her innocence and the trial continued, it was up to the priest to declare the outcome of the ordeal. Were the burns really healing, or had the proband really sunk? His judgement was critical, and the clergy could be sympathetic. Indeed, some people complained that the medieval clergy rarely declared anyone to be guilty.

The Tibetans used almost exactly the same processes with hot iron and boiling water as their medieval European counterparts.[21] But ingenious communities came up with other ways to invite a sign from the deities in their ordeals. In Iceland, the proband had to walk under a strip of turf that had been raised above the ground and balanced perilously on sticks.[22] He failed if he knocked it over. But when Christian missionaries arrived in the year 1000, the Icelanders adopted their techniques of using hot iron and boiling water. In the early twentieth century, anthropologists and colonial officials recorded the ordeals still being practised by groups scattered throughout sub-Saharan Africa and the Caucasus, among Bedouin tribes, and in the Hindu Kush.[23] While many used forms of burning or scalding, several African communities also resorted to poison. As with the European evidence, accounts of what could be done in such cases were much more common than records of actual incidents. The anthropologist Edward Evans-Pritchard, who conducted extensive fieldwork among the Azande of southern Sudan in the 1920s, said that he only came across good evidence of one poisoning ordeal.[24] A man had accused another of poisoning his father, and the Zande princes consulted the poison oracle, who declared that the accused must undertake poisoning as an ordeal. As an upper-class man, he was able to avoid the test by sending one of his servants to drink the poison in his stead, but when the boy died he was declared guilty.

ALTHOUGH PEOPLE AROUND the world have resorted to elaborate and generally painful ways of determining the truth, it stands to reason that people in a small and relatively close-knit community would be well aware of who was doing what, who might be responsible for a crime, and whose word could be trusted. A thorough process of inquiry should, in the last resort, have resolved any lingering doubts. Perhaps the ordeals were designed to terrify, not actually to be carried out. Although the Icelandic lawbook refers to ordeals, for example, suggesting that the process developed informally, the only descriptions of these ordeals are found in the sagas, the semi-mythical stories written several centuries after the law texts.[25] They describe several women obliged to undergo an ordeal to prove a paternity claim, and one who voluntarily offered to undergo such a test to prove her descent and right to an inheritance. At best, the ordeal was a last resort, something to which the parties turned when other evidence proved inconclusive. In one Icelandic account, the parties walked away from an ordeal because the priest's interpretation of the results was ambiguous; in another, a clever protagonist blatantly tried to rig the process.[26] One can see how an ordeal could easily find a place in these stories, as it could help to bring a narrative to a dramatic conclusion, heighten tension, and provide a theatrical twist to a tale. But this does not mean that they were merely narrative devices, a fiction of the storyteller's imagination. Ordeals provided drama because the listeners were familiar with what they involved and what they meant, even if, as in medieval Europe, they were threatened more often than carried out. Small communities would have found an ordeal attractive because it provided a direct sign from God or the local divinities, proving guilt and justifying the resulting punishment. Its finality might bring an end to a period of hostility, even if it merely confirmed what most people already knew. It demonstrated to everyone that justice had been done.

In medieval Europe it also provided reassurance to the judges who conducted more elaborate legal cases. Both kings and lords sanctioned the processes and expected their clergy to conduct them. In the ninth century, Charlemagne declared that all should 'believe in the ordeal'. This was the period during which Germanic and Frankish kings were amassing power and status, trying to limit blood feuds, and taking responsibility for processes of justice. An ordeal, conducted and interpreted by a member of the clergy, took the process beyond their control and weakened the authority of the judges. But it provided an answer where the evidence was genuinely contradictory or inconclusive, particularly if it involved an event that had allegedly happened in private, such as a sexual crime, a clandestine theft, or a surreptitious murder. Even more importantly, it allowed judges to avoid taking responsibility for what was a deeply problematic process, sitting in judgement on their fellow men and women.

Making a judgement was especially problematic if it meant condemning someone to death. In medieval Christendom, as well as in the Islamic world, Vedic India, and premodern Tibet, theological concerns placed a heavy moral burden on the shoulders of a judge. Christian writers made it clear that a judge who acted 'against his conscience' by wrongly condemning an accused person faced damnation. In *The Divine Comedy*, Dante graphically portrayed the torments of sinful judges in the lower hell. Imposing a blood punishment, whether execution or mutilation, was fraught with peril.[27] Seeking a direct sign from God was one way of averting these dangers.

Medieval Christian theologians liked to quote St. Augustine, who had declared that judges must act justly, which meant 'pursuant to the law' (*iuris ordine servato*). If a judge acted justly, and an accused was executed, it was the law that killed him, not the judge.[28] When a medieval judge took office, he had to swear an elaborate oath on holy relics that he would give just judgements. But although 'the law' gave judges some protection, it could hardly help when the evidence was thin or contradictory. Medieval jurists had not developed laws of evidence with concepts like the 'burden of proof'. The ordeal offered the judge a way around this problem by providing a divine indication of guilt. A judge could then make an order for punishment secure in the knowledge that God had indicated it was just. Following Roman procedures, judges also insisted on a direct accusation before they could hand down a criminal judgement, however good the circumstantial evidence. But, like the judges, most witnesses did not want to take moral responsibility for the resulting blood judgement. So a judge might hear rumours and learn that people harboured suspicions about an offender, but find that no one was prepared to come forward with a direct accusation. An ordeal allowed the divine to solve the problem by providing direct evidence.

WIDESPREAD THOUGH ORDEALS and oath-taking were, religious leaders in both the Christian and Islamic worlds came to disapprove of these practices. Ordeals were most problematic, but so were some practices of oath-taking. Although they helped judges and witnesses avoid serious moral dilemmas, it was a long time before they developed the jury and inquisitorial systems we rely upon today.

Christian clergy conducted most of the European ordeals in the early Middle Ages, but by the thirteenth century church leaders had become deeply uncomfortable with these processes.[29] In the code of laws he wrote for the Armenian people in the twelfth century, Mxit'ar Goš stipulated that oaths should only be taken in serious cases between Christians, and only in the absence of sufficient witnesses.[30] He criticized all the 'pointless swearing' that happened in court and the 'frightful way' in which some people made oaths, and he declared that children, the elderly, the sick, women near childbirth, and penitents should not take oaths. Instead, they should find relatives to represent them. He also banned tax officers and sinners from the courts and stipulated that drunkards should wait until they were sober. And, like the Tibetans, he declared that priests and monks should not take oaths; in fact, they should not even enter the courtroom.

The Fourth Lateran Council made similar pronouncements soon afterwards. In April 1213, Pope Innocent III summoned all the senior clergy of the Christian church to a general council. Seventy-one patriarchs and metropolitan bishops, 412 ordinary bishops, and 900 abbots and priors made the journey to Rome the following year, and Emperor Frederick II, Henry of Constantinople, and the kings of France, England, Aragon, Hungary, Cyprus, and Jerusalem all sent envoys. The delegates assembled for three weeks to consider seventy canons presented by the pope. These decrees, he explained, would combat vice, stamp out heresy, settle discord, establish peace, and foster liberty. They also included new directions about legal procedures. Judges were now to have the authority to investigate wrongdoing and summon suspected criminals to their courts, rather than relying upon an accuser. Pope Innocent had also decided that members of the clergy should no longer take part in judicial ordeals. The delegates agreed. There were two problems with ordeals, the church determined. First, ordeals 'tempted God': that is, they tested the divine by demanding a sign of guilt or innocence. Second, if the process might end with a punishment of mutilation or death, it involved the clergy in 'blood practices'.[31]

This seemingly innocuous decree set in train a series of reforms that eventually led to the rules of evidence used in practically every modern state legal system. But in the short term, the ban created practical problems for judges and moral dilemmas for witnesses and jurors. Replacing blood punishments with other penalties was not a practical option. Imprisonment was expensive, compared to mutilation and execution, and the Old Testament also made it clear that justice meant proper punishment. God had said to Moses, 'Thou shalt not suffer evildoers to live.' And in 1203, Pope Innocent had himself declared that criminals should be punished in the public interest.[32] So judges feared public unrest if they failed to prosecute and punish crime. The theological problems of crime and blood punishment remained acute.

The church's decision had the most immediate effect in England, where Henry III, newly appointed to the throne after the disastrous reign of King John, ordered that his judges must find new means of adjudicating disputes.[33] The solution they came up with was to place the burden and moral responsibility for declaring guilt onto a jury. The Anglo-Saxon kings had used groups of witnesses to assist in inquests, and the Norman kings had turned them into 'juries of presentment'. When the judges travelled around the country, they summoned twelve men from each hundred (a division of the shire) and four from each vill (roughly equivalent to a manor) to 'present' cases. They had to declare whether they knew of anyone from their area who was guilty, or suspected of being guilty, of a serious crime such as robbery, murder, or theft. These crimes attracted blood punishment. So English peasants and townspeople were already used to being summoned to make accusations against one another. Most probably hated informing on their neighbours, but Henry III's declaration made their task dramatically worse. It forced them not just to bring accusations against their fellow men but also to decide on the question of their guilt. In practice, this meant that they had to send some criminals to the gallows, with terrifying consequences for their consciences. Not surprisingly, many refused, or tried to refuse, but the king's officers could charge them with *amercement* if they failed to bring a case forward. Many found ways to avoid the worst punishments. They could grant an accused priest 'benefit of clergy', for example, because clergymen could not be given a blood punishment. Or they could find the accused guilty of a lesser offence—for example, by devaluing the goods he or she had stolen. But it was still a deeply uncomfortable process, and it caused moral anguish to many.

The English system of jury trial soon spread into the civil sphere. By using the new writ of novel disseisin, a landowner could bring a property claim in the royal court, and here a jury of *recognitors* would adjudicate on the claim.[34] Over the following centuries, the courts of the manors, markets, boroughs, ports, and forests all adopted the jury. The system went through changes, but the basic principles remained the same.[35] In 1382, concerned about immorality among the inhabitants of the expanding capital city, the mayor and aldermen of London issued a set of ordinances that gave local courts the power to prosecute 'bawds', 'common women', adulterers, and 'common scolds'.[36] Each of the capital's wards selected its own aldermen and juries, who could send offenders to the pillory and stocks or banish them from the neighbourhood.

By demanding that twelve people agree on a verdict, the courts did provide some comfort to the jurors and their consciences, and officials would keep searching for jurors until they found twelve who could agree. The system also provided some safeguards for the accused. By the seventeenth century, at least, judges were directing juries that they had to be 'sure' of guilt, and even that evidence of a felony had to be 'so manifest, as it could not be contradicted'.[37] But Tudor monarchs took the view that they ought to crack down on crime, and limited the methods that juries could use to lighten sentences. And in the eighteenth century, the British Parliament dramatically increased the number of crimes subject to the death penalty. This was largely to protect the interests of the new landowning classes, their great estates, and deer parks. In a series of criminal statutes, Parliament created new capital offences for hunting and stealing deer, poaching, damaging all sorts of property, committing arson, shooting, and even sending threatening letters.[38] The notorious Black Act of 1723 specified fifty distinct capital offences, and over the following decades new acts protected rivers, sea banks, hop fields, and coal mines. The Parliament was now using the terror of capital punishment as a means of social control. The problems faced by jurors, who were expected to send convicts to their deaths, became extreme. By the late eighteenth century, many citizens had become convinced that the law too readily prescribed capital punishment. So sympathetic clerks, prosecutors, and judges helped jurors find means to excuse conduct, downgrade punishment, and identify mitigating circumstances.[39]

Before long, the pendulum was swinging the other way. Many critics complained about the reluctance of juries to convict, even in what seemed like clear cases. The judges now began to talk of 'reasonable doubt' as the test that juries should use when deciding their verdicts.[40] They would direct jurors that it was their duty to convict if all the 'moral probabilities' of the evidence was against the accused and they had no 'reasonable doubts' about the facts. This not only protected the accused but also reassured jurors that they could convict with a clear conscience if the evidence was, in their judgement, sufficiently strong. A principle that we now associate firmly with protection of the accused was originally designed to salve the consciences of the jury. Finally, the law was addressing the moral concerns that English jurors had wrestled with since the thirteenth century.

The same practices made their way across the Atlantic to the new colonies in what became the United States of America. Here, in the early nineteenth century, judges were still instructing jurors to convict if they had 'moral certainty'. As one chief justice explained, this meant certainty that satisfied their consciences. Inconsequential doubts they could disregard, but moral concerns they should take seriously. Nineteenth-century American juries, brought up in a strongly Christian tradition, were still troubled by the moral and theological consequences of a guilty verdict.[41]

THE PRONOUNCEMENT OF the Fourth Lateran Council did not have such an immediate effect in continental Europe, where courts continued to use ordeals for several decades.[42] But judges faced several problems: according to the principles established in Roman law, an accuser needed direct proof of a crime and the support of at least two witnesses before a court could convict. This made it almost impossible to prosecute a crime committed in private, however compelling the circumstantial evidence. So

Pope Innocent III's declaration that crime needed to be punished in the public interest prompted scholars to rethink the whole basis of criminal evidence. Gratian, the great twelfth-century scholar of canon law, had already proposed that judges could sentence someone for a 'notorious' crime, one which was firmly suspected by a large number of people, without an accusation or direct proof. And some judges began to hand down lesser sentences when they felt that the evidence was short of conclusive. When the Lateran Council directed that judges could summon suspected offenders to their courts, some theologians proposed that they should also be able to compel witnesses to give evidence. In doing so, they began laying a foundation for practices of judicial torture.

As in England, and undoubtedly for the same reasons, witnesses were often reluctant to go through the alarming and perilous ritual of accusing someone of a crime or other misdeed under oath. The scholars, accordingly, developed rules about 'half-proof'. In these cases, the judge could torture an accused in order to extract a confession. The attraction of this method was that it provided proof of the crime. If the accused confessed, the judge did not need to worry about the quality of the evidence, so his conscience could rest easy. The judges were soon using their newfound powers to summon witnesses and torture people accused of serious crimes. And they began meting out extremely harsh forms of justice. Reassured by the pope's declaration that it was important to punish crime, they decided that beatings, blindings, brandings, the slashing of nostrils, and hangings were all in the public interest.[43] Theologians and other writers continued to debate the justification for these punishments and some expressed doubts about the use of judicial torture. But by the sixteenth century a class of professional judges had developed who routinely used these methods, apparently without too much concern. It was only in the eighteenth century that judges felt able to do without the certainty provided by a confession and to sentence, albeit on a lesser scale, on the basis of 'suspicion'. Gradually, judicial torture was abandoned and the inquisitorial process as we know it today took shape.

THE EUROPEAN JURISTS were not the only ones to search for alternatives to oaths and ordeals in criminal cases, but everywhere, the scholars found it a challenge to develop legal rules for the processes of evidence-gathering and judgement. In China, Confucius disapproved of the harsh legal processes advocated by the 'legalist' scholars and promoted new ideas about moral education. But even he and his followers recognized the need for punishment in the interest of social order. Rather than resorting to ordeals, Chinese government officials came up with the idea of judicial torture several centuries before their European counterparts. It was already well established in the third century BCE, when the Qin drafted their legal code. We do not know for sure if Chinese officials had similar concerns to their Christian counterparts about the consequences of wrongful conviction, but it is clear that corrupt earthly judges could expect divine retribution in the underworld, where spiritual judges heard petitions, took evidence, and meted out justice.[44] Chinese magistrates were acutely aware that a confession was not foolproof, because many convicts appealed on the grounds that they had only confessed under the pain of the torture, and the higher courts did punish magistrates who wrongly convicted people. But they presumably still felt that a confession provided the best and safest justification for a blood punishment. Many also hoped for divine intervention to help solve difficult cases. They might interrogate a recalcitrant witness in front of an image of their city god in order to terrify him into confessing, for example, or even stage the trial in a temple. But these activities were not sanctioned as part of the official justice system. The lawmakers never prescribed oath-taking; nor did magistrates resort to ordeals. They had to extract confessions directly in order to justify punishing even a known criminal.

Indian Buddhists, meanwhile, took an extreme view of the problem of blood punishment.[45] In the classic account of his life, the Buddha renounced his wealth and family to become a wandering ascetic, casting doubt on the activities of the ruling classes. The Jataka tales, widely read moral stories dating from about the same period, recount the story of a prince who realizes that he cannot succeed his father as king without waging war and meting out blood punishments. It is, he concludes, impossible to be a good king and a good Buddhist at the same time. So, like the Buddha, he renounces his birthright. Buddhist writers developed sophisticated accounts about the wider moral purposes of punishment, which could be justified on the basis of reform and deterrence, but the purists among them continued to maintain that all blood punishment was sinful. Even at the beginning of the twentieth century, the highest monk officials in the Dalai Lama's government refused to sign a warrant for the mutilation of a minister they had just declared to be guilty of treason—and whose sentence was, in fact, carried out—on the ground that it would be inappropriate for them to do so as Buddhist monks.[46]

The Hindu brahmins managed to avoid these concerns, at least in their more extreme form, by declaring it to be the duty of the kshatriya class to govern, wage war, and mete out justice.[47] The laws of karma promised a miserable rebirth for anyone who led a sinful life, so the kings and their judges must have had similar concerns to their European counterparts about wrongful convictions. But the brahmins assured them that it was their dharma to maintain peace and order, and offered them detailed rules about how to go about prosecuting and punishing criminals. 'If the king punishes those who deserve punishment and puts to death those who deserve capital punishment, it is as if he has performed a hundred thousand sacrificial offerings', declares one medieval text.[48] The author then goes on to describe the many factors that should affect the assessment of the right punishment. It explains how a trial had to go through the stages of plaint, reply, evidence, and decision, during which the judge had to consider the qualification of the witnesses and examine them thoroughly, and weigh up and assess other forms of evidence and proof. 'Human trials', as the text put it, relied upon witnesses, documents, and inferences, while 'divine trials' used forms of what we would consider chance, along with oaths and ordeals. In his review of the scholarship on criminal procedures, the writer gives little indication that the Hindu judges suffered the same theological anxieties as those in medieval Christendom, and he repeatedly emphasizes that judges should only turn to 'divine' proof as a last resort. The appropriate form of the test depended on the caste of the witness, who had to undertake it after fasting in the presence of both a king and a brahmin. Presumably the detailed directions about the trial processes and the means of assessing the evidence allowed the judges to convict with a clear conscience in all but the most problematic cases.

Meanwhile, the early jurists of the Islamic world also formalized traditional practices of oath-taking. But these were hardly sufficient for the more centralized and sophisticated legal systems that the Abbasid sultans and caliphs established. The Quran gave them only the briefest guidance about punishing crimes and about the kind of evidence required to convict someone of adultery, rape, or murder, offences that merited a blood punishment. Over the centuries, the jurists developed a more extensive set of procedural rules and principles. But instead of helping the judges convict in difficult cases, by the eleventh century they were calling on judges to avoid criminal punishments in all cases of doubt.[49] The jurists saw themselves as heirs to the tradition of the Prophet and, from a very early date, distinguished their role from that of the caliph and his officials. The government's judges, the qadis, could hand down criminal sentences, which their officials would enforce, but most scholars were reluctant to act as judges themselves. Although they had the authority to say what the law was, they considered that the work of the judges was morally ambiguous, marred by corruption, coercion, and error.[50] Their role was to form a 'pious opposition', as they put it, to the use of political power.[51]

When the Seljuks swept down from Central Asia into Persia, ousting the Abbasid rulers, they established an administration based in what is now Turkey. Powerful and autocratic, the new rulers urged their judges to mete out harsh forms of justice and to make free with orders for execution, flogging, public shaming, and imprisonment. In their madrasas, at some remove from the power of government officials, Islamic jurists were concerned and felt they needed to provide checks and balances on the Seljuk's excessive use of executive power. They scoured records of cases, from early Medina to contemporary Yemen, to find precedents related to the principle of doubt, in an attempt to restrict the legitimacy of criminal punishments. The Arabic word for doubt, *shubha*, was broad, and they decided it could refer to doubts about the facts of a case, doubts about the law, or doubts about the morality of a proposed punishment. Seeking to give the principle a firm theological foundation, the jurists attributed it to a report from the Prophet's life. This was at best equivocal, but the scholars boldly declared that in a case involving any degree of doubt, the judge should demand multiple confessions. He should carry out an investigation into mitigating circumstances and resolve any textual uncertainty in favour of the accused.[52]

The Islamic jurists were obviously motivated by the same moral anxieties as their Christian counterparts, but they produced rules with a very different purpose. While the European doctrine of 'reasonable doubt' and the use of oaths, judicial torture, and juries helped judges decide when blood punishment was justified, the Islamic rules told judges when they ought to harbour doubts. They reflected the jurists', rather than the judges', anxieties about the morality of punishment. Instead of providing moral comfort, they injected an element of uncertainty into the judges' work, insisting on the problematic nature of a very wide range of cases. Their object was to deter capital sentences and to curb executive power by helping a morally anxious judge resist pressure from officials to hand down capital sentences on the grounds that his hands were tied under Islamic law. Over the centuries, some Islamic judges did turn to judicial torture to secure confessions before they made capital judgements in unclear cases.[53] But their fears about the consequences in the afterlife can only have been heightened by the jurists' doctrine of doubt. And many of them cited it to justify handing down lighter sentences than the evidence might otherwise have indicated.[54]

THE PROBLEMS OF punishment and the perils of judgement arise whenever some people assume the right to discipline and punish others. Over the centuries, many have found the process of judgement fraught with difficulties. Oaths and ordeals, which invoked the threat of divine sanction and sought direct confirmation of guilt or innocence, were the most basic techniques, used the world over to confirm the justness of a punishment. Gradually, some people established alternative practices, from the judicial torture of the Chinese to the juries of England, from the inquisitorial practices of European courts to the doctrine of doubt in the Islamic world. Eventually, more bureaucratic states established rules of evidence, which relieved the discomfort of judges and juries by defining what it meant to act legitimately. They also constrained the power of the judges and officials. This is one of the most dramatic ways in which modern laws, after so many centuries of trial and error, have offered new ways to fulfill the promise of justice.

Since the first lawmakers wrote out grand statements on stone slabs, people have repeatedly turned to law in the search for justice, not least by controlling the powers of their judges and officials. Objective rules offer a sense of certainty, that there is a right way to do things. The reasons for such an endeavour may be utterly pragmatic, such as the desire to establish and regulate mercantile relations through commercial laws. But laws may promise justice and confirm autonomy, sometimes by consolidating local custom, as they did among the Irish, the Icelanders, the Indian communities, and the Daghestani tribes. Laws can also create a sense that, by observing their rules, people are participating in a wider cosmological order, or following God's path for the world, as they did for those who observed the great religious systems. But in most legal systems, the laws also defined and limited how power should be exercised, giving people at least the possibility of challenging the actions of those who governed them. This is the rule of law, a dynamic that has run through history since the time of Hammurabi. Only in China did the emperors who presided over a disciplinary system resist this idea.

In the modern world, the rule of law has become an ideal to rival the religious and cosmological visions of the ancient legal systems. How they faded and European laws came to dominate the world is the story of the third part of this book.

PART III

ORDERING THE WORLD

CHAPTER TWELVE

FROM KINGS TO EMPIRES
The Rise of Europe and America

T he state laws that now dominate the world are largely based on those developed in European countries and America from the seventeenth century onwards. During that period, law has come to be firmly associated with the state and its processes of government in ways that combine law's disciplinary potential with its promise of justice and order. According to powerful international institutions, such as the United Nations and World Bank, laws should support democratic structures, efficient regulation, private property regimes, and individual rights, with an independent judiciary to resolve disputes and decide on criminal sanctions. And modern states should exercise sovereign jurisdiction within clearly demarcated borders. It is a remarkably successful and powerful model. But how did it emerge?

In the seventeenth century, Europe's monarchs were still waging debilitating wars over political borders, and the world's major political powers and most sophisticated legal systems were to be found in Asia. The Manchu Qing rulers, then establishing a new regime in imperial China, went on to preside over the most elaborate and bureaucratic legal system anywhere in the world for over two centuries. The Muslim Mughals had extended their control over most of northern India, where they enjoyed unchallenged political power and prosperity. The Safavids, who also recognized Islamic law, ruled in Persia, and the Ottomans were reaching the height of their powers in Constantinople. Having toppled the remnant of the Byzantine Empire in 1453, they controlled Mesopotamia, Egypt, Greece, and the Balkans and had made large parts of North Africa into vassal states; and in 1683, they reached the gates of Vienna. The Ottomans also established their own *kanun*, a code of civil law loosely based on the shari'a. As one scholar has put it, 'Islamic law sheltered a world economy and an international commercial culture pioneered by Armenians, Hindus, and Greeks, which was as developed as that of Europe'.[1]

European monarchs were acutely aware of Ottoman power and the sophisticated civilizations of the Mughals, the Qing, and the Safavids, with whose merchants they were eager to trade. And in the eighteenth century, Montesquieu was not alone in acknowledging the superiority of Chinese law.[2] But Europeans were already convinced of the excellence of their own legal and religious traditions and the benefits that these bestowed on their people. When they sent settlers to the Americas, many declared that they should send their laws, too. Given the disorganized nature of these laws, this confidence in their ability to order distant parts of the world was remarkable.

In the seventeenth century, European laws were partial, overlapping, and unsystematic. Yet, over the course of the next two centuries, movements for codification in continental Europe transformed the civil law into a number of organized national legal systems, while judges in England rationalized and expanded the reach of the common law. Their work was also taken up on the other side of the Atlantic, where the new American colonies were enthusiastic proponents of law in their quest for

CALECHVT CELEBERRI-
MVM INDIÆ EMPORIVM.

licut in the sixteenth-century. The port was one of the most important for European
rchants trading with the Islamic and Chinese empires.

French scholar Paul Pelliot travelled
to Western China in 1908 to explore
the thousands of manuscripts in
Dunhuang, newly opened after nine
hundred years.

A page from the chronicle
of the Tibetan Wa clan,
discovered at Dunhuang.

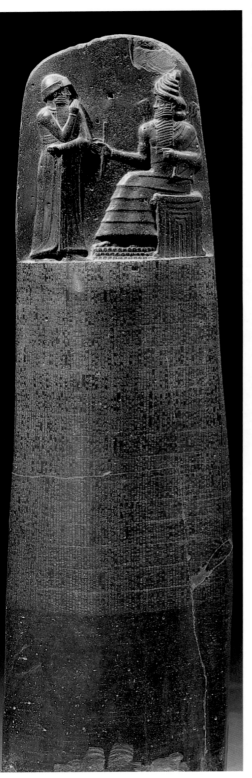

The granite law stone created for King Hammurabi of Babylon in around 1770 BCE. The king is standing before Shamash, god of the sun, and both sides of the stone are covered with laws in cuneiform script.

Ashurbanipal, king of Assyria (r. 669–c. 631 BCE), collected a vast library of texts inscribed on clay tablets. Contemporary images depict him with a stylus tucked into his belt, even when fighting a lion.

...dradaman, second-century
...r of Saka in western India,
...o commissioned a lengthy
...cription in Sanskrit. This
...ed to secure the authority
...he brahmins and their
...l texts.

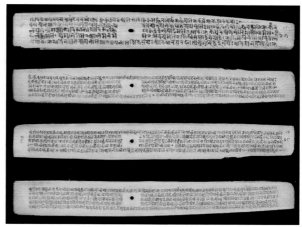

A fifteenth-century copy of the Naradasmrti,
a Dharmashastra text that concentrates on legal
matters, made for the Himalayan Malla kings.

Shivaji, a seventeenth-
century rajput warlord,
had to commission a legal
opinion from a renowned
brahmin to confirm his
royal status.

Tang Emperor Taizong (r. 626–649) receives Gar Tongtsen Yülsung, ambassador of the Tibetan Empire, at his court. Copy of an original painted in 641.

A Tang dynasty exam paper from Turfan or Dunhuang, reused for a funeral shoe.

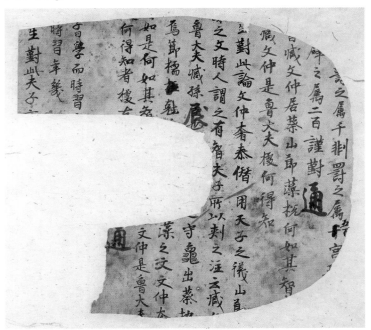

Upper-class Romans lived and worked in elegant villas decorated with frescoes. These Pompeian women are encouraging a girl to read.

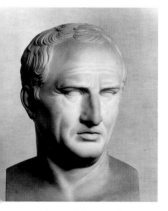

arcus Tullius Cicero, the at legal scholar and orator.

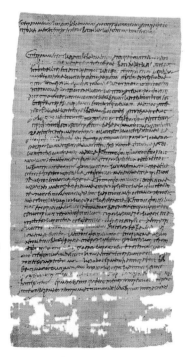

Papyrus recording the registration of property, prepared for the Roman census of Arabia in 127. It was hidden in a cave by a Jewish woman fleeing from the Romans after the Bar Kokhba revolt.

Learning and literacy flourished under the Abbasid caliphate. Scholars in a library in Baghdad, from a thirteenth-century manuscript.

Senior Jewish scholars also made Baghdad a centre of learning, remaining there into the twentieth century. Photograph from 1910.

Alfonso X of Castile commissioned the legal text known as the *Siete Partidas*, inspired by Justinian's *Corpus Iuris Civilis*, in 1265.

Denarius representing Charlemagne as Roman emperor after his coronation in 800.

The laws of the Anglo-Saxon king Aethelstan, written in the tenth century, reflected the expanding reach of royal government. From the later Leges Angliae.

This aestal, or pointer, was made for King Alfred, to help readers to follow the manuscripts he distributed throughout his kingdom in the ninth century.

Thingvellir, site of the Althing, where the Icelanders gathered every year to listen to and promulgate new laws.

Grágás, 'the grey goose', the Icelandic book of laws collected during the twelfth century.

The baptism of Rurikid prince Vladimir in the tenth century, depicted in a fifteenth century vers of the Russian Primary Chronicle. The event marked the beginning o an era of lawmaking in Rus.

The Armenian priest and teacher, Mxit'ar Goš, began work on his legal text in 1184. This monastery, at Tatev, was then already three centuries old.

Legal manual discovered in a Geniza, the storeroom of a synagogue, at Fustat, in Egypt from the eleventh or twelfth centuries. It sets out the conditions for debt agreements.

Irrigation channels in a central Algerian oasis just north of the Touat region. The villagers kept thousands of documents using Islamic legal forms.

The village of Tindi, in Daghestan, in the late 1890s.

The Song emperors, here Emperor Huizong (1082–1135), hosted elegant banquets for their scholar officials.

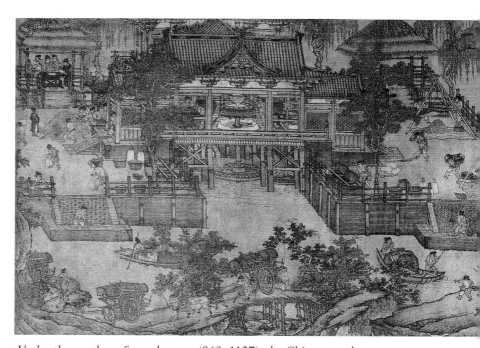

Under the northern Song dynasty (960–1127), the Chinese made numerous technological innovations, including harnessing hydraulic power to drive a grain mill.

English law students kept commonplace books in which they copied out important legal texts and decisions. This book, from the fifteenth or sixteenth centuries, contains the Natura Brevium, a commentary on the application of writs.

Manorial court roll from Assheton of Downham, in the Wapentake of Blackburn, from 1621–1622.

Lostwithiel Palace, in Cornwall, constructed by the Earls of Cornwall for the stannary administration in the late thirteenth century. It housed the Convocation Hall, smelting houses, the coinage hall, stannary courts, and the stannary prison. Engraving from the eighteenth century.

In 1470, a boy named Hans Hegenheim was convicted for theft and as punishment thrown into the Reuss River bound with a rope and pulled behind a boat. He survived, and was considered to have atoned for his crime, and went on to live a long life.

Kunigunde of Luxembourg, wife of Holy Roman Emperor Heinrich II, was accused of adultery in around 1010. To prove her innocence she walked over red-hot ploughshares, as depicted in this bas-relief from Bamberg Cathedral.

The ordeal by hot iron, as depicted in a twelfth-century European manuscript.

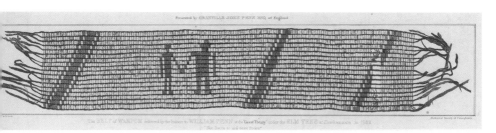

When they entered into the Treaty of Shackamaxon with William Penn in 1682, the Lenape people presented him with a belt of wampum, a symbolic object used by Native Americans to confirm important agreements.

The representatives of the English king confirmed and recorded their treaties in their own ways.

William Blackstone published the volume of his *Commentaries he Laws of England* in 1765.

"COLLARED!!"

"I BEG THAT YOU WILL LOOK UPON ME SIMPLY AS REPRESENTING THE EXECUTIVE POWER, AND THE AUTHORITY OF THE LAW."—*The Premier's Speech at the Guildhall, Thursday, October 13.*

By the late nineteenth century, the law and its executives had become matters for satire in publications such as *Punch* magazine.

A QUAND LE RÉVEILLON DES PEUPLES

Warren Hastings (1732–1818), British colonial administrator, was considered one of the founders of the British Empire in India. In this portrait by Sir Joshua Reynolds, he is shown with a pile of papers and a seal with Persian script.

This cartoon of the Berlin conference from 1884 depicts Belgian King Leopold II dividing up the pumpkin that is the Congo, flanked by German Emperor William I and the crowned bear of the Russian Empire.

British colonial administrators employed local Nigerians as officials. This court clerk is surrounded by his messengers. Photo from October 1914.

Abu al-Sa'ud (1490–1574), one of the chief Ottoman theologians, teaching law. Illustration from a sixteenth-century manuscript.

A qadi and a mufti (on the left) are offered refreshments during a break from their work in Afghanistan in 1960.

ty-year-old Grand Ayatollah Ali al-Sistani and Francis met in Iraq in March 2021.

Seyh Suleyman Kaslioglu, Turkish Mufti of Rhodes, in 1957.

In the Tibetan areas of Ladakh, villagers turned their backs on law and legal records, even in the twenty-first century.

In the eastern Tibetan region of Amdo, respected mediators resumed their work of resolving feuds after the end of the Cultural Revolution.

independence. Amidst wars, revolution, and colonial conquests, the rising European states developed powerful new forms of law.

DURING THE MIDDLE Ages, most European courts applied an amalgam of the civil law and their own customary rules. In France, the kings ordered that every community should have its own *coutumes*, a code of customary laws, and the Coutume de Paris, published in 1510, became the standard applied throughout France. Meanwhile, the Parisian courts adopted Romanocanonical procedures, those developed by the church and based on Roman precedents, and a new class of professional lawyers emerged to implement them. In Spain, too, the monarch ordered a new compilation of laws to supplement the *Siete Partidas*, which had been modelled on Justinian's code. Customary norms and processes remained important, particularly in the lands that made up the Holy Roman Empire, by now the dominant political power in Europe.[3] Here, the emperors presided over a loose confederacy of Germanic principalities and free cities, most of which had their own courts, and they regularly referred to the Lehnrecht, the feudal law codified by the Lombards in the twelfth century.

Gradually things changed. The emperors passed a few general laws, particularly concerning the election of the emperor and the role of his electors, and in 1495 Emperor Maximillian I had sought to institute a 'perpetual peace' by forbidding the feud and other unauthorized violence.[4] He also established a new supreme court, the Reichskammergericht, to which appeals could be brought from all over the empire. A few decades later, in 1532, Emperor Charles V issued a criminal code, the *Carolina*, based on Italian precedents. He required judges who were not legally trained to seek advice from scholars—those in Prague,

Vienna, Heidelberg, and Cologne were particularly renowned—entrenching both their authority and that of Roman law. Many German princes, keen to establish more effective administrations, now saw the civil law as a useful tool for building a bureaucratic state as well as a means to counter the independence of the more powerful feudal lords. Subsequent emperors recognized the potential for the civil law to unify their disparate territories and required that the judges of the Reichskammergericht be trained jurists and apply Roman-canonical procedures. As the professional lawyers flourished, their authority and social pretentions drew criticism from some, but influential reformers praised the Roman law for its ability to stand above petty factionalism.[5] It represented, for many, the impartial law of peace and order.

At the outbreak of the Thirty Years' War, in 1618, the Holy Roman Empire included most of modern Germany along with parts of what are now the Netherlands, Italy, Belgium, the Czech Republic, and Poland. Its monarchies, duchies, principalities, bishoprics, counties, imperial abbeys, and villages may have maintained their own courts, but they all recognized the civil law. Lawyers quoted passages from Justinian's *Corpus Iuris Civilis* in the courts of Paris, Valladolid, and Vienna. In Scotland, too, James V confirmed that judges trained in the civil law should sit in the Court of Sessions.[6] The Scottish judges accepted continental written procedures in place of common law remedies and turned to Justinian's text to supplement Scots law, citing its 'equity' and 'rationality'. The civil law had come to provide a point of reference and source of common principles for a vast array of local courts, rulers, customs, and legal processes.

IT WAS DIFFERENT south of the Scottish border. In the mid-sixteenth century, England was hardly an important world power, and its law was still an uncoordinated set of codes, courts, principles, and procedures.[7] Since the establishment of central courts by Henry II in the twelfth century, the English monarchs and their parliaments had issued statutes to expand and improve their government, raise revenue, and improve the society and economy. But the substance of the law applied in the higher courts was largely shaped by writs, the forms of words that litigants had to use when they presented their cases, and this 'common law' was far from comprehensive. Ordinary people largely followed, and expected others to follow, regional customs.

Even the central courts, in which the common law formed something like a system, varied in composition and jurisdiction, sometimes competing for cases. The judges of the King's, or Queen's, Bench heard cases involving the Crown; the Court of Common Pleas considered private disputes; and the Court of Exchequer dealt with revenue matters. During the twice-yearly assizes, twelve royal judges travelled around the country to hear cases that originated in the regions. The chancellor, the highest of the royal ministers, established his own court, known as Chancery, which allowed petitioners more flexible procedures than the rigid writs of the kings' courts, as did the Exchequer and the Court of Requests, which heard small claims.[8] There was also a High Court of Chivalry, which heard claims about distinctions of honour, using Roman law procedures, while the court of the Lord High Admiral had maritime jurisdiction.

In practice, the ability of the monarchs' ministers to regulate people's lives was limited, and the central courts could not adjudicate all their disputes. The church courts, albeit now subject to royal authority, issued marriage licenses, granted probate, heard matrimonial disputes, adjudicated on tithes, and considered allegations of sexual misconduct. The manorial courts continued to hear local cases, record land transactions, and recognize local customs and institutions, although these were gradually overshadowed by the borough courts, established in the towns, to which people took most debt claims. In these urban courts, justices of the peace also considered allegations of petty crime, while a range of other local tribunals considered disputes that arose in the markets, fairs, and forests.

Both lawyers and judges nevertheless talked about 'the law and custom of the realm' when they presented and argued their cases and negotiated their way through the technical details of writs and pleadings. If pushed, most judges would probably have agreed that the 'common law' was found in the learning of the legal professionals and the reasoning they used in the higher courts.[9] In the fifteenth century, Sir Thomas Littleton, a judge of the Common Pleas, had produced his *Treatise on Tenures*, in which he tried to make sense of the complicated system of landholdings and tenancies.[10] He wrote of 'the common learning of the lawyers' and their 'understanding of the law'. Also in the fifteenth century, Sir John Fortescue, chief justice of the King's Bench, wrote a eulogy on the English law, in fact a polemic against the introduction of new courts. In it, he praised the qualities of English legal reasoning, emphasizing the fundamental principles that judges expressed as legal maxims.[11] The legal scholar Christopher St. German crafted another polemical tract in 1523, this time against Henry VIII's adviser Thomas Wolsey. St. German linked the common law with God's will and his eternal laws. Unsystematic though it may have been, both scholars and judges were keen to emphasize the qualities, and also the ancient origins, of the English common law.

Even the magistrates in the lower courts talked frequently of the 'excellence' of the English law and the 'liberties' of the people that it upheld.[12] To a large extent they were thinking of the safeguards of the courts' procedures, above all jury trial. In the early seventeenth century, the lawyer and politician Francis Ashley declared that the phrase *nullus liber homo* (no free man) came to the mind of every Englishman who felt threatened or oppressed. Clause 29 of Magna Carta, with its declaration that 'no free man' should be imprisoned or condemned in court, save by the judgement of his peers or the law of the land, still stood as a fundamental declaration of the liberties of the English.[13]

By the end of Elizabeth's reign in the early seventeenth century, local magistrates could consult cheaply produced treatises on law and its history and on equity and jurisprudence along with practical manuals and extracts from statutes.[14] These works provided guidance about procedures, which was what the magistrates most needed to know, along with some discussion on the substance of the law. And people flocked to the courts, initiating more cases per capita than during any other period in their history.[15] But even the 'common law', applied by the higher courts, hardly formed a systematic body of rules and principles. There were no textbooks which even tried to be comprehensive, and success in court depended on using the right writ. Procedure was everything. During their training at the Inns of Court, law students listened to 'readings' (lectures) on statutes, discussed hypothetical cases, and noted down legal arguments in their 'Year Books' and collections of pleadings, while judges felt that they ought to follow the reasoning and judgements of their predecessors. But case reports were sketchy, and the system of precedent, which renders an earlier decision binding on a later judge, was far from firmly established.[16]

ALTHOUGH ENGLISH LAW was an imperfect system, there was a sense that law was important, something with its own authority. This led to political tensions between the monarch and the judiciary in the early seventeenth century. Both Henry VIII and his daughter, Elizabeth, had tried to strengthen the 'royal prerogative', which allowed them to bypass Parliament by using their Council to issue charters and proclamations. Elizabeth used it to grant patents to merchants, which gave them monopolies over certain types of international trade. Citing the threat of foreign invasion, along with local conspiracies, she also expanded the work of her court, the Star Chamber, which provided a summary form of justice, and boldly claimed that 'exhorbitante offenses were not subjecte to an ordinayre course of law'.[17] But she did not entirely turn her back on common law institutions. And even a staunch supporter of her royal supremacy, the cleric Richard Hooker, argued that the law should guide the queen (or king), not the other way around. The commonwealth, the English state, would then, he claimed, be like 'a harp or melodious instrument, the strings whereof are tuned and handled all by one'.[18] This left the door open for others to use the law to challenge unpopular royal initiatives.

In the early seventeenth century, James I, less politically astute than his predecessor, claimed that the king was the source of all law, that he owned it, and that he had the right to define, regulate, and administer it. Neither Parliament nor the king's judges could accept these claims, and even James's chancellors, Lord Ellesmere and Sir Francis Bacon, argued that the king's legal powers ultimately derived from the common law. Sir John Davies, the attorney general in Ireland, made extravagant statements about the law being the 'common custome of the realme', ancient and immemorial. Following his lead, the parliamentarian Thomas Hedley argued, in 1610, that the common law was the product of reason and immemorial custom which had evolved in response to the particular experiences of England and its people. It was the common law, he maintained, that had established the authority of Parliament to make statutes.[19]

In the same year, Sir Edward Coke, chief justice of the Common Pleas, considered a dispute about the jurisdiction of the London College of Physicians, *Dr Bonham's Case*.[20] In his judgement, Coke famously declared that the courts would not enforce any parliamentary statute that was 'against common right and reason, or repugnant, or impossible to be performed'. The common law, he said, would 'control it' and 'adjudge it to be void'.

Coke had already had an argument with James about legal jurisdiction, in which he declared that the king had to obey the law because 'the law protected the king'. This was to put the authority of the highest judges above that of the king, and it provoked James to 'high indignation'. Coke had to apologise to James, falling 'flat on the floor' to seek his pardon, as a contemporary report puts it.[21] But the standoff between the two men continued. It came to a head in 1616, during a tussle over the jurisdictions of the King's Bench and Chancery. In *The Case of Commendams*, Coke persuaded the other judges to declare that the king's attempt to prevent them from reaching a decision was invalid. Furious, James summoned the judges, ripped up their judgement, and declared that he knew the common law to be 'the most favourable to kings'. The other judges bowed to the pressure, begging the king's forgiveness, but Coke defended his duty to do what he considered to be right and was dismissed as chief justice. Later writers may have exaggerated Coke's determination to confront the monarch and resist royal absolutism, but there is no doubt that the judge was convinced of the superiority of the common law. The idea that the law imposed limits on the authority of the king, the 'rule of law', continued to resonate in legal and political circles over the decades. Coke's arguments would also be taken up, to dramatic effect, on the other side of the Atlantic.

Amidst all these debates and arguments, some expressed concern that, over the centuries, the common law had become a tangle and needed to be synthesized. But, resisting calls for codification, Sir Edward Coke insisted that its flexibility and refinement made the common law superior to the civil law.[22] And, following his dismissal as a judge, he set out to describe the 'frame of the ancient common laws of this realm' in his *Institutes of the Laws of England*, a title that deliberately invoked Justinian.[23] Coke's first volume, published in 1628, concerned property and inheritance and was largely based on Littleton's

Tenures. The second set out the statutes that were 'declaratory of the principal grounds of the fundamental laws of England'. The third discussed the criminal law, and the fourth presented a 'map' of 'all the high, honourable, venerable, and necessary tribunals, and courts of justice within his majesties realms and dominions'. Coke recognized the canon law and civil law along with forest law, law of marque, and law merchant; the laws and customs of Jersey, Guernsey, and Man; the laws of the stannaries; and the laws of the East, West, and Middle Marches, as well as the authority of custom.[24]

While Coke's work went some way towards finding system and order in this tangle of English laws, other writers felt that an alphabetical list was the way forward. Yet others tried to synthesize legal procedures, concerned about notorious delays in court proceedings.[25] Calls for codification continued, but scholars who tried to produce general accounts later in the century gave up in despair.[26] One judge, Sir Matthew Hale, argued that, in the fourteenth century, Edward III had extracted 'one law, to be observed throughout the kingdom', from diverse customary and provincial laws, and that it had become 'the complexion and constitution of the English commonwealth'.[27] But, as he lamented, 'the particulars thereof are so many, and the connexions of things so various therein, that as I shall beforehand confess that I cannot reduce it to an exact logical method, declare that I do despair at the first, yea, the second or third essay'. It was over a century before Sir William Blackstone compiled a work that would supplant Coke's volumes.

MOST EUROPEAN STATES had adopted some aspects of the civil law by the seventeenth century, particularly in terms of procedure. But when James I, as king of both England and Scotland, attempted to unify their divergent legal traditions on the basis of

Roman law, judges objected strenuously on both sides of the border.[28] England had its own 'common law', 'the common custom
of the realm', which protected the liberties of all Englishmen. It
was the birthright of the English and could not be extended to
the Scots. Earlier, as he had consolidated his power over Wales,
Henry VIII had passed the Laws in Wales Acts, which declared
that 'the laws, ordinances and statutes of this realm of England'
were to replace the 'divers and discrepant' laws and customs of
Wales. But the judges took a different view with regards to Scotland. In 1608, they decided that a Scotsman could bring a case in
an English court to claim land in England, but that the English
courts could not exercise jurisdiction over land in Scotland.[29]
This posed a considerable dilemma when the English monarchs
sent settlers across the Atlantic. What was to happen to the laws
and customs of the colonized lands? Could their new inhabitants
continue to enjoy the protection of the English law?

Following the pioneering activities of Spanish and Dutch explorers, English adventurers began to organize expeditions to
North America in the late sixteenth century. Elizabeth I issued
charters allowing them to establish settlements, and James I followed suit. In 1606, he granted a charter to the London Company
authorizing it to establish a permanent settlement in Virginia.
The company was to 'make, ordain, and establish all manner of
orders, laws, directions, instructions, forms, and ceremonies of
government and magistracy, fit and necessary for and concerning the government of the said colony'. Settlers, often Quakers
and Puritans, were soon establishing small communities in other
territories as well under charters which granted them power to
make their own laws as long as they were 'near', 'agreeable', and
'not repugnant' to the laws of England.[30]

The English governments were distracted by the upheavals of
the English Civil War in the mid-seventeenth century, and for a
while they left the colonies largely free to govern themselves.[31]
Many developed forms of local justice emphasizing informality

and consensus. But as their populations expanded, most established courts that followed English models, selecting local leaders to act as magistrates. Already in 1618, the London Company had introduced a system of property tenures that followed common law principles, and Virginia lawyers began to refer to the texts of Littleton and Coke in property disputes. They also found useful precedents in the laws of the councils of the English border regions. In practice, those who acted as lawyers in the new American settlements had rarely received much training. Many were simply laymen who took an interest in the law, reading English practice manuals and commentaries on legal texts, while the magistrates studied guides created for justices of the peace and treatises on wills. But the settlers found the new courts useful and flocked to them in large numbers. In the seventeenth century, the courts of Massachusetts heard cases brought by merchants, debtors, creditors, Swedes, Quakers, farmers, artisans, servants, and even slaves.[32]

Back in England, there was considerable debate over the status of the American settlements, which largely centred on the question of whether the English Parliament had jurisdiction over their territories or the Crown could administer them directly. The issue had some significance in the tensions between king and Parliament, which culminated with the execution of Charles I in 1649. Some judges backed the king and his claims to rule without any constraints, and it seemed for a while as if this might undermine the authority of the common law and its ability to control monarchical absolutism, for which Coke had argued so strenuously. In his *Leviathan*, published in 1651, Thomas Hobbes famously called for a strong ruler who would impose order through law.[33] But the common law and its judges survived. Oliver Cromwell committed himself and his regime to upholding the common law—he needed its legitimacy—even as scholars debated whether he had 'usurped' the crown.[34]

After the Glorious Revolution of 1688, when James II was deposed in favour of his daughter Mary and her husband William of Orange, the parliaments began to take a more active role in the government of the country, debating and passing new statutes. But the kings' courts successfully maintained their authority and now made a deliberate effort to expand their jurisdiction.[35] They took over more of the cases traditionally handled by the church courts and developed the law relating to commercial activities, to some extent assimilating it with the laws applied in continental Europe. This meant assuming jurisdiction in the application of the Lex Mercatoria, the legal practices followed by merchants. Chancery remained a separate jurisdiction, as did the admiralty courts, but the king's judges successfully restricted their remit, eventually drawing both into the system of the common law.

Taking an interest in the changing dynamics of local government, the King's Bench judges also expanded their capacity to pass judgement on the activities of officials. From the Tudor period, urban governments had begun to expand their responsibilities, taking charge of roads and bridges, licensing alehouses, enforcing labour regulations, and caring for paupers and illegitimate children. Royal charters granted them powers to hold markets and raise tolls, and many created long sets of bylaws. In Leicester, for example, the town's laws confirmed rights to common fields, required Sabbath observance, and took measures to ensure the supply of tallow for candles, a stock of coal for sale to the poor, and leather buckets for firefighting. They regulated the repair of pavements and the weighing of wool for sale, and forbade the sale of bread and gloves by 'foreigners', that is, anyone from another county.[36] Urban authorities now regulated the lives of town dwellers more than the local groups that made up their guild and manor courts. Enclosures and drainage in the Fens, meanwhile, caused social unrest, encouraging those who were dislocated to try to disrupt schemes that primarily, as they saw it, benefitted wealthy Essex landowners. They launched complaints against members of the drainage commissions along with town councillors and justices of the peace and found the royal courts ready to hear their cases. The King's Bench duly developed new forms of action which allowed people to complain about 'misgovernment' and to argue that officials should uphold the common good, and officials themselves often brought cases against their peers. The higher courts were now sitting in judgement on officials and their administration.

Both judges and magistrates continued to emphasize the liberties granted by Magna Carta, along with the Petition of Right, the statement of civil liberties Parliament sent to Charles I in 1638, and the Habeas Corpus Amendment Act of 1679.[37] Together, these laws guaranteed people freedom from arbitrary arrest, equal treatment before the courts, and trial by a jury of their peers. As one scholar has put it, the educated classes associated the legal regime centred on the common law and the courts with ideas of justice, equality of process, and active consent, which elevated them above the oppressed condition of other European peoples.[38] In practice, too, the cumulative effect of the new legislation was a relatively uniform set of principles for such things as relief for the poor and regulation of labour. Meanwhile, many local courts adopted forms of action and procedure from the common law, including the use of juries instead of oath-helpers.[39] All this, along with the involvement of the King's Bench in local government, contributed to at least some sense of a common system of justice. But it was still not unified.

MOST AMERICAN SETTLERS also believed in the benefits of the English common law, but by the late seventeenth century some were already arguing that they should not be subject to the laws of its Parliament.[40] They were, after all, a long way from

London. But the post-Restoration parliaments were not inclined to give up control over their foreign possessions or the benefits of the transatlantic trade, to which the French posed a threat. Various government bodies tried to assume more direct control, granting charters to new colonies, such as Pennsylvania, which required the governors to send legislation for approval by the Privy Council. The Board of Trade, meanwhile, set up to regulate the colonies and their commerce, reviewed colonial legislation for conformity with the common law, although the older colonies had more freedom to pass new laws as long as they were 'not repugnant to the laws of Great Britain'.

Some governors now invited English lawyers to join their administrations, but many sent back alarming reports about the state of the colonies' laws. The Earl of Bellomont, when he arrived as governor of New York in 1698, declared that the attorney general of Rhode Island was 'a poor illiterate mechanic, very ignorant', while his predecessor was 'very corrupt, brutish, with no principles in religion'.[41] And one English barrister commented that Virginia's courts combined the work of Chancery, the King's Bench, Common Pleas, and Admiralty, so 'the sense of the law was mistaken, and the form and method of proceeding was often very irregular'.[42] The Board of Trade directed that governors and other administrators should take steps to ensure proper legal standards among the settlers. Under this pressure, American lawyers began to refer more closely to English laws and customs. The Rhode Island Assembly acquired and consulted a book of English statutes. Lawyers and judges studied Coke's work on property, which was frequently republished and circulated widely. Gradually, the colonies consolidated their legal institutions into more unified systems, recognizing the common law, while their lawyers undertook more specialist training. Indeed, free of the historical complexities of English legal institutions, American lawyers could often develop more systematic and coherent procedures than their counterparts across the Atlantic.[43]

Some English writers were still troubled by the idea that English law, which they regarded as a privilege as much as a form of governance, should not be applied directly overseas. The judge and jurist Sir William Blackstone maintained that the American colonies were conquered lands, so the common law could not apply to them directly. Their laws were similar, he argued, simply because they had been copied from the English. This, incidentally, meant that they could maintain slavery, something that was already subject to debate in England. But when Blackstone published the first volume of his monumental *Commentaries on the Laws of England*, in 1765, American lawyers eagerly ordered copies and studied it avidly.[44] Its contents were disorganized, but Blackstone had made a heroic effort to bring order to the rules of the common law. And this was just the text that Americans needed to develop their nascent legal systems. The English publisher sold 1,000 copies in America before a local edition appeared, which quickly sold another 1,400. The most eminent lawyers subscribed, and the renowned Chief Justice John Marshall claimed he had read it four times by the age of twenty-seven. More than lawyers, Blackstone had intended it for laymen. Farmers, merchants, cabinetmakers, cordwainers, soldiers, and tavern keepers all consulted its pages. Initially, some of the more independence-minded American politicians objected to Blackstone's view that they did not enjoy common law rights, and legal scholars supplemented his text with commentaries on the new American laws. But no one doubted that Blackstone was the starting point for anyone keen to understand, follow, and develop the law in America.[45]

IN ENGLAND, MEANWHILE, a combination of political and judicial activities continued to develop the common law. Parliament held more regular sessions after 1688 and found itself responding to increasing numbers of petitions for new legislation. Concerned about social problems, justices of the peace, members of a growing middle class, and new voluntary associations all lobbied for new laws, better methods of policing, and more effective penalties. They introduced bills to penalize gin drinking and practices of prostitution, which they saw as both symptom and cause of spiralling poverty, lawlessness, and disorder, particularly in London, and they lobbied for new criminal offences with extremely harsh punishments. Moral panic about crime was matched by anxiety about overregulation and abuses of power in a pattern all too familiar to the modern world. But by the 1750s, parliamentarians had accepted the necessity of legislating for the day-to-day government of their nation. People came to see law in the decisions of their Parliament as much as in the ancient principles of the common law.[46]

Still, the idea that the common law had an existence and authority of its own, apart from that of the monarchs and their parliaments, did not disappear. Both Radicals and Whigs, when they were in opposition, cited the common law as a guarantor against arbitrary and tyrannical rule. It represented a series of fundamental rights, they claimed, which the government was bound to protect and which it could not alter without the people's consent. They took inspiration from theories developed by philosophers and legal scholars about natural rights.[47] Hugo Grotius, the Dutch legal philosopher, had laid the basis for these ideas in the early seventeenth century in his influential work on natural law, which he had equated with Christian principles. The English philosopher John Locke further developed these ideas in the seventeenth century in his influential writings on property ownership. He argued that individuals had natural rights to own property on the basis of the labour they put into it.

These ideas about natural laws and rights, particularly as they concerned property, had a tremendous influence across the Atlantic.[48] Following the conclusion of its very expensive wars with France, the British Parliament tried to extract more revenues from its flourishing American colonies. Inevitably, this led to resentment and resistance, and although there was now a sense of a common legal heritage, more and more Americans became determined to achieve autonomy, many lawyers among them. Several seized upon Coke's ideas about liberties and property rights, along with his famous statements in *Dr Bonham's Case*, which seemed to put the authority of the law above the power of the king. A number of them talked of the 'fundamental rights' of Englishmen and declared that the legal control exercised by the English monarch and his government was against the principles of natural equity. Even though Coke and his contemporaries had never seriously questioned the authority of Parliament, American activists talked of the common law in the same terms as natural law. It promised individuals a set of fundamental rights, they maintained, and guaranteed their freedom. Rather than substantive rules handed down by the ruler, the law required the consent of the people.

These arguments took their place alongside claims that the settlers had purchased their lands from the Indigenous peoples and improved them with their labour, that the Crown could not revoke its charters, and that the colonialists provided valuable benefits to England in its defence against the French and their popery. These arguments successfully appealed to American people across religious and regional divides, helping to create a shared political and legal culture. Blackstone's insistence on the importance of natural, inherent, and inalienable rights provided valuable support.[49] By the mid-1770s, John Adams was declaring that the laws of New England derived not from Parliament, or even from the common law, but from the law of nature. 'Our ancestors', he maintained, 'were entitled to the common law of England when they emigrated', but just so much of it as they pleased. The Preamble to the Declaration of Independence, ratified in 1776, appealed to the principles of natural law, proclaiming the 'self-evident' truth that 'all men are created equal' and 'endowed by their Creator with certain unalienable rights', including 'Life, Liberty, and the Pursuit of happiness'.

In practice, after Independence, American states continued to use and develop the common law they had inherited from their English forebears. By the time of the Declaration, the English common law was so well established in the American courts and their procedures, in the arguments made by lawyers, and in the maxims cited by judges that there was no question of trying to establish any other system.[50] People could no longer take appeals to the Privy Council in London, but they continued to read Blackstone's *Commentaries* and to cite English cases in their courts. Ideas about natural law and rights had come together with the practices and principles of the English common law to form the basis for what was to develop into one of the dominant legal systems of the modern world.

BUT ENGLISH COMMON law was not without its critics. In 1811, the English scholar and social reformer Jeremy Bentham wrote to James Madison, the fourth president of the United States, offering to create a new legal code for America. This, he claimed, would free the new country from 'the yoke' of the wordless, boundless, shapeless common law 'which remains about your necks'.[51] He was one of a number of reformers who believed passionately in the need for written legal codes on both sides of the Atlantic. Their arguments largely fell on deaf ears in England and America, but it was different in continental Europe. Here, powerful movements for codification were already coming to a head.

France's descent into revolutionary chaos and the disintegration of the Holy Roman Empire in the late eighteenth century, along with the discovery and settlement of the Americas, seem to have inspired European writers and reformers to pursue new debates about the sovereignty of national parliaments and the authority of their laws. How, some wondered, was the idea of parliamentary sovereignty to be reconciled with the idea that natural law protected individual freedom against tyranny? Was the legislature supreme, or could judges disregard a statute that offended against principles of natural law? Could individuals rely on their inherent rights to avoid the tyranny of a ruler or government?

These debates built on theories about natural laws and rights that scholars had developed over the centuries, and that John Locke and other political reformers in England had now taken up. For their part, continental scholars formulated the idea of the 'law of nations', a body of general principles that were supposed to apply to all people wherever they lived. They built on the Roman concept of the *ius gentium*, the laws common to all nations, which were distinct from the legal privileges enjoyed by Roman citizens. In the sixteenth century, the French legal scholar Charles du Moulin had laid the groundwork for the new ideas by trying to synthesize the idea of customary law with Roman laws and principles. Then Hugo Grotius, in the early seventeenth century, argued that natural law could be discovered by observing rules common to the laws of all civilized people. The theories of Grotius and his colleagues soon commanded respect throughout Europe, and scholars began to look for principles of natural law in Roman texts. Some, like the German jurist Samuel von Pufendorf, sought to align the idea of natural law with Christian theology. God, he argued, had created natural law for man. But not all scholars were so theologically minded. The German mathematician and philosopher Gottfried Leibniz advocated a system of laws based on logic. And, in his work on the civil law published in 1689, the French scholar Jean Domat recast Roman law according to what he argued were the logical principles of natural law. As in England, continental scholars were developing powerful ideas about a form of law that transcended political authority and, in this case, political divides, whether it was rooted in ancient tradition, Christian theology, logic, or common humanity.

The turmoil of the Thirty Years' War in the seventeenth century encouraged scholars to think more pragmatically about the purposes of the law and what it could achieve. Many became convinced that they needed a system of impartial law that could transcend the 'human passions' and antagonisms of their rulers, whose wars had done so much to devastate lives and livelihoods in northern Europe. On the other hand, the *Corpus Iuris Civilis* was the work of a Roman emperor, and Justinian had asserted exclusive lawmaking power. Roman maxims asserted that the prince was 'absolved from the laws' ('legibus solutus'), and that 'what pleases the prince has the force of law' ('quod principi placuit legis habet vigorem'). Although the Roman jurist Ulpian had originally been expressing somewhat different ideas, scholars in medieval and early modern Europe quoted these maxims as simple statements of royal authority.[52] The rationalist natural law scholars, as they came to be known, advocated the creation of a complete set of laws, which could be stated simply and logically, based on the will of the ruler. In this way, they tried to align the notion of the ruler's sovereign power with the idea of natural and impartial law. Not surprisingly, the leaders of the European states that emerged from the Peace of Westphalia, which ended the wars, were enthusiastic about the idea of developing national codes of law, viewing them as aids to unifying their territories and limiting the power of local lords and judges. The Coutume de Paris and the criminal code of the Holy Roman Emperors were hardly up to the task.

Some writers objected to the idea that law could be fixed in a single code, notably the judge and philosopher Montesquieu. In his *De l'esprit des lois* (The spirit of laws), published in 1748, he argued that any law must relate to its own society, with its particular climate, economy, traditions, manners, and religion. Looking for universal ideas in the principles of natural law or theology was a mistake. But most rulers pushed ahead with plans for comprehensive legal codes. The first, published by the Duchy of Bavaria in 1756, presented a German-language version of the civil law. This was followed by an immense code commissioned by Frederick the Great of Prussia and completed under his son in 1794. It ran to some nineteen thousand articles. In Austria, the Holy Roman Empress Maria Theresa ordered a code of private law in 1753. The *Codex Theresiana* had over eight thousand articles but was extensively revised by her successors. It was eventually published in 1812, after the Holy Roman Empire had already collapsed.[53]

By this time, momentum for a comprehensive codification had already built in France, supported by the revolutionaries who were keen to implement their radical schemes for a new world order. When he seized power as First Consul in 1799, Napoleon Bonaparte lost no time in appointing a small panel of commissioners to create a civil code.[54] This text, he declared, was to bring law and order to his people alongside a new calendar, a system of metric measurements, and educational reforms. He presided over the commission's discussions himself. The code, Napoleon maintained, would abolish feudalism and make all Roman laws obsolete in a new spirit of unity, uniformity, and simplicity. In practice, Roman precedents substantially shaped the structure and content of the new code. The committee followed the structure of Justinian's Institutes, and critical laws on private property were based on Roman ideas. Napoleon also emphasized the 'reason' on which his legal structure was based, a concept firmly associated with Roman law.

And Napoleon was nothing if not imperial in his ambitions. Looking to Rome for inspiration, he incorporated a toga and sword into his wardrobe and established a Senate and Tribunate in his government. He enthusiastically adopted Justinian's view that the will of the ruler should constitute the law. As one scholar has commented, he was, like Justinian, obsessed by a belief in his mission to master and reorder the world and to rule, godlike, over his creation.[55] Napoleon insisted that the law itself was not to be changed: legal experts would apply his laws, but judicial interpretation was forbidden. And, like the Roman emperor thirteen centuries earlier, he was quick to brush aside academic arguments that any law could transcend the authority of the ruler, arguing instead for absolute imperial power. But the French jurists were not remotely impressed. Following Napoleon's defeat at Waterloo and the reestablishment of the monarchy in 1815, they reviewed and revised the law to suit the new constitution. In exile on St. Helena, Napoleon was appalled by their changes, but the revised code endured and still forms the basis for French law today.

Elsewhere, the ideas promoted by Montesquieu, that any law must be rooted in the context of its own society, had powerful advocates. Fierce debates arose in universities across Europe between those who advocated codification, on the one hand, and, on the other, members of the German Historical School, led by Friedrich Carl von Savigny, who argued against codification, saying that law emerged, and should be allowed to emerge, from its social and historical context. But it was the former group who eventually triumphed, persuading the rulers of the new German Reich to create a comprehensive code, which they published in 1900. This followed another wave of European codifications, many of them explicitly based on the French *Code Civil*. The French *Code Civil* also shaped the laws of Louisiana, not to mention the many colonial territories to which it was exported over the following decades.

★

BY THE BEGINNING of the twentieth century, the Mughals had been vanquished, the Ottomans were teetering, and the Chinese Qing dynasty was in its dying days. In Europe, the system of states was more or less established, and the common and civil laws were being transplanted around the world. The United States, meanwhile, was gathering economic and military strength. It was barely two centuries since European laws had been a disorganized mass of rules, customs, principles, and institutions. But ambitious governments had developed laws that would help them administer large territories, transforming them into tools of discipline by creating an array of crimes and punishments. The chaos of civil war had also encouraged many to look to law as an instrument that would help strong rulers impose order on restive populations. As these ideas worked themselves out, many people experienced legal processes as oppressive and unjust. But judges and lawyers still held idealistic visions of what law was and could do. Legal scholars aspired to the rationality and intellectual sophistication of the Roman civil law; natural lawyers appealed to Christian theology and ideas of a common humanity; and English judges claimed they were upholding the ancient traditions of the common law. Influential theorists argued that law should be rational and reasonable, that it could protect individuals, define property, and promote commerce. It was a source of rights as much as an instrument of control. These were the ideas developed by Blackstone and taken up so enthusiastically in America. They were also the ideas that colonial governments relied upon when they maintained that their laws would bring order and civilization to the people they regarded as the unenlightened inhabitants of the rest of the world.

CHAPTER THIRTEEN

COLONIALISM
Exporting the Law

Europeans were not the first to impose systems of law and government on new places and populations. Hammurabi ended his military campaigns by erecting law stones throughout his empire; Chinese emperors established centralized bureaucracies throughout their vast territories; the Roman emperor Caracalla declared that all subjects of his empire were to enjoy the benefits of Roman law; and the Mughals brought Persian forms of law and government to India. And from the earliest days, lawmakers borrowed and copied new styles of law from distant traditions and precedents.

Historically, new laws generally coexisted more or less harmoniously with already established legal traditions: medieval Jews and Muslims lived side by side, observing different laws; the Mughals allowed Hindu kings to continue to administer their own territories and apply their own laws; and princes, bishops, and merchants in early Rus created parallel rules for their own domains. But European colonialism and its laws came to dominate a greater area, and more comprehensively, than any other form of law in global history. This was, of course, largely due to geopolitical events as they unfolded during the eighteenth and nineteenth centuries. But the European powers had developed effective new forms of bureaucratic government, relying on law as both a tool of discipline and a means of regulation, and the 'rational' legal systems they introduced soon overshadowed and marginalized the historical laws in most of the colonies.

IT ALL BEGAN just months after Christopher Columbus's voyage to America in 1492. At the request of the Spanish monarchs, Pope Alexander VI issued a papal bull in which he granted them 'dominium' over all territories in the Western Hemisphere. King Ferdinand and Queen Isabella had recently 'reconquered' Granada, the last enclave in Spain held by the Nasrid emirs, and their combined kingdoms enjoyed unsurpassable military strength. Now they lost little time in despatching armies across the Atlantic. Their conquistadors confronted the Aztec Empire in Mexico, followed by the Maya, before moving south to Peru, gradually defeating armies, deposing rulers, and destroying cities. The European armies eliminated sophisticated civilizations, burned their records, and brought disease and famine to their people, so little is known about legal practices in these South American kingdoms. Although few written records survive, we do know that the Aztecs recorded some of their criminal rules, and that all of these kingdoms had systematic structures of government and administration.

The brutality of the Spanish conquest is well established. What is less well known is the fierce opposition voiced by Spanish theologians and philosophers and the protracted debates they conducted about the legitimacy of these ventures.[1] Most were appalled by the suffering unleashed on the Indigenous populations, and many were alarmed by the vision of Roman imperium, the emperor as lawgiver, which lay behind the pope's declaration. By granting the Spanish monarchs dominium, he was acting as if he had authority to grant sovereignty over any part of the world. Fransiscus Vitoria, a Dominican professor of theology, delivered a forthright and critical lecture in 1539, and scholars in the universities of Salamanca and Coimbra followed suit. They developed legal arguments about the ius gentium, the law common to all people, which ought to apply to relations between the Spaniards and Indigenous people.[2] Vitoria's colleague, the Dominican friar Bartolomé Las Casas, maintained that the conquest was not just tyrannical and unjust but also unlawful. This eventually prompted the emperor Charles V to convene a debate in 1550 between Las Casas and the humanist scholar Juan Ginés de Sepúlveda, who sought to defend the legitimacy of the conquest on the basis that Indigenous customs were against the laws of nature. Las Casas largely got the better of his rival, but the emperor would not declare a winner or halt the conquest. It was too late to save the Indigenous civilizations.

One result of the conquest was that the Spanish throughout South America, along with the Portuguese in Brazil, imposed new forms of government on the Indigenous people.[3] Having declared that the conquerors would maintain local legal traditions that did not conflict with Castilian law, Charles V established the Royal and Supreme Council of the Indies to exercise legal jurisdiction over the American territories. The council's ordinances mandated the observance of Castilian law throughout the empire. This effectively meant the *Siete Partidas*, along with subsequent legislation, and new laws and decrees that Spain enacted specifically for America.

The Spanish conquests were the first in a series of colonial ventures that eventually exported European forms of law throughout the world. But debates about the legitimacy of these projects continued. The Europeans may have enjoyed superior military and economic power, but they still felt the need to justify their activities. Scholars appealed to Christianity, rationality, and natural law to promote models of civilization, and these laid the basis for modern ideas of statehood and the rule of law.

SEPÚLVEDA ARGUED THAT conquest was a first step towards preaching Christianity to the infidels. The French used the same justification when they launched their expeditions to North America. So did early English explorers. In the sixteenth century, the influential writer Richard Hakluyt promoted colonization by talking of the duty to evangelize among the pagans. When James I granted the Virginia Company a charter in 1609, he proclaimed that it should propagate Christianity to such people 'as yet live in darkness and miserable ignorance of the true knowledge and worship of God', so that it 'may in time bring them . . . to humane civility'.[4] In the courts, Sir Edward Coke declared that the laws of the Indigenous peoples were extinguished upon conquest, since they were 'against the law of God and nature'. And the writer William Strachey drew parallels with the Roman conquest of 'our barbarous Island'. The English, he said, had a duty to civilize 'infidels and savages'.[5]

But outright conquest was hard to defend, as the Spaniards had found, and the North American settlers sought new arguments to justify their activities.[6] They claimed to be making 'improvements' to 'unoccupied' lands, and said that the American territories were 'almost uninhabited', so the settlers had occupied them peacefully. In reality, they had encountered people living in villages and cultivating fields and had negotiated to buy parts of their hunting and fishing grounds. Initially, the Indigenous people were happy to sell, using the proceeds to purchase tools, weapons, and decorative items. But as more settlers arrived, many challenged their rights of occupation. North America was so vast, and the existing population so small, that arrivals from an overcrowded England, as they saw it, were justified in taking advantage of the practically deserted abundance.

Philosophers, meanwhile, were developing new ideas about property and found reasons to doubt Indigenous people's rights. Thomas Hobbes, in his *Leviathan* (1651), argued that property rights depended on effective government, while John Locke, in *Second Treatise on Government* (1689), linked property rights firmly to cultivation. It followed that if the Indigenous people were not cultivating their land, only hunting over it, settlers could legitimately move in. Once they had begun to lay out fields, to 'mix their labour with the land', in Locke's terms, the new occupiers had rights to possession. Other writers seized on these ideas. The Swiss legal scholar Emer de Vattel wrote an influential treatise on the 'law of nations' (*le droit des gens*) in which he talked of people's obligation under natural law to cultivate their land. So, although the conquest of the civilized empires of Peru and Mexico had been 'a terrible usurpation', he said, the establishment of colonies in North America might, 'if done within just limits', be entirely lawful.[7]

These arguments would later justify European expansion into the prairies, but most of the Indigenous groups on the East Coast were farmers, so the settlers continued to negotiate contracts to purchase their land. At the same time, they readily denigrated the Indigenous people as 'uncivilized' and 'lawless'. Ideas about human progress were then taking hold, and in the settlers' eyes, the Indigenous people were at an earlier stage of development, yet to discover writing and develop the arts of government.[8] Law, and the lack of it, was becoming an important symbol of civilization. In the *Odyssey*, after all, Homer had described the Cyclopes as arrogant and 'lawless' beings.[9] Some argued that even if the Indigenous people did not consent to the occupation, they would be thankful for the benefits brought by the settlers, who would transform 'their wild manners of life to the civil and polite customs of Europe'.[10]

In practice, many settlers tricked the people they dealt with into signing contracts they did not understand. They negotiated with 'representatives' who did not speak for their whole group, or they simply threatened force. The main problem for the Indigenous people was that the power to prevent illegal land seizures lay in the English-controlled courts. But at least there was a mechanism, which they could, and at times successfully did, resort to. Recognizing the abuses perpetrated by many settlers, in 1763 George III issued a royal proclamation to forbid private land sales. Only the colonial governments could now acquire land, under properly negotiated treaties. Most governors, anxious to maintain the profitable fur trade, accepted that they had to respect the Indigenous territories. But the proclamation also had the indirect effect of distancing the settlers from the Indigenous people and any sense of their land rights.

For the Indigenous people of North America, things took a turn for a worse after the colonists' struggle for independence. During the American Revolution most of the Indigenous people had supported the British, whose government at least recognized their rights, so the new Confederation's governors were not inclined to look favourably on their interests. At first, the new federal government of the United States, along with many of the individual state governments, pursued an aggressive land policy, dictating 'treaties' to the Indigenous groups which effectively confiscated their lands without compensation. In the 1780s they started purchasing again, declaring that they recognized the property rights of the 'Indians', but settlers who wanted to move into new territories constantly pressured the new governments to ease the restrictions. Hard-pressed officials resorted to unscrupulous techniques, such as selling goods on credit to Indigenous people and then demanding land transfers as a means of settling the debts, as well as other kinds of trickery and downright coercion. Many, especially in the East, genuinely wanted to treat the Indigenous people properly, but those living difficult lives on the frontiers resented the people who were roaming freely over lands they wanted to cultivate.

A legal decision in 1823 finally stripped the Indigenous people of their land rights. In the famous case of *Johnson v. M'Intosh*, the judges decided that they had rights of occupation, rather than property. This was a crucial distinction. It made it much easier, legally, for the federal and state governments to pursue policies of removal, reservation, and allotment. Although the legal arguments were complex, behind them lay the fact that, by now, settlers had debilitated most of the eastern Indigenous groups and the frontier had moved westwards, to the prairies inhabited by nomadic populations. Lawyers could now claim that the Indigenous people were 'wandering savages', who 'traversed the wilds of America' and hardly indulged in agriculture, their occupation mainly warfare.[11] Now the arguments of John Locke proved particularly useful. John Quincy Adams, who would go on to become the sixth US president, maintained that Indigenous land rights were limited to the tiny fraction of land they actually cultivated. During treaty negotiations in 1814, he told a British delegation that 'to condemn vast regions of territory to perpetual barrenness and solitude that a few hundred savages might find beasts to hunt upon it' would never be tolerated by the people of the United States.

Adams's successor as president, Andrew Jackson, was even less sympathetic. He pursued a policy of removal, forcing most of the eighty thousand Indigenous people in the East to migrate west of the Mississippi River. In his State of the Union Address in 1830, he justified his policies on the basis of 'progress': 'What good man would prefer a country covered with forests and ranged by a few thousand savages to our extensive Republic, studded with cities, towns, and prosperous farms, embellished with all the improvements which art can devise or industry execute, occupied by more than 12,000,000 happy people, and filled with all the blessings of liberty, civilization, and religion?'

Civilization meant progress, and progress meant property rights. The United States had now established a system of land ownership, based on the English common law, by which the government enjoyed ultimate ownership of all American territory. And this allowed it to pursue policies of dispossession against the Indigenous people who hunted, fished, and followed ancient ways of life. Behind all this was a sense of the fundamental importance of private property for both development and progress.

The same ideas lay behind many of the projects of colonization that Europeans pursued over the following century.

WHILE THE COLONIES in North America were slipping from their grasp, the British were already consolidating successful trading ventures in Asia and the Middle East.[12] The first expeditions around the Cape of Good Hope in the fifteenth century had brought Portuguese and Dutch sailors into contact with the flourishing empires of the Safavids and Mughals. The Europeans were awed by their technological advances and dazzled by the splendour of the Muslim courts in Isfahan and Delhi, which rivalled even the Ottomans' magnificent capital in Constantinople. Meanwhile, around the Indian Ocean, Chinese merchants were doing business with Indians, Persians, Ottomans, and Arabs.

By the middle of the seventeenth century, internal tensions and conflicts were weakening all three of the great Muslim empires. Regional power-holders challenged the sultans' control, and European powers used their military strength to dominate the trading networks. The British, who had come late to the game, put their ventures in the hands of the East India Company, which established trading posts around the Indian coastline. Eventually, the company consolidated its activities in Calcutta, and from there it entered into more or less amicable relations with the Mughal court. When the Persian ruler Nader Shah sacked Delhi in 1739, the East India Company was free to expand its activities. After quashing resistance from the Nawab of Bengal in 1757, it soon extended its influence over the whole of northeastern India. Just a few years later, following extensive negotiations, the Mughal emperor Shah Alam granted the company the *diwani*, the right to collect taxes throughout Bengal and Bihar. This effectively made it the ruling power in the region.

The company's armies, under Robert Clive, now embarked on a programme of military expansion in India, confronting and defeating local rulers and effectively seizing their lands. Many Europeans saw the Muslim regimes as terrifying despotisms, in which private property and the merchant classes were crushed under the weight of a military government and exploited in the interests of imperial luxury. So initially Clive received high praise in Britain. The Whig politician Robert Macaulay declared that he 'gave peace, security, prosperity and such liberty as the case allowed of to millions of Indians, who had for centuries been the prey of oppression'. But governing the lands of 'Moorish despotism' was quite another matter. Company administrators, sent to tax the populations, found technical accounting records written in Persian which reflected complex property relations. Baffled, they severely overtaxed the Indian population, leading to a terrible famine in Bengal in the 1770s. As well as causing millions of deaths, it pushed the company to the brink of insolvency. British politicians now turned on the venture, lambasting the company's representatives for enriching themselves at the expense of the local populations. An outraged Horace Walpole condemned the 'iniquities of the East India Company and its crew of monsters'.

These iniquities were not lost on Indian observers, who could only look on helplessly as their country's wealth was exported to Britain.

Determined to hang on to British interests in India, the new prime minister, Lord North, took steps to exert more control over the company. He appointed Warren Hastings as governor of Bengal in 1772 and established a Supreme Court in Calcutta, with judges appointed by the Crown.[13] Many in Britain continued to criticize the company's treatment of the 'natives' and feared that corrupt officers would import practices of 'oriental despotism' to their own country. And the defeat of the company's armies by Hindu Marathas a few years later did nothing to help matters. But in 1784, Parliament strategically reduced duties on Chinese tea, which stimulated a vast rise in imports and transformed the economic fortunes of the company. The next governor, Lord Cornwallis, introduced new rules for taxation and property ownership, after which he could argue that the company's government was now guided by 'all the rules and systems of European policy'.[14]

The East India Company's armies also regrouped after their earlier setback and turned on Delhi, wresting control of the emperor from the Marathas in 1803. Mughal rule was now reduced to little more than a fiction. The company's charter, renewed in 1813, referred to the Crown's 'undoubted sovereignty' over all its territories in India.[15]

THROUGHOUT THESE DEVELOPMENTS, continuing resistance and what the colonialists regarded as the instability of local states led many to argue that peace could only be guaranteed by absolute paramountcy.[16] New ideas about racial superiority and the evolution of government reinforced these attitudes. By the nineteenth century, population expansion, economic developments, and political reforms in Britain had seen the rise of a more unified national elite. Operating through Parliament, it used regulation and audit to control and coerce rather than relying on old aristocratic rights and privileges. Benefitting from agrarian improvements, a rise in land values, and the growth of a property market, the ruling classes were easily convinced of the superiority of their model of government and systems of private property, which they felt should be exported to the colonies.

Influential politicians and officials denigrated the Indian governments as 'arbitrary', 'founded neither on law, nor upon the opinions and attachments of mankind', and talked of the 'perverseness and depravity' of the Indians.[17] One East India Company employee reported that 'law' in India was nothing more than the will of the Muslim rulers. In the local courts, petitioners would plead for justice, he explained, but the judges would make arbitrary decisions, unconstrained by rules or proper records.[18] The British, by contrast, were a 'governing race', fit to rule because of their 'moral independency', a phrase constantly heard in political circles. In 1800, a new governor, Lord Wellesley, explained that the company's officers had initially copied the despotic methods of the Indian princes but had now reformed their methods 'on principles drawn from the British constitution'. Imperial expansion in India could now be presented as a crusade to introduce civilized forms of government and law to those who had suffered under Mughal rule.

The British were reflecting ideas now circulating widely in Europe. French merchants and adventurers had established fortified towns and trading enclaves along the African coasts from the sixteenth century. Here, they encountered 'wild Arabs', as Montesquieu described them, who were little more than a race of 'roaming thieves'.[19] Later, the philosopher and mathematician Nicolas de Condorcet argued that the interests of the Africans, 'les Noirs', should be respected, but that they were still people 'waiting to be civilized'.[20] Throughout Europe, ideas about conquest and conversion of the 'infidels' had given way to projects of civilization. In the late eighteenth century, the German philosopher Immanuel Kant argued that colonial activities would open up trade routes and communications, which would create a truly cosmopolitan world order. He echoed Condorcet's call for a global civilization that would unite people across racial, religious, and cultural divides. But for both men, this meant order based on European legal and political principles.[21]

IN INDIA, DESPITE the denigration of the 'Oriental despots', British officials knew they had to exercise caution. Having learned from their experiences in America, they were unwilling to promote large-scale settlement, seize territory, or exploit indigenous and slave labour.[22] They knew that the Mughals had established complex systems of taxation, and most British officials were fully aware of the perils of trying to intervene in, and manage, a territory with a sophisticated government of its own, even if it was in disarray. It became East India Company policy to respect local laws and structures of government. The problem was how to understand them. The company employees sent to assess and collect land revenues found a mass of quasi-feudal rights and obligations that defied interpretation in Western terms. The intricacies of Persian estate law baffled them, and they struggled to master the language of the medieval texts that described property ownership. It did not help that the Indians seemed to place just as much emphasis on oral tradition, custom, and local usage as on their written records.[23]

The Mughal emperor's diwani had stipulated that the company must govern its new possessions 'agreeably to the rules of Mahomen and the law of the Empire'. So, when Warren Hastings arrived as governor in 1772, he declared that the administration should be conducted 'agreeably to the old constitution of the Empire'.[24] He encouraged his more junior colleagues to study Sanskrit, Persian, and Arabic, the languages of Indian learning and administration, in order to create structures of government that would work with Indian laws and institutions. Hastings was familiar with the Mughals' methods, and he had studied the *Ain-i-Akbari*, a fifteenth-century Persian text on the arts of government. This set out rules and regulations for taxation and the administration of justice as well as detailed discussions on the qualities of a good ruler. Indian systems were to be respected, Hastings declared, and his employees should identify and record local landholdings. The problem was that English categories did not always fit indigenous ideas and arrangements.

When a British parliamentary committee argued for the introduction of British law and institutions throughout the company's territories, Hastings lobbied hard against the idea, arguing that the 'ancient constitution' of Bengal was very much intact. The Hindus, he said, 'had been in possession of laws which continued unchanged, from remotest antiquity'. He instructed the officers stationed in local districts to get to know 'the natives', as well as raising taxes, maintaining order, and meting out justice.[25] In the district courts, they were to sit with Hindu and Muslim experts who could advise them on the relevant law. Hastings believed, correctly, that the Hindu and Muslim populations had sophisticated systems of law and justice, but he assumed that in a 'theocratic state' religious scholars must have worked out rules of conduct which they applied as law. These must have been written down in codes, he felt, or could at least be compiled into sets of rules, which could then be read and applied by British judges. He was impressed by the ancient Dharmashastras, which he understood to be codes of law rather than the amalgams of brahminical learning, wisdom, religious principles, ritual guidelines, and directions for practical administration that they were. The shastras, he maintained, were known to all brahmins and respected by Muslim rulers, so what was needed was an English version, which the British could apply in their district courts. It only remained for him to commission such a text. Because there were no Europeans in Calcutta who knew Sanskrit, he employed a team of Bengali scholars (*pandits*) to translate the most relevant Dharmashastras into Persian, from which one of the company's employees translated them into English. He published the result in 1776, as *A Code of Gentoo Laws, or Ordinations of the Pundits.*

Hastings's approach was continued by Sir William Jones, appointed to the Calcutta Crown Court in 1783. Jones had studied both Arabic and Persian and argued that although British law was superior to Indian, it could not be imposed without tyranny. 'The laws of the natives must be preserved inviolate', he declared, and the courts' decrees must conform with their legal traditions. The problem, as far as Jones was concerned, was that there was no authoritative text on Indian law equivalent to Justinian's *Corpus Iuris*, which meant that the judges were reliant on Indian scholars who kept the laws in their heads. He worried that they could not be trusted. Although Jones had trained in the English tradition, in which the common law crystallised out of previous cases and could, in practice, adapt to changing circumstances, he held the view, as Hastings had, that Hindu customs had been fixed since ancient times. This meant that the earliest legal texts had the greatest authority. As Jones could see, the Dharmashastras were religious as much as legal texts. So he proposed to build on Hastings's work by compiling a complete digest of Hindu and Muslim law, and he commissioned a number of pandits to extract the relevant legal principles from the most ancient texts. They were to arrange them in a scientific order, under headings he specified, such as on contracts, succession, and property ownership. This was, of course, just like Justinian, who had ordered his scholars to compile a new text from older Roman material. Jones declared that the British government would, in this way, give to the natives of India 'security for the due administration of justice among them, similar to that which Justinian gave to his Greek and Roman subjects'. They should then, he declared, be able to live content and productive lives under British rule. He was interpreting Indian law in European terms, as if it could be divorced from its religious foundations.

It was Jones's successor, H. T. Colebrook, who finished the translation of the Digest after Jones's death in 1794.[26] He had studied Sanskrit and had a much better grasp than Jones of the nature of Hindu and Muslim law, appreciating the variety of legal texts in the Hindu tradition and the principles of interpretation, which militated against the establishment of any fixed and certain set of norms. He concluded that he needed to establish a system according to which the judges could work out which were the most authoritative legal texts. But time, resources, and the demands of his administrative duties did not allow him to complete this project, and the aims of British governors to discover and apply Indian laws finally stalled.

In the meantime, the Permanent Settlement of 1793 had established an independent judiciary in India and, at least in theory, the rule of law.[27] The law was supposed to define and protect the private rights of all subjects. Over the following decades, some of the Indian elite were able to take advantage of the new property rights, adapting their commercial activities accordingly. But although, when faced with Indian litigants, judges and officials were supposed to 'discover' and recognize customary and religious norms, in the absence of useful texts they largely relied on the advice of Indian pandits. The image of the unreliable native continued to hold sway, particularly among new arrivals to the subcontinent, fresh from their schooling in Britain. In history lessons they might have read James Mill's monumental *History of British India*, published in 1817, with its disparaging remarks about the 'mendacity and perjury' of the Indians. Mill, who had never even set foot in the country, did not appreciate that the British system baffled the pandits, and even more, most petitioners, who were often treated with contempt, leading to confusion and suspicions of perjury and fabrication. Even the more conscientious and fair-minded officials struggled with what they saw as local variations in custom and a lack of precision in legal norms, as well as differences between Hindu practices and Islamic laws.[28] Of course, the English common law had developed out of just such a varied and imprecise set of customs and practices, but British officials believed it to be more rational than it actually was.

During the nineteenth century, British judges and officials effectively developed the civil law they applied in the Indian courts on common law principles. They supported market-oriented rules and entrenched private property relations in place of rights and relations based on status.[29] The brahmin pandits continued to insist upon the importance of caste, which reinforced many inequalities, not least in taxation, and their new powers as legal experts allowed them to entrench the caste hierarchy, disastrously for many sections of the population. Meanwhile, Indian merchants operated through kin and caste networks, while much land was in communal ownership. But the courts decided to recognize these lands as 'ancestral', subject to a form of 'trust', thereby transforming complex and historical Indian property relations into categories familiar to English lawyers. Meanwhile, the colonial judges adopted the system of precedent, with which they were familiar from Britain, looking to earlier cases as sources of guidance and authority.

Thomas Macaulay, charged with educational reform in India, proposed an Indian Penal Code in 1837.[30] He took the view that 'a single shelf of a good European library was worth the whole native literature of India and Arabia', and he argued for the replacement of Persian by English as the language of administration. His criminal code, eventually passed in 1860, following the British declaration of empire, was in theory based on first principles, but in practice it incorporated a good many Indian social and religious norms, which the judges realized they needed to respect if their judgements were to have any effect. Officials soon argued that they needed means to punish violent acts more severely and more quickly than the code allowed, particularly in the northwest frontier, now part of Pakistan, where sixteen Europeans had been killed or injured by 1867. Here, those who committed 'murderous attacks' needed 'a lesson of obedience', and local commissioners were allowed to exceed their legal powers to address the 'special danger' of multiple murders.[31] The Murderous Outrages Act was passed to suppress murderous outrages by 'fanatics'. With great irony, the philosopher John Stuart Mill, who worked for the East India Company, declared that Indians were not ready for representative government. He wrote that 'a vigorous despotism is in itself the best mode of government for training the people in what is specifically wanting to render them capable of a higher civilization'.[32]

Eventually, the colonial authorities dismissed the pandits and codified practically all commercial, criminal, and procedural laws, while the judges used case reports, following the English system of precedent. Despite the best efforts of Warren Hastings and Sir William Jones to discover and preserve the indigenous legal systems of India, and despite all the opinions and advice of the pandits, the British authorities ended up establishing a form of English common law throughout India. Traditional Indian laws and legal practices, decentralized as they were, and based on centuries of esoteric textual and religious scholarship, could never have fitted into the structures established by the colonial authorities, even had the administrators better understood them. European ideas about legal certainty and rationality, along with assumptions about final authority and structures of enforcement, were a world away from the rules and practices of the Hindu Dharmashastras and the Islamic shari'a. Legalistic though they were, and authoritative though their scholars and judges might have been, the ancient laws of India could not withstand the onslaught of British 'rationality' and the determination to 'improve' and 'civilize' the lands of 'Oriental despotism'.

AFTER SPAIN AND Portugal lost the last of their South American territories in the 1830s, Britain and France expanded their imperial ambitions.[33] For centuries, Portuguese and Dutch merchants had traded with their Asian counterparts from enclaves in India, Malaysia, and the East Indies while the Spanish and French concentrated on the African coastline. Now the British and French were able to dominate much of this trade. So they established consular jurisdictions in China, Meiji Japan, Siam (Thailand), Zanzibar, Muscat, and the weakening Ottoman Empire. The new arrangements reduced trading tariffs and allowed Europeans to avoid local courts and laws.

Elsewhere, they forcibly annexed new territory, including in Burma, which was incorporated into British India in 1826, and the Malaysian enclave of Malacca, ceded to Britain by the Dutch in 1824 and soon forcibly 'pacified'. By this time they had also seized Singapore. The British had been settling parts of Australia since the late eighteenth century and now extended their domains to New Zealand, signing the Treaty of Waitangi with the Maori in 1840. Meanwhile, the French invaded and conquered Algeria, the first of their African territories, and forcibly occupied most of Indochina (now Vietnam, Cambodia, and Laos). The Dutch East India Company, too, established settlements in South Africa and Indonesia, where they had formerly maintained trading posts.

The French navy had taken Algiers in 1830, and eventually the government decided to claim the whole territory as part of France.[34] Settlers inevitably wanted the French government to grant them land, but Algeria had a substantial population, and around half of its farmland was held under Islamic trusts, waqf.

Some of these supported religious establishments, while others were essentially family property. French scholars were already writing treatises on North African Islamic law and now they produced dubious arguments to the effect that the family waqf were both immoral and illegal, preventing the 'efficient' exploitation of land. This notion justified the confiscation of all such land in 1844, although most Muslims refused to deal with it as private property. The French administration also took over responsibility for funding religious establishments, which were gradually starved of resources. The French government ultimately decided to support an Islamic legal system in Algeria, 'le droit musulman-algérien', partly to avoid allowing Muslims to claim full political rights. But by centralizing and subjecting it to bureaucratic structures and processes, at odds with the fluid and segmented character of the shari'a, they turned it into something else. Like the British in India, they constructed a new form of law based on a European model.

By the late nineteenth century, Britain, along with Italy and Germany, had followed the French into Africa, where they all claimed large tracts of territory. Fearing another debilitating conflict among European powers, the German chancellor, Otto von Bismarck, convened a conference in 1884 to establish guidelines for the acquisition of African territory. So began the 'scramble for Africa', which, over the next three decades, saw almost 90 percent of the continent come under European control. Following its incursions into Algeria, France instituted a mission to West Africa, where it consolidated several territories under a governor general based in Dakar. Its armies confronted the rulers of the Savannah states and eventually took on the formidable Tukulor Empire, which had recently been founded by a Muslim cleric.[35] Finally, they overcame the disciplined army of the Fon kingdoms of Dahomey, which had established large palm oil plantations worked by slaves. By the early twentieth century, the French ruled over a vast area which included most of modern

Mauritania as well as Senegal, the Ivory Coast, Guinea, Burkina Faso, Mali, Niger, and Benin.

In an effort to overcome Muslim 'fanaticism', the French introduced schools and hospitals into Algeria. By the 1870s, they were pursuing a programme of cultural change through education, courts, and ministerial offices. They rolled out the same policies in West Africa, initially constructing a network of railways and launching programmes of hygiene in an explicitly 'civilizing' mission. As Ernest Roume, governor general in the early 1900s, declared, the idea was to go beyond maintaining order and promoting commerce: 'We have a higher ambition and a significantly broader intention: we wish truly to open Africa to civilization.'[36] This meant expanding communications, providing medical assistance, promoting hygiene, offering education, developing agriculture, and, 'last but not least, the guaranteed enjoyment of individual rights and of the most sacred right of all, that of individual freedom'.[37]

On Roume's view, to institute a fair and humane system of justice and guarantee the rule of law, it was necessary for the colonizers to wield ultimate power to settle disputes. But their new courts were to respect African customs. The object was not to turn Africans into Frenchmen. In the urban areas, they would apply French law, save in family matters, for which Muslims could also go to shari'a courts. But in treaties with African chiefs, the colonial powers agreed to respect custom, so in the rural areas local courts staffed by African chiefs were to apply customary or Islamic laws to the African populations. Above them, the 'circle court', presided over by a French administrator, tried serious crimes and heard appeals.

Despite the ostensible respect for African custom, Roume felt that natives needed a guarantee of the good administration of justice, which he thought only French officials could provide. He ordered that his administrators investigate and record local customs on marriage, contracts, descent, and inheritance and classify them 'with a clarity they too often lack'. This meant modifying them according to fundamental principles of natural law as 'the original source of all legislation'. In criminal cases, corporal punishments were to be replaced by prison sentences and the use of ordeals was to be eliminated, so that the processes would 'conform to the principles of criminal law that apply to all countries, regardless of their level of civilization'.[38] The goal of respecting African custom only extended to recognizing practices that conformed to French legal principles.

THE BRITISH IN Africa were, at least initially, less explicit about their 'civilizing mission'. They established 'protectorates' in areas they considered to be without organized government, but they generally took a dim view of indigenous institutions and soon decided they would have to implement new systems of law.[39] Administrators instructed local officials to apply English law; they were only to recognize African law in cases arising between Africans, and as long as it was not 'repugnant' to English legal principles. The new officials were rarely experienced administrators, and they lacked the resources to introduce elaborate courts and legal procedures. The more junior took up their posts with some trepidation, often feeling isolated and insecure in the African savannah. Unsure about how to keep the peace among Africans, whose lives and conflicts they barely understood, these officials generally meted out justice as they saw fit, trying to judge according to 'natural justice'. They were endlessly puzzled by Africans' demands for compensation, instead of punishment, for what they considered to be crimes, including murder. And they were horrified at the use of poison ordeals, which many Africans readily offered to undergo when accused of wrongdoing. Feeling they had to suppress violence, many officials resorted to summary justice, simply telling the local populations that certain things were 'prohibited', meting out harsh punishments, and punishing petty infractions, such as 'wasting time buying food' or 'sitting around the fire instead of working'.[40] Ignoring African ideas about wrongdoing did nothing to enhance their authority in African eyes.

By the early years of the twentieth century, the British colonial authorities recognized that the ideal of a superior 'white man's justice' was not being realized. Although many officials genuinely tried to implement 'prompt and efficient justice', the reality was very different. In Northern Rhodesia (now Zambia), persistent complaints by lawyers persuaded the British government to appoint a Royal Commission. 'It is the duty of the Government to civilize and maintain peace and good order', the commission declared, which meant introducing British concepts of wrongdoing. It recommended the sanctions of imprisonment and fines in place of traditional African systems of compensation, since these were accepted by all 'civilized nations'. But many of the local administrators objected to the commission's recommendations, realizing that they would mean imposing alien ideas about justice on Africans. Most preferred the idea of 'indirect rule' promoted by Lord Lugard, governor general of Nigeria. Lugard characterized native institutions as 'crude tribunals of primitive pagans', but he recognized that it was only by supporting them that colonial governments could ensure respect for their own authority.

Lugard's arguments were heard, and, in 1929, the Native Courts Ordinance granted authority over criminal issues to local African courts. The governments of other British colonies followed suit. In practice, this meant that colonial officials had to recognize the authority of African chiefs, whose status and powers they strengthened in the process. Possibly with the image of a hereditary aristocracy in their minds, they encouraged the chiefs to act as petty monarchs, receiving petitions and dispensing wisdom. But their procedures were hardly legalistic. African petitioners would present their problems and argue about the consequences of events at the same time, invoking notions of right and wrong in the context of particular social relations, rather than trying to use legal principles and questions of fact to reach a reasoned conclusion.[41] The African processes had their own logic, but they hardly formed a system of rules that could be put into writing and applied directly, as the local administrators wished.

During the early decades of the nineteenth century, many Africans had been involved in wars, suffered invasions, and participated in the slave trade, all of which had upset traditional power structures, norms, and processes of conflict resolution. Yet the colonial powers talked as if customary African law had a fixed substance which could be formalized into rules and applied in the courts. British officials also expected chiefs to adjudicate on new offences they introduced in regulations on taxation, forestry, sanitation, and agricultural production. Now, the chiefs were forced to consider the regulations separately from the facts of a case, and they began to talk in terms of 'laws'. Their courts began to consult documents and keep written records. They began to prohibit ordeals and to insist on a distinction between crimes and torts, eventually referring to the idea of *mens rea*, intent, which had not been important in traditional negotiations for compensation. Without even realizing it, the chiefs were creating a new sort of law on a British model.

Impressed by the Europeans' military and organizational powers, many members of the African elite decided to support the colonialists' project to 'legalize' the administration of justice. Some district officers and traditional leaders did realize the benefits of a more flexible administration of justice, and debates continued over the wisdom of the new legal projects. But the nationalist leaders who campaigned for independence generally argued that African law should be applied in 'proper' courts and objected to the idea of a two-tier system.

By the 1960s, when many of the former British colonies had achieved independence, representatives of the new countries met in Dar es Salaam to discuss the role and jurisdiction of their courts.[42] The delegates agreed that 'customary law' should continue to be a significant part of their legal systems, but they confirmed the importance of creating a 'unified' body of laws. These laws would integrate African customary law with the rules and procedures they had inherited from the colonial administrations. Implicit in their conclusions was the assumption that African customary laws still survived, in much the same form as they had taken in the past, and that they could be recorded and integrated seamlessly into the new structures of government. But, as in India, this was to assume that historical and traditional systems were much closer to European forms than they ever had been.

India and Africa were not the only territories in which colonial administrations struggled to understand, record, and apply indigenous laws. In the twentieth century, legal scholars in Dutch-controlled Indonesia persuaded their colonial government to record, recognize, and apply the local law, 'adat.[43] This effectively formalized and fixed what had been a shifting set of customs, practices, and norms. No less important for that, it was hardly a good basis for colonial administration. And when an independent Indonesia eventually established its national legal system, it followed the models introduced by the Dutch colonialists, with only faint recognition of the ancient systems of 'adat which had shaped—and still shape—the lives of indigenous populations.

THROUGHOUT THE WORLD, colonial projects to record and apply local laws were supported by local elites who embraced the new projects of government. The existence of law had by now become an important marker of development, so no one wanted to deny that their ancestors had had their own laws, even if they were not written down. This meant that they effectively had to create a new type of law, which they called 'customary', or 'traditional', out of the fluid norms and practices that had characterized traditional systems of government.

Even in India, with its ancient and sophisticated legal traditions, the local elite soon embraced European ideas about law and government. Among the first casualties of the East India Company's activities were members of the Mughal ruling classes, who saw their world turned upside down after the grant of the diwani. 'Every heart was aflame with grief and every eye brimmed with tears', as one Muslim poet put it. Hindu intellectuals saw the seizure of power by 'white faced upstarts' as heralding a new age of demons.[44] Turning around the language of the British to critique the project of their colonial overlords, the Indian Muslim preacher Shah Ismail Shahid declared that those who acted without regard for the shari'a or for custom were 'despots'. But resourceful Indians learned to live with the new political order, and high-caste Bengali Hindus were able to profit from the new framework of landed property rights, entering the world of commerce and trade and sending their sons to acquire an English education in Calcutta. Many supported the British in their wars with Napoleon, and one Indian, Ram Mohun Roy, born in 1772, launched an ambitious and influential movement to reform traditional Indian practices such as widow-burning. In the long run, familiarity with English ideas about rights and liberty gave Indian nationalists the confidence to stand up to personal indignities and complain that the privileges of English law were confined to the ruling classes. From the early nineteenth century, they consistently used the language of law and rights in their agitation for self-determination.[45]

In all these ways, European colonial powers introduced new social and political ideas into their territories, and these continued to shape the postcolonial constitutions, especially in the hands of an indigenous elite keen to participate in the emerging international order. The new nation-states had clearly bounded territories, languages, religious conventions, and their own laws. Behind it all lay ideas about universal progress and an international order that recognized the 'comity of nations', a concept emphasizing mutual respect for laws in a world of equal political entities. With this model, European forms of government, law, and property rights took hold in the far more fluid and segmented societies that had formed the civilizations of Asia and Africa.

During the twentieth century, these ideas became so dominant that new states and postcolonial regimes around the world turned to European models of law. Even those that had not been colonized chose the French *Code Civil* as the basis for new legal systems, which they hoped would allow them to participate more readily in the new economic and commercial order. Postcolonial states in Latin America had already adopted European models. Brazil's laws were largely derived from the Portuguese, and these, in turn, influenced Argentina. Meanwhile, the Chilean Civil Code of 1855 was based on the Napoleonic code and the Spanish *Siete Partidas*, along with elements of canon law. Japan's nineteenth-century Meiji constitution was based on a German (Prussian) model, and Thailand's constitutional monarchy, established in 1932, replaced laws derived from the Hindu Dharmashastras with codes based on civil law principles. Similar developments took place in the countries that emerged from the quasi-colonial protectorates of the Middle East which had been established after the fall of the Ottoman Empire in the early twentieth century. Even China, which resolutely followed its own path under Mao, eventually adopted legal forms and practices that essentially followed European forms. As China developed its economy and engaged in international commerce in the late twentieth century, its leaders found they needed laws that international partners could understand. The longest lasting of the ancient legal systems had finally given way to a European model.

★

THE LAWS THAT the European powers exported and imposed around the world were primarily instruments of government designed to support new colonial administrations, regulate commerce, and impose order on large populations. Officials may have paid lip service to the ancient laws of India and the customs of Africa, but they could only recognize those that would fit into their new bureaucratic structures. Morality and religion, and with them, the sophisticated religious laws of the Hindus, Jews, and Muslims, as well as the more fluid and negotiated processes used by many Africans to resolve disputes, largely became confined to a separate realm.

But the colonial project was not an entirely pragmatic one. Europeans felt they needed to justify their activities, and they did so by making claims about the transformations their laws would bring about: efficient administration, private property regimes, individual rights, and the rule of law. It was a promise of civilization. Rulers of the states that later gained their independence, and even those that had never been colonized, eventually came to accept this model of law, turning their backs on centuries of sophisticated legal scholarship and the dynamics by which their own predecessors had maintained order. By the late twentieth century, most had adopted European models and taken their seats at the United Nations. But this form of law, powerful as it was, did not totally eclipse all that had preceded it.

CHAPTER FOURTEEN

IN THE SHADOW OF THE STATE
Islamic Law in the Modern World

B y the end of the nineteenth century, the rising European states were promoting a new international order. The 'Great Powers', led by France and Britain, had established systems of bureaucratic government, law, and landholding in their colonies and dependencies, where governors were supposed to promote 'civilized' regimes. In India, the rules of the Dharmashastras and the authority of the brahmin pandits were reduced to matters of 'personal law', codified and applied in specialist family courts. Even the Chinese legal system was swept away when the Nationalist government overthrew the remnants of the Qing dynasty in 1911, and Mao's communist regime finally turned its back on all vestiges of imperial law in the 1950s.

But Islamic law was not so easily overcome. By the early twentieth century, the great Muslim empires had largely disintegrated, along with their networks of courts, judges, and jurists. Ottoman sultans, Egyptian leaders, and Iranian shahs had all embarked on extensive reform programmes, with modernity and European examples in mind. But the scholars had not lost all status and influence. In fact, the twentieth century saw a resurgence in appeals to the shari'a and calls for return to government by Islamic law. Muslim-majority states throughout the Middle East and North Africa still claim to recognize Islamic law, while political movements hostile to westernized forms of government, including the Muslim Brotherhood in Egypt and the Wahhabis of Saudi Arabia, have called for its strict application.

Observers and scholars have debated whether these political movements are trying to implement anything that could truly be called 'Islamic law', and most doubt that an Islamic state is even a possibility.[1] The problem faced by those trying to implement Islamic laws is that the shari'a was never wholly, or even partly, a state system. Its scholars, the ulama, distanced themselves from the control of political rulers. They pronounced fatwas and advised judges, but they regarded themselves as morally superior to state-appointed officials. In practice, people observed the shari'a in many areas of their daily lives, where the rules and principles of Islamic law, the fiqh, mingled with local customs and practices. Here, social regulations were barely distinguishable from the rules of morality and ritual requirements, which mediators invoked as they sought pragmatic and effective solutions to people's disputes. These practices have been disrupted by state-building and the introduction of new courts and laws, and contemporary governments struggle to incorporate them into state structures. But in many settings shari'a courts continue to hear family disputes and Islamic scholars retain their authority. And the most charismatic continue to foment popular movements, even revolution. Islamic law is still a force to be reckoned with.

BETWEEN THE FIFTEENTH and eighteenth centuries, the Safavid, Mughal, and Ottoman rulers generally treated one another with respect, corresponding in Persian and following accepted protocols and customs. The Ottoman Empire had its origins in Anatolia, where Oghuz Turkic tribes had established a base in the fourteenth century.[2] When he captured Constantinople in 1453, Mehmed the Conqueror embarked on a period of imperial expansion, which his successors extended into Central Asia and North Africa. The ancient cities of Mecca, Medina, and Jerusalem had all fallen under Ottoman sway by 1517, and their leaders persuaded the Abbasid caliph to move to Constantinople. The Ottoman sultans quickly realized that in order to secure popular legitimacy, they needed to co-opt the Islamic religious scholars, the Hanafi ulama. So they channelled substantial resources into the madrasas, effectively centralizing religious education in Constantinople. The chief mufti, the sultan's adviser, retained the power to declare that an unfit ruler should be deposed, something that did occasionally happen, but the sultans could claim to be upholding the justice of the shari'a.

The rules of the fiqh, Islamic law, had taken shape almost a millennium earlier in the deserts of Arabia, however, and they hardly provided the legal resources needed by a rising military power. So, in the sixteenth century, Suleiman the Lawgiver, known in the West as 'the Magnificent', issued a raft of new laws. His *kanun*, from the Greek *canon*, provided rules and penalties on highway robbery, theft, injury, homicide, adultery, usury, taxation, and land tenure, and he established administrative courts. Suleiman was careful to obtain approval from the ulama, and his new rules confirmed many aspects of Islamic law, but they necessarily remained distinct from the shari'a. Suleiman also appointed a chief qadi to every major provincial town, granting him authority to adjudicate legal cases, including complaints against government officials. He was trying to ensure a more standard application of both his kanun and the shari'a.

By the end of Suleiman's reign, in 1566, his empire was the largest and most powerful in the Islamic world. But over the following century its administration fragmented and military discipline weakened. The seventeenth century saw a partial recovery, when Ottoman armies laid siege to the city of Vienna for the second time, but by the early nineteenth century they suffered defeat at the hands of the Russians. Arabia broke away, and an Albanian military leader, Muhammad Ali, took control in Egypt. Facing the threat of European power, in 1838 the Ottoman rulers signed a treaty with the British agreeing to a programme of economic liberalism and administrative reforms. In the Edict of Gülhane, announced with much fanfare at the Topkapi Palace in Constantinople in November 1839, Sultan Mahmud II introduced a series of measures 'to bring the benefits of good administration to the provinces of the Ottoman Empire'. His successors reformed the banking system, reorganized the army, founded new schools, and established bureaucratic institutions for their government. They took more control of the madrasas, confiscated their incomes, appointed salaried officials to government posts in place of Islamic scholars, and established a secular university. They also established a new legislature with the power to make kanun regulations independently of the ulama.

The Tanzimat reforms, as they became known (from the Turkish for 'reorganization'), were supposed to introduce European standards of law and administration into the Ottoman Empire, ensuring civil equality and liberties in place of the principles found in the Quran and shari'a. They failed to impress Europeans, who mocked Ottoman attempts to adopt Western customs and styles of dress, but they did usher in the ideas and forms of Western law. Mahmud had promised a new French-style penal code, and his son established commercial courts along with a Ministry of Justice, which had authority over both the shari'a and the new civil courts. Legal reformers had come to see shari'a jurisprudence as problematically vast, difficult to access, and unsuitable for the times, 'an ocean without shores', as they commonly described it. The new code, the *Mecelle*, was written in Ottoman Turkish. Its sixteen volumes, containing 1,851 articles, were eventually completed in 1876.[3] 'Islamic in content but European in form', its drafters claimed it was the Turkish equivalent to the civil law of 'civilized nations'.

In Egypt, meanwhile, Muhammad Ali pushed through his own reforms in the early nineteenth century.[4] He encouraged Egyptian manufacturers and traders to participate in international markets, and his successor pursued an enthusiastic programme of modernization. He promoted French culture among the elite as well as welcoming European commercial interests. But the Egyptian economy struggled in the new world order, leading to popular resentment, and in 1881 the army, encouraged by many of the middle classes along with younger members of the ulama, rebelled and tried to eliminate European influence. To safeguard their interests, the British stepped in to support the now unpopular ruler. Their Resident in Cairo, Lord Cromer, was able to act almost like a colonial administrator, benevolent but condescending towards the Egyptians, as he introduced new systems of land ownership and ambitious infrastructure projects. Like his counterparts in Africa, Cromer planned to civilize Egypt by making it more European.

Farther east, Iranian shahs were pursuing their own programmes of modernization, albeit with less success. Tensions between powerful shahs and influential Islamic leaders had characterized the regime since the days of Safavid imperialism.[5] The great Shah Abbas, who commanded the empire at the turn of the sixteenth and seventeenth centuries, had declared himself to be a representative of the Shi'i Imam, the historical religious leader. He brought the most influential judges into his court and promoted the application of customary, rather than Islamic, law in criminal cases. The Quran and hadiths, after all, had very little to say about criminal punishments. But the leading ulama retained their influence, insisting on an orthodox version of Shi'ism. In the early eighteenth century, incompetent administrators and petty feuds weakened the shahs' control, and the empire fell to invading Afghans before being taken over by Qajar tribal leaders, originally from the Caucasus. The new Qajar shahs invested heavily in religious institutions, but they never completely succeeded in co-opting the Shi'i ulama. Legal scholars, who continued to dominate the education of the judges, resisted legal reforms in the 1830s and again in the 1870s, insisting that their fatwas could pronounce any imperial decree to be invalid.

By the late nineteenth century, then, the former Islamic empires were being transformed. India was under British colonial rule, while the Ottoman, Egyptian, and Persian rulers pursued their own plans for modernization. Even if they claimed to base their new laws on the shari'a, all these rulers had a vision of European statehood firmly in their sights. But the Persian ulama were not alone in resisting these moves. Before the discovery of oil, Arabia was still something of an economic backwater, although it remained important to all Muslims as the birthplace of the Prophet. In the mid-eighteenth century, when the Ottomans still ruled the Arabian Peninsula, Muhammad ibn 'Abd al-Wahhab, a jurist of the Hanbali school of Sunni Islam, gathered a large following behind calls for a holy war.[6] Realizing the potential of this movement, a local prince, Muhammad bin Saud, declared a new state in which he enforced ibn 'Abd al-Wahhab's vision of the shari'a. He suppressed tribal custom and persecuted those who followed the popular Sufi orders. The partnership between the Wahhabis and the House of Saud endured and, as the movement grew in strength, its leaders occupied holy cities, destroyed ancient tombs, and massacred Muslims who refused to conform to their vision of Islam. The Ottomans tried to suppress the movement in 1818, but by then it had already spread. Many pilgrims had been impressed by the Wahhabis' promises to purify Islam and had founded similar movements throughout the Middle East and North Africa. These would develop into the Islamist campaigns of the following century.

Not all Islamic reformers advocated the same path, however. In the late nineteenth century, concerned about European influence, the scholar and political activist Jamal al-Din al-Afghani called for Muslims everywhere to embrace modernization and undertake technical and scientific training while also adhering to Islamic principles.[7] Travelling widely, he successfully encouraged political activism among his supporters, and one of his collaborators, Muhammad 'Abduh, was appointed as Egypt's Grand Mufti in 1899. 'Abduh promoted an explicitly modernizing agenda, arguing for a flexible approach to Islam and the fiqh, which should be adapted, he maintained, to the social, economic, and political conditions of the era. 'Abduh had great influence on a subsequent generation of Middle Eastern scholars, who were emboldened to criticize orthodox Islam. As they explored the possibility of incorporating Islamic legal principles into new constitutional frameworks, however, there were others who rejected more flexible understandings of Islam, labelling them 'corrupt deviations from the straight path'. These fault lines caused rifts in the Islamic world which linger to this day.

By the early twentieth century, movements for reform were taking different directions in the Middle East. Explicitly modernizing leaders embraced European styles of politics and law and Islamic reformers tried to adapt Islam to the changing world, while reactionary forces insisted on more traditional and less accommodating versions of the shari'a. Their successors followed different paths during the twentieth century as more states with significant Muslim populations formed or gained independence from colonial rule in North Africa, the Middle East, and South Asia.

AFTER THE FIRST World War, the new president of Turkey, Kemal Atatürk, distanced his government decisively from Islamic establishments and authorities. Pursuing an explicitly secular agenda, he abolished Sufi orders, closed madrasas, and stopped training the ulama. He also replaced the *Mecelle* with a new law code based on the Swiss civil law. He prefaced it with a critical statement on the deficiencies of the shari'a and its unsuitability in the modern world.[8] The leaders of Egypt finally freed themselves from direct British influence in 1922 and decided to create their own civil legal code, which was eventually published in 1948. Adopting a rather more conciliatory tone than Atatürk, its drafter, Abd el-Razzak el-Sanhuri, explained that his aim was to reinstall in Egypt a modernized shari'a, taking a civil law form but with shari'a-derived content.[9] Most of the new states of the Middle East followed similar paths. Syria closely copied Egypt's code; Iraq and Kuwait asked Sanhuri to advise on the drafting of their own laws; and Jordan's code, enacted in 1976, followed the same pattern, as did the code made by the United Arab Emirates. The Egyptian laws required judges to consider principles of Islamic shari'a, to the extent that the code and custom combined gave them insufficient guidance, and the Jordanian code required judges to rely directly on the fiqh to fill lacunae. But in form, all of these were European-style civil codes.

In Iran, popular unrest and dissatisfaction among the religious leaders weakened the Qajar regime in the early twentieth century, and the country was occupied by Ottoman, Russian, and British forces during the First World War.[10] With British support, the Pahlavi Reza Khan staged a military coup in 1921 and deposed the last Qajar shah. The Qajars had drawn up a constitution, based on a Belgian model, which provided for an elected assembly, the Majlis. With the support of this body, along with scholars who argued for a more flexible approach to Islamic law, Reza Shah set about establishing modern institutions. He built new factories and government buildings, banned the veil, introduced Western clothing, and forced nomadic tribes to settle, undermining their independence and, catastrophically, their livelihoods. He established a system of state courts and introduced new legislation on civil procedures. Although some of the principles of the shari'a lingered in family laws, over the next twenty years the shah effectively transformed Iran's legal system. He also confiscated the resources of the ulamas' institutions and brought them under government control. Not surprisingly, discontent among the more conservative religious elements ran high, many of whom continued to insist on a more orthodox version of the shari'a. Of all the modernizing regimes in the Muslim world, it was the Iranian that was to prove the most fragile, subject to a British and US-led coup in 1953 and then dramatically overturned in the revolution of 1979.

Just to the west, a prince from the House of Saud reunited the Arabian Peninsula after its occupation during the First World War, establishing the kingdom of Saudi Arabia in 1932.[11] The Saudi kings continued to work closely with Wahhabi-inspired religious leaders, who now commanded great respect among the general population. Determined to maintain the supremacy of the shari'a courts, the ulama were able to limit the administrative structures and regulations that the Saudi kings tried to introduce in the 1950s and 1970s. They restricted new rules to novel social issues, such as the definition of nationality, provision of social insurance, and regulation of motor vehicles and firearms, and they ensured that even these measures only acquired the status of regulations. The ulama resisted moves for legal codification and the establishment of new courts. The one exception was the Board of Grievances, established by the king in 1955 to hear complaints against the government and enforce foreign judgements. Explicitly drawing on shari'a traditions, the board was, and still is, tolerated by the ulama. The exploitation of oil dramatically changed the region's economy, requiring new commercial regulations, and the kings persuaded the ulama to cooperate over their implementation. And in the 1980s, the Board of Senior Ulama issued a detailed fatwa about how different crimes should be dealt with. They also allowed the Board of Grievances to hear commercial disputes. But the religious scholars continued to insist on the superiority of the shari'a courts and retained effective control over constitutional and legal reforms into the twenty-first century.

Saudi Arabia is the only state in the Islamic world to have so extensively resisted the movements for reform and in which the ulama retain so much of their traditional authority. In Yemen, the Ottomans tried to introduce the *Mecelle* when they controlled the southern region from 1872.[12] Scholars of the dominant Zaidi school objected to the laws, based as they were on Sunni Islam, and when the region became independent again in 1919, Yemen's political leaders returned to more traditional forms of governance. But a revolution led to the establishment of a republic in 1967, and the new government embarked on administrative and legal reforms, declaring that the shari'a was 'the source of all laws'. In 1975, the government established a commission of jurists to formulate a comprehensive set of new laws. The resulting codes claim that their laws have been taken from Islamic shari'a principles and that shari'a jurisprudence must guide their interpretation. Still, as in most of the Middle East, simply introducing a written code undermined the authority of traditional Islamic scholars and their methods of interpreting and applying the fiqh.

After the Second World War, movements for independence swept the European empires, and several Muslim-majority states emerged in Africa. Libya, after a brief period of Italian colonization, was occupied by the Allies during the war. When King Idris returned in 1951, he asked Sanhuri, the author of the Egyptian code, to approve a new set of laws for his country. In Morocco, Muhammad V codified the family law, citing the interests of 'unity and clarity', and encouraged Western-trained lawyers. Effectively displacing the Islamic legal scholars, the new legal professionals tended to regard the fiqh as obscure, complicated, disorderly, and inaccessible.[13] In Sudan, Tunisia, and

Mauritania, Muslims also formed a majority, but despite popular support for the shari'a, none of their leaders embraced anything like traditional forms of Islamic law. However much they may have resented being colonized, the local elite, often trained in European schools and universities, had generally come to admire European forms of government and law. Despite making reference to Islam and the shari'a in their constitutions, they affirmed the structures of government and systems of law that European colonialists had bequeathed. In any event, there were hardly practical alternatives if they wanted to join the United Nations.[14] The French administered Algeria as part of France until the War of Independence in 1962.[15] They had reorganized property holdings in the nineteenth century, abolishing the waqf, the charitable trusts that provided the endowments of many religious establishments. They had also centralized control over Islamic education and limited the funding of the madrasas, which dramatically depleted their numbers along with the influence of Islamic jurists. The constitution of the newly independent Algeria did not even claim to be based on the shari'a.

MOST NEW MUSLIM-MAJORITY states affirmed Islam as the official religion and recognized the shari'a in their constitutions. Some even claimed that their laws were based on the shari'a. But many scholars, both Islamic and non-Islamic, have doubted the coherence of these claims. Attempts to implement Islamic laws, they maintain, including the 1948 Egyptian civil code, merely put shari'a-derived rules into a civil-law framework and ignored the fundamentally different forms of use and reasoning demanded by Islamic law.[16] Even codifying the shari'a distorts the law and undermines its open quality, as well as the ability of jurists to interpret and explain it.[17] Shari'a is God's law, after all, so the jurists' work can only be interpretive, not definitive. And although legislators can pass laws for Islamic ends, these can never be definitive or comprehensive, as modern state law inevitably aspires to be. While some maintain that reformed principles of Islamic law can, and should, be incorporated into modern legal systems, others say that without fixed doctrine, it is entirely unsuitable for state structures.[18] The shari'a integrates ritual, moral, social, and political norms which set the authority of the scholar above that of any king or minister. Shari'a is an 'anti-state project', they maintain, in which the law stands above everything.

The shari'a also does not incorporate the sorts of laws essential to a modern nation-state.[19] It offers no general theory of contracts, for example, instead having specific rules for different types of contracts which are too limited for today's commercial world. It also has no general theory of torts, let alone laws that would allow for the establishment of limited companies or partnerships. Sanhuri's code imported civilian laws to fill these gaps, and even Saudi Arabia has introduced new rules for commercial disputes.

Still, Muslims throughout the Islamic world, including minorities in the United States, the United Kingdom, and elsewhere, continue to turn to their religious leaders for advice and to Islamic courts for resolution of family disputes, and calls for new shari'a courts are growing.

OTHER ISLAMIC REFORMERS, meanwhile, have called for a return to more orthodox religious and legal practices. At times they have successfully forced their governments to take their claims to uphold the shari'a more seriously. In the early twentieth century, alongside the Wahhabi-inspired Salafi in Egypt, a rather different Islamic movement took shape. Hasan al-Banna, a young Egyptian schoolteacher and imam, became appalled, on his own account, by the injustice suffered by Muslim workers on the Suez Canal.[20] So, in 1928, he launched a campaign to contest Western imperialism, successfully gathering popular support and establishing a movement he called the 'Muslim Brotherhood'. Al-Banna advocated a reformed Islamic law, one adapted to a changing world, and forcefully opposed the dominance of the conservative ulama at Cairo's Al-Azhar University. Al-Banna never set out explicitly what form the new shari'a was to take, but the *hakimiyya*, God's domain, was its main goal. He told his followers to concentrate on duties and beliefs, making no distinction between governmental and religious rules. The movement grew quickly, attracting around five hundred thousand members within a decade, with branches throughout Egypt and beyond. Al-Banna focused primarily on establishing religious morality and Islamic law, but the Egyptian government, concerned about his popularity, banned the Muslim Brotherhood in 1948. As well as persecuting the movement's leaders, the reforming president, Gamal Abdel Nasser, took control of Al-Azhar University, nationalized much of its property, and excluded its scholars from the national courts. But the Muslim Brotherhood continued to spread throughout the Middle East, North Africa, and beyond, reaching Pakistan, Malaysia, and Indonesia and flourishing under al-Banna's influential successor, the prolific writer Sayyid Qutb.

After the Suez crisis and Egypt's defeat by Israel in 1967, the Muslim Brotherhood was able to regroup. The new Egyptian president, Anwar Sadat, released many of its members from prison and redrafted the constitution to describe Islamic law as 'a principal source of legislation'. But both Parliament and the judiciary were staffed by liberal secularists, so members of the Brotherhood took several cases to the Supreme Constitutional Court, where they argued that some of Egypt's laws were 'un-Islamic'. They found the judges generally unsympathetic and unwilling to define what it might mean for law to conform to the shari'a. But eventually, in 1993, the court declared that new legislation had to be consistent with the broad legal principles of the Quran as defined by the consensus of Muslim jurists over the centuries. Most importantly, it said, no law should be harmful to Muslims. Lower court judges, it also confirmed, should refer to the opinions of the Hanafi fiqh. In practice, however, the legal training of most judges gave them little knowledge of the shari'a or its modes of reasoning, let alone skills in classical Arabic. Even in the Supreme Constitutional Court, the judges continued to cite pragmatic concerns more than the classical fiqh, and they only referred to Islamic doctrine when they considered it consistent with the purposes and principles of the constitution.[21]

Egypt's popular revolution in February 2011 provided new opportunities for the Muslim Brotherhood. Its leader, Mohamed Morsi, was elected president in June 2012. Morsi now declared that there was no contradiction between the principles of the shari'a and the structures of a modern nation-state, which could promote the values of Islam alongside the rule of law, individual freedom, and equal opportunities. Egyptian Salafists disapproved of this flexible interpretation of Islamic law and set up a new party, al-Nour, to promote even stricter implementation of the shari'a, declaring its goal to be the establishment of an Islamic state.[22] The military then deposed Morsi, in July 2013, and banned the Brotherhood.

While the Wahhabis, the Salafis, and the Muslim Brotherhood were promoting rival visions of Islamic law in the Middle East, their Shi'i counterparts were pursuing a rather different reform project farther to the east.[23] Having mounted a revolution in Iran and overthrown the regime of the last Pahlavi Shah in 1979, Ruhollah Khomeini, a Shi'i Imam, set about introducing a new political order based on Islamic principles. His constitution established a jurist-in-charge to represent the original Shi'i Imam, and Khomeini himself initially took this position. Recognizing one of the most fundamental principles of Islamic law, Khomeini also declared that he would treat the established law of the shari'a as unchangeable. His government initially concentrated on introducing visible symbols of Islam, insisting that women use the veil, and outlawing nightclubs, alcohol, music, and dancing. It only gradually tried to reform the structures of the state, and it largely allowed the legal system to continue to operate on the patterns introduced by the Pahlavis, using the same civil code. Eventually Khomeini began to speak of law as an instrument for justice in society, rather than a superior system that could challenge the highest political authority. He declared that, as the Imam's representative, he had supreme authority to pronounce on the law. This even extended to challenging the central pillars of Islam if the interests of Iran's Islamic state required it. It was a dramatic reversal of his original position, effectively putting his own authority above that of the shari'a.

At the same time, Khomeini's regime continued to rely on Western legal forms. It implemented the Quran's penal laws, limited as they were, but introduced statutory penalties for other offences rather than allowing the judges to use their discretion, as was traditional under the Islamic doctrine of ta'zir. Khomeini set up a Court of Guardians to review new legislation, but it was formed by both shari'a and Western-trained lawyers. In practice, too, many of the regime's new laws were inspired by Western models, and Iran continued to participate in the international legal order, entering into treaties with other states. At best, Iran's legal regime incorporated some Islamic legal principles within an essentially Western legal framework.

Elsewhere, Islamic scholars embarked on less revolutionary tactics, trying to reform family laws to comply more closely with Islamic principles. With the exploitation of oil and its dramatic rise in value from the 1970s, the issue of interest also came to the fore. When the Gulf states began to participate more extensively in the international economic order, it became evident that the Islamic legal prohibition on usury would prove a problem.[24] So lawyers set about developing financial instruments that would allow Muslims to participate in financial and banking transactions without violating the shari'a. Building on earlier Egyptian efforts to create a system of Islamic banking, they devised forms of commercial partnership that would allow their members to share profits without charging interest. They also used the *murabaha*, a sale contract compatible with Islamic principles, which came close to a traditional Western finance agreement. Over the subsequent decades, the banking and financial centres in the Middle East expanded dramatically, offering 'screened' financial products which promised that investors could profit from commercial ventures while committing themselves to shari'a values. International institutions set up shari'a boards incorporating prominent Islamic scholars to advise on transactions involving Muslim participants. Of course, more traditional Islamic scholars have criticized these new financial instruments on the basis that they contravene the objectives of the shari'a, which include avoiding profit, hoarding, bribery, and speculation. In Saudi Arabia, where the ulama retain greatest influence, these objections have effectively restricted the new instruments to matters of private contract, on which special committees in the banking sector can advise and adjudicate.[25] But these voices have not deterred large and powerful sectors of the Muslim world from investing heavily in the modern commercial order.

ATTEMPTS TO ADAPT Islamic law to changes in the modern world have taken very different forms, then. While Islamic businesspeople have used creative methods to overcome the ban on interest, the more fundamentalist attitudes of the Wahhabis and Salafis have inspired a series of dramatic conflicts, and Islamist groups have called for violent jihad against the West. The Taliban, which effectively ran Afghanistan from 1996 to 2001, first emerged among a group of classically trained students who claimed to promote a strict interpretation of Islamic law.

In northern Nigeria, where Muslims form a majority in several states, Boko Haram has now taken hold. Founded in 2002, this Islamist group objects to Western-style education and engages in violent confrontations with the Nigerian government. Al-Shabaab, another radical movement, was established in Somalia in 2006 amidst the region's long-running political turmoil. Al-Qaeda arose from Salafist movements in the Middle East, and in 2013 Sunni jihadists with links to al-Qaeda launched their own insurgency against Syria's president, Bashar al-Assad, which they called *Daesh*. By 2014 they had declared a worldwide caliphate under their leader Abu Bakr al-Baghdadi. But they were activists, rather than ulama, and embarked on a military movement and state-building project that owed little to Islamic principles, at least of the more orthodox kind. Their main gesture towards Islam was to insist on the importance of personal morality. Military success enabled them to introduce administrative regulations, and they granted charters to major towns, promising security and services in exchange for loyalty and proper Islamic conduct. Inevitably, they were moving towards the structures of a modern nation-state more than a traditional Islamic caliphate.[26]

Whether or not a true caliphate can exist in the modern world, the ulama still exercise overwhelming legal authority within the Saudi regime. In more local contexts, too, the Islamic fiqh still provides useful rules for merchants, including in Somalia, which barely has a functioning state. Many merchants have turned to Islamic laws to organize commercial affairs, finding them well suited to relatively small-scale transactions, especially where the parties are members of the same social networks.[27] Other countries have allowed spaces for uncodified shari'a to flourish. Sudan, where the colonial and postcolonial regimes recognized a diversity of legal traditions, did not try to control all legal practices or sources of authority.[28] Pakistan, Mauritania, Yemen, Libya, and Sudan have tried to incorporate shari'a-based laws into their states' legal systems, while others, including Indonesia,

Malaysia, and Algeria, allow shari'a courts to exercise authority in family matters, even if they barely refer to the shari'a in their constitutions.

Amidst all these upheavals and movements for reform, shari'a courts have quietly continued their work, in many places doing their best to resolve disputes according to the practices and principles of the dominant version of Islamic law.[29] From Malaysia to Morocco, they hear cases about marriage, divorce, wills, inheritance, custody, and maintenance. In Lebanon, for example, a varied population claims adherence to numerous religions, including the Druze faith, Judaism, different forms of Christianity, and several sects of Islam, and the government recognizes fourteen different family courts. These administer their own laws and appoint their own judges. Both the Shi'i and Sunni courts have their origins in the Ottoman era, and the Lebanese government has exercised light control over their work, although, in 1962, it directed that both must adopt civil law procedures.[30] This means that in the Shi'i appeal courts, the presiding *shaykh*, a classical jurist, sits alongside a civil judge, who advises him on matters of procedure. But the shaykh's clerical regalia of turban and robes leaves no one in doubt about the substance of the law he is applying. In practice, Shi'i litigants in Lebanon first turn to one of the shaykhs, who hear cases in their simple offices. As one of them explained, they must garner respect by acting as good Muslims, and this means that they must not flaunt too much wealth; in court they should display humanity and adopt 'brotherly' attitudes. To be a true shaykh, he said, they must engage personally with those facing moral difficulties. As traditional Muslim judges, they should develop enhanced moral attitudes so that they can embody the principles of the shari'a, not just apply its rules. In accordance with Lebanon's laws, they must also observe its bureaucratic procedural rules, however, which can present dilemmas arising from what they describe as a tension between the shari'a and the state law.

The shari'a contains its own procedural rules, but contemporary judges may be castigated by civil lawyers if they make procedural mistakes. At the same time, members of the general public may object to this legalism: 'He shouts at you, throws you out, that's not right', one disappointed litigant complained of a firm judge.[31] People feel that shaykhs should be kind and gentle. In fact, shari'a judges have always faced criticism in such terms, which has encouraged the best Islamic scholars to prefer the moral authority of the mufti to the legal authority of the qadi. But the dilemmas of the shaykhs have only been sharpened in the modern state.

For all these tensions, shari'a courts are popular throughout the Islamic world, even where they are not recognized by the state. In East Africa, the British and German imperial powers allowed the qadis' courts to continue their work when they divided up territory between them in the 1890s.[32] On independence, the Kenyan government did the same, and the courts remained popular, although they became subject to constitutional debate, as well as a focus for tensions between Muslims and Christians in the early twenty-first century. Tanzania, meanwhile, abolished its shari'a courts on independence but has faced strong calls for their reestablishment since the 1990s. In India, Muslim clerics set up their own courts in the nineteenth century as an alternative to the colonial system, and judges trained in Islamic seminaries continue to hear and adjudicate in family cases.[33] India's state courts can, in theory, apply Islamic law, but this has never been codified, and the shari'a courts represent a popular alternative. Islamic councils have also been established in the United Kingdom, where, even without enforcement powers or the status of qadis, respected Islamic mediators pressure parties to reach a solution compatible with Islamic law. Some Islamic scholars help Muslims adhere to Islamic norms in family arrangements by creating complex prenuptial agreements, which may be effective even if not enforced in the state's legal system.[34]

Whether part of a state's legal system or not, all these Islamic courts and councils try to apply principles of Islamic law and recognize the authority of the scholars. Ironically, it is in some overtly Islamic countries that the judges can use the now codified shari'a to consider new forms of claims.[35] After the Iranian Revolution of 1979, Ayatollah Khomeini repealed the family laws on the basis that they did not recognize Islamic women's domestic roles. Judges were then supposed to follow the shari'a, supplemented by Khomeini's own opinions. But both legal officials and litigants protested about the resulting confusion, and their calls for a more uniform family law eventually persuaded the government to reinstate European-style civil family laws. New courts, established in the 1990s, were staffed by judges trained in civil procedures, assisted by law clerks with university training. Here, educated Iranian women found they could insist on the individual rights granted them by the codified law in ways that would not have been possible in more traditional shari'a courts.

Muslims do not just encounter the shari'a in courts, of course, and the pious try to follow its rules in many areas of their daily lives. They still seek legal guidance from muftis, and Shi'i Muslims might elect to follow the guidance of a *marja*, a 'source of emulation'. Traditionally, the muftis and marjas ranged from learned and prestigious scholars, who advised sultans and senior qadis, to far more modest men who gave guidance to rural populations and local judges. The processes of modernity have changed their status, and they no longer advise judges directly, save in the shari'a courts. But, continuing the tradition of the Ottoman sultans, the Egyptian government appointed a State Mufti in 1895, and successive officeholders have reinvented their roles, issuing fatwas to support the government's modernizing agenda.[36] Some have published long opinions in the press seeking to demonstrate how the shari'a can be accommodated to modern life.

Other marjas command huge personal followings and can be influential in diplomacy. In the early twenty-first century, Shi'ites looked to three marjas in particular. Preeminent among them was Sayyid Ali al-Husseini al-Sistani, a senior cleric at the seminary of Najaf in Iraq.[37] Millions declared loyalty to Sistani, allowing him to amass immense financial resources, which he used to support offices across the world. Sistani himself was reclusive and retiring, particularly under the regime of Saddam Hussein, when the Shiʻite clergy were regularly persecuted. But he continued to publish books for his followers, including a guide for Shiʻites living in the West. During the US-led invasion of Iraq in 2003, he eventually intervened, calling for an assembly to be chosen in a general election, as against a US-appointed body. When his influence over Iraq's Shiʻi population became apparent, the United States altered its policy, and in 2004 he successfully brokered a cease-fire. Having been catapulted briefly into the limelight, Sistani then returned to his position of aloof authority.

In Lebanon, the marja Ayatollah Muhammad Husayn Fadlallah was much more politically engaged than Sistani. He promoted education among the young and advocated 'anti-imperial' politics through a network of charitable and educational organizations. He maintained his own radio station and an active website, gave regular lectures, and published prolifically, including twenty-five volumes of Quranic exegesis and fifteen works on jurisprudence. Although adopting a classical style, he tried to make his legal writing accessible to a lay audience, explaining technical terms and the reasoning behind his rulings. He engaged in contemporary issues, giving opinions on medical and scientific ethics, such as the admissibility of DNA evidence. He also issued numerous fatwas in response to individual requests for advice. Like Sistani, he exercised enormous influence over the Muslims who read his books, consulted his website, and sought his opinions.

Alongside these famous scholars, the Muslim world is populated by an array of other scholars and leaders who are less ambitious and play more traditional roles. Although they occasionally become involved in politics, they typically focus on offering advice to personal petitioners, sometimes taking advantage of modern media. Yemen was historically governed by a Shi'i Imam who combined scholarship with politics in a role distinctive to this brand of Islam. Other Yemeni scholars and prestigious jurists, meanwhile, kept their distance from government, acting as independent muftis, authorities on shari'a interpretation. After Yemen's revolution and the codification of its laws in the 1970s, the muftis continued their work.[38] The Yemeni Ministry of Justice appointed a Mufti of the Republic, similar to Egypt's State Mufti, who was based in the capital, Sanaa, and it supported regional muftis in the provinces.

One anthropologist was introduced to a mufti in Ibb, a provincial town in the southern highlands, in the 1970s. The mufti was still receiving petitioners every afternoon in an upper room of his house, where local townsmen would gather to watch the proceedings. Chewing qat, a mildly narcotic local leaf, they leaned against low cushions and chatted about local affairs while petitioners arrived to seek advice on disputes or to ask the mufti to certify documents for a court case. Farmers in open-necked shirts and loosely wrapped turbans, with cracked hands and bare feet, would bow low before the mufti and ask about a marriage or divorce, a problematic inheritance, or contributions to a religious endowment. The mufti, in his indoor dress of skullcap, white gown, and waistcoat, having left his scholar's turban, dagger, and outer coat by the door, would give immediate advice. Using a traditional reed pen, he wrote his fatwas as notes on their petitions, using an abbreviated, even cryptic, form which the less educated might need assistance to interpret. He advised on property transactions, legal disputes, and marital arrangements until his retirement in the 1990s.

Meanwhile, in Sanaa, the Mufti of the Republic also received petitioners in his house. He also participated in a weekly radio fatwa show. Here, four scholars would consider questions that listeners sent in. Broadcast to thousands, the show required that they give fatwas that were easy to understand. As one explained, while the traditional mufti would inscribe a short note that the recipient could ponder, the radio audience had to understand their words immediately, and they had to assume that some members of the audience had little education. But by using modern media, the muftis' fatwas could reach a much larger population. On television, too, fatwa shows brought together bearded old men in turbans and robes to dispense wisdom in response to viewers' questions.

The shari'a continues to shape Muslim lives in numerous ways. Muftis use fatwas to give direct advice, qadis hand down rulings in the shari'a courts, and senior muftis and marjas wield political influence. In Senegal, for example, traditional Sufi leaders, *marabouts*, became wealthy from peanut production and could use their religious status to exert considerable influence in domestic politics. Islamic legal norms shape daily lives in more indirect ways, too, as people debate moral problems and seek informal advice about how to behave as good Muslims. The guidance of the shari'a extends to matters of personal morality as well as setting out requirements for family, property, and commercial relations, and enterprising campaigners find new ways to bring its rules and principles to ordinary people.

In Cairo, a women's mosque movement was initiated in the wave of Islamic revival that swept the Muslim world in the 1970s.[39] It had its origins in the work of Zaynab al-Ghazali, who trained women preachers in the first half of the twentieth century. Although her organization was disbanded by Nasser at the same time as the Muslim Brotherhood, later, as neighbourhood mosques proliferated in Cairo, so did female teachers, *da'iyat*. Concerned above all to guide women in matters of piety, they gave teaching and advice on standards of dress and speech, suitable entertainments for adults and children, household management and finances, care for the poor, and appropriate terms for public debate. They stopped short of advocating reinstatement of the shari'a in place of Egyptian civil law, but they did insist that proper religious conduct had an impact on worldly and legal affairs.

The Cairo movement was able to take advantage of mass media and general literacy, which made Islamic classics widely available in Egypt. New manuals proliferated in which writers explained the rules on religious obligations, matters of character formation, and issues of moral uprightness; street vendors offered booklets on fiqh and a widely read three-volume compendium commissioned by the Muslim Brotherhood; and people could buy tape-recorded sermons and find religious instruction on radio and TV programmes, which often transmitted popular fatwas. The women's movement used the fiqh manuals, in particular, to formulate practical guidance for their audiences. In the more middle-class neighbourhoods, classically trained da'iyat drew on the long tradition of scholarly legal commentary to present a range of juristic opinions, emphasizing that members of the audience must make their own choices about which of these to follow. Meanwhile, in working-class neighbourhoods, da'iyat interspersed their talks with devotional phrases and short Quranic verses. Like the muftis in Yemen, the Cairo da'iyat hardly distinguished matters of law, morality, religious observance, and personal piety. They were careful to avoid conflict and kept out of ongoing tensions between Islamists and secularists. But their teachings were deeply rooted in traditional Islamic sources and the authority of the shari'a.

THE SHARI'A HAS always been more than a legal system, offering ritual and moral guidance to individuals throughout the Muslim world. It does not aspire to provide a fixed body of laws or a single coherent doctrine, as state systems do. Rather, it offers rules for guidance, which are open to interpretation by specialist scholars. They concentrate, above all, on individual duties, hardly straying into criminal offences, matters which were originally left to the caliphs. The object is not so much to impose order, or even to promise justice, although the fiqh can be, and regularly is, used to resolve disputes. It is a moral programme, intended to guide people along God's path for the world. It offers a very different vision of order from that of the modern state.

Many Muslims consider that the shari'a could and should have more authority in the modern world, a counterweight to the limitations and irreligion of modern governments and states. Muslim-majority countries have tried to incorporate its principles into their civil legal systems and claim that they uphold the shari'a, but they have generally also undermined the institutions and authority of traditional jurists. The idea of an Islamic state is deeply problematic, and the example of Daesh has hardly proved otherwise. But the authority of Islamic law stems from God, and its religious scholars continue to offer more persuasive guidance and more effective solutions to legal disputes than bureaucratic institutions can do. And some have proved able to intervene dramatically in international conflict.

Islamic scholars stand apart from political rulers, claiming that their laws and principles should guide even the most powerful ruler. Although these dynamics cannot easily be aligned with the structures of a state, it is a form of the rule of law. And, while the most eminent scholars command the respect of millions, Islamic law retains both power and influence.

CHAPTER FIFTEEN

TURNING THEIR BACKS ON THE STATE

Tribes, Villages, Networks, and Gangs

W hen world leaders take their seats at the General Assembly of the United Nations, they symbolize a globe divided neatly into sovereign states. Each takes responsibility for its own populations, economy, and environment and maintains its own legal system. These often aim to regulate the minutest aspects of people's lives, from the way they buy and sell goods to the safety of their houses and public spaces, the organization of their family relations, and the efficiency of their financial systems. Maintaining peace and order is supposed to be a national project. But the reach of these legal systems, however powerful they may be, is less extensive and less effective than our governments would generally have us believe. Islamic law and legal scholars are not the only alternative sources of order in the modern world.

Tibetan tribesmen still make and follow laws in defiance of the Chinese state; village communities scattered throughout the world preserve their own constitutions; and even at the heart of the modern United States, trade associations discourage their members from turning to state courts. The dynamics of law and legalism have not been wholly co-opted by the modern state. At the same time, while very small communities formulate rules to provide a source of predictability, order, and autonomy, not all organized groups turn to legalism. Making rules explicit means making them visible, and some prefer to hide their rules and structures from view, seeking to avoid scrutiny. Anti-legalism is also a powerful tool by which gangs and mafia organizations defy the state.

★

ON THE GRASSLANDS of Tibet, now in modern China, feuds still break out among nomadic yak herders, as they have for centuries. In a pattern common to pastoralists in Asia, the Middle East, and Africa, a dispute can set up a cycle of violence and counterviolence, a feud, which tribal leaders must work hard to end. Skilled mediators may need to persuade tribesmen to accept compensation instead of taking further revenge. Centralized states inevitably try to force nomads to settle, imposing their own laws and criminal sanctions in place of tribal customs, and the modern Chinese state is no exception. But on the grasslands of Qinghai and Gansu provinces, Tibetan nomads continued their practices of feuding and mediation well into the twenty-first century.[1]

Pastoralists brought sheep and goats onto the vast Tibetan Plateau many centuries ago and domesticated the wild yaks that roamed its pastures. In the valleys, where melting glaciers and snowfields allowed them to irrigate fields and cultivate barley, people gradually settled in villages and established monasteries. Some of these tribes came together to form the empire that dominated the region between the sixth and ninth centuries. But on the higher pastures, nomads continued to tend flocks of yak, sheep, and goats. Images of pastoralism pervade Tibetan poetry, stories, and religious texts, and modern herders in sheepskin coats still tether their horses outside black tents, where women in heavy coral jewellery churn milk into butter. The winter months are difficult, as wind sweeps the dusty plains and temperatures plummet, but in the summer, the nomads lounge in their spacious tents, woven from the hair of their own yaks. Men congregate on carpets around the central stove, sipping milky tea and melting rich butter and cheese into barley meal, or they bask in the sun as they tend the grazing livestock while women tend to the bulk of the household tasks.

During China's devastating Cultural Revolution, all farming and herding activities were collectivized, but in the 1980s the government allowed Tibetan pastoralists to regroup into tribes. Most reverted to historical patterns. More recently, Chinese authorities have made strenuous efforts to persuade the nomads to settle, complaining of pasture degradation, although in reality they are more uncomfortable with the nomads' 'backward' lifestyles and ability to escape taxation and control. But in the early twenty-first century, many Tibetan tribes still practised raiding and feuding in time-honoured patterns.

In Amdo, the historically Tibetan region that makes up much of Qinghai province, each tribe has several thousand tents divided into encampments of around forty. The Amdo nomads eat, socialize, and sleep on the grass floor of their tents. In early spring the women create tiny huts next to the sheep pens where the young men sleep in order to guard their livestock against raids. They keep fierce mastiffs to deter intruders, and many adults bear the scars of tooth-marks from when they suffered bites as careless children. But, despite their vigilance, raids do occur. A man discovers that some sheep have gone missing overnight and announces his intention to ride off in pursuit. He declares that he will gather companions to track down and fight the thief and is barely restrained by the rest of his family, who send a child racing to find the local headman. A raid is an insult to the victim, and custom dictates that the head of the tent take immediate revenge. All men carry knives, which hang ostentatiously in decorated sheaths around their waists, and their herding tasks are not onerous. While their mothers, sisters, and wives undertake the majority of the labour around the tent, as well as the child care, men are able, if necessary, to drop everything to ride off and avenge a raid. They are constantly 'prepared for war'.[2]

Neighbours often quarrel over grassland, and minor feuds break out between encampments. But when raiders appear from a different tribe, a single incident can easily lead to a fight, and then a war, as each side gathers companions to meet attack with counterattack, each more severe than the last. In the most serious feuds, leaders summon men from all parts of a scattered tribe to mount a full-scale offensive. In the early twenty-first century, Amdo nomads were still, intermittently, engaged in a feud that had its roots in a pasture dispute dating back to the 1950s. Mothers wept as they talked of sons lost in shootings, while a headman described the difficulty of recruiting men from encampments close to the border, where many had married into families from the enemy tribe. That was no excuse, he explained. Loyalty to one's family, one's encampment, and one's tribe is everything.

Most feuds are settled before they get to this stage. Everyone can recall incidents in their tribes, often serious ones involving knives and even killings, that have been swiftly resolved through payment of compensation. Everyone knows that it is much better to negotiate and avert a cycle of vengeance, angry though the young men may be, and must be seen to be. Stolen property must, of course, be returned, and blood money or wound price paid as compensation for the loss of life or injuries. In a serious case, the elders first negotiate a truce, sometimes with the help of local monks, and then call on the services of a respected mediator. An American missionary who lived among the nomads in the 1930s described the camps set up on the grasslands, the different sides in separate tents, while a group of mediators shuttled between the two. Here, they listened to impassioned arguments about injury and status and tried to persuade angry nomads to think of accepting compensation.[3] These are age-old patterns. A legal text from the fourteenth century describes the arguments about 'greatness' that mediators encountered and the skilful arguments they had to employ to calm passions and bring parties to an agreement.[4] Now, as before, wronged and angry tribesmen start by refusing compensation. Honour demands that they take direct revenge. Then skilled mediators go patiently between the two sides, now more likely to gather in different rooms of a hotel in the local town, listening to defiant speeches, citing high principles, and gradually wearing down obstinate refusal to compromise. Slowly and patiently, family members, fellow tribesmen, and mediators exert pressure until the parties finally accept compensation. In the most intransigent feuds, they may have to call on a senior Buddhist lama, one who has earned high respect for his skills in mediation, and whose involvement may finally allow an injured tribesman, after a show of the greatest reluctance, to accept a compromise.

The mediators approach each case on its own facts and negotiate appropriate compensation, with the amount depending on the seriousness of the injury and the circumstances of the incident as well as the status of the different parties. In the modern world, the police might also intervene. It is hard to keep a major dispute from their attention, and those responsible for a serious injury may face arrest, a court hearing, and a prison sentence. Even so, among the tribesmen, the family still has to pay compensation. They may complain about double punishment—their son is already in gaol and the compensation will devastate their herds— and the mediators are sympathetic. But, as one mediator pointed out, the government system does not 'do justice'—it gives nothing to the victim. 'Someone subject to two laws is like a horse with two saddles', he explained, encapsulating the problem in a traditional maxim. Justice, then, must be negotiated. It depends on the circumstances of the incident, the status of the victim, and the eloquence of his advocates. The most renowned mediator cannot simply apply a rule, and even the highest lamas can fail to resolve an intractable case. And that includes the grassland dispute from the 1950s that continued into the twenty-first century after innumerable attempts at settlement had failed.

These practices are not remotely legalistic. Justice must be negotiated. But the Tibetan nomads do have laws. In Golok, a wild and inhospitable region in southern Qinghai, home to the fiercest and most independent Tibetan nomads, a member of one of the leading tribes proudly referred to their ancient laws. The ruling families of the Golok tribes claim to be descended from three brothers. Historically, their groups occasionally formed confederacies to face a threat from outsiders, but fights and feuds have always marred relations among them. Experienced mediators explained the skills they need to employ to settle the most intractable disputes, the importance of oratory, the flamboyant displays of rhetoric, and the protracted negotiations that conciliation required. But they also referred to their tribes' laws. One described a complicated set of rules bearing a loose resemblance to the processes of negotiation he had just described. He did not claim that the rules were applied, or even referred to, during mediation, and yet they were obviously important and had been written down. Local bookshops sold a two-volume history of the region written in the 1980s which included a version of these laws. One of its authors confirmed that the Golok tribes had always kept written laws. Although all the copies had been lost in the upheavals of the Cultural Revolution, he explained, his team had compiled a new version from interviews with tribal leaders, who knew them well.

The printed laws are detailed and explicit, specifying exact amounts of compensation for people with different statuses. Like the ancient Tibetan texts, the modern laws promise justice through compensation. They also require elaborate procedures: a killer has to give up the horse and the gun he used in the attack before a truce can be called, a rule still followed by the Golok nomads. But it is evident that the laws are not applied directly, or even referred to during mediation processes, while the sharp status hierarchy they outline bears little relation to the relatively egalitarian status of nomads. Why then, did anyone go to the trouble of writing them out, and why do mediators still refer to them with such reverence?

While the farmers of central Tibet lived in estates, where most were effectively serfs, bound to aristocratic families or the local monastery, the Golok tribes long guarded their independence from centralized control. They resisted Mongol and Muslim invaders and even insisted on paying voluntary tribute, rather than taxes, to their local monasteries. In the early twentieth century, a Russian traveller recorded the words of a Golok tribesman who announced, contemptuously, and with probably only a little exaggeration, that while other Tibetans followed the rules of the Dalai Lamas of China, and of any number of their petty chiefs, 'we Goloks recognize only our own laws'.[5] Drawing up their own laws was a mark of independence. Still, they did not entirely turn their backs on Lhasa and the authority of Buddhist institutions. They supported the monasteries generously, sent their sons to become monks, and treated the highest lamas with the utmost respect. And, like all Tibetans, they revered and still revere the Dalai Lama. The laws begin with a reference to the ancient Tibetan king, Songtsen Gampo, and the religious principles on which he had supposedly based his laws. The Golok tribesmen had considered these principles, so the authors claim, and then made their own laws. In this way they were linking their code to the traditional, but largely apocryphal, account of the first Buddhist king, who is said to have brought civilization, through religion and law, to Tibet. In fact, there is no correspondence between these early Tibetan laws—or what they were supposed to contain—and the rules that follow in the Golok code. But the authors were obviously keen to link their laws to the legal traditions of central Tibet and give them a Buddhist veneer.

What, then, were they for? In former times, as another of the mediators explained, the leading families in the area used to gather to discuss their laws. In this way, they probably standardized the principles on which mediators settled disputes. But the rules make the negotiation of compensation seem far more tidy and rule-bound than it can ever have been. And maybe that was the point. Life on the Tibetan grasslands was always unsettled, punctuated by raids, violence, cycles of feuding, and uncertain tribal loyalties as well as the interference of officials from central Tibet, or now, the state. Even if they were never directly applied, the neatness and order of these laws, setting out the principles on which compensation ought to be negotiated, created a sense of moral order. It was an order rooted in tribal autonomy, but morally linked to the legal and religious traditions of central Tibet. Carefully preserved, even under Chinese rule, the laws tell the tribesmen how life ought to be.

THE TIBETAN NOMADS are not the only pastoralists to have made laws. In the highlands of northern Yemen, tribes wrote out elaborate agreements of accord and cooperation in the eighteenth century.[6] Like the Tibetan rules, these specified the ways in which revenge could be conducted and compensation negotiated based on a complicated system of protection and guarantee. Farmers in more settled communities have also made laws. In the highlands of Kabylia, in northeastern Algeria, the Berbers historically formed distinct villages, clustering in stone houses amidst their fields and olive groves.[7] The area nominally fell under Ottoman rule in the sixteenth century, but only the areas most accessible to visiting officials ever paid taxes or provided recruits for their armies. Berber villagers visited markets and travelled to the ports on the coast to look for work, but they remained culturally and linguistically distinct from their lowland neighbours and managed their own internal affairs. This meant maintaining order within their own communities and carefully regulating their relations with outsiders. In most villages, an elected headman convened an assembly once a week, which all adult men attended, and he formed a village council together with his assistants and the village imam. Here, they discussed and developed village rules, *qanun*, as they called them, which the imam might help them to formulate, sometimes recording them in writing along with other important documents. Each village also formed part of a larger tribe, a loose association of communities that arranged weekly markets.

When the French army conquered Kabylia in an early wave of colonial expansion in 1857, they sent back reports of fiercely independent communities. The French public quickly assumed that these fitted their image of ideal peasants, living self-sufficient and harmonious lives, and scholars soon arrived to record examples of their 'customary laws'. They compiled volumes of rules from the local qanun as dictated to them by the local imams. After translating them into French, often using legal categories from the Napoleonic Civil Code, they sent the results to the colonial magistrates, who were supposed to consult them when managing Berber affairs.

The many qanun recorded by the French are varied, obviously reflecting different village customs, but most follow a relatively standard form. The imams seem mainly to have explained the regulations of the largest village of each tribe, almost certainly adding an Islamic veneer to the laws. It is unclear to what extent the qanun were written down before this date, but the rules were certainly there in some form, as in lists of offences and punishments that defined how people ought to behave, both individually and collectively. In each text, an introductory paragraph refers respectfully to religious scholars, the Islamic qadi, the Quran, and sometimes even the Ottoman sultan. It then sets out a long list of offences with corresponding fines. The rules demand that villagers participate in collective activities, such as roadbuilding and maintaining watercourses, and that they attend communal events, such as the weekly village meetings, funerals, and common prayers. They require that the villagers coordinate their agricultural activities, and they include rules about dress, sumptuary laws designed to restrain conspicuous competitive displays, and prohibitions on the waste of household resources. Most qanun demand small payments to village funds at times of birth, circumcision, marriage, or death. They fix the amounts to be paid as dowries and what families can spend on wedding celebrations, and some even stipulate that women must not marry below their status.

The rules are evidently designed to maintain peace in the community. They generally specify that a fine must be paid by anyone who quarrels or engages in any form of violence. Curiously, they have little to say about homicide and physical injuries. But the Berbers had long traditions of retaliation and compensation not dissimilar from those of the Tibetan tribesmen, and these must adequately have regulated the related processes. The village community had to step in when those traditions could not apply, such as when a killing occurred within a family. Several qanun allow the assembly to confiscate all of a family's property in such cases—for example, when someone has killed a relative to secure an inheritance. Other rules regulate the conduct of the headman and village officials, imposing fines on those who have not fulfilled their functions properly or who have misappropriated village funds. The amounts collected from all the fines are supposed to be spent on collective meals and village improvements. The rules also require that the villagers respect their officials, on pain of further fines.

Within these qanun, numerous rules attempt to enforce good public behaviour. They prohibit any villager from leaving dung or other rubbish in the streets, from contaminating the village fountain by washing clothes in it, and from diverting water, urinating against the mosque, or running races or singing lewd songs in the streets. People should not lie or listen at other people's doors. Women had to dress appropriately, covering their heads, and deviant sexual behaviour was particularly sanctioned. So was fighting, and some qanun go into great detail about the different sorts of weapons the villagers were not supposed to use, which attracted a range of different fines. Some rules impose particularly harsh penalties on anyone who takes sides in the quarrels of others; others punish people who fail to intervene and restrain the violence. The qanun also make it clear that to appeal to the sultan for justice would bring dishonour to the whole village, a wrong that attracted a serious fine, as did an attempt to seek justice from another village, or allowing strangers to intervene in village matters. In these ways, the qanun formed village constitutions, regulating and controlling life within the community and creating a sense of distance from outsiders.

Berber farmers regularly married people from other villages or migrated to different regions in search of work. Thus almost all qanun contain rules specifying that they still have obligations to contribute to local funds if they retain property in it. Some prohibit sales of land to outsiders. In this way, the qanun define the boundaries of village membership. They also carefully regulate the provision of hospitality. The village, as a whole, has to be able to offer protection to outsiders, and villagers incur fines if they do not offer lodging and sustenance to a stranger, even more if they harm someone who has taken refuge with them. But it is clear that individual households had to be careful about inviting people in, especially if those people were fleeing vengeance. Village honour depended on guarding the community against outsiders, who were generally assumed to be causes of disorder, corruption, and gossip, and this meant carefully managing their relations with all those with whom they came into contact.

By the time the French armies arrived in Kabylia, the Berbers had long since converted to Islam, and they unequivocally respected the authority of their imams. But they recognized that their community might, on occasion, need to depart from the rules of the shari'a. One set of regulations makes this explicit: although Islamic law demands that a hand be cut off as punishment for theft, it declares, this is not our custom. Equally, many qanun recognize that not allowing women to inherit—as was Berber custom, probably to avoid the difficulty of land passing to outsiders—is against the shari'a, without condemning the practice. The qanun, that is, serve to distinguish the village and its customs from the wider world of Islamic law and authority, just as they distance it from neighbouring villages and outsiders of all sorts.

The political changes of the late nineteenth and twentieth centuries, when the French military administration was followed by a civil colonial regime, brought changes to village life and rulemaking. As the government extended its control into the highlands, the villagers began to incorporate new terms, borrowed from colonial administrators, into their rules. Villages were no longer supposed to deal with murder and theft or to banish a miscreant and appropriate his property, and they adapted their rules accordingly. But the communities largely retained their autonomous character. After the Second World War, when the French recognized certain villages as 'municipal centres' with their own 'mayors', the villagers enthusiastically produced new rules, firmly based on their old qanun. The forces of modernity, which followed hot on the heels of Algerian independence in the 1960s, made it more difficult for the villagers to control their members, many of whom took the opportunity to study in the capital, migrate to Paris, or simply leave to find work elsewhere.

Still, most villages continued to insist on contributions for local projects, proudly showing their paved roads, electricity supplies, and water pipes, funded by the community, to a visiting anthropologist. They also held out against the forces of militant Islam, effectively requiring young people to shave off their beards and remove their headscarves when they returned from the towns. A movement for the revival of Berber culture in the mid-1990s encouraged a number of villages to enter into a collective agreement to control the expenses of festivals and celebrations. Like the sumptuary laws, which formed such an important part of the old qanun, the new rules placed limits on the presents they could offer during engagement ceremonies and the expenses they could devote to a wedding. The new rules do not seem to have ever been enforced, at least not in detail, but the villagers continue to talk about them with some pride. If nothing else, they remain a marker of village autonomy and the ability of the inhabitants to turn their backs on the state and the militant movements that now threaten them.

SMALL COMMUNITIES THE world over have made laws to regulate internal affairs and maintain a sense of distinctiveness and autonomy. The Berber constitutions find parallels in sixteenth-century Spain, where villagers created and maintained their own laws, which distanced the kings and priests who tried to meddle in their affairs.[8] Jewish communities in medieval Cairo used their own rules to regulate internal matters, while medieval Italian cities drew up their own charters.[9] The ability to make laws, even quite mundane ones, seems often to have been an important marker of independence.[10] The patterns, of course, vary. Towns in medieval Germany had their own ordinances, but by the fourteenth century some were asking legal officials from neighbouring towns to advise on what their laws should be, entering into what they called 'mother-daughter' relationships.[11] Here, legal practices established relations of voluntary dependence rather than determined independence.

Other communities turn their backs on laws and legalism altogether, managing local affairs according to unwritten rules and customs even when sources of legalism are readily available. At the other end of the Tibetan Plateau from the grasslands of the Golok tribes, the Himalayan region of Ladakh was for long an independent kingdom, although it paid tribute to the Dalai Lamas in Tibet. Now part of India, the region is still sparsely populated, with difficult roads and tracks though the mountains, which are blocked for months by winter snow. The Ladakhi population forms distinct villages, which cluster around the lands their farmers irrigate by diverting the water from melting glaciers into a network of small channels. These channels clearly mark out their fields and village boundaries. In the early twenty-first century there were still no roads in many areas, which meant that any journey to the local town—for example, to visit government offices, access health care, buy household goods, collect the food rations provided by the government, or accompany children to the local boarding school—involved a difficult trek over high passes. In winter, it meant traversing a treacherous gorge, where ice cover created a navigable path. Not surprisingly, visits by teachers, medical officers, development workers, and others were rare.

Although historically many Ladakhi villagers paid taxes to local monasteries and landowners, they always managed their own affairs, and after Indian independence their villages became practically self-governing. At the turn of the twenty-first century, headmen still managed local affairs in the remoter villages, and their positions rotated annually among the major households.[12] Most agricultural matters followed well-established patterns. Numerous other village obligations rotated, too, but the visit of a high-ranking lama, repairs to the local temples, and decisions about major festivals required the agreement of a full meeting. In these cases, the headman would assemble all the adult men, as he also did when a major conflict arose, something that all Ladakhis took extremely seriously. They would negotiate suitable communal arrangements or patiently persuade angry villagers to reconcile their differences, shake hands, and move on. But, unlike the Berber and Spanish villages, the Ladakhis did not draw up local rules. They spoke of their 'customs', by which they meant traditional forms of dress, food preparation, and hospitality, and they followed a strict calendar of religious and other festivals, whose dates were determined by the village astrologer. They had rules for inheritance, regulated the rotation of responsibilities, and had clear expectations about how conflict should be resolved. Yet the headmen maintained practically no records. In one village, they kept in a slim file of collective decisions, which largely concerned property matters, but there was no written constitution.

The Ladakhi villagers could perfectly well have written their own constitutions. Many were literate—Buddhist monks had established monasteries in the region almost a thousand years previously, bringing with them a tradition of scholarship. The Ladakhi kings and nobility kept libraries and archives, and villagers had a high regard for scholarship, sending sons to the local monasteries. Even before the government established schools in the region there was a tradition of literacy, generally passed from father to son, which enabled villagers to read religious texts. By the early twenty-first century the majority could read and write. It must, then, have taken a deliberate effort on the part of the villagers to turn their backs on the legalism that surrounded them in the monasteries, palaces, and government offices, and to continue to manage their affairs according to unwritten rules and customs. This, in itself, may have been a reaction against outsiders, including the landowners to whom they had had to pay taxes during the era of the Ladakhi kings. A written constitution

would have made the village organization more visible and potentially liable to external interference. As it was, the villagers
could pay the greatest respect to outsiders and officials, as they
do still to the development workers who visit to try to introduce
agricultural and other improvements. The villagers can agree to
all their demands and quietly ignore them when the visitors have
gone on their way.

Throughout the world, independent villages have developed
their own forms of government with their own logic. Internal
rules and precedents always govern village affairs, but only some
write them down. Written rules and records of legal cases are
visible, and many want to avoid scrutiny.[13]

SIMILAR PATTERNS CAN be found at the heart of one of the
most legalistic societies in the modern world. In the 1970s, a
legal anthropologist who had been working among African
tribes in postcolonial states noticed parallels with the ways in
which members of the fashion industry in New York maintained
a distance from the state.[14] Here, a network of manufacturers
and merchants could largely avoid state-sanctioned union regulations by establishing personal relations among key people.
The fashion business, then as now, was volatile. The vagaries
of changing seasonal trends could suddenly create huge demand
for certain items, while just a few months later, retailers would
struggle to shift to a similar garment. At the top end of the market, where dresses retailed for over $300, then a significant sum,
clothes were designed and produced by fashion houses, whose
representatives enjoyed the industry name of 'jobbers'. The fashion houses sent the bulk of their manufacturing work out to
subcontractors, who ran workshops which employed teams of
seamstresses. As retailers coped with fluctuating demands, they
would send orders to a jobber, who might suddenly commission

large quantities of a garment from the subcontractor. The workshop would have to demand that its team put in long hours over several days to complete the order on time, going far beyond what union regulations permitted.

In theory, working practices in the industry were governed by contracts between the association of contractors and jobbers and the International Ladies' Garment Workers' Union (ILGWU). The ILGWU specified appropriate wages for the seamstresses and limited their working hours. Its business agent would visit each workshop regularly to discuss business and see that both sides were complying with the agreed terms. The agent's main point of contact was the subcontractor's floor manager, often called a 'floor lady', who supervised the team in the workshop, bargained with the jobber and the jobber's representatives over prices and orders, and maintained good relations with the union. In practice, the agent understood how the business worked, and knew that the subcontractors had to ask their teams to work far longer hours than the union agreements allowed. They had to meet unexpected demand and make up for the fact that at other times they would be effectively unemployed. Everyone expected that the agent would not, in fact, enforce the working hours specified in the agreement. In return for the agent's 'reasonableness', the subcontractor's floor manager would send an agent carefully chosen gifts, such as bottles of whisky at Christmas, an expensive dress, or a present for a child's birth, graduation, or marriage. Both the subcontractor and the floor manager developed personal relations with each agent, even stepping in to provide advice about medical issues or employment possibilities for a child, and the floor manager would personally supervise the making of garments for, say, an agent's wife. They maintained similar relations with the jobber's representatives, who commissioned and checked the finished garments, effectively controlling the work that flowed to the subcontractor. At the same time, the seamstresses had to be willing to work the extra hours, which

409

they generally did, presumably realizing that it was effectively a condition of their employment.

In these ways, relations between the subcontractors and the union agents followed clearly established but unwritten rules which allowed them to ignore the union's requirements. Cash-flow difficulties, meanwhile, might mean that the subcontractor had to seek a loan from the workers, which they were often able to provide. And the jobber might in turn look to the subcontractor for a source of funds to pursue some private business venture. Everyone colluded to avoid the terms of the employment contracts and subvert the protection it was supposed to give its members. On either side, parties would also extend credit or wait to call in a loan or payment for work done in times of need. Most people were aware of their legal rights, but no one expected to enforce them.

Within the fashion industry, then, the owners and agents of the most successful businesses carefully built up a web of personal relations. If these were managed properly, people could expect that favours would be extended and contractual rights would not be insisted upon. The union's agent could have insisted on enforcement of his agreement, and anyone could have turned to the state courts to insist on payment under the terms of their contractual arrangements. But those who wished to flourish had to follow an alternative set of rules, giving gifts, extending favours, and expecting the same from their colleagues in the industry.

IN ANOTHER PART of the city, meanwhile, a network of traders, many of Jewish origin, controlled the market in diamonds.[15] The New York Diamond Dealers Club was, and still is, the largest and most important diamond trading network, or 'bourse', in the United States. It brings together importers, wholesalers, manufacturers, and brokers, and in the 1980s, when one researcher

investigated the network, around 80 percent of the rough diamonds coming into the United States passed through the club,
along with a fair proportion of the polished stones. Membership
was limited, and even nonmembers sought to conduct deals on
its premises in the heart of Manhattan, though anyone who did
had to obtain a suitable introduction and secure sponsorship
from a member.

Membership of the club offered access to important networks
and a reputation for trustworthiness. It also meant complying
with a set of bylaws, which set out the membership requirements.
Dealers had to have been in the industry for at least two years,
and they had to comply with requests for information from the
club's directors. Any member could object to a prospective member, and those admitted had to undergo a two-year probation.
An initial payment of $5,000 was followed by an annual fee of
$1,000. Membership was highly prized, as it signalled that the
dealer could be trusted. But the limits of space, and probably a
sense of exclusivity, encouraged the directors to limit their numbers to around two thousand. The rules for membership were
not particularly onerous, but there was always a waiting list.

More favourable rules governed the admission of sons, daughters, sons- and daughters-in-law, and members' widows. This
reflected the club's origins in the Jewish family networks that
still dominated large parts of the international diamond trade.
Jewish merchants have controlled parts of the trade since the
late fifteenth century, when they and their families settled in the
trading centres of Amsterdam and Antwerp. Many of the club's
bylaws, which specified how transactions could and should be
conducted, were ultimately derived from Jewish laws and the
commercial customs they had developed over the centuries.
The rules provided, for example, that a dealer could accept
an oral offer by using the term 'Mazel und Broche', a Yiddish
phrase literally meaning 'luck and blessing', or a similar form of
words. Dealers also had to respect unwritten rules and customs,

including procedures that allowed them to establish the state of the market and the appropriate price before committing themselves to a transaction. A buyer would, for example, make an offer for a stone but allow the seller time to accept it. Meanwhile, the seller would place the stone in an envelope, which he folded and sealed in a specific way and signed with the terms of the offer. Sellers used a similar process to give an option to a buyer for a limited period. In each case, the parties understood that the arrangements, although unwritten, were binding.

The bylaws required that each member sign an arbitration agreement promising to take any dispute to the club, rather than to the state courts, for settlement. The club's directors appointed a number of arbitrators to a 'Floor Committee' which considered most disputes. As one of them explained, the arbitrators would take the club's rules into account, but they would also consider trade custom, common sense, a little Jewish law, and, when they thought it appropriate, the common law principles that applied in the state courts. They sought to broker compromises, but they did not make findings of fact. This made it difficult for dealers to appeal to the state system. Instead, an Appeals Board, made up of the club's arbitrators, would consider appeals internally. In any event, the state courts recognized the exclusive nature of the arbitration agreements that the club's members signed and generally refused to entertain appeals. Some dealers complained of the arbitrary nature of the committee's decisions, but most saw the advantages of a process that was cheap and quick, certainly compared to the lengthy procedures of the state courts. Even some nonmembers brought their disputes to the club for arbitration, valuing the privacy of the process, which helped to safeguard their reputations.

The club also had procedures for managing those who got into financial difficulties and could not pay their debts, thereby keeping cases away from the bankruptcy courts. But while the state's insolvency procedures generally allowed debtors to pay a certain percentage of their outstanding debts and then wipe the slate clean, the club was not so lenient. Conscious of the reputation its members needed to maintain in the national and international industries, it effectively required 100 percent payment of all debts on pain of permanent expulsion from the club. The club had no direct means of enforcing its rules and decisions, but it did have the very powerful sanctions of suspension, expulsion, and reputational damage. Under its bylaws, the Floor Committee could fine or temporarily suspend anyone who failed to fulfil his or her obligations or who otherwise engaged in conduct it felt was 'unbecoming'. Moreover, it could publish the picture of any dealer who failed to comply with an arbitration award. As a last resort, the club could ask a Jewish rabbinical court to intervene and threaten expulsion from the Jewish Orthodox community. In an industry where trust and reputation were everything, these were powerfully effective sanctions.

In the mid-1980s, the club was experimenting with new technologies, and some of its younger members were using written contracts in place of the oral agreements relied upon by their elders. And the club has doubtless changed in significant ways over the subsequent decades. But it still functioned like a mutual aid society and was dominated by its Jewish members. Its premises included a kosher restaurant and a synagogue, offered medical services and the assistance of a social committee, and negotiated discounts for group travel during the monthlong annual closure. The personal connections that these activities fostered undoubtedly helped to cement relations of trust among its members and encouraged observance of the unwritten rules that governed many of their commercial activities. They also reinforced the secrecy that shrouded many of the club's operations, including its arbitration awards. All of this reduced external competition and helped to ward off governmental regulation.

★

THE DIAMOND DEALERS Club published its rules in bylaws, which it made available to all its members as well as the inquisitive researcher. Carefully formulated and explicit, they had to be respected, even by the club's directors and committees. In this way, the club's officers recognized a form of rule of law. But some of the club's activities, including arbitration awards and bankruptcy arrangements, were hidden from the outside world. As well as enhancing the prestige and air of mystery that surrounded the club and the reputations of its members, this tactic kept the state at bay. Another group of New York families used similar methods of concealment, albeit to hide much more nefarious activities.

The mafia was formed by families of mainly Italian origin. Over the years, they developed a complex network through which they engaged in the elaborate, lucrative, and illegal business of 'protection'. In doing so, they enforced a code of secrecy that successfully shielded the majority of their activities as well as the organization itself, and its membership, from the attention of law enforcement. The New York mafia was related to an older cousin across the Atlantic, the Sicilian Cosa Nostra. This crime syndicate had an even longer history of providing 'protection' services to the local populations. It controlled businesses and extracted payment for protection against threats, either real or of its own making. It offered to enforce extralegal contracts, mediate disputes, and ensure a form of order. Scholars have long debated whether the Sicilian and other mafias mimic the state and exercise an alternative form of government—and if so, to what extent—or simply operate as businesses or 'brotherhoods'.[16] Some have even claimed that mafia structures and organizational principles are law-like, and that their members have to follow strict norms of behaviour, as described by *pentiti*, those who turn their backs on the organization and give evidence to state prosecutors. But these norms are never written up into laws or codes, and neither are the internal structures and hierarchies of the organization. The norm of secrecy, *omertà*, makes these rules and structures inexplicit and obscure, sometimes even from a mafia organization's own members. It stops them, in fact, from becoming law-like.

The Sicilian mafia had its origins in the early nineteenth century. Sometimes genuinely stepping in where the state was unable to protect businesses from raids and bandits, local strongmen gradually developed more organized forms of protection. They demanded payments from legitimate businesses and sheltered others involved in illegal activities. By the early twentieth century, judges were talking about the mafia as having law-like practices (*ordinamento giuridico*). 'Cosa Nostra' literally means 'Our Thing', and the organization was formed of different 'families' based in different regions, which selected their own leaders. Some were dominated by extended families, although all incorporated people unrelated by blood. Until the 1970s, members captured by the authorities steadfastly denied that they belonged to an organization, local or regional, merely claiming they were 'men of honour' bound by common rules of proper behaviour. But with anti-mafia campaigns and prosecutions came the discovery of a superior organization. Some pentiti finally admitted that the leaders of each Sicilian 'family' formed a committee that met to regulate violence between them and, to a limited extent, coordinate their activities. Each family also had its own committee, leaders, and deputies along with rules and rituals for membership. And each demanded absolute loyalty and strict secrecy.

Informers described the obligations of the mafia's members to respect one another and take care not to allow outsiders to infiltrate their organization. Some even talked of the 'ten commandments' of Cosa Nostra, and researchers gradually pieced together a set of commonly accepted norms.[17] These included the principle that members should never introduce themselves to one another directly, to avoid the danger of infiltrators, that they should not be involved in prostitution, that they should respect one another's wives, and that they should always tell the truth. Nor could they ever change their 'family'. Above all, they had a duty of omertà, silence. This meant that they should not know, or try to find out, too much about other parts of the organization, and that they should use signs, symbols, and metaphors to communicate, avoiding explicit statements about sensitive information. These rules of secrecy and communication were in effect designed to obscure details of the organization's structures and practices from the outside world. Complicated though the organization of Cosa Nostra was, with its councils and hierarchies, none of its structures, rules, or procedures were ever reduced to writing. Indeed, it was an absolute rule that nothing relating to the organization should be written down.[18] In all these ways, the mafia kept its existence and procedures largely hidden from the attention of state authorities. There are parallels in other extralegal organizations, whose members use codes to signal to one another in order to avoid more explicit means of communication.[19]

The mafia 'families' do not need laws in order to exercise power. They extract resources from both legal and illegal businesses and manage many of their activities effectively, relying largely on their own reputations, not least for the ability to use or order the use of violence. They exercise their power to provide 'protection', enforce agreements, and mediate disputes. But they do not establish bureaucracies, and their members rarely play fixed roles or perform explicit duties, as officials in modern administrations do. This allows their most powerful members to change the rules when it suits them. In the early 1980s, a coalition of 'families' headed by the chief of the Corleone group, Salvatore (Totò) Riina, took over much of the Sicilian mafia. Riina was able to turn it into a quasi-dictatorship until he was imprisoned in 1993. During this period, some of his most powerful allies flagrantly breached the rules that had formerly been held sacrosanct—for example, those concerning marital fidelity and keeping women out of mafia affairs—and murdered several of their rivals along with their wives, sisters, and mothers.[20] When rules are not written they cannot constrain the abuse of internal procedures. The mafia does not recognize the rule of law.

★

IN THE CONTEMPORARY world, many tribes, villages, and clubs, along with mafia organizations, turn their backs on the state and its administrative control more or less successfully. Some use written laws to reinforce patterns of solidarity and exclusion, while others reject legalism, relying on unwritten rules and expectations. Some use perfectly legal means to keep disputes out of the state courts, while others resort to secrecy and violence as they pursue projects of protection and extortion. All, in different ways, limit the power of the state and its mission to regulate and impose order on its citizens' lives.

Some of these dynamics are thoroughly legalistic and it would be illogical to dismiss them as mere rules. They may not have the disciplinary power and means of enforcement deployed by the modern state, but legalism has its own force. The Tibetan tribesmen, Berber villagers, and diamond traders all created law-like rules which effectively regulated and controlled their members' lives and activities. Making them explicit gave the rules a life of their own, the ability to promise order, justice, and predictability. They constrained village headmen, specified the fines they could impose, or placed limits on the sanctions that the diamond traders club could apply. And would the young Berber graduates have been quite so diligent about making contributions to village funds if they were not aware that a historical qanun required it?

But social order has never depended upon law. The unwritten norms of the Ladakhi villagers, the expectations of the New York garment traders, and the commands of the mafia bosses were also effective means of ordering lives and activities, albeit producing very different dynamics. Unwritten norms can be changed, misremembered, and ignored, while explicit written rules can be quoted against those who would flout them, requiring justification and inviting condemnation. Those who want to exercise autocratic forms of control and oppression need to avoid making their rules explicit. The lengths to which mafia bosses went to deny their organization and its structures was testament to the power and potential of written rules. Whether or not we call them 'laws', legalistic practices can be used to limit power as well as offering an effective means of ordering the world. Avoiding them is one route to autocracy.

CHAPTER SIXTEEN

BEYOND THE STATE
International Laws

T he New York Diamond Dealers Club went to great lengths to keep disputes away from the state courts and maintain its own rules and regulations. But by publishing its bylaws, it was also presenting itself as a reputable organization with fair and transparent processes of self-government. Beyond the structures and power of the state, numerous international organizations do the same, including the International Diamond Manufacturers Association. Trade associations, financial organizations, international corporations, and the bodies that regulate the Internet and international sport all make laws that transcend national borders, providing means of coordination, common standards, and even disciplinary procedures for their members and networks. Their ambitions are surprisingly similar to those of the merchants who formulated pragmatic rules for international trade many centuries before states took their present shape.

These laws do not have the backing of direct enforcement mechanisms as state laws do. Nor is there a world government to ensure compliance with international conventions and resolutions.

The United Nations can exert pressure on its members, but defiant leaders flout conventions, manipulate resolutions, and commit acts of aggression in the face of condemnation. So why do the UN delegates persist, and why do pressure groups continue to lobby for new international laws? Campaigns to eliminate oppression, uphold human rights, alleviate poverty, and protect a region's cultural heritage often culminate in new laws. These projects are not so different from those of the Mesopotamian kings, who promised justice to their people by writing out sets of laws even if they were probably never applied in detail. Beyond the disciplinary authority of the state, law and legalism have a power of their own.

THE RULES CRAFTED to facilitate international commerce have ancient precedents. Merchants who carried goods along the silk roads over two thousand years ago developed systems of writing to keep accounts and records. When they made complex bargains with partners from distant countries, traders needed to be confident that goods would be delivered, money accounted for, and losses apportioned in ways they had previously agreed. The rules and instruments they developed laid the groundwork for some of the earliest written laws. By the Middle Ages, Arab merchants were bringing spices from the Indies to Alexandria; African caravans were transporting gold across the Sahara to Tunisia; and Mongolian camel drivers were unloading Chinese silks and porcelain at Crimean ports, where ships took them on to North Africa and southern Europe.

For a while, Jewish merchants dominated this trade, forming colonies in towns on both sides of the Mediterranean and using standard agency and partnership agreements when they sent merchandise to distant lands.[1] Their partners took many of these exotic goods on to the great trade fairs in Champagne, in northern France, where large numbers of merchants congregated to exchange local wares for rare luxuries. Here, they could also take disputes to specialist courts, where the judges were familiar with standard loan agreements, pledges, and agency arrangements and could quickly pronounce decisions before the traders went on their way. As they came to displace the Jews and control long-distance trade, Italian merchants copied their partnership arrangements and developed increasingly sophisticated contracts and bills of exchange which allowed them to receive payment in different currencies. Specialist notaries drafted agreements that anticipated difficulties and disagreements, helping the parties avoid the courts while introducing legal formulae to create binding obligations.[2]

In the Far East, Taiwanese merchants bought up stocks of the island's rice, sugar, and camphor, which they shipped to the Chinese mainland. Into the nineteenth century, they relied on trade practices to determine responsibility for losses and defects, drawing up intricate legal documents to specify their rights and duties, especially when contracting with trading partners they had never met. Merchants on both sides of the Taiwan Strait went to great lengths to ensure that their legal documents were sufficiently clear, and detailed enough to avoid the delays and parochialism of the local courts. Chinese magistrates did not always understand the commercial contexts of these transactions, and the law did not provide much help in enforcing their terms.[3] The International Diamond Manufacturers Association is just one modern equivalent. Numerous other commercial and financial networks create their own rules, conventions, and treaties, some of which have their roots in long-established patterns of cooperation.

The nineteenth century saw the rise of formalized international lawmaking. As European states defined their boundaries, international merchants, financiers, and economists became concerned that the new borders would present barriers to free trade.

So, in 1847, a Belgian association invited political economists from different countries to an international meeting. The delegates agreed to encourage their governments to draft commercial treaties and negotiate agreements on tariffs.[4] Meanwhile, technical developments encouraged scientists and engineers to standardize tools, techniques, and measures for international use.[5] In 1865, after engineers laid a submarine telegraph wire between Britain and France and then the first transatlantic cable, representatives of twenty countries gathered in Paris to form the International Telegraph Union. They agreed it should standardize equipment, set uniform operating instructions, and lay down common tariffs and accounting rules. The invention of the telephone prompted another conference, held in Berlin, where the delegates drew up international rules for phone use. Five minutes was to be the unit of charge, and calls were to be limited to ten minutes if there were other requests to use the line.[6] Electrical engineering also required standardization, and scientists from national physics laboratories met to tackle the difficult task of developing precise electrical units. Meanwhile, British and American institutes established the International Electrotechnical Commission in 1906 to maintain industrial standards. The birth of aviation led to a further need for international cooperation, including agreement on universal radio call signs. By the beginning of the First World War, in 1914, dozens of organizations were coordinating the development and use of international infrastructure for the telegraph, the postal system, railways, and roads. European governments and international institutions convened one conference after another to formulate standards for weights and measures, protect intellectual property, and coordinate scientific study.

Humanitarian concerns also prompted international lawmaking. In the early nineteenth century, following the successful movement to abolish slavery within British dominions, campaigners set up the British and Foreign Anti-Slavery Society with the aim of eliminating slavery worldwide. The society convened a World Anti-Slavery Convention in 1840, and Anti-Slavery International, as it is now known, remains the oldest humanitarian organization in existence.[7] Other conventions made recommendations for prison reform, while the international labour movement met to discuss global standards for workers.[8] But it was warfare that generated the most concerted humanitarian activity. When Henry Dunant, a Swiss businessman, witnessed the aftermath of the Battle of Solferino in 1859, he was horrified by the suffering of both soldiers and injured civilians, who had to cope without adequate medical attention. Returning to Switzerland, he formed a small committee to campaign for a neutral organization to provide care for the war wounded. In 1863, he convened an international conference at Geneva, and the following year the Swiss government invited representatives of all European countries, together with the United States, Brazil, and Mexico, to attend a conference. Here, they adopted what became known as the first Geneva Convention, 'for the Amelioration of the Condition of the Wounded in Armies in the Field'. This was the beginning of the International Committee of the Red Cross and the first of the conventions that regulate warfare to this day.

Inspired by the success of Geneva, and fearing the consequences of a European arms race, Tsar Nicholas II of Russia convened an international peace conference at The Hague in 1899. The resulting multilateral treaty, the first of the Hague Conventions, established laws for the treatment of wounded combatants and prisoners of war as well as prohibiting armies from looting, killing those who had surrendered, attacking undefended places, forcing civilians in occupied territories into military service, and engaging in collective punishment (that is, punishment of entire classes or groups of people). The delegates also decided that international disputes should be settled by a Permanent Court of Arbitration.

In the meantime, American missionaries in China had been shocked by the pernicious effects of opium use and initiated a campaign against the international narcotics trade. Eventually they gained the support of the US Congress and President Theodore Roosevelt, who convened the International Opium Commission in Shanghai in 1909. This was followed by an international conference at The Hague in 1912, where nine European nations, along with Japan, Persia, Russia, and Siam (now Thailand), signed a convention agreeing to 'use their best endeavours to control, or to cause to be controlled, all persons manufacturing, importing, selling, distributing, and exporting morphine, cocaine, and their respective salts'.

Realizing that all these international initiatives were creating new forms of law, a group of scholars and lawyers gathered to create an institute for the study of international law. They founded the Institut de droit international (Institute of International Law) in 1873 and launched a journal in which scholars debated the nature of the new laws and the ways in which they departed from the legal models developed by earlier philosophers. On a more practical level, and concerned about the warfare that had recently erupted between Prussia, Austria, and France, they hoped to make laws that would limit the ability of states to perpetrate violence.[9] One member of the group, Tobias Asser, promoted a new system of private international law to harmonize the rules under which one country would recognize the laws of another, primarily in cases of marriage and commercial agreements. In 1893 he convened the first Hague Conference on Private International Law, at which representatives of several states agreed to harmonize their laws on marriage, divorce, and guardianship.

THE HOPES OF Henry Durant and the international lawyers that international initiatives could restrain warfare were confounded by the horrors of the First World War. But the war led to new

424

attempts to create an organization that could ensure international peace. The Paris Peace Conference, attended by diplomats from thirty-two countries, agreed to establish a new League of Nations. Its permanent members were France, Britain, Italy, and Japan.[10] The League's founding covenant declared that its mission was to maintain world peace and prevent wars by promoting collective security and disarmament, as well as encouraging the settlement of international disputes through negotiation and arbitration. It also established a Permanent Court of International Justice at The Hague to resolve disputes between states, which was initially popular and well used, and the Hague Conferences confirmed its jurisdiction to interpret their conventions.

But the League's objectives were not just about war and peace. It set up agencies to address other global issues and promoted new free trade agreements. The war had dramatically increased the use of aircraft, and the League sponsored an International Air Convention in 1919 to debate the difficult but crucial legal issue of who owned the skies. It also set up the International Commission for Air Navigation (ICAN) to make rules for air traffic, aircraft identity, and flight safety.[11] In 1926, members of the League decided they needed to do more to harmonize national laws, supplementing the efforts of the Hague Conferences by setting up an International Institute for the Unification of Private Law, later UNIDROIT.[12] This institute drew up conventions, some for other organizations, such as ICAN, and established model laws, principles, and contractual guides for the sale of goods, commercial contracts, and financial instruments. It continues to this day, recently promulgating rules for securities in emerging markets, space assets, satellite systems, mining and construction equipment, and cultural objects.[13]

The Paris Peace Conference took up the work of the international labour movement and established the International Labour Organization (ILO), which campaigned to restrict working hours, end child labour, and make shipowners liable for accidents affecting their crews. The League of Nations went on to establish an International Commission on Intellectual Cooperation, the precursor to UNESCO, a Commission for Refugees, a Slavery Commission, and a Permanent Central Opium Board. Its Health Organization continued the work initiated by the many conferences on sanitation that had already developed measures to combat cholera, yellow fever, and the bubonic plague. In this wave of international cooperation, a number of national associations also formed the International Federation of National Standardizing Associations in 1926 to devise technical standards. This was the precursor to the International Organization for Standards (ISO).

Alongside the League of Nations, the International Committee of the Red Cross continued its humanitarian work and convened further meetings every few years. These were attended by members of national organizations, government representatives, and technical experts. In 1929 the committee formulated a new Geneva Convention on the Treatment of Prisoners of War.[14] Although twenty national associations concerned with human rights had established the International Federation for Human Rights (Fédération internationale des ligues des droits de l'Homme) in 1922, its work was largely overshadowed by the humanitarian efforts of the Red Cross and the ILO. The notion of human rights as a force in international law had not yet come of age.

THE SECOND WORLD War proved a severe challenge to the robustness of the Geneva conventions. In June 1941, Germany declared that the conventions did not apply to its activities on the eastern front because the Soviet Union had not signed them.[15] But even while they were waging an explicitly genocidal war, Germany's leaders continued to pay lip service to the laws of war. They also maintained a legal department, which discussed the war crimes supposedly committed by their enemies. Rather than undermining faith in international law, the conflict encouraged many to argue for new measures. Even while German bombs were still falling on southern England, Hersch Lauterpacht, an international lawyer who had fled Poland, spoke of the 'essential and manifold solidarity' of the modern world. States, he said, had a common interest in the elimination of both private violence and war. In the aftermath of the conflict, he argued relentlessly for the recognition of 'crimes against humanity' and measures to strengthen the rule of law. Other lawyers argued for stronger rules to control violence and prevent atrocities.[16]

When the Allied powers set up the Nuremberg Trials to try prominent leaders from Nazi Germany, Lauterpacht's arguments for the recognition of 'crimes against humanity' emerged into the spotlight. The court decided that it could judge the defendants according to general principles of justice, and that these principles overrode whatever national laws and internal orders had sanctioned their activities. This seemed to be leading to new developments in international law, possibly even an international criminal court. But meanwhile, the Allied powers had turned to the idea of a new world organization of 'united nations' to ensure peace and global security. Discussions began during the war about how to the replace the League of Nations, which had so strikingly failed to prevent the current catastrophe. The United States and Britain invited representatives from the Soviet Union and China to help convene the first international meeting, in April 1945. Here, representatives of fifty national governments approved a founding charter. It declared the aims of the new United Nations to be international peace and security, the promotion of friendly relations among nations, international cooperation, and harmonization of their activities. Among its five major institutions was the Security Council, with a remit for peace and security. Its diplomatic meetings, attended by national representatives, went on to formulate treaties on nuclear weapons, disarmament, chemical weapons, and land mines.

At its third session, in 1948, the UN General Assembly adopted the Universal Declaration of Human Rights. It also established an International Court of Justice to replace the Permanent Court of International Justice at The Hague. Encouraged by Sir David Maxwell-Fife, head of the British prosecution team at the Nuremberg Trials, the European countries created a Council of Europe, which adopted its own convention on Human Rights in 1953, and established a Court of Human Rights in 1959. But despite the initial enthusiasm, no international criminal court was established. UN structures affirmed state sovereignty and agreements between them rather than promoting a set of international legal principles that would supervene over the laws and activities of individual states.[17]

Some members of the United Nations were meanwhile making a concerted push for a new economic order. The United States invited representatives of the forty-four Allied nations to a conference at Bretton Woods, in New Hampshire, in July 1944. The delegates discussed how to regulate the international monetary and financial order after the war and drew up agreements establishing the International Monetary Fund (IMF) and what would become the World Bank. Both became UN agencies when it was founded the following year. The United Nations then convened a conference on trade and employment, which established the General Agreement on Tariffs and Trade (GATT). GATT reduced tariffs on cross-border trade and held new rounds of talks every few years, finally establishing the World Trade Organization (WTO) as an independent body in 1995. The United Nations General Assembly also established a Commission on International Trade Law (UNCITRAL) to harmonize and unify commercial arrangements. Like UNIDROIT, UNCITRAL sponsored conventions and drew up model laws and legislative guides. But UNIDROIT continued its work, as did the Hague Conference, which established itself as a permanent organization, the Hague Conference on Private International Law (HCCH), in 1955.[18] The United Nations also set up and worked with subsidiary bodies and agencies to coordinate and regulate activities in specialist areas, such as the International Atomic Energy Agency (IAEA), founded as an autonomous body in 1957, and the International Civil Aviation Organization (ICAO), founded as a UN agency in 1947.

As well as these commercial and technical projects, the United Nations promoted social and humanitarian interests through specialist agencies such as the Food and Agriculture Organization (FAO) and the World Health Organization (WHO), set up in 1945 and 1948, respectively. Later, the two combined to established the Codex Alimentarius Commission, based in Rome, which creates international food standards and addresses disputes concerning consumer safety and protection. In 1946, the United Nations General Assembly also set up its Children's Fund (UNICEF) to provide emergency food and health care to children; in the same year, it established the Educational, Social, and Cultural Organization (UNESCO). Two years later, UNESCO's director general encouraged government representatives and conservation organizations to form the International Union for the Conservation of Nature, which published a list of endangered species in consultation with UNESCO and the Council of Europe. It sponsored an African Convention on the Conservation of Nature and Natural Resources in 1968, which was followed by a Convention on the International Trade in Endangered Species of Wild Fauna and Flora (CITES), in 1974.[19]

THE RANGE OF international conferences, conventions, and organizations sponsored by the United Nations and its agencies continues to expand. But although it works in a vast range of fields and has unrivalled capacity to bring together representatives of states and global organizations, it does not have a monopoly on international agreements and lawmaking. Alongside the United Nations, other groups and organizations have continued to promote rules, standards, and procedures for international cooperation and coordination, many, but not all, in the sphere of finance.[20]

The Bank for International Settlements (BIS), based in Basel, Switzerland, had its origins in a Hague Conference of the 1930s. The representatives of ten countries set up the bank to supervise the reparations payments imposed on Germany. After the Second World War, in cooperation with the IMF, it took on the task of stabilizing national currencies. Then, in the 1970s, with the rapid growth of international financial markets and the collapse of major banks in Germany and the United States, central bank governors from the G10 group of nations, those that had originally combined to create the IMF, formed the Basel Committee on Banking Supervision. In association with the BIS, this committee brought together banking supervision authorities from around the world to agree on common rules and standards. Over the following decades, the BIS sponsored the formation of further international committees to promote financial and banking standards and worked with the International Association of Insurance Supervisors to create standards for the insurance industry. In 2008, the global credit crisis prompted a group of nineteen countries, along with the European Union, to form the G20, which largely replaced the G10, to promote financial stability.

Basel had now become the centre of global financial supervision, but international financial initiatives have continued to proliferate. The International Organization of Securities Commissions, based in Madrid, regulates the world's securities and futures markets, and in 1989, the G7 group of countries—the world's largest economies—set up the Financial Action Task

Force to combat money laundering. An International Competition Network was also established, in 2001, to facilitate cooperation between the competition law authorities of different countries.

Security concerns have led to international initiatives such as the Wasenaar Arrangement on Export Controls for Conventional Arms and Dual-Use Goods and Technologies, which brought together several countries from the former Soviet Union in 1990. In 2003, on the initiative of US president George Bush, a number of countries agreed to the Proliferation Security Initiative and its principles for information sharing on weapons of mass destruction. The United Nations continues to sponsor arrangements in response to ethical concerns in international trade. Concern about the trade in 'blood diamonds', for example, led to the Kimberley Process Certification Scheme in 2003. There are also regional bodies overseeing competition networks, including the Andean Community in South America, organized in 1969; Asia-Pacific Economic Cooperation, established in 1989; and the Organization for the Harmonization of Business Law in Africa, formed in 1993.[21]

At times, different organizations embark on parallel projects in response to a global problem. The transnational effects of bankruptcy came to prominence in the 1990s, for instance, with the global economic recession and the insolvencies of a number of high-profile corporations. By 1999, different transnational insolvency rules had been developed by the Asian Development Bank, the European Bank for Reconstruction and Development, the IMF, the World Bank, and UNCITRAL.[22] But by 2012, UNCITRAL had settled on a single set of norms that is now recognized by all the other organizations. At other times, international organizations deliberately combine their efforts. In 2015, for example, UNCITRAL, UNIDROIT, and the HCCH embarked on an ambitious project to coordinate rules for international sales law.[23] At the same time, several different organizations have responded to the need to protect cultural objects and return stolen artefacts to their places of origin. UNESCO developed an international code of ethics for dealers in cultural property, while the International Council of Museums creates lists of missing and illegally transferred objects.[24]

Most of these organizations are now dominated, or at least influenced, by state representatives and members of national supervisory authorities, but private organizations also establish international agreements and rules. Derivatives dealers established the International Swaps and Derivatives Association in 1985, for example, to create standard contracts and forms of language for their transactions, and in 2008, an international group of wealth fund managers formed the International Forum of Sovereign Wealth Funds. Like the International Diamond Manufacturers Association, these create standards for best practice. Numerous trade associations have also been established, such as the International Air Transport Association (IATA), and these can play important roles in regulating different industries. The International Council for the Harmonization of Technical Requirements for Pharmaceuticals for Human Use, for instance, brings together members of the pharmaceutical industry and international regulators. All these organizations seek to smooth out international transactions, establish trust, and provide means for dispute resolution, goals that are not so dissimilar from those of the medieval merchants who created standard forms of contract and rules for international trade five hundred years ago.

SOME RESEARCHERS AND lawyers have expressed concerns about the proliferation of these international rules and agreements and the difficulty of establishing hierarchies among them.[25] Others have looked at the informal laws produced by trade associations, asking how they can be made more democratic and more accountable. But these are concerns prompted by the ideals of state law. It is inevitable that organizations, conventions, and processes will continue to emerge in ad hoc ways; indeed, their efforts are necessary to global development.

The Internet, now of unquestioned global importance, is a case in point. It was initially managed by the engineers and researchers who created it. They established the Internet Engineering Task Force (IETF), with support from the US government, in 1986, to set technical standards for its development. But, concerned about a broader array of issues, some of the Internet pioneers set up a new organization, the Internet Society, in 1992, with the aim of promoting free, equitable, universal, and stable development of the World Wide Web and ensuring beneficial use by all. The IETF now operates under the auspices of the Internet Society and continues to convene working groups to establish new standards, largely acting through consensus. The Internet Society, meanwhile, accepts global membership and has grown to include over a hundred thousand organizations and individuals. Tim Berners-Lee, one of the Internet's founders, also established the World Wide Web Consortium (W3C), which provides another forum for the discussion of technical standards. It regularly consults with the IETF and the Internet Society, and all three cooperate with the ISO and the International Electrotechnical Commission.

One of the biggest sources of disputes among Internet users, and thus a major point of controversy for Internet organizations, has been the Domain Name System, or DNS, which assigns numerical addresses to the names that allow users to create and manage websites.[26] Initially, a single individual based in California performed this task. It was only in 1998 that the National Telecommunications and Information Administration (NTIA) of the US Department of Commerce announced that it would improve the system by setting up an International Corporation for Assigned Names and Networks (ICANN). This is technically an international nongovernmental organization, managed by a global board of directors, which carries out DNS functions under contracts with the US Department of Commerce and the IETF. A year after its founding, ICANN finalized a Uniform Domain Name Dispute Resolution Policy setting out criteria for determining, among other things, what amounts to the abusive and bad faith registration of domain names, sometimes called 'cybersquatting'. Some scholars have termed this area of policy and its application 'Internet law'. In practice, ICANN encourages users to turn to an established arbitration service.[27]

Until 2016, ICANN remained a sui generis public-private partnership over which the US government, through the NTIA, exercised some control. But a meeting of ICANN, IETF, and the Internet Society in 2013 called for its 'globalization', and the delegates resolved to create 'an environment in which all stakeholders, including all governments, participate on an equal footing'.[28] The process proved to be long and complicated, but eventually the NTIA relinquished its control to an unincorporated association based in California, made up of the supporting organizations already within ICANN and organizations representing endusers.[29] More national governments have since become involved in issues of Internet governance, but lengthy negotiations surrounded the resolutions of the World Summit on the Information Society in 2003 and 2005 and the World Conference on International Telecommunications in 2012. Many of those involved have chosen to promote their own guidelines, model laws, and general principles.[30] Ideals of transparency, accountability, and fair representation are only gradually working their way into this system of international regulation.

Also with its own international bodies and arbitration procedures is the realm of international sport.[31] The national associations of seven European countries formed the International Federation of Association Football (FIFA) in 1904 to oversee international football (soccer) competition. The federation soon expanded beyond Europe and within a decade encompassed associations from South Africa and the Americas. It now takes responsibility for organizing major tournaments, notably the World Cup, which was first held in 1930. It also enforces the 'Laws of the Game'. But these remain the responsibility of the International Football Association Board, established in 1886 by the associations of England, Scotland, Wales, and Ireland, which continue to provide half its members.

In the same era that FIFA took shape, a French educator and historian, Baron Pierre de Coubertin, set up a small committee to organize a modern Olympic Games. This was the beginning of the International Olympic Committee (IOC), which continued to meet after the successful 1896 Athens games. The IOC selects its own members, of whom there are currently around one hundred, from a range of different countries. It recognizes national Olympic committees, making rules for their constitutions and activities, and sets up an organizing committee for each Games. Along with the international federations for each sport, these organizations form the 'Olympic Movement'.

The IOC established the Court of Arbitration for Sport in 1984 to hear disputes arising in connection with the Olympic Games. But the issue of doping soon presented a problem for sports worldwide. In 1989, the Council of Europe established an Anti-Doping Convention, which maintains a list of prohibited substances and methods and creates regulations to combat drug use in all sports. A decade later, the IOC convened an international conference, which recognized the importance of 'the fight against doping in sport' and set up the World Anti-Doping Agency (WADA).[32] The agency formulated the World Anti-Doping Code in 2004 to harmonize anti-doping regulations in all sports and countries worldwide.

The IOC had, meanwhile, turned its Court of Arbitration for Sport into an independent body, governed by an international council, which expanded its jurisdiction from the Olympics to all international sports.[33] A large amount of its work has been concerned with doping allegations, particularly after the establishment of the WADA. It is busy during each Games and had to convene an ad hoc court just days before the 2016 Summer Olympics to hear doping cases that had just come to light. But it has also considered cases of sex verification, Gibraltar's membership in the Union of European Football Associations, and a dispute between the football associations of Northern Ireland and the Republic of Ireland about the eligibility of their players.

These international organizations all develop legal rules and principles, and sometimes also courts, to meet practical needs, rather than waiting for their governments to enter into international agreements. They are often linked to national organizations, and it would be hard for many of them to operate if national governments did not recognize their rules and decisions. In the case of the Anti-Doping Code, for example, UNESCO organized a convention in 2005, quickly ratified by most countries, under which they agreed to be bound by the rules of the code, and the IOC has observer status at the United Nations. But substantial and influential sets of rules, associations, and processes continue to be set up, largely without official representation from national governments. Some, like ICANN, can be extremely powerful, effectively controlling access to one of the most important global resources.

Creating international laws requires time and effort, and even the UN conventions and multilateral treaties do not always achieve global reach. China has effectively challenged the authority of the IMF to control exchange rate practices, for example.[34] But many agreements and rules are effective even though they are not backed by enforcement mechanisms. They lay down rules, such as those concerning the registration of domain names, and set standards that technicians and other users have to recognize. And, like the IOC, the Diamond Manufacturers Association, and ICANN, many have to deal with disputes, set up arbitration mechanisms, and develop procedural rules to address the issues of justice and fairness that inevitably arise.

Scholars continue to express concerns about the purposes and effects of these new legal regimes. Many international organizations, they argue, support international capitalism for the benefit of a new global elite. The legal structures that promote free trade, international financial regimes, and economic liberalism, along with those that justify armed intervention in the affairs of other states, they say, are creating a new imperial order.[35] And they point out that even laws with explicitly idealistic goals, those that promote human rights and justice, tend to represent the values and ideals of the West. The explosion of rights talk since the end of the Cold War risks imposing alien values where they do not belong. And they have a point.

AFTER THE INITIAL euphoria that surrounded the Universal Declaration and European Convention on Human Rights at the end of the Second World War, belief in the power of rights as the basis for an international legal order largely faded. The United Nations continued to work on the formulation of laws that would enshrine civil and political rights, which it made the subject of a convention in 1966, along with a parallel convention on economic, social, and cultural rights. But the Cold War between the United States and the Soviet Union overshadowed these initiatives, and the international conference held in Tehran to mark the twentieth anniversary of the Universal Declaration, in 1968, was regarded by many as a failure. It did not help that it became mired in controversy between Israel and various Muslim-majority countries.

The late 1970s saw renewed interest in human rights. The United Nations established conventions and declarations against gender discrimination (1979) and torture (1984) and to create rights to religious freedom (1981), for children (1989), and for refugees (1990). US president Jimmy Carter's ethical vision for foreign policy encouraged social movements disillusioned with communism, socialism, and other global ideals to renew their efforts to promote international rights, and this, in turn, revived interest among international lawyers.[36] The end of the Cold War and the collapse of the Soviet Union in 1989, and with it the ideological power of communism, generated further enthusiasm for the idea of human rights. A number of social movements successfully campaigned for international conventions and resolutions to protect the rights of minorities (1992), those subject to racism (2001), those with disabilities (2006), indigenous people (2006), and peasants (2018), and there were declarations on the 'right to development' (2006) and LGBT rights in 2014.[37] The United Nations established a Commission on Human Rights in 1993, now the International Human Rights Commission. Advocacy groups the world over have invoked human rights in arguments and campaigns to promote new protections for minorities, refugees, prisoners, the victims of war, and the subjects of human trafficking.

In practice, the principles of many human rights conventions and declarations are virtually unenforceable. General and vague, they also lack the support mechanisms of courts and effective international institutions. The UN Convention against Torture, for example, requires that signatory states criminalize and prosecute all acts of torture. When Britain ratified the convention in 1988, it duly created a crime of torture under its Criminal Justice Act of that year.[38] Yet, in the following three decades, no British citizen was charged with torture. The only person to be convicted was an Afghan 'warlord' for crimes he committed in Afghanistan. Even after a group of British soldiers beat an Iraqi detainee to death in Basra during the Iraq conflict of 2003–2004, British prosecutors charged them with other crimes. Manslaughter, inhuman treatment, assault, and actual bodily harm were more specific and easier to prove than the vague crime of torture.

Not everyone has been convinced by the language of 'human rights'. Although the concept of 'les droits de l'homme' was deeply engrained in the Francophone world, to many English speakers the phrase sounded new and unfamiliar when it was used at UN sessions in the 1940s.[39] The Saudi Arabian delegation to the drafting committee for the Universal Declaration protested that its members had 'for the most part taken into consideration only the standards recognized by Western civilization'. It was not the committee's task 'to proclaim the superiority of one civilization over all others or to establish uniform standards for all the countries of the world'. The Saudis were particularly concerned about the guarantees of freedom of religion and for the right of women to choose their marriage partners.[40] Anthropologists were also highly critical of the notion of universal rights. In 1947, the president of the American Anthropological Association warned that the promotion of 'universal values' would encourage people to overlook cultural differences and lead to a lack of respect for the alternative ideas and ideals of those who did not think in terms of human rights.[41] Since then, many have accused human rights laws and their champions of imposing Western cultural values on people and places in which they do not belong. At the 1993 World Conference on Human Rights, held in Vienna, representatives of several Asian countries renewed the debate, arguing for the recognition of distinct 'Asian values'.[42]

The criticisms of 'universal values' have some justification. Many of the pioneering human rights lawyers believed in the superiority of Western civilization and its values. In a letter to the *New York Times*, one of them even described the 1966 conventions as 'a tribute to Western values' and to 'our [US] ideology'.[43] Historically, people seeking to defend their interests and livelihoods did not turn to the idea of rights, even in Western Europe.

The indigent who petitioned for relief in early modern England, to which they had some entitlement under the Poor Laws, for example, did not use the language of rights, and most of them hardly even expressed a sense of entitlement.[44] Even today, Ladakhi villagers negotiate relations within their community and with representatives of the state without appealing to any concept of rights.[45] Buddhists are taught to deny the substance of the self and its emotions in complex philosophical ways that do not sit happily with the concept of the rights-bearing individual. Yet the language of human rights has proliferated. Buddhists in Nepal campaigning for a secular, rather than Hindu, state, marched under banners proclaiming that 'secularism is a human right' in 1994.[46] They presented themselves as people with entitlements even though they adhered to a religion that taught them to deny attachment to worldly things.

This has been one of the paradoxes of the human rights movement. The Nepalese Buddhists were using the concept of human rights to catch the attention of the state, probably also conscious of the international currency of the language, and they apparently had no difficulty in distancing the instrumental language of their political arguments from the concepts they used to talk about themselves as followers of the Buddhist path. Indigenous groups the world over, from the Amazonian rainforest to the African savannah, have invoked their 'rights to self-determination', quoting phrases from the Declaration on the Rights of Indigenous People.[47] A movement for sovereignty in Hawai'i was already using the language of rights in the 1980s. Conflicts over land and a new cultural awareness had encouraged the Kanaka Maoli people, descendants of the Polynesians who came to the island in the eighteenth century, to campaign against US imperialism, and soon they were quoting phrases from UN documents and declarations on human rights. Members of the movement organized a tribunal in 1993 to 'try' the United States for its takeover of their sovereign nation. Here, prosecutors laid charges against the United States under the laws of the Kanaka Maoli nation, also citing international treaties, the US Constitution, and UN declarations. They were appropriating forms of Western law to draw attention to their struggle, using language that powerful people in other countries would understand.

Many of these campaigns are led by the educated elite who feel comfortable with international legal language. There are others, particularly in the Islamic world, who continue to resist what they see as Western imperialism. They are often particularly concerned about the promotion of rights and equality for women, which they see as contradicting their religious values. But indigenous, marginalized, and impoverished people everywhere have come to appreciate the power of human rights language and adopt its idioms. This may not be how they would initially have thought to discuss their interests and problems, but it is a language that people in positions of power can hear.

On the international stage, human rights laws have time and again provided powerful tools for argument. And this is how the law often works. Litigants turn to lawyers to transform their claims into arguments that a judge will hear, even if it sometimes seems to distort their stories, omit things that concern them most, and use phrases they barely understand. And this happens in national courts as well as international contexts. But while litigants in local courts often have pragmatic reasons for pursuing legal cases, those who appeal to human rights laws are often trying to make moral arguments, to draw attention to their cause in a long-term campaign for social reform. Indeed, a Lebanese philosopher on the drafting committee of the 1948 Declaration justified the vagueness of the article that prohibited torture on the basis that it was primarily a moral statement. It would explain in an international instrument, he said, 'that the conscience of mankind had been shocked by inhuman acts in Nazi Germany'.[48]

While the Internet pioneers largely had the practical goals of international coordination in mind for their lawmaking, human rights campaigners argue for new laws that make moral statements in long-term campaigns to make the world a better place. Both find that the simple technique of creating explicit rules gives them a powerful resource.

THE END OF the Cold War and renewed interest in human rights encouraged campaigners to revive the idea of an international criminal court. They responded to the atrocities committed during the Balkan Wars, which erupted in 1991, by persuading the United Nations to establish the International Criminal Tribunal for the Former Yugoslavia (ICTY).[49] Over twenty-four years, the ICTY received indictments against 161 people involved in the conflicts, from common soldiers to generals and police commanders, all the way up to the prime minister, Slobodan Milošević. It held 111 trials, resulting in 90 convictions. It was followed by a Criminal Tribunal for Rwanda, set up in 1994, and finally the establishment of a permanent International Criminal Court (ICC) in 2003, which has jurisdiction over war crimes, genocide, crimes against humanity, and aggression.

Some of the new enthusiasm for international laws and courts crystallised around the idea of 'transitional justice', and campaigners established an International Center for Transitional Justice in New York in 2001. The organization advocates measures to 'redress the legacies of massive human rights abuses' in countries 'transitioning' from conflict or state repression. It promotes criminal prosecutions, reparations for victims, institutional reforms, and truth commissions to address victims' rights and 'to see the perpetrators punished, to know the truth, and to receive reparations'.[50] But it has proved notoriously difficult to prosecute anyone for war crimes. Following the violence that surrounded the Kenyan presidential elections in 2007, which left more than one thousand dead, campaigners both inside and outside the country argued strenuously that those responsible should be brought to justice. The ICC's prosecutor duly announced that there should be 'no impunity' for crimes against humanity, promising to bring prosecutions against the leading perpetrators unless Kenya's own justice system took action. When it failed to do so, the prosecutor brought charges against several former politicians. The Kenyan government ostensibly cooperated with the ICC, but after two of the accused were elected as the president and deputy president of the country, the prosecutor found it more difficult to gather evidence and the proceedings foundered.[51]

Despite this and similar setbacks, enthusiastic campaigners have continued to promote justice in the aftermath of wars and conflict, seeking to bring perpetrators to account and secure reparations for victims. In Colombia, Rwanda, and Sierra Leone, advocacy groups advise members of war crimes tribunals, set up programmes for victims, and promote the rehabilitation of offenders. But their optimistic campaigns have had patchy success. In Sierra Leone, combatants from the eleven-year civil war, which ended in 2002, were often afraid to participate in the truth and reconciliation commission because they feared criminal prosecution.[52] The peace accords had pronounced a general amnesty, but the United Nations declared that this could not extend to anyone guilty of genocide, crimes against humanity, or other serious violations of human rights, and no combatant wanted to run this risk. A UN representative later declared the commission to have been a success, but in practice, local communities had often developed strategies to reintegrate ex-combatants which were substantially at odds with the processes demanded by transitional justice norms. The Sierra Leoneans were more concerned about whether former combatants would act as good community members than about holding them accountable for the past. The ideals of transitional justice did not sit comfortably with the pragmatic concerns of local communities.

Tensions have emerged within international processes themselves about the extent to which the pursuit of peace clashes with the requirements of justice. These were rehearsed at length in the context of South Africa's Truth and Reconciliation Commission, and peacemakers there and elsewhere continue to be confronted with a dilemma: Should they promote amnesties or criminal proceedings? Since 1999, the United Nations has issued a number of guidelines for those involved in processes of conflict resolution, including for the treatment of anyone subject to an arrest warrant from the ICC.[53] Trying to negotiate a way through these difficulties, international organizations have developed what one scholar has described as 'the law of peace'. They are establishing norms and guidelines for peace processes which draw on the laws of human rights, humanitarian laws, and international criminal law.[54] Whether or not this is the right terminology, an international network pursuing the goal of justice in the aftermath of conflict is at least trying to create rules and standards for general application. Whatever the practical difficulties faced by these initiatives, faith in the power of the law and legal processes remains strong.

DISCIPLINARY CRIMINAL LAWS, backed by effective means of detection, trial, and punishment, are the achievement of the modern state. Along with elaborate laws that seek to regulate numerous aspects of social life, they lay the basis for new social programmes and promote economic development. States everywhere claim to be the source of peace, order, and prosperity. But a world divided neatly into nation-states, each with its own political and legal jurisdictions, is a relatively recent development in global history. Laws have long crossed borders as merchants developed practical rules and instruments for long-distance trade and missionaries sought to guide their followers along God's path for the world. In the modern world, international organizations create rules with pragmatic aims, seeking to promote coordination and regulation among large networks. And alongside them are initiatives with idealistic goals as campaigners seek to make the world a better place.

Autocratic rulers regularly use law to control, oppress, and exclude, and international conventions can seem like vain attempts to restrain their worst excesses. But passing a resolution at the United Nations may be an act of international condemnation, which even the most determined dictator cannot entirely ignore. On the international stage, many laws are more important for what they represent than for how they actually restrain government power. Human rights and associated international laws stand as moral statements, which many find appealing and powerful, as they translate the messy reality of conflict, discrimination, injury, and oppression into a more direct language. They offer ideas that anyone can appeal to as they seek to make their arguments heard. A similar enthusiasm surrounds the international criminal trials, which have symbolic importance, however difficult it may be to prosecute and convict anyone guilty of crimes against humanity. Behind all this lies a continuing faith in the capacity of law to bring about a more ordered and more civilized world. The possibilities of law far exceed the disciplinary power and enforcement mechanisms of the modern state.

THE RULE OF LAWS

Law is a deceptively simple means of ordering the world. It makes explicit the general rules we use to describe how our societies ought to be and those that lie behind our judges' decisions. This is all the ancient Mesopotamian kings and the earliest Chinese lawmakers were doing when they inscribed rules onto clay tablets and wrote out lists of punishments on long bamboo strips. Their laws were thoroughly unspectacular statements. But, once spelled out and held up for all to see, they made possible a new way to order their societies. Pragmatic statements about compensation, punishment, and duties promised a fairer social order, illustrated the ways in which judges ought to decide cases, spelled out the rulemaking powers of kings, and directed officials on how they should mete out punishments. By making rules explicit, the authors turned their words into laws, and law itself became a social force.

The social ambitions of the earliest lawmakers in Mesopotamia were quite different from those of the ancient Chinese rulers, and those of the Chinese rulers different again from those of the Hindu brahmins. When mounting debt threatened to destabilize his society, Ur-Namma wrote out casuistic statements about crimes and compensation ('If a man divorces his first wife, he shall pay her one measure [about 430 grams] of silver'), intending them to reinforce his promise to bring justice to his people. In war-torn China, the Qin rulers drew up lists of crimes and punishments as a means of imposing discipline and imperial unity on populations that were still fragmented and divided. On the plains of the Ganges, the brahmins crafted elaborate texts combining basic rules for their followers with narratives about the principles of dharma, and this also confirmed their elite status at the top of a social hierarchy in which they were ritually superior to the kings. These three projects built on different fundamental principles: justice in Mesopotamia, discipline in China, and duty in India. But they collectively established a foundation for practically all the laws that have since been created.

The Middle Eastern tradition has had the longest and most far-reaching legacy. The laws crafted in Mesopotamia inspired Israelite priests, Greek and Roman citizens, and eventually Islamic scholars. Later still, Roman law inspired lawmaking throughout Europe. By that time, the Jewish and Islamic legal traditions had developed along quite different paths, but they still had common roots in Ur-Namma's promises to his people. Meanwhile, Hindu laws had spread throughout Southeast Asia, carried by brahmins and copied even by Buddhist scholars, who used them to found legal systems for their own kings. Successive Chinese emperors used their laws to hold together an expanding empire and directed their officials to impose the same laws on very diverse people in far-flung places. These traditions continued along divergent paths for over two thousand years. It is only in the past few centuries that the laws established in Western Europe have come to dominate practically the whole world.

During all these developments, people in very different places and times exported, borrowed, and copied laws and legal forms. Small communities and even tribesmen grasped the possibilities of this technique and turned it to multiple ends. Medieval Jewish merchants used laws to regularize their trading relations; Irish scribes enjoyed writing esoteric tracts about bees; Berber villagers drew up constitutions to regulate marriage celebrations and the use of wells; Islamic legal scholars created small masterpieces of intellectual intricacy; and an Armenian priest published a law code to try to protect his people from ascendant Seljuk judges. The simple act of spelling out general rules can order human societies in multiple ways.

AT THEIR MOST basic, laws provide means to order social life. Legal systems everywhere punish murder, compensate injuries, regulate marriage and inheritance, relieve debtors, and provide for the maintenance of children. These are issues that arise whenever people live together. Most laws also offer rules for property transactions and trading relations. Laws help governments and merchants in their projects of coordination and regularization: they direct how we should drive down the street to avoid accidents and create uniform standards for international technologies. But not all laws need the backing of direct enforcement in order to be effective. Daghestani villagers, who did not have a police force or prisons, wrote out rules to regulate the use of common property. Most medieval merchants respected the decisions of mercantile courts, when they could easily have fled. In the contemporary world, international trade organizations with no direct enforcement powers publicize the standards they expect their members to observe.

Rulers turn to laws because they put people and things, along with their activities, into categories and classes and specify relations between them, enabling more extensive and more effective government. They use laws to define what counts as a crime and an appropriate punishment; they specify how property may be sold, leased, and inherited; they define the conditions for a binding contract or a valid marriage; they confirm social hierarchies, specify who belongs or not, and spell out the unequal rights and duties of those in different classes. Laws, in this way, support regimes of discipline, hierarchy, and centralized control.

But rules are not just practical means of social ordering and government. Laws have also symbolized the societies that lawmakers have wanted to bring about, promising justice and fairness, a vision of civilization—usually that of a ruler or priest—as much as achieving anything concrete. Early medieval European kings and their advisers copied the high Latin of Roman law and carefully inscribed the illogical results on precious parchment. Burmese legal scholars copied the Dharmashastra texts of the Hindu brahmins, even though the caste distinctions made little sense in a Buddhist society. Impractical though they may have been, these laws were important. They were aspirational documents more than practical ones. They were attempts to copy grander civilizations or reproduce the order of a prestigious historical regime. They reflected cosmological ideals and created the vision of a civilized world.

Ordinary people have also turned to law for varied reasons. Often they have been seeking justice. Berber villagers in the Atlas Mountains repeatedly took their disputes with neighbouring villages to local judges in their efforts to prove they had better rights to water. Two Jewish girls insisted that their brothers' unfair behaviour should be brought to the synagogue in medieval Cairo. Laws indicate the right way to do things. English peasants copied the legal procedures of the kings' courts when they judged their neighbours in the manor courts, and Indian artisans' guilds made rules to standardize their craftsmanship. For the Armenians who established trading colonies in distant lands, laws were a matter of identity. The fact that some laws represent the sense of a higher order and a civilized world explains why farmers in the tiny oases of the Touat adopted the complex Islamic laws on property even if it meant they had to sell their donkeys in fractions. Laws offered, and still offer, a language of propriety. It is also a language that gives people a way to object to injustice and oppression and stand up to the powerful. Roman citizens realized this when they demanded laws on debt and punishment in the fifth century BCE. They were seeking, for neither the first nor the last time, the rule of law. The simple technique of writing out general rules using abstract categories creates conceptual order, and this order can be a powerful symbol of justice.

Behind the legal systems of the most powerful, there generally hovers a sense of divine right, cosmological order, or natural law. And rulers inevitably promise to prevent or correct disorder and injustice. The Chinese emperors claimed that their people needed to be disciplined in the interests of the peace and stability that they themselves embodied as representatives of heaven; Indian kings patronized the brahmins, who maintained that Hindus needed to act according to the requirements of their dharma to avoid a miserable rebirth; and modern states everywhere justify punitive regimes by insisting that chaos and disorder will ensue if 'criminals' are not punished. We are still heirs to Hobbes's view of life without a state as 'nasty, brutish, and short'.[1]

Rulers have everywhere claimed to promote peace, order, and prosperity, maintaining that they are in the best position to pursue these goals, if only people will follow their lead and grant them sufficient power. Promulgating laws is a means to make these goals explicit, to spell out the ways in which they will manage resources, suppress crime, and redistribute wealth—or accomplish whatever currently exercises the public imagination.

In little more than three hundred years, law has come to be associated firmly with the nation-state. Models and systems developed in Western Europe now dominate the world. Of course, state systems are not as comprehensive, effective, or coherent as our governments would have us believe. Small communities continue to live by their own rules, Muslims follow the legal guidance of their muftis, and international organizations create sets of rules that unite people across borders. But European rulers brought together disciplinary practices, pragmatic techniques, and idealistic visions, the innovations of the first lawmakers in Mesopotamia, China, and India, to create a powerful model of law. Behind it lay ideas about natural law and common humanity. Remarkable economic, technological, and military expansion then allowed them to export their laws around the world, claiming that they would bring 'civilization' to indigenous people and sweep away outdated models of 'despotic' or 'primitive' order. In the twentieth century, this has become the vision of an international order in which properly elected governments promote peace and prosperity, uphold democracy, and respect human rights. It is the equivalent of the cosmological order invoked by the Chinese emperors and the order of the dharma elaborated by the Hindu brahmins that the colonizing powers were so keen to replace.

By MAKING THESE promises, rulers throughout history have also made laws that their citizens can rely upon. And, despite the disciplinary techniques of the most autocratic rulers, many ordinary people have continued to put their faith in the power of law to produce a just social order. It was not just the Roman citizens who gathered in vast assemblies to pass new laws that they hoped would curb the powers of corrupt officials. Medieval French peasants quickly grasped the possibility of standing up to their lords, and even viscounts and bishops, in their local courts; Daghestani tribesmen made their own laws in defiance of the local khans and even shaykhs; a Russian traveller was impressed by the Tibetan herdsman who claimed that his tribal laws were vastly superior to those of China, the Dalai Lama, and 'any of your petty kings'; and Hawaiian nationalists established their own court to 'try' the United States for crimes of colonial aggression.

Laws do not possess any inherent power for good or for evil. Over history, many legal projects have been thoroughly cynical and manipulative. The Germanic kings were trying to acquire the power and status of Roman emperors; Hammurabi was a ruthless warlord who wanted to bequeath a benign image for posterity; lawmaking priests and their institutions often amassed power and resources for their own benefit; authoritarian leaders regularly cite the law to legitimate their actions; and contemporary governments try to convince us that they are more in control of a crisis than they really are. A vision of civilization, competence, and human rights may be a screen for ambition and greed, or simply power. But visions and screens only work if people believe in the values they project. And once laws set out a vision that people believe in, they can also be used against any power-holder who tries to ignore them. This is what gives law its ability to both legitimate and limit power.

Once made explicit, laws are rules that people can quote, rely upon, and use to object to corruption and abuse. Hammurabi declared that any person should be able to read the laws on his granite stone and seek justice. He also described the terrible curses that would descend on any of his successors who flouted these rules. He was graphically illustrating the rule of law. And legal experts have almost always been able to stand up to political power. Indian brahmins upheld a vision of dharma that was so powerful they could refer to their laws to declare that a king was illegitimate. Medieval popes claimed authority to define the jurisdiction of European kings. In the Islamic world, while the qadis enjoyed the backing of powerful caliphs, the muftis kept themselves apart, claiming superior authority. Both caliphs and qadis had to respect their legal opinions if they wanted to secure popular support. And the reclusive Islamic cleric Ali al-Sistani was able to intervene decisively in the 2003 conflict in Iraq to insist upon an elected government, to the embarrassment of the US authorities who had wanted simply to appoint one. European colonialists embarked on projects to administer the territories they had seized and imposed their own rules with little regard for ancient laws and customs, fairness, or justice. Indeed, they often stipulated that indigenous people remain outside the protective cover of the law. But eventually local elites were able to turn the new laws and legal principles against their colonizers in powerful arguments for independence. If laws spell out a ruler's vision for the world and legitimate his power, they can also be used to curb or overturn it.

This is why, over the course of human history, tensions have repeatedly arisen between those who exercise political power and the scholars and judges who claim authority to declare what the law is. In England, Sir Edward Coke threw down the gauntlet to James I by declaring that the king could not interpret the law. In doing so, he set a precedent for Lady Hale, when she sat in the Supreme Court four centuries later and told Boris Johnson's government that it had acted unlawfully by proroguing the British Parliament.[2] Powerful governments chafe when their judges declare executive activities to have been illegal and mutter darkly about the judiciary 'exceeding its powers' and 'straying into politics'. No rulers like to have their power constrained, but this is how law has been used repeatedly over the course of history.

LAW CAN MAKE a social vision concrete and explicit, holding it up for all to see. This may be the promise of a king, a religious elite, a community, or a state, and it may be the means by which they seek to legitimate power. But once made explicit, that vision has a life of its own. Publicizing rules and judicial precedents gives them a fixity, hence authority, of their own. This is why law can be both an instrument of power and a means of resisting it. Heavy-handed rulers may be able to bend law to their will, use it to control and oppress, and justify what they do. But most find that their laws can eventually be turned back against them by anyone who can cite a rule and demonstrate that it has been broken, as long as they can gain access to legal structures and procedures and be heard. Rules can be quoted against the actions of those who would flout them. Dictators may tear up the rulebook, but they cannot do it unnoticed. Obscurity, imprecision, and secrecy are the tools of the autocrat, the mafia boss, and the despot.

The exception, as so often, has been China. Here, for centuries, powerful emperors managed to avoid the rule of law by claiming that they were both the source of their elaborate legal system and the ultimate object of its protection. Their achievement was to establish a sense not just that social order depended upon the discipline they could impose through punitive laws, but that they themselves were the representatives of heaven. They combined the roles of king and priest, the forces of might and right, in a pattern that endured through successive dynasties, and that no other ruler has been able to emulate so successfully or for so long. The European doctrine of the divine right of kings had a very short life. Unscrupulous rulers have repealed their laws, sacked their judges, closed the madrasas, or just declared, as Ayatollah Khomeini did, that they were above the law, but none has had the success of the Chinese rulers. Even now in China, the idea of 'the rule of law' implies the obligation of government officials to abide by the state's rules, rather than acting as an explicit constraint on party leaders.[3] This is rule *by* law, not the rule *of* law.

There is nothing inexorable about the rule of law, however widespread and however repeatedly it has emerged over the course of human history. The question is not whether law is a force for good or for evil, or even the extent to which the dynamics of the rule of law can successfully restrain abuses of power. Law can act as a check on power, but the powerful can often avoid its effects. The question is, rather, how law does what it does, and how any of us can use its promise and potential to make the world a better place. People repeatedly put their faith in law, grasping its capacity to transform their experiences of unfairness and injustice into arguments that will be heard. But laws on their own cannot transform the world. To ensure justice, laws need to be enforced. The Mesopotamian citizen who stood before Hammurabi's law stone needed a judge to listen as he quoted the laws. Roman citizens had to struggle for decades to establish the political institutions that would ensure the justice promised by their laws, and by the time Justinian had them codified, those political rights had long been lost. Rulers in the modern world need to respect their judges if they are to claim, with any conviction, that they uphold the rule of law. Courts need to be accessible, and laws need to be fair. How this can and should be achieved are practical questions that go far beyond the scope of this book. But we, the ordinary citizens, need to demand the rule of law, and for this, we need to understand what law is and how it works.

The rule of law has a long history. It is an achievement of the past four thousand years. But that is a short time in the history of humankind. It has emerged time and again to confront and challenge those who wield power, but it is neither inevitable nor invulnerable. It is also ours to lose.

ACKNOWLEDGEMENTS

The intellectual origins of this book lie in the *Oxford Legalism* project. Between 2009 and 2018 a group of inspiring colleagues from many different disciplines and institutions presented papers and case studies which stimulated debates about the nature and history of laws and produced four edited volumes (*Legalism*, OUP). In doing so, they laid the ground for the arguments that would develop into the present book. I owe a particular debt to the initiative and insights of Paul Dresch and Judith Scheele within that project and I am grateful to the several Oxford institutions that supported it. The result was empirically-grounded, exploratory scholarship of the most productive kind.

The University of Oxford is generous in its provision of sabbatical leave and allowed me a year in which to work on the manuscript, while my colleagues at the Centre for Socio-Legal Studies kindly covered my teaching and administrative duties during that period.

Embarking on a substantial book project, which travels in new directions and seeks to reach new audiences, is a daunting task and I depended heavily on the encouragement of several friends. I must particularly thank Neil Armstrong, Nick Stargardt, Andrew Post, Rosemary Cameron, and Mark

Roseman for their support and help in bringing speculative ideas together into a convincing book proposal.

The important thing was that it convinced my agent, Chris Wellbelove, who is as wonderful as his name. He saw the potential of the book and was willing to help an academic through the challenging process of becoming a trade author. And he persuaded two excellent editors, Ed Lake at Profile and Brian Distelberg at Basic, to take it on. The manuscript was infinitely improved under the expert guidance of all three, not to mention the tricky issue of the title, on which we probably exchanged more emails than on everything else put together.

A number of friends and colleagues took the time to read draft chapters and offered detailed and expert advice, often saving me from egregious errors and omissions. For those that remain, I must, of course, take full responsibility. At different times, Andrew Post, Gilead Cooper, David Gellner, and Michael Lobban offered perceptive comments and suggestions on the introduction and conclusion. Ulrich Borges gave advice on early Jewish law, David Gellner (again) on the Hindu world, Ernest Caldwell on early China, Christian Sahner on the Islamic world, Tom Lambert on Anglo-Saxon law, Alice Rio on medieval Europe, Marina Kurkchiyan on early Rus, James McComish on medieval England, and Judith Scheele on modern Islam. I must particularly mention Georgy Kantor for correcting and improving my attempt to condense the history of Roman law into twenty-six pages and Mike Macnair who performed an equally heroic task on the chapter on early modern Europe. I am lucky to count them all as colleagues and friends and I offer them my heartfelt thanks.

The manuscript benefitted greatly from the careful editing of Kyle Gipson at Basic, whose liberal use of 'fascinating' and 'wow' alongside perceptive suggestions for improvement was immensely encouraging. Sandra Assersohn stepped in at a moment's notice to source a large number of images with great efficiency and the whole team at Basic has been a pleasure to work with.

Nick Stargardt was there at the outset and stayed to the end. One house project later, he is still offering invaluable advice and has read (almost) all the manuscript.

Finally, I must acknowledge all those scholars on whose shoulders I have dared to stand in writing this book. It is only possible to range so widely over time and space because of the decades of scholarship that have produced the knowledge we now have about the people, societies, and laws of the past. Unravelling the mysteries of ancient languages and the meanings of fragmentary and obscure texts with the barest of archaeological context requires hours of painstaking work, often pursued in difficult and unrewarding circumstances. Other scholars have mastered mountains of evidence to tell us about recent legal developments, offering perceptive analyses of global events. Many of the publications mentioned in this book have been produced in university faculties of archaeology, classics, history, and ancient languages, as well as my own subject of anthropology. While funding for the humanities is relentlessly squeezed (and anthropology fares little better) this important scholarship is implicitly devalued. Whenever departments close, we risk losing the opportunity to learn from the fragile resources that survive about our past. This book is a tribute to those scholars who are still prepared to face the obstacles and tackle the most difficult of historical sources, not least in Oxford's (still quaintly named) Oriental Institute. The bibliography cannot do them all justice.

NOTES

INTRODUCTION: THE PROMISE OF LAW

1. For a readable contemporary account, see Glen Ames, *Em nome de deus: the journal of the first voyage of Vasco da Gama to India, 1497–1499*, Leiden: Brill, 2009. Calicut is now Kozhikode.
2. There is considerable debate about the writing of the Pentateuch, but the scribes almost certainly drew on earlier sources. See John Barton, *A history of the Bible: the book and its faiths*, London: Allen Lane, 2019, ch. 1.
3. The rules are found in Leviticus 9 and Deuteronomy 14.
4. The question was raised by Mary Douglas in 'The abominations of Leviticus', in *Purity and danger: an analysis of the concepts of pollution and taboo*, London: Routledge and Kegan Paul, 1966.
5. Aurel Stein gave an account of his expedition and discoveries in *Ruins of desert Cathay: personal narrative of explorations in Central Asia and westernmost China*, London: Macmillan, 1912. The reasons it was sealed up are still not clear.
6. These texts are discussed in Brandon Dotson, 'Divination and law in the Tibetan Empire', in M. Kapstein and B. Dotson

(eds), *Contributions to the cultural history of early Tibet*, Leiden: Brill, 2007; Fernanda Pirie, 'Oaths and ordeals in Tibetan law', in D. Schuh (ed.) *Secular law and order in the Tibetan Highland*, Andiast, Switzerland: International Institute for Tibetan and Buddhist Studies, 2015.

7. This is to borrow from the anthropologist Clifford Geertz, who described religion as a 'cultural system' that provided models *for*, rather than *of*, society. See his *The interpretation of cultures*, New York: Basic Books, 1973.

8. Pauline Maier, *American scripture: making the Declaration of Independence*, New York: Knopf, 1997.

9. See, for example, Kay Goodall, 'Incitement to racial hatred: all talk and no substance?', *Modern Law Review* 70: 89–113, 2007; Secret Barrister, *Fake law: the truth about justice in an age of lies*, London: Pan Macmillan, 2020.

10. See Sandra Lippert, 'Law (definitions and codification)', in E. Frood and W. Wendrich (eds), *UCLA Encyclopedia of Egyptology*, Los Angeles, 2012, https://escholarship.org/uc/item/0mr4h4fv; Christopher Eyre, *The use of documents in Pharaonic Egypt*, Oxford University Press, 2013.

11. Eyre, *The use of documents*, 9, 15.

1. MESOPOTAMIA AND THE LANDS OF THE BIBLE

1. Martha T. Roth, *Law collections from Mesopotamia and Asia Minor*, Atlanta: Scholars Press, 1995, 16–17.

2. For background, see Amanda H. Podamy, *The ancient Near East: a very short introduction*, Oxford University Press, 2014.

3. Podamy, *Ancient Near East*, 33.

4. Jerrold S. Cooper, *Sumerian and Akkadian royal inscriptions*, vol. 1, New Haven, CT: American Oriental Society, 1986.

5. Records of instructions by a prophet of the gods to the later Zimri-Lin in Roth, *Law collections*, 5.

6. Hammurabi's laws are presented and analysed in Roth, *Law collections*, 71–142; Jean Bottéro, *Mesopotamia: writing,*

reasoning, and the gods, trans. Z. Bahrani and M. Van De Mieroop, Chicago: University of Chicago Press, 1992. Another translation can be found in M. E. J. Richardson, *Hammurabi's laws: text, translation, glossary,* Sheffield, UK: Sheffield Academic Press, 2000. The translations are based on Roth, using the standard numbering for the laws.

7. See David Graeber, *Debt: the first 5,000 years,* New York: Melville House, 2011, 214–17.
8. Roth, *Law collections,* 133–42.
9. Laws 59 and 60.
10. Law 48.
11. Law 135.
12. Law 170.
13. Sophie Démare-Lafont, 'Law I', in *Encyclopedia of the Bible and its reception,* vol. 15, Berlin: de Gruyter, 2017; Bernard S. Jackson, *Wisdom laws: a study of the Mishpatim of Exodus 21:1–22:16,* Oxford University Press, 2006, 12n50.
14. Laws 1, 6, 14, and 129. For example, 'If a man should kidnap the young child of another man, he shall be killed' (Law 14); 'If the owner of lost property cannot produce witnesses who can identify it, he is a liar who has perpetrated falsehoods, and he shall be killed.' (Law 11).
15. Laws 195–201.
16. Laws 215–17.
17. Laws 218–20.
18. Law 278.
19. Law 206.
20. Laws 266–67.
21. Sophie Démare-Lafont, 'Judicial decision-making: judges and arbitrators', in K. Radner and E. Robson (eds), *The Oxford handbook of cuneiform culture,* Oxford University Press, 2011, 335–57.
22. Roth, *Law collections,* 213ff.
23. Roth, *Law collections,* 153ff.
24. Hannah Harrington, 'Persian law', in B. A. Strawn (ed.) *The Oxford encyclopedia of the Bible and law,* Oxford University Press, 2015.

25. On early Athens and its laws, see A. Andrews, 'The growth of the Athenian state', in J. Boardman and N. G. L. Hammond (eds), *The Cambridge ancient history*, 2nd ed. vol. 3, pt. 3, Cambridge University Press, 1982.

26. Raymond Westbrook, 'Barbarians at the gates: Near Eastern law in ancient Greece', in Westbrook, *Ex Oriente Lex: Near Eastern influences on Ancient Greek and Roman law*, ed. D. Lyons and K. Raaflaub, Baltimore: Johns Hopkins University Press, 2015.

27. For general background, see John Barton, *A history of the Bible: the book and its faiths*, London: Allen Lane, 2019; Michael Coogan, *The Old Testament: a very short introduction*, Oxford University Press, 2008.

28. Scholars have conducted extensive debates about the origins of the Pentateuch and the relations between different versions. See Barton, *History of the Bible*, ch. 1.

29. Exodus 19–23. Deuteronomy 12–26 contains a similar set of laws and seems to be an updated version, maybe written under Josiah in the second century BCE.

30. Exodus 21:3–4. The translations are based on the Revised Standard Version of the Bible.

31. Exodus 21:1–22:16. The text does not distinguish separate laws. Even the more discursive set of laws in Deuteronomy is far shorter than Hammurabi's code.

32. Barton, *History of the Bible*, 84.

33. My analysis largely draws on Jackson, *Wisdom laws*. Other scholars, as Jackson discusses, take different views on the origins, use, and significance of the laws.

34. Exodus 21:23–25.

35. Leviticus 25:39–46.

36. Laws 196–200.

37. David P. Wright, *Inventing God's law: how the covenant code of the Bible used and revised the laws of Hammurabi*, New York: Oxford University Press, 2009.

38. In this discussion I largely follow and build on Jackson, *Wisdom laws*.

39. Some scholars think that some passages in Deuteronomy concerning oaths of loyalty were based on Assyrian treaties. See Jeremy M. Hutton and C. L. Crouch, 'Deuteronomy as a translation of Assyrian treaties', *Hebrew Bible and Ancient Israel* 7: 201–52, 2018.

2. INDIAN BRAHMINS: THE ORDER OF THE COSMOS

1. Historical details throughout this chapter are drawn from Romila Thapar, *From lineage to state: social formations of the mid-first millennium BC in the Ganga Valley*, Bombay: Oxford University Press, 1984; Hermann Kulke and Dietmar Rothermund, *A history of India*, London: Routledge, 1986; Richard Gombrich, *Theravada Buddhism: a social history from ancient Benares to modern Colombo*, London: Routledge and Kegan Paul, 1988; Wendy Doniger, *The Hindus: an alternative history*, Oxford University Press, 2009.
2. Thapar, *From lineage to state*, 24.
3. Thapar, *From lineage to state*, 104.
4. Kulke and Rothermund, *History of India*, 44.
5. Kulke and Rothermund, *History of India*, 40.
6. Patrick Olivelle, 'Dharmaśāstra: a textual history', in Timothy Lubin, Donald R. Davis, and Jayanth K. Krishnan (eds), *Hinduism and law: an introduction*, Cambridge University Press, 2010.
7. The details in this section are largely based on Kulke and Rothermund, *History of India*, 53, and Thapar, *From lineage to state*, ch. 5.
8. Olivelle, 'Dharmaśāstra'; Albrecht Wezler, 'Dharma in the Veda and the Dharmaśāstras', *Journal of Indian Philosophy* 32: 629–54, 2004.
9. On the Arthashastra, see Timothy Lubin, 'Punishment and expiation: overlapping domains in Brahmanical law', *Indologica Taurinensia* 33: 93–122, 2007, at pp. 99–102; Kulke and Rothermund, *History of India*, 63–64.

10. Patrick Olivelle, 'Manu and the Arthaśāstra: a study in Śāstric intertextuality', *Journal of Indian Philosophy* 32: 281–91, 2004.
11. Olivelle, 'Dharmaśāstra'.
12. D. R. Davis, Jr, 'A historical overview of Hindu law', in Lubin et al., *Hinduism and law.*
13. Doniger, *The Hindus*, ch. 12.
14. On the Dharmasutras and Dharmashastras, see Patrick Olivelle, with the editorial assistance of Suman Olivelle, *Manu's code of law: a critical edition and translation of the* Mānava-Dharmaśāstra, South Asia Research, Oxford University Press, 2004; Olivelle, 'Dharmaśāstra'; Robert Lingat, *The classical law of India*, trans. D. Derrett, Berkeley: University of California Press, 1973.
15. On brahminical ideology, see Gombrich, *Theravada Buddhism*, ch. 2.
16. The code is presented and analysed by Olivelle in *Manu's code*. Another translation can be found in Oxford University Press's World Classics series, *The law code of Manu*, 2004.
17. My analysis of the Dharmashastras is based on Olivelle, *Manu's code* and 'Dharmaśāstra', along with Donald R. Davis, Jr, *The spirit of Hindu law*, Cambridge University Press, 2010.
18. Olivelle, *Manu's code* (8.47–343).
19. Olivelle, *Manu's code* (8:143–44).
20. On legal practices in medieval India, see Donald R. Davis Jr, 'Centres of law: duties, rights, and jurisdictional pluralism in medieval India', in P. Dresch and H. Skoda (eds), *Legalism: anthropology and history*, Oxford University Press, 2012; and his 'Intermediate realms of law: corporate groups and rulers in medieval India', *Journal of the Economic and Social History of the Orient* 48: 92–117, 2005; Bajadulal Chattopadhyaya, '"Autonomous spaces" and the authority of the state: the contradiction and its resolution in theory and practice in early India', in B. Kölver (ed.) *Recht, Staat und Verwaltung im klassischen Indien*, Munich: R. Oldenbourg Verlag, 1997.

21. Olivelle, 'Dharmaśāstra', 44–45.
22. Lubin, 'Punishment and expiation', 107–8.
23. Davis, *Spirit of Hindu law*, 117.
24. Olivelle, *Manu's code*, 41
25. Sheldon Pollock, *The language of the gods in the world of men: Sanskrit, culture, and power in premodern India*, Berkeley: University of California Press, 2006, 67–68.
26. Pollock, *Language of the gods*, 255–56.
27. Gombrich, *Theravada Buddhism*, 37.
28. Olivelle, *Manu's code*, 169–74.
29. Donald R. Davis, Jr, 'Recovering the indigenous legal traditions of India: classical Hindu law in practice in late medieval Kerala', *Journal of Indian Philosophy* 27: 184–91, 1999.
30. Lubin, 'Punishment and expiation', 111–14; Ananya Vajpey, 'Excavating identity through tradition: Who was Shivaji?', in S. Saberwal and S. Varma (eds), *Traditions in Motion*, Oxford University Press, 2005.
31. Richard W. Lariviere, 'A Sanskrit jayapattra from 18th century Mithilā', in R. W. Lariviere (ed.) *Studies in dharmaśāstra*, Calcutta: Firma KLM, 1984, 49–65.
32. Bajadulal Chattopadhyaya, 'Autonomous spaces'.
33. On the Vanjeri, see Davis, 'Recovering the indigenous legal traditions'.
34. Davis, 'Recovering the indigenous legal traditions', 167.
35. On the ascetics, see Whitney M. Cox, 'Law, literature, and the problem of politics in medieval India', in Lubin et al., *Hinduism and law*.
36. Shivaji is discussed by Vajpey, 'Excavating identity'.
37. Olivelle, *Manu's code* (10.74–80, 11.55–124).
38. This and the following paragraphs are largely based on Davis, 'Recovering the indigenous legal traditions'.
39. Lubin et al., *Hinduism and law*, 3.
40. Doniger, *The Hindus*, 325.
41. Ananya Vajpey, '*Śudradharma* and legal treatments of caste', in Lubin et al., *Hinduism and law*.
42. J. D. M. Derrett, 'Two inscriptions concerning the status of Kammalas and the application of Dharmaśāstra', in

J. Duncan Derrett (ed.) *Essays in classical and modern Hindu law*, vol. 1, Leiden: Brill, 1976.

43. Davis, 'Recovering the indigenous legal traditions', 197–98.
44. This section is based on Lingat, *The classical law of India*, 267–70.
45. Clifford Geertz, 'Local knowledge: fact and law in comparative perspective', in *Local knowledge*, New York: Basic Books, 1983, 200, quotation slightly amended.

3. CHINESE EMPERORS: CODES, PUNISHMENTS, AND BUREAUCRACY

1. The general historical details are based on Morris Rossabi, *A history of China*, Chichester, UK: Wiley Blackwell, 2014.
2. On the Shang social and political structures, see Yongping Liu, *Origins of Chinese law: penal and administrative law in its early development*, Hong Kong: Oxford University Press, 1998, 22–29.
3. The Kang Gao has survived in a collection of documents that claims to be based on material from this period; scholars think that it does represent the views of the Chinese nobility of the time. Liu, *Origins of Chinese law*, 43, 122–24; Geoffrey MacCormack, 'Law and punishment in the earliest Chinese thought', *Irish Jurist* 20: 335–51, 1985. For the text, see James Legge, *The Chinese classics*, vol. 3, Hong Kong: Hong Kong University Press, 1960, 48.
4. On the bronze inscriptions, see Laura Skosey, 'The legal system and legal traditions of the Western Zhou (ca. 1045–71 B.C.E.)', PhD diss., University of Chicago, 1996.
5. Liu, *Origins of Chinese law*, 50–52.
6. On the Zhou period and its laws, see Ernest Caldwell, 'Social change and written law in early Chinese legal thought', *Law and History Review* 32: 1–30, 2014; Ernest Caldwell, *Writing Chinese laws: the form and function of legal statutes found in the Qin Shuihudi corpus*, London: Routledge, 2018; Liu, *Origins of Chinese law*, ch. 5.

7. Much of what we know about this period is found in the commentary to a rather terse set of annals purported to be by the great scholar Confucius. The commentary, the *Zuo zhuan*, probably written by one of his disciples in the mid– to late Warring States period (403–221 BCE), reflects the attitudes and thoughts of a later period, but from it we can glean many details about the ideas of the Zhou. See Caldwell, 'Social change', 5–6; Liu, *Origins of Chinese law*, 128–38. For the text, see Legge, *Chinese classics*, vol. 5, 710.

8. On Confucius, see Caldwell, *Writing Chinese laws*, ch. 2.

9. Caldwell, 'Social change', 20.

10. Caldwell, 'Social change', 14–18.

11. On the Qin and the *Shangjun Shu*, said to be the work of Shang Yang, see Caldwell, *Writing Chinese laws*, ch. 3; Liu, *Origins of Chinese law*, ch. 6, esp. 175–77.

12. Ulrich Lau and Thies Staack, *Legal practice in the formative stages of the Chinese Empire: an annotated translation of the exemplary Qin criminal cases from the Yuelu Academy collection*, Leiden: Brill, 2016.

13. See, generally, the cases and commentary in Lau and Staack, *Legal practice*, particularly 27–45.

14. Debates continue about why officials were buried with texts. See Anthony J. Barbieri-Low and Robin D.S. Yates, *Law, state, and society in early imperial China: a study with critical edition and translation of the legal texts from Zhangjiashan tomb numbers 247*, Leiden: Brill, 2015, 107–9.

15. Lau and Staack, *Legal practice*, 174–87.

16. These were expressed in terms of shields or suits of armour, but in practice they were replaced by other goods or money, as documents found at Liye indicate. I am grateful to Ernest Caldwell for this fact.

17. Lau and Staack, *Legal practice*, 188–210.

18. On this period and its laws, see Barbieri-Low and Yates, *Law, state, and society*.

19. See Barbieri-Low and Yates, *Law, state, and society*.

20. Barbieri-Low and Yates, *Law, state, and society*, 99–100.

21. Barbieri-Low and Yates, *Law, state, and society*, 100–101.
22. On the Han and Sui laws, see Geoffrey MacCormack, 'The transmission of penal law from the Han to the Tang', *Revue des droits de l'antiquité* 51: 47–83, 2004.
23. MacCormack, 'Transmission', 54–55.
24. MacCormack, 'Transmission', 73–74.
25. For a translation of, and commentary on, the code, see Wallace Johnson, *The T'ang Code*, 2 vols., Princeton, NJ: Princeton University Press, 1979–1997.
26. Scholars have estimated this at 30 to 40 percent. Derk Bodde and Clarence Morris, *Law in Imperial China: exemplified by 190 Ch'ing Dynasty cases (translated from the Hsing-an hui-lan)*, Cambridge, MA: Harvard University Press, 1967.
27. Philip Huang, 'The past and present of the Chinese civil and criminal justice systems: the Sinitic legal tradition from a global perspective', *Modern China* 42: 227–72, 2016.
28. On legal practices, see Philip Huang, *Civil justice in China: representation and practice in the Qing*, Stanford, CA: Stanford University Press, 1996.
29. This was particularly the case under Hu Jintao, while Xi Jingping has encouraged greater use of law. See Taisu Zhang and Tom Ginsburg, 'China's turn toward law', *Virginia Journal of International Law* 59: 277–361, 2019.
30. Jérôme Bourgon, 'Chinese law, history of, Qing dynasty', *The Oxford international encyclopedia of legal history*, Oxford University Press, 2009, 176.

4. ADVOCATES AND JURISTS: INTELLECTUAL PURSUITS IN ANCIENT ROME

1. For early Rome, see Tim Cornell, *The beginnings of Rome: Italy and Rome from the Bronze Age to the Punic Wars (c. 1000–264 BC)*, London: Routledge, 1995; Kathryn Lomas, *The rise of Rome: from the Iron Age to the Punic Wars (1000–264 BC)*, London: Profile Books, 2017. Readable general histories are offered by Mary Beard, *SPQR: a history of ancient Rome*, London: Profile Books, 2015; Robin

Lane Fox, *The classical world: an epic history of Greece and Rome*, London: Folio Society, 2013.

2. On the early Roman temples, see Charlotte R. Potts, 'The development and architectural significance of early Etrusco-Italic podia', *BABESCH* 86: 41–52, 2011.
3. The crystallisation into two classes, patricians and plebeians, occurred gradually, but its origins were in the opposition between the wealthy political elite and the newly formed plebeian group in this period.
4. R. Westbrook, 'The nature and origins of the twelve tables', *Zeitschrift der Savigny-Stiftung für Rechtsgeschichte* 105: 74–121, 1988, argues for the influence of the Mesopotamian, rather than Greek, codes via the trading and diplomatic missions of the Phoenicians to Italy. The casuistic form is certainly similar.
5. For the text, see M. H. Crawford, *Roman statutes*, vol. 2, London: Institute of Classical Studies, School of Advanced Study, University of London, 1996.
6. On the Twelve Tables, see also Elizabeth A. Meyer, *Legitimacy and law in the Roman world*, Cambridge University Press, 2004, 26.
7. See, among others, Richard E. Mitchell, *Patricians and plebeians: the origin of the Roman state*, Ithaca, NY: Cornell University Press, 1990.
8. On early lawmaking, see David Ibbetson, 'Sources of law from the Republic to the Dominate', in D. Johnston (ed.) *The Cambridge companion to Roman law*, New York: Cambridge University Press, 2015.
9. Seth Bernard, 'Debt, land, and labor in the early Republican economy', *Phoenix* 70: 317–38, 2016.
10. Lomas, *Rise of Rome*, ch. 9.
11. Bernard, 'Debt, land, and labor'.
12. This fact, based on a single source, is much debated, but several scholars think it likely. See Cornell, *Beginnings of Rome*, 247–28; Seth Bernard, *Building mid-republican Rome: labor, architecture, and the urban economy*, Oxford University Press, 2014, 123–24.

13. Alan Watson, *Law making in the later Roman Republic*, Oxford: Clarendon Press, 1974, ch. 2.

14. Philip Kay, *Rome's economic revolution*, Oxford University Press, 2014, 10, 327.

15. This was the Lex Hortensia. See Lomas, *Rise of Rome*, ch. 14.

16. On Roman legal practice, see Richard A. Bauman, *Crime and punishment in ancient Rome*, London: Routledge, 1996; Alan Watson, *The spirit of Roman law*, Athens: University of Georgia Press, 1995, 3, although some of their conclusions, like much about early Rome, are subject to debate.

17. On the pontiffs, see Alan Watson, *The evolution of Western private law*, Baltimore: Johns Hopkins University Press, 1985, 22.

18. Watson, *Evolution*, 5–6, ch. 1.

19. In general, see Andrew Lintott, *The constitution of the Roman Republic*, Oxford University Press, 1999.

20. Callie Williamson, *The laws of the Roman people: public law in the expansion and decline of the Roman Republic*, Ann Arbor: University of Michigan Press, 2005, ch. 3.

21. Williamson, *Laws of the Roman people*, xii–xiii.

22. As Cornell put it, in *The beginnings of Rome*, 342, Rome had developed from an exclusive aristocracy to a competitive oligarchy.

23. Polybius was applying Greek political theory to the Roman constitution and his account was schematic, but he was clearly convinced that 'the people' played a vital role in overthrowing corrupt regimes and allowing the rise of a more democratic constitution. See F. W. Walbank, 'A Greek looks at Rome: Polybius VI revisited', in his *Polybius, Rome and the Hellenistic world: essays and reflections*, Cambridge University Press, 2002; Lintott, *Constitution*, chs. 3 and 12.

24. On Polybius's account they produced 35 metric tonnes each year. Kay, *Rome's economic revolution*, ch. 3.

25. Beard, *SPQR*, 199.

26. The laws are listed in Williamson, *Laws of the Roman people*, Appendix C.

27. This incident is described by Watson, *Law making*, 7–8.
28. On the praetors and their activities, see Lomas, *Rise of Rome*, 296–97; Bruce W. Frier, *The rise of the Roman jurists: studies in Cicero's* 'pro Caecina', Princeton, NJ: Princeton University Press, 1985, ch. 2; T. Corey Brennan, *The praetorship in the Roman Republic*, Oxford University Press, 2000; Watson, *Law making*, chs. 3–5.
29. The earliest known edict dates from 213 BCE. Watson, *Law making*, 1.
30. This was confirmed by the Lex Aebutia. Anna Tarwacka, 'Lex Aebutia', in the *Oxford classical dictionary*, 5th ed. Oxford University Press, 2019.
31. On legal procedures, see Frier, *Rise of the Roman jurists*, 64–65, ch. 5; A. H. J. Greenridge, *The legal procedure of Cicero's time*, Oxford: Clarendon Press, 1901.
32. Frier, *Rise of the Roman jurists*, 59–62.
33. Lintott, *Constitution of the Roman Republic*, ch. 9; A. N. Sherwin-White, 'The *Lex Repetundarum* and the political ideas of Gaius Gracchus', *Journal of Roman Studies* 72: 18–31, 1982.
34. Derek Roebuck and Bruno de Loynes de Fumichon, *Roman arbitration*, Oxford: Holo Books, 2004, ch. 5.
35. Frier, *Rise of the Roman jurists*, 157.
36. Cicero, *Topica* 65; Watson, *Law making*, 103.
37. Watson, *Law making*, 103.
38. Frier, *Rise of the Roman jurists*, 158–60, ch. 4.
39. Watson, *Law making*, 117–22.
40. On Cicero's prosecution of Verres and its context, see Frier, *Rise of the Roman jurists*, 48–50, ch. 2; Brennan, *Praetorship*, 446–50.
41. Williamson, *Laws of the Roman people*, ch. 2.
42. Brennan, *Praetorship*, 450–51.
43. Frier, *Rise of the Roman jurists*, 149. Cicero's equivalent in United Kingdom is the criminal barrister who specializes in courtroom advocacy in cases that turn largely on matters of fact, while his or her Chancery colleagues, often less brilliant in court, are more like the jurists.

44. The case is described in some detail by Frier, *Rise of the Roman jurists*, ch. 1.
45. Alan Watson, *Rome of the XII Tables: persons and property*, Princeton, NJ: Princeton University Press, 1975, 175.
46. Jill Harries, *Cicero and the jurists: from citizens' law to the lawful state*, London: Duckworth, 2006.
47. Brennan, *Praetorship*, 608.
48. On the jurists, see Frier, *Rise of the Roman jurists*, esp. ch. 4; Watson, *Law making*, 108–9.
49. In fact, Cicero did not become a jurist, and most of his fellow students were destined for other public offices, but their training must have followed similar patterns.
50. We do not know about Scaevola's properties, but the details are typical of wealthy Roman residences. Fox, *Classical world*, ch. 34; Beard, *SPQR*, 318–28.
51. Watson, *Law making*, 104–6.
52. On the fictions, see Yan Thomas, 'Fictio Legis: L'empire de la fiction Romaine et ses limites Médiévales', *Droits* 21: 17–63, 1995.
53. Clifford Ando, *Law, language, and empire in the Roman tradition*, Philadelphia: University of Pennsylvania Press, 2011, 6–18.
54. Ari Z. Bryen, 'Responsa', in S. Stern, M. del Mar, and B. Meyler (eds), *The Oxford handbook of law and humanities*, Oxford University Press, 2019, 675–77.
55. Watson, *Law making*, ch. 15.
56. Frier, *Rise of the Roman jurists*, 120–23.
57. The Latin is 'Dolus mal(us) abesto et iuris consult(i)'. See Bryen, 'Responsa', 675.
58. There is considerable debate over the figures for population and citizenship. Walter Scheidel, 'Italian manpower', *Journal of Roman Archaeology* 26: 678–87, 2013; Myles Lavan, 'The spread of Roman citizenship, 14–212 CE: quantification in the face of high uncertainty', *Past and Present* 230: 3–46, 2016, at p. 30.
59. Bryen, 'Responsa', 679.

NOTES TO CHAPTER 4

60. What he actually declared and intended by his *ius respondendi* is not, however, entirely clear. Bryen, 'Responsa'.

61. On the development of the imperial cult, see Clifford Ando, *Imperial ideology and provincial loyalty in the Roman empire*, Berkeley: University of California Press, 2000, esp. ch. 9.

62. Cicero, *De Re Publica*, 1.39.1; Ando, *Imperial ideology*, 9–11, 47–48.

63. See Ando, *Imperial ideology*, 383; Clifford Ando, 'Pluralism and empire: from Rome to Robert Cover', *Critical Analysis of Law* 1: 1–22, 2014, at pp. 9–11.

64. There is considerable literature on this edict and its implications. See, for example, Ando, *Imperial ideology*, 395, and the introduction to his *Citizenship and empire in Europe, 200–1900: the Antonine constitution after 1800 years*, Stuttgart: Franz Steiner Verlag, 2016, 9.

65. Ando, *Citizenship*; Tony Honoré, 'Roman law AD 200–400: from cosmopolis to Rechtstaat?', in S. Swain and M. Edwards (eds), *Approaching late antiquity: the transformation from early to late empire*, Oxford University Press, 2006.

66. Bruce W. Frier, 'Finding a place for law in the high empire', in F. de Angelis (ed.) *Spaces of justice in the Roman world*, Leiden: Brill, 2010.

67. On the legal reforms of this period, see Honoré, 'Roman law AD 200–400', and his *Emperors and lawyers*, 2nd ed. Oxford: Clarendon Press, 1994.

68. Ando, *Imperial ideology*, 362–83.

69. Myles Lavan, 'Slavishness in Britain and Rome in Tacitus' *Agricola*', *Classical Quarterly* 61: 294–305, 2011, at p. 296.

70. Ando, *Imperial ideology*, 339–43.

71. On law in this period, see Tony Honoré, *Law in the crisis of empire, 379–455 AD: the Theodosian dynasty and its quaestors*, Oxford: Clarendon Press, 1998.

72. Peter Stein, *Roman law in European history*, Cambridge University Press, 1999, 46, 60.

5. JEWISH AND ISLAMIC SCHOLARS: GOD'S PATH FOR THE WORLD

1. For general background, see David N. Myers, *Jewish history: a very short introduction*, Oxford University Press, 2017, and on the historical development of Jewish law, see N. S. Hecht, B. S. Jackson, S. M. Passamaneck, D. Piattelli, and A. M. Rabello (eds), *An introduction to the history and sources of Jewish law*, Oxford: Clarendon Press, 1996.
2. Peretz Segal, 'Jewish law during the Tannaitic period', in Hecht et al., *Introduction*, 101.
3. Plural of Gaon.
4. On the Geonim, see Gideon Libson, 'Halakhah and law in the period of the Geonim', in Hecht et al., *Introduction*.
5. Background details are largely drawn from Joseph Schacht, *An introduction to Islamic law*, Oxford: Clarendon Press, 1964, and Marshall G.S. Hodgson, *The venture of Islam: conscience and history in a world civilization*, vol. 1, Chicago: University of Chicago Press, 1961, along with Adam J. Silverstein's excellent *Islamic history: a very short introduction*, Oxford University Press, 2010.
6. Hodgson, *Venture of Islam*, 161ff., ch. 2.
7. Schacht, *Introduction*, ch. 3.
8. This section draws on Hodgson, *Venture of Islam*, bk. 1, ch. 3, and Schacht, *Introduction*, chs. 4–6.
9. This is a major point of scholarly debate. I largely follow Schacht rather than Hallaq, taking the view that while the Quranic tradition and practices of Muhammad's time must have laid the groundwork for later legal practices, during this period the qadis relied substantially on non-Islamic sources and their own judgement. Schacht, *Introduction*; Wael B. Hallaq, *The origins and evolution of Islamic law*, Cambridge University Press, 2005; Wael B. Hallaq, *Sharīʿa: theory, practice, transformations*, Cambridge University Press, 2009.
10. In what follows, I concentrate on the Sunnis and their law. The Shiʿi tradition developed in parallel, relying on the

works of their imams, who regarded themselves as heirs to the Prophet, on which, see works by Robert Gleave.

11. Hodgson, *Venture of Islam*, bk. 2.
12. Marina Rustow, *The lost archive: traces of a caliphate in a Cairo synagogue*, Princeton, NJ: Princeton University Press, 2020. Earlier sources claimed they had learned the techniques from Chinese captives.
13. This was one area in which the Sunni and Shi'i traditions differed, each recognizing different hadiths, but the results were not so different. Hodgson, *Venture of Islam*, 326–32.
14. Hodgson, *Venture of Islam*, 337.
15. On the laws, see Schacht, *Introduction*, ch. 7.
16. On the devices, see Schacht, *Introduction*, ch. 11.
17. The details in this paragraph are largely drawn from Hodgson, *Venture of Islam*, bk. 2, ch. 3, and Schacht, *Introduction*, 80–82 and chs. 6 and 7.
18. Schacht, *Introduction*, 80.
19. On Shafi'i, see Schacht, *Introduction*, chs. 7 and 10.
20. Hodgson, *Venture of Islam*, 326–36.
21. Schacht, *Introduction*, ch. 9.
22. By the twelfth century, some scholars were arguing that all the essential legal questions had been settled and the gates of *ijtihad* were closed. See Wael B. Hallaq, 'Was the gate of *ijtihad* closed?', *International Journal of Middle East Studies* 16: 3–41, 1984; Wael B. Hallaq, 'On the origins of the controversy about the existence of mujtahids and the gate of ijtihad', *Studia Islamica* 63: 129–41, 1986. In these works Hallaq contradicts Schacht, in *Introduction*, ch. 10, who proposes an earlier date. For a good review of the issues, see David S. Powers, 'Wael B. Hallaq on the origins of Islamic law: a review essay', *Islamic Law and Society* 17: 126–57, 2010.
23. Schacht, *Introduction*, ch. 11.
24. Schacht, *Introduction*, 84.
25. Hodgson, *Venture of Islam*, 347.
26. Hodgson, *Venture of Islam*, 349.
27. On the general history in this section, see Silverstein, *Islamic history*, ch. 1.

28. Schacht, *Introduction*, 84.
29. On the jurists, see Norman Calder, *Islamic jurisprudence in the classical era*, Colin Imber (ed.) Cambridge University Press, 2010, 161.
30. On Nawawi, see Calder, *Islamic jurisprudence*, ch. 2.
31. Calder, *Islamic jurisprudence*, 101–2.
32. Calder, *Islamic jurisprudence*, 94.
33. Calder, *Islamic jurisprudence*, 92–95, 112–15.
34. Calder, *Islamic jurisprudence*, 92.
35. On Subki, see Calder, *Islamic jurisprudence*, ch. 3.
36. Calder, *Islamic jurisprudence*, 119.
37. Calder, *Islamic jurisprudence*, 124–25.
38. Calder, *Islamic jurisprudence*, 127.

6. EUROPEAN KINGS: COURTS AND CUSTOMS AFTER THE FALL OF ROME

1. The background in the first part of this chapter is largely drawn from Peter Heather, *The fall of the Roman Empire: a new history of Rome and the barbarians*, Oxford University Press, 2005. Legal details are based on Peter Stein, *Roman law in European history*, Cambridge University Press, 1999.
2. Étienne Renard, '*Le pactus legis Salicae*, règlement militaire Romain ou code de lois compilé sous Clovis?', *Bibliotèque de l'École des chartes* 167: 321–52, 2009.
3. Patrick Wormald, 'Lex scripta and verbum regis: legislation and Germanic kingship from Euric to Cnut', in P. H. Sawyer and I. N. Wood (eds), *Early medieval kingship*, Leeds: University of Leeds, School of History, 1977, 28; Patrick Wormald, *The making of English law: King Alfred to the twelfth century*, Oxford: Blackwell, 1999.
4. Wormald, 'Lex scripta', 25–27.
5. On the Lex Salica, see Katherine Fischer Drew, *The laws of the Salian Franks*, Philadelphia: University of Pennsylvania Press, 1991. Although the king took responsibility for the laws, many probably originated with the customs

and decisions of his councils. See T. M. Charles-Edwards, 'Law in the western kingdoms between the fifth and seventh century', in A. Cameron, R. Ward-Perkins, and M. Whitby (eds), *The Cambridge ancient history*, vol. 14, *Late antiquity: empire and successors, A.D. 425–600*, Cambridge University Press, 2001, 274–78.

6. The *Digesta* is also known as 'the Pandects', from the Greek version of the name.
7. Stein, *Roman law in European history*, 40–43.
8. Arianism was based on the teachings of Arius, who lived from 256 to 336. His doctrine differed from mainstream Christianity on points involving the nature of the Trinity.
9. Matthew Innes, 'Charlemagne's government', in J. Storey (ed.) *Charlemagne: empire and society*, Manchester University Press, 2005.
10. Alice Rio, *Legal practice and the written word in the early Middle Ages: Frankish formulae, c. 500–1000*, Cambridge University Press, 2009.
11. Drew, *Laws of the Salian Franks*, 132–39.
12. Wormald, *Making of English law*, 46–47.
13. Wormald, 'Lex scripta', 23. Wormald's views are confirmed by Charles-Edwards, 'Law in the western kingdoms', but some doubts are expressed by Thomas Faulkner, *Law and authority in the early Middle Ages*, Cambridge University Press, 2016, and Rosamond McKitterick, *The Carolingians and the written word*, Cambridge University Press, 1989.
14. Translations of the Anglo-Saxon laws can be found in F. L. Attenborough, *The laws of the earliest English kings*, Cambridge University Press, 1922. A thorough analysis of the laws is provided by Tom Lambert, *Law and order in Anglo-Saxon England*, Oxford University Press, 2017.
15. Charles-Edwards, 'Law in the western kingdoms', 265–66.
16. Lambert, *Law and order*, ch. 5.
17. Wormald, 'Lex scripta', 14–15.
18. George Molyneaux, *The formation of the English kingdom in the tenth century*, Oxford University Press, 2015.
19. On Wulfstan's laws, see Lambert, *Law and order*, ch. 5.

20. Most of this section is based on Charles M. Radding, *The origins of medieval jurisprudence: Pavia and Bologna, 850–1150*, New Haven, CT: Yale University Press, 1988. On the Lombard laws, see Katherine Fischer Drew, *The Lombard laws*, London: Variorum Reprints, 1988; Charles-Edwards, 'Law in the western kingdoms'.
21. Further details are from Chris Wickham, 'Land disputes and their social framework in Lombard-Carolingian Italy, 700–900', in W. Davies and P. Fouracre (eds), *The settlement of disputes in early medieval Europe*, Cambridge University Press, 1986.
22. On Bologna and its significance, see Stein, *Roman law in European history*, ch. 2.
23. Stein, *Roman law in European history*, 54.
24. On the impact of Roman law in Europe, see also Alan Watson, *Legal transplants: an approach to comparative law*, Charlottesville: University Press of Virginia, 1974.
25. Stein, *Roman law in European history*, 54–57.
26. On the development of Angevin law, see Wormald, *Making of English law*; John Hudson, *The formation of the English common law: law and society in England from the Norman Conquest to Magna Carta*, London: Longman, 1996.
27. On the development of the royal courts, see Paul Brand, *The origins of the English legal profession*, Oxford: Blackwell, 1992.
28. Anne J. Duggan, 'Roman, canon, and common law in twelfth century England: the council of Northampton (1164) re-examined', *Historical Research* 83: 379–408, 2009, at p. 402.
29. Paul Brand, 'Legal education in England before the Inns of Court', in A. Bush and Alain Wijffels (eds), *Learning the law: teaching and the transmission of law in England, 1150–1900*, London: Hambledon Press, 1999, 54–55.
30. On legal education, see Brand, 'Legal education'; J. H. Baker, 'The Inns of Court in 1388', *Law Quarterly Review* 92: 184–87, 1976.

7. AT THE MARGINS: LAWMAKING ON THE FRINGES OF CHRISTIANITY AND ISLAM

1. For background on Ireland, see Clare Downham, *Medieval Ireland*, Cambridge University Press, 2018; Robin Chapman Stacey, *The road to judgment: from custom to court in medieval Ireland and Wales*, Philadelphia: University of Pennsylvania Press, 1994.

2. On the Irish kings, see Francis Byrne, *Irish kings and high kings*, London: B. Y. Batsford, 1973.

3. Marilyn Gerreits, 'Economy and society: clientship in the Irish laws', *Cambridge Medieval Celtic Studies* 6: 43–61, 1983.

4. On the early lawyers, see T. M. Charles-Edwards, Review of the 'Corpus Iuris Hibernici', *Studia Hibernica* 20: 141–62, 1980; Jane Stevenson, 'The beginnings of literacy in Ireland', *Proceedings of the Royal Irish Academy: Archaeology, Culture, History, and Literature* 89C: 127–65, 1989.

5. By the early eighth century, one author was distinguishing the well-read cleric, the traditional Irish scholar, and the gifted but unlearned poet. Stevenson, 'Beginnings of literacy', 161–62.

6. D. A. Binchy (ed.) *Corpus iuris hibernici: ad fidem codicum manuscriptorum recognovit*, Dublin: Institute for Advanced Studies, 1978. On the laws, see Fergus Kelly, *A guide to early Irish law*, Dublin: Institute for Advanced Studies, 1988; Charles-Edwards, Review of the 'Corpus Iuris Hibernici'; Thomas Charles-Edwards and Fergus Kelly, *Bechbretha*, Dublin: Institute for Advanced Study, 1983; Marilyn Gerreits, 'Money in early Christian Ireland', *Comparative Studies in Society and History* 27: 323–39, 1985.

7. Fergus Kelly, *Early Irish farming: a study based mainly on the law-texts of the 7th and 8th centuries* AD, Dublin: Institute for Advanced Studies, 1997.

8. Charles-Edwards and Kelly, *Bechbretha*.

9. Gerreits, 'Money', 329–30.

10. Downham, *Medieval Ireland*, 66.

11. Gerreits, 'Money'.
12. On legal practice, see Richard Sharpe, 'Dispute settlement in medieval Ireland', in Wendy Davies and Paul Fouracre (eds), *Settlement of disputes in early medieval Europe*, Cambridge University Press, 1986.
13. This difficult text is discussed by Stacey, *Road to judgment*, ch. 5.
14. Charles-Edwards, Review of the 'Corpus Iuris Hibernici'; Charles-Edwards and Kelly, *Bechbretha*, 25ff.
15. Fergus Kelly, *Marriage disputes: a fragmentary Old Irish law-text*, Dublin: Institute for Advanced Studies, 2014.
16. Kelly, *Guide to early Irish law*, 7.
17. Stacey, *Road to judgment*, 22.
18. On the laws for the kings, see Kelly, *Guide to early Irish law*, 18–26.
19. T. M. Charles-Edwards, 'A contract between king and people in early medieval Ireland? *Críth Gablach* on kingship', *Peritia* 8: 107–19, 1994.
20. Stacey, *Road to judgment*, 16ff.
21. Much of the background and detail in this section is from William Ian Miller, *Bloodtaking and peacemaking: feud, law, and society in saga Iceland*, University of Chicago Press, 1990, with further detail from Jón Jóhannesson, *A history of the old Icelandic commonwealth: Islendinga saga*, trans. H. Bessason, Winnipeg: University of Manitoba Press, 1974.
22. Miller, *Bloodtaking*, 223.
23. Miller, *Bloodtaking*, 222–23.
24. Miller, *Bloodtaking*, 227, 257.
25. Jóhannesson, *History*, 40.
26. Some scholars doubt whether all these articles, which appear in later copies, are original. But Vladimir and his son almost certainly did issue statutes of this nature. Simon Franklin, *Writing, society and culture in early Rus, c. 950–1300*, Cambridge University Press, 2002, 152–56. For analysis of the laws, see also Daniel H. Kaiser, *The laws of Rus': tenth to fifteenth centuries*, Salt Lake City: C. Schlacks, 1992;

Simon Franklin, 'On meanings, functions and paradigms of law in early Rus', *Russian History* 34: 63–81, 2007.

27. Franklin, *Writing*.

28. For the laws, see Kaiser, *Laws of Rus'*, 14–19. The dates and authorship of both versions of the *Russkaia Pravda* are very uncertain.

29. Simon Franklin and Jonathan Shepard, *The emergence of Rus, 750–1200*, London: Longman, 1996, 224.

30. On the emergence of writing, see Franklin, *Writing*, ch. 1.

31. Franklin, *Writing*, 38–39.

32. Franklin, *Writing*, 184. The letter is from the first half of the twelfth century.

33. Kaiser, *Laws of Rus'*, 20–34. The expanded version probably appeared during this period, although its authorship is unknown.

34. Franklin, *Writing*, 140.

35. Franklin, *Writing*, 149.

36. Franklin, *Writing*, 151–52.

37. Franklin *Writing*, 137.

38. These are specified in the rules imported from Byzantium for the Monastery of the Caves in the mid-eleventh century. Franklin, *Writing*, 143–44.

39. Kaiser, *Laws of Rus'*, 20–34.

40. I am grateful to Marina Kurkchiyan for this summary of the documents.

41. Elena Bratishenko, 'On the authorship of the 1229 Smolensk–Riga trade treaty', *Russian Linguistics* 26: 345–61, 2002.

42. These included the *Zakon Sudnyi Liudem*, 'Court Law for the People', originally translated by Bulgarian scholars, but based on Byzantine laws. Others went directly to the Greek texts and translated digests of the Byzantine imperial laws, known as the Ecloga and the Prochiron. Franklin, *Writing*, 137–39.

43. The text has been translated and analysed by Robert Thomson in *The Lawcode (Datastanagirk') of Mxit'ar Goš*, Amsterdam: Rodopi, 2000. Further background is provided by

Peter Cowe in 'Medieval Armenian Literary and Cultural Trends', in R. Hovannisian (ed.) *The Armenian people from ancient to modern times*, vol. 1, Los Angeles: University of California Press, 1997, 297–301.

44. Thomson, *Lawcode*, 22.
45. Cowe, 'Medieval Armenian', 299.
46. Cowe, 'Medieval Armenian', 300.
47. Cowe, 'Medieval Armenian', 301; Krikor Mahsoudian, 'Armenian communities in eastern Europe', in Hovannisian, *Armenian people*, 1:62–64.

8. EMBRACING THE LAWS OF RELIGION: THE HINDU, JEWISH, AND MUSLIM WORLDS

1. For the South Indian background, see Rajan Gurukhal, 'From clan to lineage to hereditary occupations and caste in early south India', *Indian Historical Review* 20: 22–33, 1993–1994.
2. Donald R. Davis, Jr, 'Responsa in Hindu law: consultation and lawmaking in medieval India', *Oxford Journal of Law and Religion* 3: 57–75, 2014, at p. 61.
3. Bajadulal Chattopadhyaya, '"Autonomous spaces" and the authority of the state: the contradiction and its resolution in theory and practice in early India', in B. Kölver (ed.) *Recht, Staat und Verwaltung im klassischen Indien*, Munich: R. Oldenbourg Verlag, 1997, 8–9. This phrase was repeated in the Manu *dharmashastra*. See Patrick Olivelle, with the editorial assistance of Suman Olivelle, *Manu's code of law: a critical edition and translation of the* Mānava-Dharmaśāstra, South Asia Research, Oxford University Press, 2004, 169.
4. On these local agreements and arrangements, see Donald R. Davis, Jr, 'Intermediate realms of law: corporate groups and rulers in medieval India', *Journal of the Economic and Social History of the Orient* 48: 92–117, 2005, and his 'Centres of law: duties, rights, and jurisdictional pluralism in

medieval India', in P. Dresch and H. Skoda (eds), *Legalism: anthropology and history*, Oxford University Press, 2012.

5. D. R. Davis, 'A historical overview of Hindu law', in Timothy Lubin, Donald R. Davis, and Jayanth K. Krishnan (eds), *Hinduism and law: an introduction*, Cambridge University Press, 2010, 20.

6. Davis, 'Responsa', 65.

7. On the social and economic contexts of Egypt, see S. D. Goitein, *A Mediterranean society: an abridgment in one volume*, Jacob Lassner (ed.) Berkeley: University of California Press, 1999.

8. Mark R. Cohen, *Jewish self-government in medieval Egypt: the origins of the office of Head of the Jews, ca. 1065–1126*, Princeton, NJ: Princeton University Press, 1980.

9. Shelomo Dov Goitein, *A Mediterranean society: the Jewish communities of the Arab world as portrayed by the documents of the Cairo geniza*, vol. 1, Berkeley: University of California Press, 1967, 329–30.

10. The geniza documents are comprehensively discussed in Goitein, *Mediterranean society*, 6 vols., Berkeley: University of California Press, 1967–1993.

11. On the scribes, see Eve Krakowski and Marina Rustow, 'Formula as content: medieval Jewish institutions, the Cairo geniza, and the new diplomatics', *Jewish Social Studies: History, Culture, Society* 20: 111–46, 2014.

12. Goitein, *Mediterranean society*, 2:332.

13. Goitein, *Mediterranean society*, 2:324.

14. On the Jews' courts and legal procedures, see Goitein, *Mediterranean society*, 2:1971.

15. Goitein, *Mediterranean society*, 2:323.

16. On court procedures, see Goitein, *Mediterranean society*, 2:334–44.

17. Goitein, *Mediterranean society*, 2:336.

18. Goitein, *Mediterranean society*, 2:331–32.

19. Goitein, *Mediterranean society*, 2:331.

20. Goitein, *Mediterranean society*, 2:328; 3:210–11.

21. Goitein, *Mediterranean society*, 2:328.
22. Phillip I. Ackerman-Lieberman, *The business of identity: Jews, Muslims and economic life in medieval Egypt*, Stanford, CA: Stanford University Press, 2014, ch. 2.
23. Marina Rustow, *Heresy and the politics of community: the Jews of the Fatimid caliphate*, Ithaca, NY: Cornell University Press, 2008, ch. 10, 278–80.
24. Goitein, *Mediterranean society*, 2:327–28.
25. Krakowski and Rustow, 'Formula as content'.
26. David N. Myers, *Jewish history: a very short introduction*, Oxford University Press, 2017, 17.
27. Much of this section draws on David S. Powers, *Law, society, and culture in the Maghrib, 1300–1500*, Cambridge University Press, 2002.
28. A lithograph in twelve volumes was produced by a committee of eight jurists in Fez in 1897–1898. A printed edition has been published in Rabat: Ahmad al-Wansharisi, *Al-mi'yar al-mu'rib wa-l-jami' al-mughrib 'an fatawi 'ulama' Ifriqiya wa-l-Andalus wa-l-Maghrib*, M. Hajji (ed.) Rabat, Morocco: Wizarat al-Awqaf wa-l-Shu'un al-Islamiyah lil-Mamlakah al-Maghribiyah, 1981–1983. See Powers, *Law, society, and culture*, 4–6.
29. On Salim's case, see Powers, *Law, society, and culture*, ch. 1.
30. On this dispute, see Powers, *Law, society, and culture*, ch. 3.
31. Powers, *Law, society, and culture*, 140.
32. Judith Scheele, 'Rightful measures: irrigation, land, and the shari'ah in the Algerian Touat', in P. Dresch and H. Skoda (eds), *Legalism: anthropology and history*, Oxford University Press, 2012.
33. In general, see Michael Kemper, 'Communal agreements (*ittifāqāt*) and '*ādāt*-books from Daghestani villages and confederacies (18th–19th centuries)', *Der Islam: Zeitschrift für Geschichte und Kultur des islamischen Orients* 81: 115–49, 2004. For further background, see Moshe Gammer, *Muslim resistance to the tsar: Shamil and the conquest of Chechnia and Daghestan*, London: Cass, 1994.

34. Kemper, 'Communal agreements', 121.
35. Kemper, 'Communal agreements', 127–28.
36. Kemper, 'Communal agreements', 132.
37. For these events, see Gammer, *Muslim resistance*.
38. Kemper, '*Adat* against *shari'a*: Russian approaches toward Daghestani "customary law" in the 19th century', *Ab Imperio* 3: 147–72, 2005.
39. Kemper, 'Communal agreements', 144–45.

9. IMPERIAL LAW AND DIVINE JUSTICE IN MEDIEVAL CHINA

1. Paul R. Katz, *Divine justice: religion and the development of Chinese legal culture*, London: Routledge, 2009, ch. 1.
2. Donald Harper, 'Resurrection in Warring States popular religion', *Taoist Resources* 5, no. 2: 13–28, 1994.
3. Anna Seidel, 'Traces of Han religion in funerary texts found in tombs', in Akizuki Kanei (ed.) *Dōkyō to shūkyō bunka*, Tokyo: Hirakawa, 1987.
4. On local legal practices, see Valerie Hansen, *Negotiating daily life in traditional China: how ordinary people used contracts, 600–1400*, New Haven, CT: Yale University Press, 1995.
5. Hansen, *Negotiating daily life*, ch. 2.
6. On the Sui and the Tang, see Patricia Buckley Ebrey, *Cambridge illustrated history of China*, 2nd ed. Cambridge University Press, 2010, ch. 5; Morris Rossabi, *A history of China*, Chichester, UK: Wiley Blackwell, 2014, chs. 5 and 6.
7. On the Tang code, see Wallace Johnson, *The T'ang Code*, 2 vols., Princeton, NJ: Princeton University Press, 1979, 1997.
8. On amnesties, see Brian E. McKnight, *The quality of mercy: amnesties and traditional Chinese justice*, Honolulu: University of Hawaii Press, 1981.
9. On local legal practices in the western areas, see Hansen, *Negotiating daily life*.
10. Hansen, *Negotiating daily life*, 42.

11. For background on the Song, see Rossabi, *History of China*, ch. 6; Brian E. McKnight and James T.C. Liu, *The enlightened judgments: Ch'ing-ming Chi. The Sung dynasty collection*, Albany: State University of New York Press, 1999; Ebrey, *Cambridge illustrated history*, ch. 6.
12. Marco Polo, *The description of the world*, trans. A. C. Moule, compiler Paul Pelliot, vol. 1, London: Routledge, 1938, 320.
13. Marco Polo, *Description of the world*, 1:329.
14. Further detail on this period can be found in Jacques Gernet, *Daily life in China on the eve of the Mongol invasion, 1250–1276*, London: Allen and Unwin, 1962.
15. On law and justice under the Song, see Brian E. McKnight, *Law and order in Sung China*, Cambridge University Press, 1992; Ebrey, *Cambridge illustrated history*, 150–54; Ichisada Miyazaki, 'The administration of justice during the Sung dynasty', in J. R. Cohen, R. R. Edwards, and F-M. C. Chen (eds), *Essays on China's legal tradition*, Princeton, NJ: Princeton University Press, 1980.
16. On local administration under the Song, see Rossabi, *History of China*, ch. 6; McKnight and Liu, *Enlightened judgments*, 'Introduction'.
17. This translation of *Qingmingji* is by Valerie Hansen. McKnight and Liu call it *The enlightened judgments*.
18. McKnight and Liu, *Enlightened judgments*, 63–68.
19. McKnight and Liu, *Enlightened judgments*, 417–18.
20. McKnight and Liu, *Enlightened judgments*, 146–47. The quotes are slightly adjusted for style.
21. McKnight and Liu, *Enlightened judgments*, 208–10.
22. See the cases in McKnight and Liu, *Enlightened judgments*.
23. McKnight and Liu, *Enlightened judgments*, 170–72.
24. McKnight and Liu, *Enlightened judgments*, 355–56.
25. McKnight and Liu, *Enlightened judgments*, 354.
26. See also the cases in R. H. Van Gulik, *T'ang-yin-pi-shih: 'parallel cases from under the pear tree'*, Leiden: Brill, 1956.
27. Miyazaki, 'Administration of justice'.
28. McKnight and Liu, *Enlightened judgments*, 152–53.

29. McKnight and Liu, *Enlightened judgments*, 453–54.
30. Hansen, *Negotiating daily life*, 103.
31. On the system of appeals, see Brian E. McKnight, 'From statute to precedent', in his *Law and the state in traditional East Asia: six studies on the sources of East Asian law*, Honolulu: University of Hawaii Press, 1987.
32. McKnight, *Law and order*, 17.
33. Miyazaki, 'Administration of justice', 69.
34. McKnight and Liu, *Enlightened judgments*, 213–15, 226–27.
35. Hansen, *Negotiating daily life*, 97; McKnight and Liu, *Enlightened judgments*, 154–55, 440–41.
36. McKnight and Liu, *Enlightened judgments*, 154–55.
37. McKnight and Liu, *Enlightened judgments*, 432–35.
38. McKnight and Liu, *Enlightened judgments*, 180–83.
39. Katz, *Divine justice*, 47–50. And for practice under the Qing, see Philip Huang, *Civil justice in China: representation and practice in the Qing*, Stanford, CA: Stanford University Press, 1996.
40. McKnight and Liu, *Enlightened judgments*, 226–27.
41. McKnight and Liu, *Enlightened judgments*, 150.
42. On these practice, see Matthew H. Sommer, *Polyandry and wife-selling in Qing dynasty China: survival strategies and judicial interventions*, Berkeley: University of California Press, 2015.
43. Hansen, *Negotiating daily life*, ch. 7.
44. Katz, *Divine justice*, ch. 2.
45. On local practices of justice in this period, see Huang, *Civil justice*.
46. Sommer, *Polyandry*.

10. COURTS AND CUSTOMS IN THE EUROPEAN MIDDLE AGES

1. On continental developments, see Peter Stein, *Roman law in European history*, Cambridge University Press, 1999, ch. 4.
2. On the Holy Roman Empire, see also G. Dahm, 'On the reception of Roman and Italian law in Germany', in G. Strauss

(ed.) *Pre-Reformation Germany*, New York: Harper and Row, 1972.

3. For this paragraph, see Alan Watson, *Sources of law, legal change, and ambiguity*, Edinburgh: T&T Clark, 1985.

4. Esther Cohen, *The crossroads of justice: law and culture in late medieval France*, Leiden: Brill, 1993; Paul Hyams, 'Due process versus the maintenance of order in European law: the contribution of the *ius commune*', in P. Coss (ed.) *The moral world of the law*, Cambridge University Press, 2000, 64–65.

5. On the legal practices in Septimania, see Fredric L. Cheyette, 'Suum cuique tribuere', *French Historical Studies* 6: 287–99, 1970.

6. Howard Bloch, *Medieval French literature and law*, Berkeley: University of California Press, 1977, 8–9.

7. Michael Clanchy, 'Law and love in the Middle Ages', in J. Bossy (ed.) *Disputes and settlements: law and human relations in the West*, Cambridge University Press, 1983.

8. F. W. Maitland, *Select pleas in manorial and other seignorial courts*, vol. 1, *Reigns of Henry III and Edward I*, Selden Society, London: B. Quaritch, 1889, xxxi. This was the Assize of Clarendon of 1166.

9. On the assizes, see Anthony Musson, *Medieval law in context: the growth of legal consciousness from Magna Carta to the peasants' revolt*, Manchester University Press, 2001; Anthony Musson and Edward Powell, *Crime, law, and society in the later Middle Ages*, Manchester University Press, 2013.

10. Musson, *Medieval law*, ch. 4.

11. The literature on the manorial courts is extensive. I have relied, in particular, on Zvi Razi and Richard M. Smith, 'The origins of the English manorial court rolls as a written record: a puzzle', in Z. Razi and R. M. Smith (eds), *Medieval society and the manor court*, Oxford: Clarendon Press, 1996; Lloyd Bonfield, 'What did English villagers mean by "customary law"', in Razi and Smith, *Medieval society*; John S. Beckerman, 'Procedural innovation and institutional

change in medieval English manorial courts', *Law and History Review* 10: 197–253, 1992.

12. Beckerman, 'Procedural innovation', 221.

13. Paul Hyams, 'What did Edwardian villagers understand by "law"?', in Razi and Smith, *Medieval society*, 98ff.

14. On criminal processes, see H. R. T. Summerson, 'The structure of law enforcement in thirteenth century England', *American Journal of Legal History* 23: 313–27, 1979; Hyams, 'What did Edwardian villagers understand?'.

15. This is Chapter 38. See Beckerman, 'Procedural innovation', 227.

16. On these changes, see Beckerman, 'Procedural innovation'.

17. On the later period, see Christopher Harrison, 'Manor courts and the governance of Tudor England', in Christopher Brooks and Michael Lobban (eds), *Communities and courts in Britain, 1150–1900*, London: Hambledon Press, 1997.

18. On the church courts, see Charles Sherman, 'A brief history of medieval Roman canon law in England', *University of Pennsylvania Law Review* 68: 223–58, 1920; David Millon, 'Ecclesiastical jurisdiction in medieval England', *University of Illinois Law Review* 1984, 621–38; Hyams, 'What did Edwardian villagers understand?'. Church courts might also hear serious criminal cases involving, for example, violence against church property, an assault on a prioress, or the abduction of a nun, along with the many disputes that arose over ownership of church property.

19. L. R. Poos, 'Sex, lies and the church courts of pre-Reformation England', *Journal of Interdisciplinary History* 25: 585–607, 1995.

20. On the borough courts, see Richard Goddard and Teresa Phipps, *Town courts and urban society in late medieval England*, Woodbridge, UK: Boydell and Brewer, 2019.

21. Sir Edward Coke, in *The fourth part of the institutes of the laws of England: concerning the jurisdiction of courts*, published in 1644, described seventy-six different courts in Britain, many of them regional, but others with specialist

jurisdictions, such as the courts of 'wards and liveries', the court of the commission of sewers, and the staple courts.

22. The case is described by Beckerman, 'Procedural innovation', 207–8.

23. Robert R. Pennington, *Stannary law: a history of the mining law of Cornwall and Devon*, Newton Abbot, UK: David and Charles, 1973.

24. On the forest courts, see Cyril Hart, *The verderers and the forest laws of Dean*, Newton Abbot, UK: David and Charles, 1971; Coke, *Fourth part of the institutes*, 229–37.

25. On the admiralty courts, see M. J. Prichard and D. E. C. Yale, *Hale and Fleetwood on admiralty jurisdiction*, London: Selden Society, 1993; Elizabeth Wells, 'Civil litigation in the High Court of Admiralty, 1585–1595', in Brooks and Lobban, *Communities and courts*.

26. He also appointed a warden for the Cinque Ports, the five port towns in Kent, who could hold his own court to hear local cases. See Prichard and Yale, *Hale and Fleetwood*, cxlvi.

27. Prichard and Yale, *Hale and Fleetwood*, ccxxxvii ff.

28. Wells, 'Civil litigation', 90–94.

29. Wells, 'Civil litigation', 92.

30. Prichard and Yale, *Hale and Fleetwood*, ccxliii–ccxlvii.

31. Wells, 'Civil litigation', 95.

32. W. A. Champion, 'Recourse to the law and the meaning of the great litigation decline, 1650–1750: some clues from the Shrewsbury local courts', in Brooks and Lobban, *Communities and courts*, 180.

II. THE PROBLEM OF JUDGEMENT:
OATHS, ORDEALS, AND EVIDENCE

1. Nathan Hill, 'The *sku-bla* rite in imperial Tibetan religion', *Cahiers d'Extrême-Asie* 24: 49–58, 2015.

2. Brandon Dotson, 'The princess and the yak: the hunt as narrative trope and historical reality in early Tibet', in B. Dotson, K. Iwao, and T. Takeuchi (eds), *Scribes, texts, and*

rituals in early Tibet and Dunhuang, Wiesbaden: Dr. Ludwig Reichert Verlag, 2013.

3. The meaning of some of these penalties is obscure, as I have discussed in 'Oaths and ordeals in Tibetan law', in D. Schuh (ed.) *Secular law and order in the Tibetan highland*, Andiast, Switzerland: International Institute for Tibetan and Buddhist Studies, 2015.

4. The literature is extensive. See, among others, Frederick Pollock and Frederic Maitland, *The history of English law before the time of Edward I*, 2nd ed. Cambridge University Press, 1898; James Thayer, *A preliminary treatise on evidence at the common law*, Boston: Little, Brown, 1898; Thomas A. Green, 'Societal concepts of criminal liability for homicide in mediaeval England', *Speculum* 4: 669–95, 1972; Harold J. Berman, 'The background of the Western legal tradition in the folklaw of the peoples of Europe', *University of Chicago Law Review* 45: 553–97, 1978; R. H. Helmholz, 'Crime, compurgation and the courts of the medieval church', *Law and History Review* 1: 1–26, 1983; R. C. van Caenegem, *Legal history: a European perspective*, London: Hambledon Press, 1991.

5. J. M. Kaye, 'The early history of murder and manslaughter, part 1', *Law Quarterly Review* 83: 365–95, 1967.

6. Helmholz, 'Crime, compurgation and the courts'; James Q. Whitman, *The origins of reasonable doubt: theological roots of the criminal trial*, New Haven, CT: Yale University Press, 2008.

7. Shelomo Dov Goitein, *A Mediterranean society: the Jewish communities of the Arab world as portrayed by the documents of the Cairo geniza*, vol. 2, Berkeley: University of California Press, 1971, 340.

8. Rudolph Peters, 'Murder in Khaybar: some thoughts on the origins of the *qasāma* procedure in Islamic law', *Islamic Law and Society* 9: 132–67, 2002.

9. Paul Dresch, 'Outlawry, exile, and banishment: reflections on community and justice', in F. Pirie and J. Scheele (eds),

Legalism: community and justice, Oxford University Press, 2014, 115–16.

10. Whitman, *Origins*, 75–76. Even members of the landowning classes embroiled in property disputes were sometimes reluctant to take an oath to confirm their claims, preferring to hire a champion to fight on their behalf in a trial by battle.

11. John M. Roberts, 'Oaths, autonomic ordeals, and power', *American Anthropologist* 67, no. 6, pt. 2: 186–212, 1965.

12. John S. Beckerman, 'Procedural innovation and institutional change in medieval English manorial courts', *Law and History Review* 10: 197–253, 1992; John W. Baldwin, 'The crisis of the ordeal: literature, law, and religion around 1200', *Journal of Medieval and Renaissance Studies* 24: 327–53, 1994.

13. Pirie, 'Oaths and ordeals in Tibetan law', 186.

14. Richard W. Larivière, *The Divyatattva of Raghunandana Bhaṭṭācārya: ordeals in classical Hindu law*, New Delhi: Manohar, 1981.

15. See my 'Oaths and ordeals in Tibetan Law'. The text is from the fourteenth century, but the processes it reflects were probably older.

16. Baldwin, 'Crisis of the ordeal', 336.

17. The literature is extensive: Robert Bartlett, *Trial by fire and water: the medieval judicial ordeal*, Oxford: Clarendon Press, 1986, ch. 2; Paul Hyams, 'Trial by ordeal: the key to proof in the early common law', in Morris S. Arnold, Thomas A. Green, Sally A. Scully, and Stephen D. White (eds), *On the laws and customs of England: essays in honor of Samuel E. Thorne*, Chapel Hill: University of North Carolina Press, 1981; Peter Brown, 'Society and the supernatural: a medieval change', *Dedalus* 104: 133–51, 1975; Baldwin, 'Crisis of the ordeal'; Dominique Barthélmy, 'Diversité dans des ordalies médiévales', *Revue historique* (T. 280), Fasc. 1 (567): 3–25, 1988; Whitman, *Origins*.

18. Bartlett, *Trial by fire and water*.

19. Aethelstan's Ordinances II, cap. 23, edited and translated by F. L. Attenborough, *The laws of the earliest English kings*, Cambridge University Press, 1922.

20. Susanna's story appears in the Deuterocanonical Book of Daniel.

21. Pirie, 'Oaths and ordeals'.

22. William Ian Miller, 'Ordeal in Iceland', *Scandinavian Studies* 60: 189–218, 1988.

23. Roberts, 'Oaths, autonomic ordeals, and power'.

24. E. E. Evans-Pritchard, *Witchcraft, oracles, and magic among the Azande*, Oxford: Clarendon Press, 1937, 309–12.

25. Miller, 'Ordeal in Iceland'.

26. Miller, 'Ordeal in Iceland', 194–98, 200–3.

27. Whitman, *Origins*, 'Introduction' (p. 3), ch. 1.

28. Whitman, *Origins*, ch. 2.

29. Whitman, *Origins*, ch. 3.

30. Robert Thomson, *The Lawcode (Datastanagirk') of Mxit'ar Goš*, Amsterdam: Rodopi, 2000, 92–99.

31. These included surgery. The objection ultimately stemmed from Jewish pollution concerns, which had made their way into Christian theology. For the same reasons, the church disapproved of jousting, tournaments, and trial by battle.

32. Whitman, *Origins*, 93.

33. Whitman, *Origins*, ch. 5.

34. Whitman, *Origins*, 139–44.

35. Whitman, *Origins*, ch. 6.

36. Martin Ingram, '"Popular" and "official" justice: punishing sexual offenders in Tudor London', in Pirie and Scheele, *Legalism: community and justice*.

37. See Sir Edward Coke's *Third institutes of the laws of England, Pleas of the Crown*, 137 (published in the 1640s). I am grateful to Mike MacNair for these references.

38. E. P. Thomson, *Whigs and hunters: the origin of the Black Act*, London: Allen Lane, 1975.

39. John H. Langbein, *The origins of adversary criminal trial*, Oxford University Press, 2005, 334–35.

40. Whitman, *Origins*, ch. 7.
41. Whitman, *Origins*, 'Conclusion'.
42. Whitman, *Origins*, ch. 4; Richard M. Fraher, 'The theoretical justification for the new criminal law of the High Middle Ages: "rei publicae interest, ne crimina remaneant impunita"', *University of Illinois Law Review*, 577–95, 1984.
43. Fraher, 'Theoretical justification', 588.
44. Paul R. Katz, *Divine justice: religion and the development of Chinese legal culture*, London: Routledge, 2009, ch. 2.
45. Michael Zimmerman, 'Only a fool becomes a king: Buddhist stances on punishment', in his *Buddhism and Violence*, Lumbini, Nepal: Lumbini International Research Institute, 2006.
46. Melvyn Goldstein, *A History of modern Tibet, 1913–1951: the demise of the lamaist state*, Berkeley: University of California Press, 1989, 199–212.
47. Donald R. Davis, Jr, *The spirit of Hindu law*, Cambridge University Press, 2010, chs. 5 and 6.
48. This is Vacaspatimiśra's *Vyavaharacintamani: a digest on Hindu legal procedure*, translated and edited by Ludo Rocher, Gent, 1956.
49. Intisar A. Rabb, '"Reasonable doubt" in Islamic law', *Yale Journal of International Law* 40: 41–94, 2015.
50. On qadis and muftis, see Brinkley Messick, 'The mufti, the text and the world: legal interpretation in Yemen', *Man* 21: 102–19, 1986; Brinkley Messick, *The calligraphic state: textual domination and history in a Muslim society*, Berkeley: University of California Press, 1993.
51. Rabb, '"Reasonable doubt" in Islamic law', 79–80.
52. Rabb, '"Reasonable doubt" in Islamic law', 84–85.
53. Baber Johansen, 'Vom Wort-zum Indizienbeweis: die Anermerkung der richterlichen Folter in islamischen Rechtsdoktrinen des 13. und 14. Jahrhunderts', *Ius commune* 28: 1–46, 2001.
54. David Powers, *Law, society and culture in the Maghrib, 1300–1500*, Cambridge University Press, 2002.

12. FROM KINGS TO EMPIRES:
THE RISE OF EUROPE AND AMERICA

1. C. A. Bayly, *Imperial meridian: the British Empire and the world, 1780–1830*, London: Longman, 1989, 21.
2. James Q. Whitman, 'The world historical significance of European legal history: an interim report', in H. Pihlajamäki, M. D. Dubber, and M. Godfrey (eds), *The Oxford handbook of European legal history*, Oxford University Press, 2018.
3. On the Holy Roman Empire, see also G. Dahm, 'On the reception of Roman and Italian law in Germany', in G. Strauss (ed.) *Pre-Reformation Germany*, New York: Harper and Row, 1972.
4. Maximillian was only proclaimed Holy Roman Emperor in 1507, but he had already succeeded his father as 'King of the Romans'.
5. In particular, the Lutheran Philip Melanchthon. Peter Stein, *Roman law in European history*, Cambridge University Press, 1999, 92.
6. See Mark Godfrey, *Civil justice in renaissance Scotland: the origins of a central court*, Leiden: Brill, 2009.
7. On English law in this period, see J. H. Baker, *An introduction to English legal history*, London: Butterworths, 1971; Christopher W. Brooks, *Law, politics and society in early modern England*, Cambridge University Press, 2009.
8. In the *Earl of Oxford's Case* (1615), 1 Rep Ch 1, at 6, Lord Ellesmere declared that his duty was 'to correct men's consciences for frauds, breaches of trusts, wrongs, and oppressions of what nature soever they be, and to soften and mollify the extremity of the Law'.
9. For contrasting views on English jurisprudence in this period, see J. G. A. Pocock, *The ancient constitution and the feudal law: a study of English historical thought in the seventeenth century*, Cambridge University Press, 1987; J. W. Tubbs, *The common law mind: medieval and early modern*

conceptions, Baltimore: Johns Hopkins University Press, 2000.

10. Littleton's *Expliciunt tenores nouelli* was published in London in around 1482.

11. This was *De Laudibus Legum Angliae*.

12. Brooks, *Law, politics and society*, 426.

13. Brooks, *Law, politics and society*, 432.

14. David Lemmings (ed.) *The British and their laws in the eighteenth century*, Woodbridge, UK: Boydell Press, 2005, 7–8; Richard J. Ross, 'The commoning of the common law: the Renaissance debate over printing English law, 1520–1640', *University of Pennsylvania Law Review* 146: 323–461, 1998.

15. On these various courts and litigation, see, among others, the papers in Christopher Brooks and Michael Lobban (eds), *Communities and courts in Britain, 1150–1900*, London: Hambledon Press, 1997; Brooks, *Law, politics and society*, 428. Scholars are still debating the reasons for the rise in litigation and its subsequent decline.

16. Baker, *Introduction*, 207–12.

17. James S. Hart Jr, *The rule of law, 1603–1660*, Harlow, UK: Pearson Longman, 2003, 9.

18. See his *Laws of Ecclesiastic Polity*, bk. VIII, ii, 12. On Hooker and the constitutional crisis, see Alan Cromartie, *The constitutionalist revolution: an essay on the history of England, 1450–1642*, Cambridge University Press, 2006.

19. On these debates, see Tubbs, *Common law mind*, ch. 6.

20. On Coke and his confrontation with James, see David Chan Smith, *Sir Edward Coke and the reformation of the laws: religion, politics and jurisprudence, 1578–1616*, Cambridge University Press, 2014; Tubbs, *Common law mind*, ch. 7.

21. This was the *Case of Prohibitions*, a debate about jurisdiction, rather than a legal case. Coke embellished his account of the speeches, claiming he had said that the king could not give legal judgements as he did not have the necessary 'artificial reason', that is, the ability to undertake legal reasoning. But, even if he did not make this famous statement, it

probably represents his thinking at the time. See Roland G. Usher, 'James I and Sir Edward Coke', *English Historical Review* 18: 664–75, 1903.

22. Smith, *Sir Edward Coke*, 11–16.

23. This phrase is from the preface to his reports, published later, but framing metaphors were common at the time. See Daniel J. Hulsebosch, 'The ancient constitution and the expanding empire: Sir Edward Coke's British jurisprudence', *Law and History Review* 21: 439–82, 2003, at p. 445.

24. The law of marque was a principle of medieval maritime law whereby a victim of piracy or an unpaid debt could obtain a letter from the king authorizing them to seek retribution on the compatriots of the perpetrators. See Kathryn L. Reyerson, 'Commercial law and merchant disputes: Jacques Coeur and the law of marque', *Medieval Encounters* 9: 244–55, 2003.

25. Mike Macnair, 'Institutional taxonomy, Roman forms and English lawyers in the 17th and 18th centuries', in Pierre Bonin, Nader Hakim, Fara Nasti, and Aldo Schiavone (eds), *Pensiero giuridico occidentale e giuristi Romani: eredita e genealogie*, Turin, Italy: G. Giappichelli Editore, 2019.

26. See, for example, Thomas Wood, *An institute of the laws of England, or, the laws of England in their natural order, according to common use*, published in 1720, discussed by S. F. C. Milsom in 'The Nature of Blackstone's Achievement', *Oxford Journal of Legal Studies* 1: 1–12, 1981.

27. Sir Matthew Hale, *Analysis of the civil part of the law*, written in the mid-seventeenth century and probably based on his lectures, although not published until 1713.

28. On these debates, see Hulsebosch, 'Ancient constitution', 447–49.

29. This was known as *Calvin's Case* and the judges included Sir Edward Coke.

30. On law in colonial America, see William M. Offutt, 'The Atlantic rules: the legalistic turn in colonial British America', in E. Mancke and C. Shammas (eds), *The creation of the British Atlantic world*, Baltimore: Johns Hopkins University

Press, 2005; William E. Nelson, *The common law in colonial America*, 4 vols., New York: Oxford University Press, 2008–2018.

31. On the early courts and their procedures, see also Warren Billings, 'The transfer of English law to Virginia, 1606–50', in K. R. Andrews, N. P. Canny, and P. E. H. Hair (eds), *The westward enterprise: English activities in Ireland, the Atlantic, and America, 1480–1650*, Liverpool University Press, 1978, 215–44; David Konig, '"Dale's Laws" and the non-common law origins of criminal justice in Virginia', *American Journal of Legal History* 26: 354–75, 1982; John M. Murrin, 'The legal transformation: the bench and bar of eighteenth-century Massachusetts', in S. N. Katz (ed.) *Colonial America: essays in politics and social development*, New York: Knopf, 1983; Mary Sarah Bilder, 'The lost lawyers: early American legal literates and transatlantic legal culture', *Yale Journal of Law and the Humanities* 11: 47–177, 1999; James A. Henretta, 'Magistrates, common law lawyers, legislators: the three legal systems of British America', in M. Grossberg and C. Tomlins (eds), *The Cambridge history of law in America*, vol. 1, *Early America (1580–1815)*, Cambridge University Press, 2008.

32. David Konig, *Law and society in Puritan Massachusetts: Essex County, 1629–1692*, Chapel Hill: University of North Carolina Press, 1979, 57–88.

33. Thomas Hobbes, *Leviathan or the matter, forme and power of a common-wealth ecclesiasticall and civil*, published in 1651.

34. Alan Cromartie, *Sir Matthew Hale, 1609–1676: law, religion and natural philosophy*, Cambridge University Press, 1995, ch. 5. He even attributes the failure of the Republic to the survival of the common law (p. 58).

35. J. H. Baker, 'The law merchant and the common law before 1700', *Cambridge Law Journal* 38: 295–322, 1979; J. H. Baker, 'The common lawyers and the Chancery', *The Irish Jurist* 4: 368–92, 1969; J. H. Baker, *The legal profession*

and the common law: historical essays, London: Hambledon Press, 1986; Baker, *Introduction*, 108.

36. Edith G. Henderson, *Foundations of English administrative
law: certiorari and mandamus in the seventeenth century*,
Cambridge, MA: Harvard University Press, 1963, 39.

37. Lemmings, *The British and their laws*, 1–2.

38. David Lemmings, *Law and government in England during
the long eighteenth century: from consent to command*,
Basingstoke, UK: Palgrave Macmillan, 2011, 15–16.

39. This made litigation much more expensive and may have led
to its decline in the seventeenth and eighteenth centuries. See
W. A. Champion, 'Recourse to the law and the meaning of
the great litigation decline, 1650–1750: some clues from the
Shrewsbury local courts', in Brooks and Lobban, *Communities and courts*, 186.

40. On these developments, see Hulsebosch, 'Ancient constitution'; Offutt, 'Atlantic rules'; Nelson, *The common law in
colonial America*, vols. 2 and 3; and Mary Sarah Bilder,
*The transatlantic constitution: colonial legal culture and the
empire*, Cambridge, MA: Harvard University Press, 2004,
'Introduction' and ch. 2.

41. Bilder, *Transatlantic constitution*, 15.

42. Offutt, 'Atlantic rules', 171.

43. Offutt, 'Atlantic rules', 168–69.

44. On Blackstone in America, see Albert W. Alschuler, 'Rediscovering Blackstone', *University of Pennsylvania Law Review* 145: 1–55, 1996, at pp. 4–19.

45. Alschuler, 'Rediscovering Blackstone', 6–7. In the early nineteenth century, a young Abraham Lincoln discovered a copy
by chance in a barrel of goods he had bought from a traveller; he claimed later that it had inspired his political career.

46. On this period, see Lemmings, 'Introduction', in *The British and their laws*; his *Law and government in England*;
and the papers in Lee Davison, T. Hitchcock, T. Keim, and
R. Shoemaker (eds), *Stilling the grumbling hive: the response
to social and economic problems in England, 1689–1750*,
London: St. Martin's Press, 1992.

47. Michael Lobban, 'Custom, nature, and judges: high law and low law in England and the empire', in Lemmings, *The British and their laws*, 52–57.
48. On these developments, see Nelson, *The common law in colonial America*, vol. 4.
49. Alschuler, 'Rediscovering Blackstone', 15–16.
50. Bilder, *Transatlantic constitution*, ch. 9.
51. Andrew P. Morriss, 'Codification and right answers', *Chicago-Kent Law Review* 74: 355–92, 1999, at p. 355.
52. Stein, *Roman law in European history*, 290.
53. Henry E. Strakosch, *State absolutism and the rule of law: the struggle for the codification of civil law in Austria, 1753–1811*, Sydney University Press, 1967.
54. On Napoleon and his code, see Jean-Louis Halpérin, *L'impossible Code Civil*, Paris: Presses universitaires de France, 1992; Donald R. Kelley, 'What pleases the prince: Justinian, Napoleon, and the lawyers', *History of Political Thought* 23: 288–302, 2002.
55. Kelley, 'What pleases the prince', 289.

13. COLONIALISM: EXPORTING THE LAW

1. Anthony Pagden, *Lords of all the world: ideologies of empire in Spain, Britain, and France, 1500–1800*, New Haven, CT: Yale University Press, 2005, 46ff.
2. Peter Stein, *Roman law in European history*, Cambridge University Press, 1999, 94–95. Vitoria also rejected the argument that the Spanish territories were *res nullius*, unoccupied. Even if their inhabitants were pagan, he argued, they had rights under natural law.
3. On Spanish law in South America, see Sonya Lipsett-Rivera, 'Law', in D. Carrasco (ed.) *The Oxford encyclopedia of Mesoamerican cultures*, Oxford University Press, 2001; C. H. Haring, *The Spanish Empire in America*, New York: Oxford University Press, 1947; Ana Belem Fernández Castro, 'A transnational empire built on law: the case of the commercial jurisprudence of the House of Trade of Seville

(1583–1598)', in T. Duve (ed.) *Entanglements in legal history: conceptual approaches*, Frankfurt: Max Planck Institute for European Legal History, 2014.

4. On these debates, see Pagden, *Lords of all the world*, 64, and his 'Law, colonization, legitimation, and the European background', in M. Grossberg and C. Tomlins (eds), *The Cambridge history of law in America*, vol. 1, *Early America (1580–1815)*, Cambridge University Press, 2008.

5. Daniel J. Hulsebosch, 'The ancient constitution and the expanding empire: Sir Edward Coke's British jurisprudence', *Law and History Review* 21: 439–82, 2003, at pp. 461–62.

6. On North America, see Stuart Banner, *How the Indians lost their land*, Cambridge, MA: Harvard University Press, 2005, ch. 1.

7. Emer de Vattel, *Le droit des gens, ou, principe de la loi naturelle, appliqués à la conduite et aux affaires des nations et des souverains*, London [Neuchâtel], 1758, bk. 1, ch. 3, §81. See Pagden, *Lords of all the world*, 78–79.

8. Pagden, *Lords of all the world*, 5.

9. Bk. IX. See Peter Fitzpatrick, *The mythology of modern law*, London: Routledge, 1992, 72.

10. Jeremiah Dummer, *A defence of New England charters*, 1721, 20–21, cited in Pagden, *Lords of all the world*, 87.

11. Banner, *How the Indians lost their land*, 150–51.

12. On the British in India, see C. A. Bayly, *Imperial meridian: the British Empire and the world, 1780–1830*, London: Longman, 1989; H. V. Bowen, 'British India, 1765–1813: the metropolitan context', in P. J. Marshall and A. Low (eds), *The Oxford history of the British Empire*, vol. 2, Oxford University Press, 1998; Rajat Kanta Ray, 'Indian society and the establishment of British supremacy, 1765–1818', in Marshall and Low, *Oxford history of the British Empire*, 512–15.

13. The East India Company Act of 1773. See Bowen, 'British India', 439–40.

14. Ray, 'Indian society', 521.

15. Bowen, 'British India', 547.

16. On these developments, see Bayly, *Imperial meridian*, chs. 3 and 4.
17. Ray, 'Indian society', 525. For further background, see Bernard S. Cohn, 'Law and the colonial state in India', in J. Starr and J. F. Collier (eds), *History and power in the study of law: new directions in legal anthropology*, Ithaca, NY: Cornell University Press, 1989, 137–39.
18. Bayly, *Imperial meridian*, 109.
19. Bayly, *Imperial meridian*, 154.
20. Pagden, *Lords of all the world*, 4.
21. Pagden, *Lords of all the world*, 61, 189.
22. Pagden, *Lords of all the world*, 6.
23. Ranajit Guha, *A rule of property for India*, Paris: Mouton, 1963, 13.
24. On the activities of Hastings and his successors, see Cohn, 'Law and the colonial state'; J. Duncan M. Derrett, *Religion, law and the state in India*, London: Faber and Faber, 1968.
25. Cohn, 'Law and the colonial state', 135.
26. It was named *The digest of Hindu law on contracts and succession*, Calcutta, 1798.
27. D. A. Washbrook, 'Law, state and agrarian society in colonial India', *Modern Asian Studies* 15: 649–721, 1981.
28. On these tensions, see Ray, 'Indian society', 525; Radhika Singha, *A despotism of law: crime and justice in early colonial India*, Delhi: Oxford University Press, 1998.
29. On the later development of law in India, see Washbrook, 'Law, state and agrarian society'; Marc Galanter, 'The displacement of traditional law in modern India', in his *Law and society in modern India*, Delhi: Oxford University Press, 1989.
30. The Indian Penal Code, 1860, and the Code of Criminal Procedure, 1861. On Macaulay's legal and educational reforms, see Singha, *Despotism of law*.
31. Elizabeth Kolsky, 'The colonial rule of law and the legal regime of exception: frontier "fanaticism" and state violence in British India', *American Historical Review* 120: 1218–46, 2015.

32. See John Stuart Mill, *Considerations on representative government*, London: Parker, Son, and Bourne, 1861.
33. On these developments, see C. A. Bayly, *The birth of the modern world, 1780–1914: global connections and comparisons*, Oxford: Blackwell, 2004; Matthew Craven, 'Colonialism and domination', in B. Fassbender and A. Peters (eds), *The Oxford handbook of the history of international law*, Oxford University Press, 2012.
34. On the French in Algeria, see Wael B. Hallaq, *Sharī'a: theory, practice, transformations*, Cambridge University Press, 2009, ch. 15, 432–38.
35. On French colonialism, see Alice Conklin, *A mission to civilize: the republican idea of empire in France and West Africa, 1895–1930*, Stanford, CA: Stanford University Press, 1997.
36. Conklin, *Mission to civilize*, 51.
37. Conklin, *Mission to civilize*, 73.
38. Conklin, *Mission to civilize*, 90–93.
39. On British law and colonialism in Africa, see Martin Chanock, *Law, custom and social order: the colonial experience in Malawi and Zambia*, Cambridge University Press, 1985, ch. 4. This is largely based on material from Malawi and Zambia, although it draws on reports from other parts of British colonial Africa.
40. Chanock, *Law, custom and social order*, 72–78, 106–8.
41. O. Adewoye, *The judicial system in Southern Nigeria, 1854–1954: law and justice in a dependency*, London: Longman, 1977; Chanock, *Law, custom and social order*, 58.
42. Eugene Cotran, 'African conference on local courts and customary law', *Journal of Local Administration Overseas* 4: 128–33, 1965.
43. On Indonesia, see M. B. Hooker, *Adat law in modern Indonesia*, Kuala Lumpur: Oxford University Press, 1978; Daniel S. Lev, 'Colonial law and the genesis of the Indonesian state', *Indonesia* 40: 57–74, 1985.
44. Ray, 'Indian society', 508.
45. Ray, 'Indian society', 526–28.

14. IN THE SHADOW OF THE STATE: ISLAMIC LAW IN THE MODERN WORLD

1. Abdullahi Ahmed An-Naʻim, *Islam and the secular state: negotiating the future of shariʻa*, Cambridge, MA: Harvard University Press, 2008; Wael B. Hallaq, *The impossible state: Islam, politics, and modernity's moral predicament*, New York: Columbia University Press, 2013.
2. On the Ottoman Empire, see Marshall G.S. Hodgson, *The venture of Islam: conscience and history in a world civilization*, vol. 3, Chicago: University of Chicago Press, 1974, bk. 5, ch. 3; Wael B. Hallaq, *An introduction to Islamic law*, Cambridge University Press, 2009, ch. 6.
3. On the *Mecelle*, see Brinkley Messick, *The calligraphic state: textual domination and history in a Muslim society*, Berkeley: University of California Press, 1993, ch. 3, 54–56.
4. On Egypt, see Hodgson, *Venture of Islam*, bk. 6, ch. 1.
5. On Iran, see Hodgson, *Venture of Islam*, bk. 5, ch. 1, and bk. 6, ch. 5; Hallaq, *Introduction*, 106–9, 152.
6. On the Wahhabis, see Hodgson, *Venture of Islam*, vol. 3, bk. 5, ch. 4; Hallaq, *Introduction*, ch. 9.
7. On the reformers, see Wael B. Hallaq, *Sharīʻa: theory, practice, transformations*, Cambridge University Press, 2009; Nathan J. Brown and Mara Revkin, 'Islamic law and constitutions', in A. M. Emon and R. Ahmed (eds), *The Oxford handbook of Islamic law*, Oxford University Press, 2018, 790.
8. Messick, *Calligraphic state*, 63–64.
9. On Sanhuri and his influence, see Nabil Saleh, 'Civil codes of Arab countries: the Sanhuri codes', *Arab Law Quarterly* 8: 161–67, 1993.
10. On Iran, see Hodgson, *Venture of Islam*, bk. 5, ch. 1, and bk. 6, ch. 5; Hallaq, *Introduction*, 106–9, 152.
11. On Saudi Arabia, see Frank E. Vogel, *Islamic law and legal system: studies of Saudi Arabia*, Leiden: Brill, 2000.
12. On Yemen, see Messick, *Calligraphic state*, ch. 3.

13. Hallaq, *Sharīʿa*, ch. 15.
14. Mark Fathi Massoud, 'How an Islamic state rejected Islamic law', *American Journal of Comparative Law* 68: 579–602, 2018; Brown and Revkin, 'Islamic law and constitutions', 781–83.
15. On Algeria, see Hallaq, *Sharīʿa*, ch. 15.
16. Messick, *Calligraphic state*, ch. 3.
17. Joseph Schacht, 'Problems of modern Islamic legislation', *Studia Islamica* 12: 99–129, 1960; Joseph Schacht, *An introduction to Islamic law*, Oxford: Clarendon Press, 1964, ch. 15.
18. An-Na'im, *Islam and the secular state*; Hallaq, *Impossible state*.
19. Haider Ala Hamoudi, 'The death of Islamic law', *Georgia Journal of International and Comparative Law* 38: 293–338, 2010.
20. On the Muslim Brotherhood, see Hallaq, *Introduction*, 143–47; Saba Mahmood, *Politics of piety: the Islamic revival and the feminist subject*, Princeton, NJ: Princeton University Press, 2005, 62–64.
21. Baber Johansen, 'The constitution and the principles of Islamic normativity against the rules of fiqh: a judgment of the Supreme Constitutional Court of Egypt', in M. K. Masud, R. Peters, and D. S. Powers (eds), *Dispensing justice in Islam: qadis and their judgements*, Leiden: Brill, 2006.
22. Hallaq, *Impossible state*, 172.
23. On Iran, see Hallaq, *Introduction*, ch. 9.
24. On Islamic law and finance, see Anver M. Emon, 'Islamic law and finance', in Emon and Ahmed, *Oxford handbook of Islamic law*.
25. Vogel, *Islamic law and legal system*, 306ff.
26. Mara Revkin, 'Does the Islamic state have a "social contract"? Evidence from Iraq and Syria', Working paper no. 9, Program on Governance and Local Development, University of Gothenburg, 2016.
27. Hamoudi, 'Death of Islamic law', 318.

28. Jeffrey Adam Sachs, 'Seeing like an Islamic state: shari'a and political power in Sudan', *Law and Society Review* 52: 630–51, 2018.
29. The literature on shari'a courts is extensive. See the references in John R. Bowen, 'Anthropology and Islamic law', in Emon and Ahmed, *Oxford handbook of Islamic law*; Morgan Clarke, 'The judge as tragic hero: judicial ethics in Lebanon's shari'a courts', *American Ethnologist* 39: 106–21, n. 6, 2012.
30. On the Lebanese shari'a courts, see Clarke, 'Judge as tragic hero'.
31. Clarke, 'Judge as tragic hero', 112.
32. John A. Chesworth and Franz Kogelmann (eds), *Shari'a in Africa today: reactions and responses*, Leiden: Brill, 2013. On Kenya, see Susan F. Hirsch, *Pronouncing and persevering: gender and the discourses of disputing in an African Islamic court*, Chicago: University of Chicago Press, 1998. On Zanzibar, see Erin E. Stiles, *An Islamic court in context: an ethnographic study of judicial reasoning*, London: Palgrave Macmillan, 2009.
33. Katherine Lemons, *Divorcing traditions: Islamic marriage law and the making of Indian secularism*, Ithaca, NY: Cornell University Press, 2019.
34. John R. Bowen, *On British Islam: religion, law, and everyday practice in shari'a councils*, Princeton, NJ: Princeton University Press, 2018.
35. Arzoo Osanloo, *The politics of women's rights in Iran*, Princeton, NJ: Princeton University Press, 2009, ch. 4.
36. Jakob Skovgaard-Petersen, *Defining Islam for the Egyptian state: muftis and fatwas of the Dār al-Iftā*, Leiden: Brill, 1997.
37. On the marjas, see Morgan Clarke, 'Neo-calligraphy: religious authority and media technology in contemporary Shiite Islam', *Comparative Studies in Society and History* 52: 351–83, 2010.
38. On the mufti in Yemen, see Messick, *Calligraphic state*, ch. 7; 'The mufti, the text, and the world: legal interpretation

in Yemen', *Man* 21: 102–19, 1986; and 'Media muftis: radio fatwas in Yemen', in M. K. Masud, B. Messick, and D. S. Powers (eds), *Islamic legal interpretation: muftis and their fatwas*, Cambridge, MA: Harvard University Press, 1996.

39. On the Cairo movement, see Mahmood, *Politics of piety*.

15. TURNING THEIR BACKS ON THE STATE: TRIBES, VILLAGES, NETWORKS, AND GANGS

1. These details are based on my own ethnographic fieldwork in the region between 2003 and 2007. See my 'Legal dramas on the Amdo grasslands: abolition, transformation or survival?', in K. Buffetrille (ed.) *Revisiting rituals in a changing Tibetan world*, Leiden: Brill, 2012; 'Rules, proverbs, and persuasion: legalism and rhetoric in Tibet', in P. Dresch and J. Scheele (eds), *Legalism: rules and categories*, Oxford University Press, 2015; 'The limits of the state: coercion and consent in Chinese Tibet', *Journal of Asian Studies* 72: 69–89, 2013. 'Tribe' is a useful, if somewhat controversial, term for the pastoralists' social groups.

2. Robert B. Ekvall, 'The nomadic pattern of living among the Tibetans as preparation for war', *American Anthropologist* 63: 1250–63, 1961.

3. Robert Ekvall, 'Peace and war among the Tibetan nomads', *American Anthropologist* 66: 1119–48, 1964; Robert Ekvall, *Fields on the hoof*, Prospect Heights, IL: Waveland, 1968.

4. Fernanda Pirie, 'The making of Tibetan law: the *Khrims gnyis lta ba'i me long*', in J. Bischoff, P. Maurer, and C. Ramble (eds), *On a day of a month of the fire bird year*, Lumbini, Nepal: Lumbini International Research Institute, 2020.

5. P. K. Kozloff, 'Through eastern Tibet and Kam', *Geographical Journal* 31: 522–34, 1908.

6. Paul Dresch, *The rules of Barat: tribal documents from Yemen*, Sanaa, Yemen: Centre Français de d'Archéologie et de Sciences Sociales, 2006.

7. On the Berbers, see Judith Scheele, 'A taste for law: rule-making in Kabylia (Algeria)', *Comparative Studies in Society and History* 50: 895–919, 2008; Judith Scheele, 'Community as an achievement: Kabyle customary law and beyond', in F. Pirie and J. Scheele (eds), *Legalism: community and justice*, Oxford University Press, 2014.

8. Ruth Behar, *The presence of the past in a Spanish village: Santa María del Monte*, Princeton, NJ: Princeton University Press, 1986.

9. Patrick Lantschner, 'Justice contested and affirmed: jurisdiction and conflict in late medieval Italian cities', in Pirie and Scheele, *Legalism: community and justice*.

10. John Sabapathy, 'Regulating community and society at the Sorbonne in the late thirteenth century', in Pirie and Scheele, *Legalism: community and justice*.

11. Alan Watson, *Sources of law, legal change, and ambiguity*, Edinburgh: T&T Clark, 1985, 31–39.

12. I conducted ethnographic fieldwork in Ladakh over eighteen months from 1999. A road did not reach the village until 2012. See my *Peace and conflict in Ladakh: the construction of a fragile web of order*, Leiden: Brill, 2007.

13. For other examples, see James C. Scott, *The art of not being governed: an anarchist history of upland Southeast Asia*, New Haven, CT: Yale University Press, 2009.

14. Sally Falk Moore, 'Law and social change: the semi-autonomous social field as an appropriate subject of study', *Law and Society Review* 7: 719–46, 1973.

15. Lisa Bernstein, 'Opting out of the legal system: extralegal contractual relations in the diamond industry', *Journal of Legal Studies* 21: 115–57, 1992. The author, somewhat bizarrely, does not describe her sources, but does refer to an interview conducted in 1989.

16. On the mafia, see Diego Gambetta, *The Sicilian mafia: the business of private protection*, Cambridge, MA: Harvard University Press, 1993; Letizia Paoli, *Mafia brotherhoods: organized crime, Italian style*, New York: Oxford University Press, 2003.

---

17. Gambetta, *Sicilian mafia*, 118–26; Paoli, *Mafia brotherhoods*, ch. 3.
18. Paoli, *Mafia brotherhoods*, 112.
19. Diego Gambetta, *Codes of the underworld: how criminals communicate*, Princeton, NJ: Princeton University Press, 2009.
20. Paoli, *Mafia brotherhoods*, 136–40.

16. BEYOND THE STATE: INTERNATIONAL LAWS

1. Avner Greif, 'Reputation and coalitions in medieval trade: evidence on the Maghribi traders', *Journal of Economic History* 49: 857–82, 1989.
2. M. M. Postan, *Medieval trade and finance*, Cambridge University Press, 1973; Robert S. Lopez and Irving W. Raymond, *Medieval trade in the Mediterranean world: illustrative documents*, London: Geoffrey Cumberlege, 1955.
3. Rosser H. Brockman, 'Commercial contract law in late nineteenth-century Taiwan', in Jeremy Alan Cohen, R. Randle Edwards, and Fu-Mei Chang Chen (eds), *Essays on China's legal tradition*, Princeton, NJ: Princeton University Press, 1980.
4. Gordon Bannerman and Anthony Howe (eds), *Battles over free trade*, vol. 2, *The consolidation of free trade, 1847–1878*, London: Routledge, 2008, 73ff.
5. On these different agreements, see Craig N. Murphy, *International organization and industrial change: global governance since 1850*, Cambridge: Polity, 1994.
6. See the web pages of the International Telecommunications Union, www.itu.int.
7. See its website, www.antislavery.org.
8. Markku Ruotuola, 'Of the working man: labour liberals and the creation of the ILO', *Labour History Review* 67: 29–47, 2002.
9. Martii Koskenniemi, *The gentle civilizer of nations: the rise and fall of international law, 1870–1960*, Cambridge University Press, 2001.

10. Even though the US president from 1913 to 1921, Woodrow Wilson, had played a leading role in establishing the League of Nations, the United States never joined, although it did send delegates to important meetings.

11. Albert Roper, 'The organization and program of the international commission for air navigation (C.I.N.A.)', *Journal of Air Law and Commerce* 3: 167–78, 1932.

12. Lena Peters, 'UNIDROIT', in the *Max Planck Encyclopedia of International Law*, 2017, https://opil.ouplaw.com /view/10.1093/law:epil/9780199231690/law-97801992 31690-e536.

13. See its website, www.unidroit.org.

14. Jean S. Pictet, 'The new Geneva Conventions for the Protection of War Victims', *American Journal of International Law* 45: 462–75, 1951.

15. On Germany's attempts to justify its war of aggression, see Jacques Schuhmacher, 'The war criminals investigate,' DPhil. diss., University of Oxford, 2017.

16. Martii Koskenniemi, 'What is international law for?' in Malcom Evans (ed.) *International law*, Oxford University Press, 2003.

17. Samuel Moyn, *The last utopia: human rights in history*, Cambridge, MA: Harvard University Press, 2001, ch. 5.

18. The acronym comes from 'Hague Conference' and 'Conférence de La Haye'. See its website, www.hcch.net.

19. See its website, www.cites.org.

20. For an overview, see David Zaring, 'Finding legal principle in global financial regulation', *Virginia Journal of International Law* 52: 683–722, 2012.

21. Joost Pauwelyn, Ramses A. Wessel, and Jan Wouters, 'An introduction to informal international lawmaking', in *Informal international lawmaking*, Oxford University Press, 2012.

22. Terence C. Halliday and Gregory Shaffer, *Transnational legal orders*, Cambridge University Press, 2015; Susan Block-Lieb and Terence C. Halliday, *Global lawmakers: international*

organizations in the crafting of world markets, Cambridge University Press, 2017.

23. Peters, 'UNIDROIT'. The HCCH website publishes a 2016 document in which it lists all the conventions and related instruments drawn up by HCCH, UNIDROIT, and UNCI-TRAL, effectively recognizing that they are pursuing similar aims.

24. See 'The 1995 UNIDROIT Convention', UNESCO, www .unesco.org/new/en/culture/themes/illicit-trafficking-of -cultural-property/1995-unidroit-convention, and the website of the International Council of Museums, https://icom .museum.

25. Martii Koskenniemi, 'Fragmentation of international law: difficulties arising from the diversification and expansion of international law, a report of the study group of the UN's International law commission', 2006. Some have doubted whether they are really law. See Zaring, 'Finding legal principle', 684: 'Both legal traditionalists and their critics tend to discount any international arrangement that is not accompanied by a treaty and a court.'

26. On the DNS, see Gianpaolo Maria Ruotolo, 'Fragments of fragments: the domain name system regulation. Global law or informalisation of the international legal order?', *Computer Law and Security Review* 33: 159–70, 2017.

27. David Lindsay, *ICANN and international domain law*, Oxford: Hart, 2007.

28. Ruotolo, 'Fragments of fragments', 161.

29. Roxana Radu, *Negotiating Internet governance*, Oxford University Press, 2019, ch. 6.

30. Radu, *Negotiating Internet governance*, ch. 7.

31. Franck Latty, *La lex sportiva: recherche sur le droit transnational*, Leiden: Brill, 2007.

32. The Lausanne Declaration on Doping in Sport, issued on February 4, 1999.

33. See its website, www.tas-cas.org.

34. Halliday and Shaffer, *Transnational legal orders*, 30.

35. Michael Hardt and Antonio Negri, *Empire*, Cambridge, MA: Harvard University Press, 2000.

36. Moyn, *Last utopia*.

37. Moyn, *Last utopia*; Martii Koskenniemi, 'Expanding histories of international law', *American Journal of Legal History* 56: 104–12, at p. 106. And see the web pages of the Office of the UN High Commissioner for Human Rights, www.ohchr.org/EN/pages/home.aspx.

38. Tobias Kelly, 'Prosecuting human rights violations: universal jurisdiction and the crime of torture', in M. Goodale (ed.) *Human rights at the crossroads*, Oxford University Press, 2013. Section 134(1) of the act provides that 'a public official or person acting in an official capacity, whatever his nationality, commits the offence of torture if in the United Kingdom or elsewhere he intentionally inflicts severe pain or suffering on another in the performance or purported performance of his official duties'.

39. Moyn, *Last utopia*, 215–16.

40. Anthony Pagden, 'Human rights, natural rights, and Europe's imperial legacy', *Political Theory* 31: 171–99, 2003.

41. R. A. Wilson, *Human rights, culture and context: anthropological perspectives*, London: Pluto Press, 1997.

42. Interventions by Singapore and China on the difference between 'Asian values' and Western human rights sparked an immense debate among scholars, activists, and politicians. See, for example, Yash Ghai, 'Human rights and governance: the Asia debate', *Australian Year Book of International Law* 15: 1–34, 1994; Amartya Sen, 'Human rights and Asian values: what Kee Kuan Yew and Li Peng don't understand about Asia', *New Republic* 217, nos. 2–3: 33–40, 1997.

43. This was Louis Henkin in 1977. Moyn, *Last utopia*, 205–6.

44. Steven King, *Writing the lives of the English poor, 1750s–1830s*, Montreal: McGill-Queen's University Press, 2019.

45. Fernanda Pirie, 'Community, justice, and legalism: elusive concepts in Tibet', in F. Pirie and J. Scheele (eds), *Legalism: community and justice*, Oxford University Press, 2014.

46. Lauren Leve, '"Secularism is a human right": double binds of Buddhism, democracy and identity in Nepal', in M. Goodale and Sally E. Merry (eds), *The practice of human rights: tracking law between the global and the local,* Cambridge University Press, 2007.

47. Sally Engle Merry, 'Legal pluralism and transnational culture: the Ka Ho'okolokolonui Manaka Maoli tribunal, Hawai'i, 1993', in Wilson, *Human rights, culture and context.*

48. This was Charles Malik. See Kelly, 'Prosecuting human rights violations', 95–96.

49. Richard Ashby Wilson, 'Judging history: the historical record of the International Criminal Tribunal for the Former Yugoslavia', *Human Rights Quarterly* 27: 908–42, 2005.

50. See its website, www.ictj.org.

51. Lionel Nichols, *The international criminal court and the end of impunity in Kenya,* New York: Springer, 2015.

52. Rosalind Shaw, 'Linking justice with reintegration? Ex-combatants and the Sierra Leone experiment', in R. Shaw and L. Waldorf (eds), *Localizing transitional justice: interventions and priority after mass violence,* Stanford, CA: Stanford University Press, 2010.

53. These are reviewed by Martin Wählisch in his 'Normative limits of peace negotiations: questions, guidance and prospects', *Global Policy* 7: 261–66, 2016.

54. Christine Bell, *On the law of peace: peace agreements and the* lex pacificatoria, Oxford University Press, 2008.

CONCLUSION: THE RULE OF LAWS

1. Thomas Hobbes's *Leviathan* was published in London in 1651.

2. The British government asked the Queen to prorogue Parliament in August 2019, an act later judged unlawful by the Supreme Court. R (on the application of Miller) (Appellant) v. The Prime Minister (Respondent); Cherry and others (Respondents) v. Advocate General for Scotland (Appellant) (Scotland), [2019] UKSC 41.

3. Taisu Zhang and Tom Ginsburg, 'China's turn toward law', *Virginia Journal of International Law* 59: 306–389, 2019, explaining, at p. 317, that China's move towards law is not a move towards the rule of law.

BIBLIOGRAPHY

Ackerman-Lieberman, Phillip I. *The business of identity: Jews, Muslims and economic life in medieval Egypt*, Stanford, CA: Stanford University Press, 2014.

Adewoye, O. *The judicial system in Southern Nigeria, 1854–1954: law and justice in a dependency*, London: Longman, 1977.

Alschuler, Albert W. 'Rediscovering Blackstone', *University of Pennsylvania Law Review* 145: 1–55, 1996.

Ames, Glen. *Em nome de deus: the journal of the first voyage of Vasco da Gama to India, 1497–1499*, Leiden: Brill, 2009.

Ando, Clifford. *Imperial ideology and provincial loyalty in the Roman Empire*, Berkeley: University of California Press, 2000.

——. *Law, language, and empire in the Roman tradition*, Philadelphia: University of Pennsylvania Press, 2011.

——. 'Pluralism and empire: from Rome to Robert Cover', *Critical Analysis of Law* 1: 1–22, 2014.

——. *Citizenship and empire in Europe, 200–1900: the Antonine constitution after 1800 years*, Stuttgart: Franz Steiner Verlag, 2016.

Andrews, A. 'The growth of the Athenian state', in J. Boardman and N. G. L. Hammond (eds), *The Cambridge ancient history*, 2nd ed. vol. 3, pt. 3, Cambridge University Press, 1982.

An-Na'im, Abdullahi Ahmed. *Islam and the secular state: negotiating the future of Shari'a*, Cambridge, MA: Harvard University Press, 2008.

Attenborough, F. L. *The laws of the earliest English kings*, Cambridge University Press, 1922.

Baker, J. H. 'The common lawyers and the Chancery', *Irish Jurist* 4: 368–92, 1969.

———. *An introduction to English legal history*, London: Butterworths, 1971.

———. 'The Inns of Court in 1388', *Law Quarterly Review* 92: 184–87, 1976.

———. 'The law merchant and the common law before 1700', *Cambridge Law Journal* 38: 295–322, 1979.

———. *The legal profession and the common law: historical essays*, London: Hambledon Press, 1986.

Baldwin, John W. 'The crisis of the ordeal: literature, law, and religion around 1200', *Journal of Medieval and Renaissance Studies* 24: 327–53, 1994.

Banner, Stuart. *How the Indians lost their land*, Cambridge, MA: Harvard University Press, 2005.

Bannerman, Gordon, and Anthony Howe (eds). *Battles over free trade*, vol. 2, *The consolidation of free trade, 1847–1878*, London: Routledge, 2017.

Barbieri-Low, Anthony J., and Robin D.S. Yates. *Law, state, and society in early imperial China: a study with critical edition and translation of the legal texts from Zhangjiashan tomb numbers 247*, Leiden: Brill, 2015.

Barthélmy, Dominique. 'Diversité dans des ordalies médiévales', *Revue historique* (T. 280), Fasc. 1 (567): 3–25, 1988.

Bartlett, Robert. *Trial by fire and water: the medieval judicial ordeal*, Oxford: Clarendon Press, 1986.

Barton, John. *A history of the Bible: the book and its faiths*, London: Allen Lane, 2019.

Bauman, Richard A. *Crime and punishment in ancient Rome*, London: Routledge, 1996.

Bayly, C. A. *Imperial meridian: the British Empire and the world, 1780–1830*, London: Longman, 1989.

————. *The birth of the modern world, 1780–1914: global connections and comparisons*, Oxford: Blackwell, 2004.

Beard, Mary. *SPQR: a history of ancient Rome*, London: Profile Books, 2015.

Beckerman, John S. 'Procedural innovation and institutional change in medieval English manorial courts', *Law and History Review* 10: 197–253, 1992.

Behar, Ruth. *The presence of the past in a Spanish village: Santa María del Monte*, Princeton, NJ: Princeton University Press, 1986.

Bell, Christine. *On the law of peace: peace agreements and the lex pacificatoria*, Oxford University Press, 2008.

Berman, Harold J. 'The background of the Western legal tradition in the folklaw of the peoples of Europe', *University of Chicago Law Review* 45: 553–97, 1978.

Bernard, Seth. *Building mid-republican Rome: labor, architecture, and the urban economy*, Oxford University Press, 2014.

————. 'Debt, land, and labor in the early Republican economy', *Phoenix* 70: 317–38, 2016.

Bernstein, Lisa. 'Opting out of the legal system: extralegal contractual relations in the diamond industry', *Journal of Legal Studies* 21: 115–57, 1992.

Bilder, Mary Sarah. 'The lost lawyers: early American legal literates and transatlantic legal culture', *Yale Journal of Law and the Humanities* 11: 47–177, 1999.

————. *The transatlantic constitution: colonial legal culture and the empire*, Cambridge, MA: Harvard University Press, 2004.

Billings, Warren. 'The transfer of English law to Virginia, 1606–50', in K. R. Andrews, N. P. Canny, and P. E. H. Hair (eds), *The westward enterprise: English activities in Ireland, the Atlantic, and America, 1480–1650*, Liverpool University Press, 1978.

Binchy, D. A. (ed.) *Corpus iuris hibernici: ad fidem codicum manuscriptorum recognovit*, Dublin: Institute for Advanced Studies, 1978.

Bloch, Howard. *Medieval French literature and law*, Berkeley: University of California Press, 1977.

Block-Lieb, Susan, and Terence C. Halliday. *Global lawmakers: international organizations in the crafting of world markets*, Cambridge University Press, 2017.

Bodde, Derk, and Clarence Morris. *Law in Imperial China: exemplified by 190 Ch'ing dynasty cases (translated from the Hsing-an hui-lan)*, Cambridge, MA: Harvard University Press, 1967.

Bonfield, Lloyd. 'What did English villagers mean by "customary law"', in Z. Razi and R. M. Smith (eds), *Medieval society and the manor court*, Oxford: Clarendon Press, 1996.

Bottéro, Jean. *Mesopotamia: writing, reasoning, and the gods*, trans. Z. Bahrani and M. Van De Mieroop, Chicago: University of Chicago Press, 1992.

Bourgon, Jérôme. 'Chinese law, history of, Qing dynasty', *The Oxford international encyclopedia of legal history*, Oxford University Press, 2009.

Bowen, H. V. 'British India, 1765–1813: the metropolitan context', in P. J. Marshall and A. Low (eds), *The Oxford history of the British Empire*, vol. 2, Oxford University Press, 1998.

Bowen, John R. 'Anthropology and Islamic law', in A. M. Emon and R. Ahmed (eds), *The Oxford handbook of Islamic law*, Oxford University Press, 2018.

———. *On British Islam: religion, law, and everyday practice in shari'a councils*, Princeton, NJ: Princeton University Press, 2018.

Brand, Paul. 'Legal education in England before the Inns of Court', in A. Bush and Alain Wijffels (eds), *Learning the law: teaching and the transmission of law in England, 1150–1900*, London: Hambledon Press, 1999.

———. *The origins of the English legal profession*, Oxford: Blackwell, 1992.

Bratishenko, Elena. 'On the authorship of the 1229 Smolensk–Riga trade treaty', *Russian Linguistics* 26: 345–61, 2002.

Brennan, T. Corey. *The praetorship in the Roman Republic*, Oxford University Press, 2000.

Brockman, Rosser H. 'Commercial contract law in late nineteenth-century Taiwan', in Jeremy Alan Cohen, R. Randle Edwards, and Fu-Mei Chang Chen (eds), *Essays on China's legal tradition*, Princeton, NJ: Princeton University Press, 1980.

Brooks, Christopher. *Law, politics and society in early modern England*, Cambridge University Press, 2009.

Brooks, Christopher, and Michael Lobban (eds). *Communities and courts in Britain, 1150–1900*, London: Hambledon Press, 1997.

Brown, Nathan J., and Mara Revkin. 'Islamic law and constitutions', in A. M. Emon and R. Ahmed (eds), *The Oxford handbook of Islamic law*, Oxford University Press, 2018.

Brown, Peter. 'Society and the supernatural: a medieval change', *Dedalus* 104: 133–51, 1975.

Bryen, Ari Z. 'Responsa', in S. Stern, M. del Mar, and B. Meyler (eds), *The Oxford handbook of law and humanities*, Oxford University Press, 2019.

Byrne, Francis. *Irish kings and high kings*, London: B. Y. Batsford, 1973.

Caenegem, R. C. van. *Legal history: a European perspective*, London: Hambledon Press, 1991.

Calder, Norman. *Islamic jurisprudence in the classical era*, Colin Imber (ed.) Cambridge University Press, 2010.

Caldwell, Ernest. 'Social change and written law in early Chinese legal thought', *Law and History Review* 32: 1–30, 2014.

———. *Writing Chinese laws: the form and function of legal statutes found in the Qin Shuihudi corpus*, London: Routledge, 2018.

Champion, W. A. 'Recourse to the law and the meaning of the great litigation decline, 1650–1750: some clues from the Shrewsbury local courts', in Christopher Brooks and Michael Lobban (eds), *Communities and courts in Britain, 1150–1900*, London: Hambledon Press, 1997.

Chanock, Martin. *Law, custom and social order: the colonial experience in Malawi and Zambia*, Cambridge University Press, 1985.

Charles-Edwards, T. M. Review of the 'Corpus Iuris Hibernici', *Studia Hibernica* 20: 141–62, 1980.

———. 'A contract between king and people in early medieval Ireland? *Críth Gablach* on kingship', *Peritia* 8: 107–19, 1994.

———. 'Law in the western kingdoms between the fifth and seventh century', in A. Cameron, R. Ward-Perkins, and M. Whitby (eds), *The Cambridge ancient history*, vol. 14, *Late antiquity: empire and successors*, A.D. *425–600*, Cambridge University Press, 2001.

Charles-Edwards, T. M., and Fergus Kelly. *Bechbretha*, Dublin: Institute for Advanced Study, 1983.

Chattopadhyaya, Bajadulal. '"Autonomous spaces" and the authority of the state: the contradiction and its resolution in theory and practice in early India', in B. Kölver (ed.) *Recht, Staat und Verwaltung im klassischen Indien*, Munich: R. Oldenbourg Verlag, 1997.

Chesworth, John A., and Franz Kogelmann (eds), *Shari'a in Africa today: reactions and responses*, Leiden: Brill, 2013.

Cheyette, Fredric L. 'Suum cuique tribuere', *French Historical Studies* 6: 287–99, 1970.

Clanchy, Michael. 'Law and love in the Middle Ages', in J. Bossy (ed.) *Disputes and settlements: law and human relations in the West*, Cambridge University Press, 1983.

Clarke, Morgan. 'Neo-calligraphy: religious authority and media technology in contemporary Shiite Islam', *Comparative Studies in Society and History* 52: 351–83, 2010.

———. 'The judge as tragic hero: judicial ethics in Lebanon's shari'a courts', *American Ethnologist* 39: 106–21, 2012.

Cohen, Esther. *The crossroads of justice: law and culture in late medieval France*, Leiden: Brill, 1993.

Cohen, Mark R. *Jewish self-government in medieval Egypt: the origins of the office of Head of the Jews, ca. 1065–1126*, Princeton, NJ: Princeton University Press, 1980.

Cohn, Bernard S. 'Law and the colonial state in India', in J. Starr and J. F. Collier (eds), *History and power in the study of law: new directions in legal anthropology*, Ithaca, NY: Cornell University Press, 1989.

Conklin, Alice. *A mission to civilize: the republican idea of empire in France and West Africa, 1895–1930*, Stanford, CA: Stanford University Press, 1997.

Coogan, Michael. *The Old Testament: a very short introduction*, Oxford University Press, 2008.

Cooper, Jerrold S. *Sumerian and Akkadian royal inscriptions*, vol. 1, New Haven, CT: American Oriental Society, 1986.

Cornell, Tim. *The beginnings of Rome: Italy and Rome from the Bronze Age to the Punic Wars (c. 1000–264 BC)*, London: Routledge, 1995.

Cotran, Eugene. 'African conference on local courts and customary law', *Journal of Local Administration Overseas* 4: 128–33, 1965.

Cowe, Peter. 'Medieval Armenian Literary and Cultural Trends', in R. Hovannisian (ed.) *The Armenian people from ancient to modern times*, vol. 1, Los Angeles: University of California Press, 1997.

Craven, Matthew. 'Colonialism and domination', in B. Fassbender and A. Peters (eds), *The Oxford handbook of the history of international law*, Oxford University Press, 2012.

Crawford, M. H. *Roman statutes*, vol. 2, London: Institute of Classical Studies, School of Advanced Study, University of London, 1996.

Cromartie, Alan. *Sir Matthew Hale, 1609–1676: law, religion and natural philosophy*, Cambridge University Press, 1995.

———. *The constitutionalist revolution: an essay on the history of England, 1450–1642*, Cambridge University Press, 2006.

Dahm, G. 'On the reception of Roman and Italian law in Germany', in G. Strauss (ed.) *Pre-Reformation Germany*, New York: Harper and Row, 1972.

Davis, Donald R., Jr. 'Recovering the indigenous legal traditions of India: classical Hindu law in practice in late medieval Kerala', *Journal of Indian Philosophy* 27: 159–213, 1999.

————. 'Intermediate realms of law: corporate groups and rulers in medieval India', *Journal of the Economic and Social History of the Orient* 48: 92–117, 2005.

————. 'A historical overview of Hindu law', in Timothy Lubin, Donald R. Davis, and Jayanth K. Krishnan (eds), *Hinduism and law: an introduction*, Cambridge University Press, 2010.

————. *The spirit of Hindu law*, Cambridge University Press, 2010.

————. 'Centres of law: duties, rights, and jurisdictional pluralism in medieval India', in P. Dresch and H. Skoda (eds), *Legalism: anthropology and history*, Oxford University Press, 2012.

————. 'Responsa in Hindu law: consultation and lawmaking in medieval India', *Oxford Journal of Law and Religion* 3: 57–75, 2014.

Davison, Lee, T. Hitchcock, T. Keim, and R. Shoemaker (eds), *Stilling the grumbling hive: the response to social and economic problems in England, 1689–1750*, London: St. Martin's Press, 1992.

Démare-Lafont, Sophie. 'Judicial decision-making: judges and arbitrators', in K. Radner and E. Robson (eds), *The Oxford handbook of cuneiform culture*, Oxford University Press, 2011.

————. 'Law I', in *Encyclopedia of the Bible and its reception*, vol. 15, Berlin: de Gruyter, 2017.

Derrett, J. Duncan. *Religion, law and the state in India*, London: Faber and Faber, 1968.

————. 'Two inscriptions concerning the status of Kammalas and the application of Dharmaśāstra', in J. Duncan Derrett (ed.) *Essays in classical and modern Hindu law*, vol. 1, Leiden: E. J. Brill, 1976.

de Vattel, Emer. *Le droit des gens, ou, principe de la loi naturelle, appliqués à la conduite et aux affaires des nations et des souverains*, London [Neuchâtel], 1758.

Doniger, Wendy. *The Hindus: an alternative history*, Oxford University Press, 2009.

Dotson, Brandon. 'Divination and law in the Tibetan Empire', in M. Kapstein and B. Dotson (eds), *Contributions to the cultural history of early Tibet*, Leiden: Brill, 2007.

———. 'The princess and the yak: the hunt as narrative trope and historical reality in early Tibet', in B. Dotson, K. Iwao, and T. Takeuchi (eds), *Scribes, texts, and rituals in early Tibet and Dunhuang*, Wiesbaden: Dr. Ludwig Reichert Verlag, 2013.

Douglas, Mary. 'The abominations of Leviticus', in *Purity and danger: an analysis of the concepts of pollution and taboo*, London: Routledge and Kegan Paul, 1966.

Downham, Clare. *Medieval Ireland*, Cambridge University Press, 2018.

Dresch, Paul. *The rules of Barat: tribal documents from Yemen*, Sanaa, Yemen: Centre Français de d'Archéologie et de Sciences Sociales, 2006.

———. 'Outlawry, exile, and banishment: reflections on community and justice', in F. Pirie and J. Scheele (eds), *Legalism: community and justice*, Oxford University Press, 2014.

Drew, Katherine Fischer. *The Lombard laws*, London: Variorum Reprints, 1988.

———. *The laws of the Salian Franks*, Philadelphia: University of Pennsylvania Press, 1991.

Duggan, Anne J. 'Roman, canon, and common law in twelfth century England: the council of Northampton (1164) re-examined', *Institute of Historical Research* 83: 379–408, 2009.

Ebrey, Patricia Buckley. *Cambridge illustrated history of China*, 2nd ed. Cambridge University Press, 2010.

Ekvall, Robert B. 'The nomadic pattern of living among the Tibetans as preparation for war', *American Anthropologist* 63: 1250–63, 1961.

———. 'Peace and war among the Tibetan nomads', *American Anthropologist* 66: 1119–48, 1964.

———. *Fields on the hoof*, Prospect Heights, IL: Waveland, 1968.

Emon, Anver M. 'Islamic law and finance', in A. M. Emon and R. Ahmed (eds), *The Oxford handbook of Islamic law*, Oxford University Press, 2018.

Evans-Pritchard, E. E. *Witchcraft, oracles, and magic among the Azande*, Oxford: Clarendon Press, 1937.

Eyre, Christopher. *The use of documents in Pharaonic Egypt*, Oxford University Press, 2013.

Faulkner, Thomas. *Law and authority in the early Middle Ages*, Cambridge University Press, 2016.

Fernández Castro, Ana Belem. 'A transnational empire built on law: the case of the commercial jurisprudence of the House of Trade of Seville (1583–1598)', in T. Duve (ed.) *Entanglements in legal history: conceptual approaches*, Frankfurt: Max Planck Institute for European Legal History, 2014.

Fitzpatrick, Peter. *The mythology of modern law*, London: Routledge, 1992.

Fraher, Richard M. 'The theoretical justification for the new criminal law of the High Middle Ages: "rei publicae interest, ne crimina remaneant impunita"', *University of Illinois Law Review*, 577–95, 1984.

Franklin, Simon. *Writing, society and culture in early Rus, c. 950–1300*, Cambridge University Press, 2002.

———. 'On meanings, functions and paradigms of law in early Rus', *Russian History* 34: 63–81, 2007.

Franklin, Simon, and Jonathan Shepard. *The emergence of Rus, 750–1200*. London: Longman, 1996.

Frier, Bruce W. *The rise of the Roman jurists: studies in Cicero's 'pro Caecina'*, Princeton, NJ: Princeton University Press, 1985.

———. 'Finding a place for law in the high empire', in F. de Angelis (ed.) *Spaces of justice in the Roman world*, Leiden: Brill, 2010.

Galanter, Marc. 'The displacement of traditional law in modern India', in *Law and society in modern India*, Delhi: Oxford University Press, 1989.

Gambetta, Diego. *The Sicilian mafia: the business of private protection*, Cambridge, MA: Harvard University Press, 1993.

──────. *Codes of the underworld: how criminals communicate*, Princeton, NJ: Princeton University Press, 2009.

Gammer, Moshe. *Muslim resistance to the tsar: Shamil and the conquest of Chechnia and Daghestan*, London: Cass, 1994.

Geertz, Clifford. *The interpretation of cultures*, New York: Basic Books, 1973.

──────. 'Local knowledge: fact and law in comparative perspective', in *Local knowledge*, New York: Basic Books, 1983.

Gernet, Jacques. *Daily life in China on the eve of the Mongol invasion, 1250–1276*, London: Allen and Unwin, 1962.

Gerreits, Marilyn. 'Economy and society: clientship in the Irish laws', *Cambridge Medieval Celtic Studies* 6: 43–61, 1983.

──────. 'Money in early Christian Ireland', *Comparative Studies in Society and History* 27: 323–39, 1985.

Ghai, Yash. 'Human rights and governance: the Asia debate', *Australian Year Book of International Law* 15: 1–34, 1994.

Goddard, Richard, and Teresa Phipps. *Town courts and urban society in late medieval England*, 1250–1500, Woodbridge, UK: Boydell and Brewer, 2019.

Godfrey, Mark. *Civil justice in renaissance Scotland: the origins of a central court*, Leiden: Brill, 2009.

Goitein, Shelomo Dov. *A Mediterranean society: the Jewish communities of the Arab world as portrayed by the documents of the Cairo Geniza*, 6 vols., Berkeley: University of California Press, 1967–1993.

──────. *A Mediterranean society: an abridgment in one volume*, Jacob Lassner (ed.) Berkeley: University of California Press, 1999.

Goldstein, Melvyn. *A History of modern Tibet, 1913–1951: the demise of the lamaist state*, Berkeley: University of California Press, 1989.

Gombrich, Richard. *Theravada Buddhism: a social history from ancient Benares to modern Colombo*, London: Routledge and Kegan Paul, 1988.

Goodall, Kay. 'Incitement to racial hatred: all talk and no substance?', *Modern Law Review* 70: 89–113, 2007.

Graeber, David. *Debt: the first 5,000 years*, New York: Melville House, 2011.

Green, Thomas A. 'Societal concepts of criminal liability for homicide in mediaeval England', *Speculum* 4: 669–95, 1972.

Greenridge, A. H. J. *The legal procedure of Cicero's time*, Oxford: Clarendon Press, 1901.

Greif, Avner. 'Reputation and coalitions in medieval trade: evidence on the Maghribi traders', *Journal of Economic History* 49: 857–82, 1989.

Guha, Ranajit. *A rule of property for India*, Paris: Mouton, 1963.

Gurukhal, Rajan. 'From clan to lineage to hereditary occupations and caste in early south India', *Indian Historical Review* 20: 22–33, 1993–1994.

Hallaq, Wael B. 'Was the gate of *ijtihad* closed?', *International Journal of Middle East Studies* 16: 3–41, 1984.

———. 'On the origins of the controversy about the existence of mujtahids and the gate of ijtihad', *Studia Islamica* 63: 129–41, 1986.

———. *The origins and evolution of Islamic law*, Cambridge University Press, 2005.

———. *An introduction to Islamic law*, Cambridge University Press, 2009.

———. *Sharī'a: theory, practice, transformations*, Cambridge University Press, 2009.

———. *The impossible state: Islam, politics, and modernity's moral predicament*, New York: Columbia University Press, 2013.

Halliday, Terence C., and Gregory Shaffer. *Transnational legal orders*, Cambridge University Press, 2015.

Halpérin, Jean-Louis. *L'impossible Code Civil*, Paris: Presses universitaires de France, 1992.

Hamoudi, Haider Ala. 'The death of Islamic law', *Georgia Journal of International and Comparative Law* 38: 293–338, 2010.

Hansen, Valerie. *Negotiating daily life in traditional China: how ordinary people used contracts, 600–1400*, New Haven, CT: Yale University Press, 1995.

Hardt, Michael, and Antonio Negri. *Empire*, Cambridge, MA: Harvard University Press, 2000.

Haring, C. H. *The Spanish Empire in America*, New York: Oxford University Press, 1947.

Harper, Donald. 'Resurrection in Warring States popular religion', *Taoist Resources 5*, no. 2: 13–28, 1994.

Harries, Jill. *Cicero and the jurists: from citizens' law to the lawful state*, London: Duckworth, 2006.

Harrington, Hannah. 'Persian law', in B. A. Strawn (ed.) *The Oxford encyclopedia of the Bible and law*, Oxford University Press, 2015.

Harrison, Christopher. 'Manor courts and the governance of Tudor England', in Christopher Brooks and Michael Lobban (eds), *Communities and courts in Britain, 1150–1900*, London: Hambledon Press, 1997.

Hart, Cyril. *The verderers and the forest laws of Dean*, Newton Abbot, UK: David and Charles, 1971.

Hart, James S. *The rule of law, 1603–1660*, Harlow, UK: Pearson Longman, 2003.

Heather, Peter. *The fall of the Roman Empire: a new history of Rome and the barbarians*, Oxford University Press, 2005.

Hecht, N. S., B. S. Jackson, S. M. Passamaneck, D. Piattelli, and A. M. Rabello (eds), *An introduction to the history and sources of Jewish law*, Oxford: Clarendon Press, 1996.

Helmholz, R. H. 'Crime, compurgation and the courts of the medieval church', *Law and History Review* 1: 1–26, 1983.

Henderson, Edith G. *Foundations of English administrative law: certiorari and mandamus in the seventeenth century*, Cambridge, MA: Harvard University Press, 1963.

Henretta, James A. 'Magistrates, common law lawyers, legislators: the three legal systems of British America', in M. Grossberg and C. Tomlins (eds), *The Cambridge history of law in America*, vol. 1, *Early America (1580–1815)*, Cambridge University Press, 2008.

Hill, Nathan. 'The *sku-bla* rite in imperial Tibetan religion', *Cahiers d'Extrême-Asie* 24: 49–58, 2015.

Hirsch, Susan F. *Pronouncing and persevering: gender and the discourses of disputing in an African Islamic court*, Chicago: University of Chicago Press, 1998.

Hodgson, Marshall G.S. *The venture of Islam: conscience and history in a world civilization*, 3 vols., Chicago: University of Chicago Press, 1974.

Honoré, Tony. *Emperors and lawyers*, 2nd ed. Oxford: Clarendon Press, 1994.

———. *Law in the crisis of empire, 379–455 AD: the Theodosian dynasty and its quaestors*, Oxford: Clarendon Press, 1998.

———. 'Roman law AD 200–400: from cosmopolis to Rechtstaat?', in S. Swain and M. Edwards (eds), *Approaching late antiquity: the transformation from early to late empire*, Oxford University Press, 2006.

Hooker, M. B. *Adat law in modern Indonesia*, Kuala Lumpur: Oxford University Press, 1978.

Huang, Philip. *Civil justice in China: representation and practice in the Qing*, Stanford, CA: Stanford University Press, 1996.

———. 'The past and present of the Chinese civil and criminal justice systems: the Sinitic legal tradition from a global perspective', *Modern China* 42: 227–72, 2016.

Hudson, John. *The formation of the English common law: law and society in England from the Norman conquest to Magna Carta*, London: Longman, 1996.

Hulsebosch, Daniel J. 'The ancient constitution and the expanding empire: Sir Edward Coke's British jurisprudence', *Law and History Review* 21: 439–82, 2003.

Hutton, Jeremy M., and C. L. Crouch. 'Deuteronomy as a translation of Assyrian treaties', *Hebrew Bible and Ancient Israel* 7: 201–52, 2018.

Hyams, Paul. 'Trial by ordeal: the key to proof in the early common law', in Morris S. Arnold, Thomas A. Green, Sally A. Scully, and Stephen D. White (eds), *On the laws and customs of England: essays in honor of Samuel E. Thorne*, Chapel Hill: University of North Carolina Press, 1981.

———. 'What did Edwardian villagers understand by "law"?', in Z. Razi and R. M. Smith, *Medieval society and the manor court*, Oxford: Clarendon Press, 1996.

———. 'Due process versus the maintenance of order in European law: the contribution of the *ius commune*', in P. Coss (ed.) *The moral world of the law*, Cambridge University Press, 2000.

Ibbetson, David. 'Sources of law from the Republic to the Dominate', in D. Johnston (ed.) *The Cambridge companion to Roman law*, Cambridge University Press, 2015.

Ingram, Martin. '"Popular" and "official" justice: punishing sexual offenders in Tudor London', in F. Pirie and J. Scheele (eds), *Legalism: community and justice*, Oxford University Press, 2014.

Innes, Matthew. 'Charlemagne's government', in J. Storey (ed.) *Charlemagne: empire and society*, Manchester University Press, 2005.

Jackson, Bernard S. *Wisdom laws: a study of the Mishpatim of Exodus 21:1–22:16*, Oxford University Press, 2006.

Jóhannesson, Jón. *A history of the old Icelandic commonwealth: Islendinga saga*, trans. H. Bessason, Winnipeg: University of Manitoba Press, 1974.

Johansen, Baber. 'Vom Wort-zum Indizienbeweis: die Anermerkung der richterlichen Folter in islamischen Rechtsdoktrinen des 13. und 14. Jahrhunderts', *Ius commune* 28: 1–46, 2001.

———. 'The constitution and the principles of Islamic normativity against the rules of fiqh: a judgment of the Supreme Constitutional Court of Egypt', in M. K. Masud, R. Peters, and D. S. Powers (eds), *Dispensing justice in Islam: qadis and their judgements*, Leiden: Brill, 2006.

Johnson, Wallace. *The T'ang code*, 2 vols., Princeton, NJ: Princeton University Press, 1979–1997.

Kaiser, Daniel H. *The laws of Rus': tenth to fifteenth centuries*, Salt Lake City: C. Schlacks, 1992.

Katz, Paul R. *Divine justice: religion and the development of Chinese legal culture*, London: Routledge, 2009.

Kay, Philip. *Rome's economic revolution*, Oxford University Press, 2014.

Kaye, J. M. 'The early history of murder and manslaughter, part 1', *Law Quarterly Review* 83: 365–95, 1967.

Kelley, Donald R. 'What pleases the prince: Justinian, Napoleon, and the lawyers', *History of Political Thought* 23: 288–302, 2002.

Kelly, Fergus. *A guide to early Irish law*, Dublin: Institute for Advanced Studies, 1988.

———. *Early Irish farming: a study based mainly on the law-texts of the 7th and 8th centuries* AD, Dublin: Institute for Advanced Studies, 1997.

———. *Marriage disputes: a fragmentary Old Irish law-text*, Dublin: Institute for Advanced Studies, 2014.

Kelly, Tobias. 'Prosecuting human rights violations: universal jurisdiction and the crime of torture', in M. Goodale (ed.) *Human rights at the crossroads*, Oxford University Press, 2013.

Kemper, Michael. 'Communal agreements (*ittifāqāt*) and '*ādāt*-books from Daghestani villages and confederacies (18th–19th centuries)', *Der Islam: Zeitschrift für Geschichte und Kultur des islamischen Orients* 81: 115–49, 2004.

———. '*Adat* against *shari'a*: Russian approaches toward Daghestani "customary law" in the 19th century', *Ab Imperio* 3: 147–72, 2005.

King, Steven. *Writing the lives of the English poor, 1750s–1830s*, Montreal: McGill-Queen's University Press, 2019.

Kolsky, Elizabeth. 'The colonial rule of law and the legal regime of exception: frontier "fanaticism" and state violence in British India', *American Historical Review* 120: 1218–46, 2015.

Konig, David. *Law and society in Puritan Massachusetts: Essex County, 1629–1692*, Chapel Hill: University of North Carolina Press, 1979.

———. '"Dale's Laws" and the non-common law origins of criminal justice in Virginia', *American Journal of Legal History* 26: 354–75, 1982.

Koskenniemi, Martii. *The gentle civilizer of nations: the rise and fall of international law, 1870–1960*, Cambridge University Press, 2001.

———. 'What is international law for?', in Malcom Evans (ed.) *International law*, Oxford University Press, 2003.

———. 'Fragmentation of international law: difficulties arising from the diversification and expansion of international law, a report of the study group of the UN's International law commission', 2006.

———. 'Expanding histories of international law', *American Journal of Legal History 56*: 104–12, 2016.

Kozloff, P. K. 'Through eastern Tibet and Kam', *Geographical Journal 31*: 522–34, 1908.

Krakowski, Eve, and Marina Rustow, 'Formula as content: medieval Jewish institutions, the Cairo geniza, and the new diplomatics', *Jewish Social Studies: History, Culture, Society 20*: 111–46, 2014.

Kulke, Hermann, and Dietmar Rothermund. *A history of India*, London: Routledge, 1986.

Lambert, Tom. *Law and order in Anglo-Saxon England*, Oxford University Press, 2017.

Lane Fox, Robin. *The classical world: an epic history of Greece and Rome*, London: Folio Society, 2013.

Langbein, John H. *The origins of adversary criminal trial*, Oxford University Press, 2005.

Lantschner, Patrick. 'Justice contested and affirmed: jurisdiction and conflict in late medieval Italian cities', in F. Pirie and J. Scheele (eds), *Legalism: community and justice*, Oxford University Press, 2014.

Lariviere, Richard W. *The Divyatattva of Raghunandana Bhattācārya: ordeals in classical Hindu law*, New Delhi: Manohar, 1981.

———. 'A Sanskrit jayapattra from 18th century Mithilā', in R. W. Lariviere (ed.) *Studies in dharmaśāstra*, Calcutta: Firma KLM, 1984.

Latty, Franck. *La lex sportiva: recherche sur le droit transnational*, Leiden: Brill, 2007.

Lau, Ulrich, and Thies Staack. *Legal practice in the formative stages of the Chinese Empire: an annotated translation of the exemplary Qin criminal cases from the Yuelu Academy collection*, Leiden: Brill, 2016.

Lavan, Myles. 'Slavishness in Britain and Rome in Tacitus' *Agricola*', *Classical Quarterly* 61: 294–305, 2011.

———. 'The spread of Roman citizenship, 14–212 CE: quantification in the face of high uncertainty', *Past and Present* 230: 3–46, 2016.

Legge, James. *The Chinese classics*, vol. 3, Hong Kong: Hong Kong University Press, 1960.

Lemmings, David (ed.) *The British and their laws in the eighteenth century*, Woodbridge, UK: Boydell Press, 2005.

———. *Law and government in England during the long eighteenth century: from consent to command*, Basingstoke, UK: Palgrave Macmillan, 2011.

Lemons, Katherine. *Divorcing traditions: Islamic marriage law and the making of Indian secularism*, Ithaca, NY: Cornell University Press, 2019.

Lev, Daniel S. 'Colonial law and the genesis of the Indonesian state', *Indonesia* 40: 57–74, 1985.

Leve, Lauren. '"Secularism is a human right": double binds of Buddhism, democracy and identity in Nepal', in M. Goodale and S. E. Merry (eds), *The practice of human rights: tracking law between the global and the local*, Cambridge University Press, 2007.

Libson, Gideon. 'Halakhah and law in the period of the Geonim', in N. S. Hecht, B. S. Jackson, S. M. Passamaneck, D. Piattelli, and A. M. Rabello (eds), *An introduction to the history and sources of Jewish law*, Oxford: Clarendon Press, 1996.

Lindsay, David. *ICANN and international domain law*, Oxford: Hart, 2007.

Lingat, Robert. *The classical law of India*, trans. D. Derrett, Berkeley: University of California Press, 1973.

Lintott, Andrew. *The constitution of the Roman Republic*, Oxford: Clarendon Press, 1999.

Lippert, Sandra. 'Law (definitions and codification)', in E. Frood and W. Wendrich (eds), *UCLA Encyclopedia of Egyptology*, Los Angeles, 2012, https://escholarship.org/uc/item/0mr4h4fv.

Lipsett-Rivera, Sonya. 'Law', in D. Carrasco (ed.) *The Oxford encyclopedia of Mesoamerican cultures*, Oxford University Press, 2001.

Liu, Yongping. *Origins of Chinese law: penal and administrative law in its early development*, Hong Kong: Oxford University Press, 1998.

Lobban, Michael. 'Custom, nature, and judges: high law and low law in England and the empire', in D. Lemmings (ed.) *The British and their laws in the eighteenth century*, Woodbridge, UK: Boydell Press, 2005.

Lomas, Kathryn. *The rise of Rome: from the Iron Age to the Punic Wars (1000–264 BC)*, London: Profile Books, 2017.

Lopez, Robert S., and Irving W. Raymond. *Medieval trade in the Mediterranean world: illustrative documents*, London: Geoffrey Cumberlege, 1955.

Lubin, Timothy. 'Punishment and expiation: overlapping domains in Brahmanical law', *Indologica Taurinensia* 33: 93–122, 2007.

Lubin, Timothy, Donald R. Davis, and Jayanth K. Krishnan (eds), *Hinduism and law: an introduction*, Cambridge University Press, 2010.

MacCormack, Geoffrey. 'Law and punishment in the earliest Chinese thought', *Irish Jurist* 20: 335–51, 1985.

———. 'The transmission of penal law from the Han to the Tang', *Revue des droits de l'antiquité* 51: 47–83, 2004.

Macnair, Mike. 'Institutional taxonomy, Roman forms and English lawyers in the 17th and 18th centuries', in Pierre Bonin, Nader Hakim, Fara Nasti, and Aldo Schiavone (eds), *Pensiero giuridico occidentale e giuristi Romani: eredita e genealogie*, Turin, Italy: Giappichelli, 2019.

Mahmood, Saba. *Politics of piety: the Islamic revival and the feminist subject*, Princeton, NJ: Princeton University Press, 2005.

Mahsoudian, Krikor. 'Armenian communities in eastern Europe', in R. Hovannisian (ed.) *The Armenian people from ancient to modern times*, vol. 1, Los Angeles: University of California Press, 1997.

Maier, Pauline. *American scripture: making the Declaration of Independence*, New York: Knopf, 1997.

Maitland, F. W. *Select pleas in manorial and other seignorial courts*, vol. 1, *Reigns of Henry III and Edward I*, Selden Society, London: B. Quaritch, 1889.

Massoud, Mark Fathi. 'How an Islamic state rejected Islamic law', *American Journal of Comparative Law* 68: 579–602, 2018.

McKitterick, Rosamond. *The Carolingians and the written word*, Cambridge University Press, 1989.

McKnight, Brian E. *The quality of mercy: amnesties and traditional Chinese justice*, Honolulu: University of Hawaii Press, 1981.

———. 'From statute to precedent', in *Law and the state in traditional East Asia: six studies on the sources of East Asian law*, Honolulu: University of Hawaii Press, 1987.

———. *Law and order in Sung China*, Cambridge University Press, 1992.

McKnight, Brian E., and James T.C. Liu, *The enlightened judgments: Ch'ing-ming Chi. The Sung dynasty collection*, Albany: State University of New York Press, 1999.

Merry, Sally Engle. 'Legal pluralism and transnational culture: the Ka Ho'okolokolonui Manaka Maoli tribunal, Hawai'i, 1993', in R. A. Wilson (ed.) *Human rights, culture and context: anthropological perspectives*, London: Pluto Press, 1997.

Messick, Brinkley. 'The mufti, the text and the world: legal interpretation in Yemen', *Man* 21: 102–19, 1986.

———. *The calligraphic state: textual domination and history in a Muslim society*, Berkeley: University of California Press, 1993.

———. 'Media muftis: radio fatwas in Yemen', in M. K. Masud, B. Messick, and D. S. Powers (eds), *Islamic legal interpre-*

tation: muftis and their fatwas, Cambridge, MA: Harvard University Press, 1996.

Meyer, Elizabeth A. *Legitimacy and law in the Roman world*, Cambridge University Press, 2004.

Miller, William Ian. 'Ordeal in Iceland', *Scandinavian Studies* 60: 189–218, 1988.

———. *Bloodtaking and peacemaking: feud, law, and society in saga Iceland*, University of Chicago Press, 1990.

Millon, David. 'Ecclesiastical jurisdiction in medieval England', *University of Illinois Law Review* 1984: 621–38.

Milsom, S. F. C. 'The Nature of Blackstone's Achievement', *Oxford Journal of Legal Studies* 1: 1–12, 1981.

Mitchell, Richard E. *Patricians and plebeians: the origin of the Roman state*, Ithaca, NY: Cornell University Press, 1990.

Miyazaki, Ichisada. 'The administration of justice during the Sung dynasty', in J. R. Cohen, R. R. Edwards, and F-M. C. Chen (eds), *Essays on China's legal tradition*, Princeton, NJ: Princeton University Press, 1980.

Molyneaux, George. *The formation of the English kingdom in the tenth century*, Oxford University Press, 2015.

Moore, Sally Falk. 'Law and social change: the semi-autonomous social field as an appropriate subject of study', *Law and Society Review* 7: 719–46, 1973.

Morriss, Andrew P. 'Codification and right answers', *Chicago-Kent Law Review* 74: 355–92, 1999.

Moyn, Samuel. *The last utopia: human rights in history*, Cambridge, MA: Harvard University Press, 2001.

Murphy, Craig N. *International organization and industrial change: global governance since 1850*, Cambridge: Polity, 1994.

Murrin, John M. 'The legal transformation: the bench and bar of eighteenth-century Massachusetts', in S. N. Katz (ed.) *Colonial America: essays in politics and social development*, New York: Knopf, 1983.

Musson, Anthony. *Medieval law in context: the growth of legal consciousness from Magna Carta to the peasants' revolt*, Manchester University Press, 2001.

Musson, Anthony, and Edward Powell, *Crime, law, and society in the later Middle Ages*, Manchester University Press, 2013.

Myers, David N. *Jewish history: a very short introduction*, Oxford University Press, 2017.

Nelson, William E. *The common law in colonial America*, 4 vols., New York: Oxford University Press, 2008–2018.

Nichols, Lionel. *The international criminal court and the end of impunity in Kenya*, New York: Springer, 2015.

Offutt, William M. 'The Atlantic rules: the legalistic turn in colonial British America', in E. Mancke and C. Shammas (eds), *The creation of the British Atlantic world*, Baltimore: Johns Hopkins University Press, 2005.

Olivelle, Patrick. 'Manu and the Arthaśāstra: a study in Śāstric intertextuality', *Journal of Indian Philosophy* 32: 281–91, 2004.

————. 'Dharmaśāstra: a textual history', in Timothy Lubin, Donald R. Davis, and Jayanth K. (eds), *Hinduism and law: an introduction*, Cambridge University Press, 2010.

Olivelle, Patrick, with the editorial assistance of Suman Olivelle. *Manu's code of law: a critical edition and translation of the Mānava-Dharmaśāstra*, South Asia Research, Oxford University Press, 2004.

Osanloo, Arzoo. *The politics of women's rights in Iran*, Princeton, NJ: Princeton University Press, 2009.

Pagden, Anthony. 'Human rights, natural rights, and Europe's imperial legacy', *Political Theory* 31: 171–99, 2003.

————. *Lords of all the world: ideologies of empire in Spain, Britain, and France, 1500–1800*, New Haven, CT: Yale University Press, 2005.

————. 'Law, colonization, legitimation, and the European background', in M. Grossberg and C. Tomlins (eds), *The Cambridge history of law in America*, vol. 1, Cambridge University Press, 2008.

Paoli, Letizia. *Mafia brotherhoods: organized crime, Italian style*, New York: Oxford University Press, 2003.

Pauwelyn, Joost, Ramses A. Wessel, and Jan Wouters. 'An introduction to informal international lawmaking', in *Informal international lawmaking*, Oxford University Press, 2012.

Pennington, Robert R. *Stannary law: a history of the mining law of Cornwall and Devon*, Newton Abbot, UK: David and Charles, 1973.

Peters, Lena. 'UNIDROIT', in the *Max Planck Encyclopedia of International Law*, 2017, https://opil.ouplaw.com/view/10.1093/law:epil/9780199231690/law-9780199231690-e536.

Peters, Rudolph. 'Murder in Khaybar: some thoughts on the origins of the *qasāma* procedure in Islamic law', *Islamic Law and Society* 9: 132–67, 2002.

Pictet, Jean S. 'The new Geneva Conventions for the Protection of War Victims', *American Journal of International Law* 45: 462–75, 1951.

Pirie, Fernanda. *Peace and conflict in Ladakh: the construction of a fragile web of order*, Leiden: Brill, 2007.

———. 'Legal dramas on the Amdo grasslands: abolition, transformation or survival?', in K. Buffetrille (ed.) *Revisiting rituals in a Changing Tibetan World*, Leiden: Brill, 2012.

———. 'The limits of the state: coercion and consent in Chinese Tibet', *Journal of Asian Studies* 72: 69–89, 2013.

———. 'Community, justice, and legalism: elusive concepts in Tibet', in F. Pirie and J. Scheele (eds), *Legalism: community and justice*, Oxford University Press, 2014.

———. 'Oaths and ordeals in Tibetan law', in D. Schuh (ed.) *Secular law and order in the Tibetan Highland*, Andiast, Switzerland: International Institute for Tibetan and Buddhist Studies, 2015.

———. 'Rules, proverbs, and persuasion: legalism and rhetoric in Tibet', in P. Dresch and J. Scheele (eds), *Legalism: rules and categories*, Oxford University Press, 2015.

———. 'The making of Tibetan law: the *Khrims gnyis lta ba'i me long*', in J. Bischoff, P. Maurer, and C. Ramble (eds), *On a day of a month of the fire bird year*, Lumbini, Nepal: Lumbini International Research Institute, 2020.

Pocock, J. G. A. *The ancient constitution and the feudal law: a study of English historical thought in the seventeenth century*, Cambridge University Press, 1987.

Podamy, Amanda H. *The ancient Near East: a very short introduction*, Oxford University Press, 2014.

Pollock, Frederick, and Frederic Maitland. *The history of English law before the time of Edward I*, 2nd ed. Cambridge University Press, 1898.

Pollock, Sheldon. *The language of the gods in the world of men: Sanskrit, culture, and power in premodern India*, Berkeley: University of California Press, 2006.

Polo, Marco. *The description of the world*, vol. 1, trans. A. C. Moule, compiler Paul Pelliot, London: Routledge, 1938.

Poos, L. R. 'Sex, lies and the church courts of pre-Reformation England', *Journal of Interdisciplinary History* 25: 585–607, 1995.

Postan, M. M. *Medieval trade and finance*, Cambridge University Press, 1973.

Potts, Charlotte R. 'The development and architectural significance of early Etrusco-Italic podia', *BABESCH* 86: 41–52, 2011.

Powers, David S. *Law, society, and culture in the Maghrib, 1300–1500*, Cambridge University Press, 2002.

———. 'Wael B. Hallaq on the origins of Islamic law: a review essay', *Islamic Law and Society* 17: 126–57, 2010.

Prichard, M. J., and D. E. C. Yale. *Hale and Fleetwood on admiralty jurisdiction*, London: Selden Society, 1993.

Rabb, Intisar A. '"Reasonable doubt" in Islamic law', *Yale Journal of International Law* 40: 41–94, 2015.

Radding, Charles M. *The origins of medieval jurisprudence: Pavia and Bologna, 850–1150*, New Haven, CT: Yale University Press, 1988.

Radu, Roxana. *Negotiating Internet governance*, Oxford University Press, 2019.

Ray, Rajat Kanta. 'Indian society and the establishment of British supremacy, 1765–1818', in P. J. Marshall and A. Low (eds), *The Oxford history of the British Empire*, vol. 2, Oxford University Press, 1998.

Razi, Zvi, and Richard M. Smith. 'The origins of the English manorial court rolls as a written record: a puzzle', in Z. Razi and R. M. Smith, *Medieval society and the manor court*, Oxford: Clarendon Press, 1996.

Renard, Étienne. '*Le pactus legis Salicae*, règlement militaire Romain ou code de lois compilé sous Clovis?', *Bibliotèque de l'École des chartes* 167: 321–52, 2009.

Revkin, Mara. 'Does the Islamic state have a "social contract"? Evidence from Iraq and Syria', Working paper no. 9, Program on Governance and Local Development, University of Gothenburg, 2016.

Reyerson, Kathryn L. 'Commercial law and merchant disputes: Jacques Coeur and the law of marque', *Medieval Encounters* 9: 244–55, 2003.

Richardson, M. E. J. *Hammurabi's laws: text, translation, glossary*, Sheffield, UK: Sheffield Academic Press, 2000.

Rio, Alice. *Legal practice and the written word in the early Middle Ages: Frankish formulae, c. 500–1000*, Cambridge University Press, 2009.

Roberts, John M. 'Oaths, autonomic ordeals, and power', *American Anthropologist* 67, no. 6, pt. 2: 186–212, 1965.

Roebuck, Derek, and Bruno de Loynes de Fumichon. *Roman arbitration*, Oxford: Holo Books, 2004.

Roper, Albert. 'The organization and program of the international commission for air navigation (C.I.N.A.)', *Journal of Air Law and Commerce* 3: 167–78, 1932.

Ross, Richard J. 'The commoning of the common law: the Renaissance debate over printing English law, 1520–1640', *University of Pennsylvania Law Review* 146: 323–461, 1998.

Rossabi, Morris. *A history of China*, Chichester, UK: Wiley Blackwell, 2014.

Roth, Martha (ed.) *Law collections from Mesopotamia and Asia Minor*, Atlanta, GA: Scholars Press, 1995.

Ruotolo, Gianpaolo Maria. 'Fragments of fragments: The domain name system regulation. Global law or informalisation of the international legal order?', *Computer Law and Security Review* 33: 159–70, 2017.

Ruotuola, Markku. 'Of the working man: labour liberals and the creation of the ILO', *Labour History Review* 67: 29–47, 2002.

Rustow, Marina. *Heresy and the politics of community: the Jews of the Fatimid caliphate*, Ithaca, NY: Cornell University Press, 2008.

———. *The lost archive: traces of a caliphate in a Cairo synagogue*, Princeton, NJ: Princeton University Press, 2020.

Sabapathy, John. 'Regulating community and society at the Sorbonne in the late thirteenth century', in F. Pirie and J. Scheele (eds), *Legalism: community and justice*, Oxford University Press, 2014.

Sachs, Jeffrey Adam. 'Seeing like an Islamic state: shari'a and political power in Sudan', *Law and Society Review* 52: 630–51, 2018.

Saleh, Nabil. 'Civil codes of Arab countries: the Sanhuri codes', *Arab Law Quarterly* 8: 161–67, 1993.

Schacht, Joseph. *An introduction to Islamic law*, Oxford: Clarendon Press, 1964.

———. 'Problems of modern Islamic legislation', *Studia Islamica* 12: 99–129, 1960.

Scheele, Judith. 'A taste for law: rule-making in Kabylia (Algeria)', *Comparative Studies in Society and History* 50: 895–919, 2008.

———. 'Rightful measures: irrigation, land, and the shari'ah in the Algerian Touat', in P. Dresch and H. Skoda (eds), *Legalism: anthropology and history*, Oxford University Press, 2012.

———. 'Community as an achievement: Kabyle customary law and beyond', in F. Pirie and J. Scheele (eds), *Legalism: community and justice*, Oxford University Press, 2014.

Scheidel, Walter. 'Italian manpower', *Journal of Roman Archaeology* 26: 678–87, 2013.

Schuhmacher, Jacques. 'The war criminals investigate', DPhil. diss., University of Oxford, 2017.

Scott, James C. *The art of not being governed: an anarchist history of upland Southeast Asia*, New Haven, CT: Yale University Press, 2009.

Secret Barrister. *Fake law: the truth about justice in an age of lies*, London: Pan Macmillan, 2020.

Segal, Peretz. 'Jewish law during the Tannaitic period', in N. S. Hecht, B. S. Jackson, S. M. Passamaneck, D. Piattelli, and A. M. Rabello (eds), *An introduction to the history and sources of Jewish law*, Oxford: Clarendon Press, 1996.

Seidel, Anna. 'Traces of Han religion in funerary texts found in tombs', in Akizuki Kanei (ed.) *Dōkyō to shūkyō bunka*, Tokyo: Hirakawa, 1987.

Sen, Amartya. 'Human rights and Asian values: what Kee Kuan Yew and Li Peng don't understand about Asia', *New Republic* 217, nos. 2–3: 33–40, 1997.

Sharpe, Richard. 'Dispute settlement in medieval Ireland', in Wendy Davies and Paul Fouracre (eds), *Settlement of disputes in early medieval Europe*, Cambridge University Press, 1986.

Shaw, Rosalind. 'Linking justice with reintegration? Ex-combatants and the Sierra Leone experiment', in R. Shaw and L. Waldorf (eds), *Localizing transitional justice: interventions and priority after mass violence*, Stanford, CA: Stanford University Press, 2010.

Sherman, Charles. 'A brief history of medieval Roman canon law in England', *University of Pennsylvania Law Review* 68: 223–58, 1920.

Sherwin-White, A. N. 'The *Lex Repetundarum* and the political ideas of Gaius Gracchus', *Journal of Roman Studies* 72: 18–31, 1982.

Silverstein, Adam J. *Islamic history: a very short introduction*, Oxford University Press, 2010.

Singha, Radhika. *A despotism of law: crime and justice in early colonial India*, Delhi: Oxford University Press, 1998.

Skosey, Laura. 'The legal system and legal traditions of the Western Zhou (ca. 1045–71 B.C.E.)', PhD diss., University of Chicago, 1996.

BIBLIOGRAPHY

Skovgaard-Petersen, Jakob. *Defining Islam for the Egyptian state: muftis and fatwas of the Dār al-Iftā*, Leiden: Brill, 1997.

Smith, David Chan. *Sir Edward Coke and the reformation of the laws: religion, politics and jurisprudence, 1578–1616*, Cambridge University Press, 2014.

Sommer, Matthew H. *Polyandry and wife-selling in Qing dynasty China: survival strategies and judicial interventions*, Berkeley: University of California Press, 2015.

Stacey, Robin Chapman. *The road to judgment: from custom to court in medieval Ireland and Wales*, Philadelphia: University of Pennsylvania Press, 1994.

Stein, Aurel. *Ruins of desert Cathay: personal narrative of explorations in Central Asia and westernmost China*, London: Macmillan, 1912.

Stein, Peter. *Roman law in European history*, Cambridge University Press, 1999.

Stevenson, Jane. 'The beginnings of literacy in Ireland', *Proceedings of the Royal Irish Academy of Archaeology, Culture, History, and Literature* 89C: 127–65, 1989.

Stiles, Erin E. *An Islamic court in context: an ethnographic study of judicial reasoning*, London: Palgrave Macmillan, 2009.

Strakosch, Henry E. *State absolutism and the rule of law: the struggle for the codification of civil law in Austria, 1753–1811*, Sydney University Press, 1967.

Summerson, H. R. T. 'The structure of law enforcement in thirteenth century England', *American Journal of Legal History* 23: 313–27, 1979.

Tarwacka, Anna J.W. 'Lex Aebutia', in the *Oxford classical dictionary*, 5th ed. Oxford University Press, 2019.

Thapar, Romila. *From lineage to state: social formations of the mid-first millennium BC in the Ganga Valley*, Bombay: Oxford University Press, 1984.

Thayer, James. *A preliminary treatise on evidence at the common law*, Boston: Little, Brown, 1898.

Thomas, Yan. 'Fictio Legis: L'empire de la fiction Romaine et ses limites Médiévales', *Droits* 21: 17–63, 1995.

Thomson, E. P. *Whigs and hunters: the origin of the Black Act*, London: Allen Lane, 1975.

Thomson, Robert. *The Lawcode (Datastanagirk') of Mxit'ar Goš*, Amsterdam: Rodopi, 2000.

Tubbs, J. W. *The common law mind: medieval and early modern conceptions*, Baltimore: Johns Hopkins University Press, 2000.

Usher, Roland G. 'James I and Sir Edward Coke', *English Historical Review* 18: 664–75, 1903.

Vajpey, Ananya. 'Excavating identity through tradition: Who was Shivaji?', in S. Saberwal and S. Varma (eds), *Traditions in Motion*, Oxford University Press, 2005.

———. '*Śudradharma* and legal treatments of caste', in Timothy Lubin, Donald R. Davis, and Jayanth K. Krishnan (eds), *Hinduism and law: an introduction*, Cambridge University Press, 2010.

Van Gulik, R. H. *T'ang-yin-pi-shih: 'parallel cases from under the pear tree'*, Leiden: Brill, 1956.

Vogel, Frank E. *Islamic law and legal system: studies of Saudi Arabia*, Leiden: Brill, 2000.

Wählisch, Martin. 'Normative limits of peace negotiations: questions, guidance and prospects', *Global Policy* 7: 261–66, 2016.

Walbank, F. W. 'A Greek looks at Rome: Polybius VI revisited', in *Polybius, Rome and the Hellenistic world: essays and reflections*, Cambridge University Press, 2002.

Wansharisi, Ahmad al-. *Al-mi'yar al-mu'rib wa-l-jami' al-mughrib 'an fatawi 'ulama' Ifriqiya wa-l-Andalus wa-l-Maghrib*, M. Hajji (ed.) Rabat, Morocco: Wizarat al-Awqaf wa-l-Shu'un al-Islamiyah lil-Mamlakah al-Maghribiyah, 1981–1983.

Washbrook, D. A. 'Law, state and agrarian society in colonial India', *Modern Asian Studies* 15: 649–721, 1981.

Watson, Alan. *Law making in the later Roman Republic*, Oxford: Clarendon Press, 1974.

———. *Legal transplants: an approach to comparative law*, Charlottesville: University Press of Virginia, 1974.

————. *The evolution of Western private law*, Baltimore: Johns Hopkins University Press, 1985.

————. *Sources of law, legal change, and ambiguity*, Edinburgh: T&T Clark, 1985.

————. *The spirit of Roman law*, Athens: University of Georgia Press, 1995.

Wells, Elizabeth. 'Civil litigation in the High Court of Admiralty, 1585–1595', in Christopher Brooks and Michael Lobban (eds), *Communities and courts in Britain, 1150–1900*, London: Hambledon Press, 1997.

Westbrook, Raymond. *Rome of the XII Tables: persons and property*, Princeton, NJ: Princeton University Press, 1975.

————. *Sources of law, legal change, and ambiguity*, Edinburgh: T&T Clark, 1985.

————. 'The nature and origins of the Twelve Tables', *Zeitschrift der Savigny-Stiftung für Rechtsgeschichte* 105: 74–121, 1988.

————. 'Barbarians at the gates: Near Eastern law in ancient Greece', in Westbrook, *Ex Oriente lex: Near Eastern influences on ancient Greek and Roman law*, ed. D. Lyons and K. Raaflaub, Baltimore: Johns Hopkins University Press, 2015.

Wezler, Albrecht. 'Dharma in the Veda and the Dharmaśāstras', *Journal of Indian Philosophy* 32: 629–54, 2004.

Whitman, James Q. *The origins of reasonable doubt: theological roots of the criminal trial*, New Haven, CT: Yale University Press, 2008.

————. 'The world historical significance of European legal history: an interim report', in H. Pihlajamäki, M. D. Dubber, and M. Godfrey (eds), *The Oxford handbook of European legal history*, Oxford University Press, 2018.

Wickham, Chris. 'Land disputes and their social framework in Lombard-Carolingian Italy, 700–900', in W. Davies and P. Fouracre (eds), *The settlement of disputes in early medieval Europe*, Cambridge University Press, 1986.

Williamson, Callie. *The laws of the Roman people: public law in the expansion and decline of the Roman Republic*, Ann Arbor: University of Michigan Press, 2005.

Wilson, Richard A. *Human rights, culture and context: anthropological perspectives*, London: Pluto Press, 1997.

———. 'Judging history: the historical record of the International Criminal Tribunal for the Former Yugoslavia', *Human Rights Quarterly* 27: 908–42, 2005.

Wormald, Patrick. 'Lex scripta and *verbum regis*: legislation and Germanic kingship from Euric to Cnut', in P. H. Sawyer and I. N. Wood (eds), *Early medieval kingship*, Leeds: University of Leeds, School of History, 1977.

———. *The making of English law: King Alfred to the twelfth century*, Oxford: Blackwell, 1999.

Zaring, David. 'Finding legal principle in global financial regulation', *Virginia Journal of International Law* 52: 683–722, 2012.

Zhang, Taisu, and Tom Ginsburg. 'China's turn toward law', *Virginia Journal of International Law* 59: 306–389, 2019.

Zimmerman, Michael. 'Only a fool becomes a king: Buddhist stances on punishment', in *Buddhism and violence*, Lumbini, Nepal: Lumbini International Research Institute, 2006.

ILLUSTRATION CREDITS

The author would like to thank all the museums, galleries, and other owners who have allowed their images to be reproduced in this book. Every effort has been made to trace copyright holders and we apologize for any unintentional omissions.

Calicut, from the 1572 volume of the *Civitates Orbis Terrarum,* edited by Georg Braun and engraved by Franz Hogenberg.

Paul Pelliot, Magite Historic / Alamy Stock Photo.

Chronicle of Wa, British Library Or.8210/S.9498A.

Law stone, now housed in the Louvre.

Ashurbanipal, Lanmas / Alamy Stock Photo.

Dharmashastra text, Sarah Welch: CC BY-SA 4.0.

Shivaji, Historic Images / Alamy Stock Photo.

Taizong, painting by Yen Liben.

Tang dynasty exam paper, courtesy of the East Asian Library and the Gest Collection, Princeton University Library.

Pompeian fresco, The Yorck Project (2002) 10.000 Meisterwerke der Malerei.

Cicero, Bertel Thorvaldsen, 1799 copy of a Roman original, Thorvaldsens Museum, Copenhagan.

Papyrus, courtesy of The Leon Levy Dead Sea Scrolls Digital Library; Israel Antiquities Authority. Photo by Shai Halevi.

Baghdad library, Bibliothèque nationale de France

Jewish scholars, David Solomon Sassoon, 'A History of the Jews in Baghdad'.

Alfonso X, Album / Alamy Stock Photo.

Charlemagne denarius, World Imaging.

Laws of Aethelstan, © The University of Manchester. Creative Commons Licence CC BY-NC 40.

King Alfred aestal, The Ashmolean Museum/ Heritage Image Partnership Ltd / Alamy Stock Photo.

Thingvellir, courtesy of Nina Thorkelsdottir.

Grágás, The Arni Magnusson Institute for Icelandic Studies.

Russian Primary Chronicle, Sputnik/TopFoto.

Tatev monastery, Mirzoyan's Ads and Marketing.

Geniza legal manual, © The University of Manchester. Creative Commons Licence CC BY-NC 40.

Algerian irrigation channels, Sergey Strelkov / Alamy Stock Photo.

Tindi, Moriz von Déchy.

Song banquet, Taipei, National Palace Museum.

Song hydraulic grain mill, Palace Museum, Beijing.

English commonplace book, © The University of Manchester. Creative Commons Licence CC BY-NC 40.

Manorial court roll, reproduced with permission from Lancashire Archives, Lancashire County Council, ref. DDHCL/7/56.

Lostwithiel Palace, Antiqua Print Gallery / Alamy Stock Photo.

Hans Hegenheim, Diebold Schilling, from the Lucerne chronicle, Zentralbibliothek Lucerne.

Kunigunde of Luxembourg, INTERFOTO / Alamy Stock Photo.

Iron ordeal, Stiftsbibliothek Lambach Cml LXXIII f64v.

Lenape wampum belt, FLHC A29 / Alamy Stock Photo.

Articles of Peace, Swem Special Collections Research Center, William and Mary Libraries.

Sir William Blackstone, Everett Collection Inc / Alamy Stock Photo.

"Collared!!", by Tenniel. British satirical journal, *Punch*, 22nd October 1881.

Warren Hastings, Album / Alamy Stock Photo.

King Leopold II cartoon, by François Maréchal. Belgian satirical journal, *Le Frondeur*, 20th December 1884.

Nigerian court clerk, Pitt Rivers Museum: 1998.336.16.

Abu al-Sa'ud, by Mahmud 'Abd al-Baqi. Metropolitan Museum of Art. Gift of George D. Pratt, 1925: 25.83.9.

Afghan qadi and mufti, Pitt Rivers Museum: 2013.3.1280 1960.

Ayatollah and Pope, UPI / Alamy Stock Photo.

Seyh Suleyman Kaslioglu, Rivers Museum: 2013.3.16322.

Ladakh, courtesy of the author.

Tibetan mediators, courtesy of the author.

INDEX

hundred courts. *See* shire
hypothetical cases and examples,
116, 117, 143, 160

Iceland, Icelandic laws, 184–189
ideals, ideal order
in China, 73, 93, 238, 247
in India, 5, 45, 49, 53, 66–67, 69
in the Islamic world, 137–138,
220
in the modern world, 9, 96, 311,
360, 433–434, 437–439, 444,
445, 450, 452
identity, laws creating
among Armenians, 450
in Ireland, 183
among Israelites, 41, 124
in medieval Europe, 151
Inca empire, 10
Ine, King, laws of, 156, 295
Indigenous people, 440, 452, 454
in Africa, 359–362
Declaration on the Rights of,
438, 440
in North America, 332, 342–346
in South America, 340–341
inheritance
in Armenian laws, 201
in China, 83, 85, 86, 250, 252,
255
in colonial Africa, 358
in Daghestan, 232
in English laws 323
in Indian laws, 208
in the Islamic world, 129, 135,
144, 221–222, 388
in Jewish laws, 216
in Kabylia, 404
in medieval Europe, 162, 167,
267, 269, 271
in Mesopotamia, 23, 26, 55
in Rome, 100, 104, 116, 117
in Rus, 196
in shari'a courts, 384
injury, assault, wounding, 5, 439,
445, 449
in Armenian laws, 202
in China, 84, 92, 249, 250

in Daghestan, 230
in India, 55, 207, 208
in Ireland, 178
in the Islamic world, 369
among the Israelites, 35, 36, 39,
42
in Kabylia, 402
in medieval England, 155, 271
in medieval Europe, 147, 151,
156, 158
in Mesopotamia, 21, 28, 30,
35–38
in Rome, 100, 103
in Rus, 192
in Tibet, 8, 289, 396–397
See also wound price
Innocent III, Pope, 300–301, 305
Inns of Court, in London, 168, 321
inquisition, 300, 306, 310
inspiration. *See* borrowing
Institut de droit international, 424
Institutes of Gaius. *See* Gaius
insult, slander, 287
in Daghestan, 230
in India, 55, 208
in Ireland, 179
in medieval England, 155,
274–275
in Rus, 192
in Tibet, 290, 395
intellectual property. *See* property
intention
in China, 73
in medieval England, 291
in Mesopotamian laws, 30
in Yemen, 292
interdict, in Rome, 109
interest (on debts)
in China, 240, 241
in India, 56
in the Islamic world, 129, 136,
381–382
in medieval Europe, 162
in Mesopotamia, 26
in Rus, 195
International Corporation for
Assigned Names and Networks
(ICANN), 433–434, 436

Credit: David Fisher

Fernanda Pirie is professor of the anthropology of law at the University of Oxford. She is the author of *The Anthropology of Law* and has conducted fieldwork in the mountains of Ladakh and the grasslands of eastern Tibet. She previously spent almost a decade practicing as a barrister at the London bar. She lives in Oxford in the United Kingdom.